THREADS OF THE UNFOLDING WEB

THREADS OF THE UNFOLDING WEB

The Old Javanese Tantu Panggĕlaran

Translated by **Stuart Robson**
with a commentary by **Hadi Sidomulyo**

YUSOF ISHAK INSTITUTE

First published in Singapore in 2021 by
ISEAS Publishing
30 Heng Mui Keng Terrace
Singapore 119614

E-mail: publish@iseas.edu.sg
Website: <http://bookshop.iseas.edu.sg>

ISEAS Library Cataloguing-in-Publication Data

Name(s): Robson, Stuart, translator. | Hadi Sidomulyo, contributor.
Title: Threads of the unfolding web : the Old Javanese Tantu Panggĕlaran / translated by Stuart Robson with a commentary by Hadi Sidomulyo.
Other title: Tantu Panggĕlaran.
Description: Singapore : ISEAS – Yusof Ishak Institute, 2021. | Includes bibliographical references.
Identifiers: ISBN 978-981-4881-99-9 (hard cover) | ISBN 978-981-4951-00-5 (pdf)
Subjects: LCSH: Kawi literature—History and criticism.
Classification: LCC PL5158.9 T17R66

Cover
Tenggerese ritual bell (*gĕnta*), possession of *dukun* Jumat at Kenongo (Gucialit), Lumajang Regency, East Java. *Photo by Hadi Sidomulyo, 2018.*

Frontispiece
Decorative panel on the rear wall of a cave hermitage, located in the ravine of Jurang Limas on the northern slope of Mt Wilis, near the village of Joho (Pace), Nganjuk Regency, East Java. Probably identifiable with the cave reported by Verbeek (1891, p. 256, no. 512), who observed an inscription on the left wall, since collapsed. *Photo by Hadi Sidomulyo, 2019.*

Typeset by International Typesetters Pte Ltd
Printed in Singapore by Markono Print Media Pte Ltd

CONTENTS

Abbreviations vi

Preface vii

Part one – Tantu Panggĕlaran, translation by Stuart Robson

Introduction 3

A note on the divisions of the text 6

Translation 10

Part two – commentary on the text by Hadi Sidomulyo

Introduction 73

I Prologue 81

II The Heavenly Realm: Tales of the Gods 103

III The Earthly Realm: Tales of Men 149

Appendix 1
Notes on names and titles occurring in the text 182

Appendix 2
Archaeological record for the Tengger Highlands and Hyang Plateau 212

Appendix 3
The Old Javanese text of the Tantu Panggĕlaran (Pigeaud 1924, pp. 57–128) 223

Bibliography 295

Lexicographical List 303

General Index 305

About the Authors 324

ABBREVIATIONS

AV	Archaeologische Verzameling
BAKOSURTANAL	Badan Koordinasi Survei dan Pemetaan Nasional
BEFEO	Bulletin de l'Ecole française d'Extrême-Orient
BM	Bujangga Manik. Noorduyn and Teeuw (2006)
BPCB	Balai Pelestarian Cagar Budaya
DW	Deśawarṇana. Pigeaud (1960–63); Robson (1995)
Eringa	Eringa (1984)
GR	Gericke and Roorda (1901)
JBG	Jaarboek Bataviaasch Genootschap
KBW	Kawi-Balineesch-Nederlandsch Woordenboek. Van der Tuuk (1897–1912)
KITLV	Koninklijk Instituut voor Taal-, Land- en Volkenkunde
MW	Monier-Williams (1899)
NBG	Notulen van de algemeene en bestuursvergaderingen van het Bataviaasch genootschap van kunsten en wetenschappen
OJO	Oud-Javaansche Oorkonden
Par.	Pararaton. Brandes and Krom (1920)
Pig.	Pigeaud (1938)
Pigeaud	Pigeaud (1924)
OV	Oudheidkundig Verslag
ROC	Rapporten van de commissie in Nederlandsch-Indië voor oudheidkundig onderzoek op Java en Madoera
RY	Rāmāyaṇa
TBG	Tijdschrift voor Indische Taal-, Land- en Volkenkunde
TP	Tantu Panggĕlaran
Volk. Mus.	Volkenkunde Museum
Z.	Zoetmulder (1982)

PREFACE

It was during a workshop at the KITLV branch in Jakarta in 2009 that I first discussed the possibility of a revised, English language translation of the Old Javanese Tantu Panggĕlaran with Stuart Robson, now Adjunct Professor of Indonesian Studies in the School of Languages, Literatures, Cultures and Linguistics at Monash University, Melbourne, Australia. The text of the Tantu Panggĕlaran had for many years held a special interest for me, as it belonged, like Prapañca's Deśawarṇana and the Old Sundanese Bujangga Manik, to that small group of literary works which offered a wealth of topographical data. I had already taken advantage of Robson's lucid translation of the fourteenth century Deśawarṇana, published in 1995, when endeavouring to trace the course of King Rājasanagara's journey through eastern Java, and imagined that the same linguistic skills applied to the Tantu Panggĕlaran would help to draw this valuable text out of its vacuum and place it in a firmer historical and geographical context.

Happily, the idea was met with enthusiasm, and our discussion ended with a tentative plan to produce a joint publication, comprising an English translation, followed by a commentary focusing on historical topography. Professor Robson noted, however, that a new critical edition of the Tantu Panggĕlaran would hardly be possible, as the whereabouts of the two principal manuscripts used by Th. Pigeaud for his dissertation were no longer known. Instead, he said, it would be better to work directly from the romanized text of Pigeaud's 1924 publication, which includes all of the variants encountered in the five manuscripts originally consulted.

Although the interest sparked by this initial meeting led to further dialogue over the next few months, there were no concrete developments. Time went by and the communication became less frequent, and then ceased entirely, as various other commitments took precedence.

Such was the condition until 2015, when suddenly, without warning, Professor Robson wrote to enquire whether I was still interested in the Tantu Panggĕlaran, as he had completed a first draft of the translation and was willing to send it to me! This came as an unexpected surprise, and without hesitating I sent an enthusiastic reply, reconfirming my commitment to our joint project. There were, however, some technical difficulties, as I was at that time fully occupied with an intensive exploration of Mt Penanggungan in eastern Java. Notwithstanding, I allotted some time for the planned commentary and began drawing up some preparatory notes, which were sent annually to Professor Robson for his approval over the course of the next three years.

With most of the preparatory work complete by the middle of 2018, it was time to direct attention to the necessary fieldwork. In compiling my notes for the commentary, I had been able to draw on a fair amount of data gathered during past expeditions in both central and eastern Java. This, however, was insufficient for the task at hand. The specific nature of the Tantu Panggĕlaran, with its focus on isolated communities in mountainous districts, required venturing far off the beaten track, not infrequently following up nineteenth century reports of archaeological sites which appeared never to have been revisited.

In view of the difficulties presented by this kind of field work, coupled with the time factor, it was clear from the outset that a complete survey would be impossible. A decision was thus made to concentrate on the three main highland regions referred to in the text, namely the Dieng Plateau in central Java, along with the Tengger and Hyang Massifs in the eastern part of the island, each of which became the focus of a separate expedition. Taking into account the inaccessibility of these locations during the wet season (between November and March), a plan was drawn up to cover the mountains of eastern Java during the latter half of 2018, and leave the Dieng region until April of the following year.

The first two expeditions proceeded on schedule, beginning with a journey through the Tengger highlands in the company of local guides. Direct observation in the field, coupled with information supplied by a number of Tengger priests (*dukun*), helped greatly towards a mental reconstruction of this region as portrayed in the Tantu Panggĕlaran. The field trip culminated in a ritual ascent of Mt Semeru by way of the sacred site known as Arcapodo, located at an elevation of just under 3,000 m. This was followed by a survey in the Hyang Massif further east, which proved to be no less challenging. Efforts were made to identify some of the archaeological remains reported by J. Hageman in the 1860s, as well as confirm the original find spot of the Batur copper plates, discussed in Part two of this book. The latter were said to have been recovered at the end of a long valley enclosed by steep hills. Unfortunately, the expedition to Batur in mid-November was interrupted by the first heavy rain of the season, and had to be cut short.

Unfavourable weather conditions throughout the first half of 2019 caused the third and final field trip to be delayed until July. The expedition nonetheless had its rewards, serving to strengthen the conviction that the earliest *maṇḍala* communities referred to in the Tantu Panggĕlaran were situated in the vicinity of the Dieng Plateau. This in turn provided a more certain context for some of the ancient sites to be found on the northern plains of Batang and Pekalongan, where the Supreme Lord Guru was said to have established his initial residence at the foot of the historical Mt Kelāśa (or Kailāśa).

The fieldwork complete, it remained to edit the notes for the commentary and produce a coherent text, as well as work on the maps and illustrations, a task which occupied the last few months of 2019. Professor Robson, in the meantime, made some final adjustments to the translation before the manuscript was submitted for publication.

A few additional comments: Th. Pigeaud's 1924 edition of the Tantu Panggĕlaran has of course long been available to scholars, but access has been limited to those conversant with Old Javanese and Dutch. The new English language version presented here brings this important literary work within the reach of a wider audience, and at the same time offers some improvements on the translation published almost a century ago. As to the commentary, emphasis has been placed on the topographical data preserved in the text, an aspect hardly touched upon in the 1924 edition. It can thus serve as a useful supplement to Pigeaud's own extensive notes, which remain a valuable source for the specialist.

Although directed primarily to the scientific community, this book has from the outset been conceived as a popular edition, designed to draw the interest of the general reader. As such, it provides no more than the groundwork for ongoing research. One important area of study which has not received the attention it deserves is the Śaiwa tradition in ancient Java. Since this constitutes the central theme of the Tantu Panggĕlaran, it is clearly in need of a deeper investigation. The complexity of the subject, however, requires a separate study by a qualified expert.

By way of acknowledgment, I would like to extend my thanks to Terence Chong and Ng Kok Kiong at ISEAS – Yusof Ishak Institute, Singapore, for accepting the manuscript for publication, as well as to Hélène Njoto for her initial recommendation of a publisher. My two companions in the field, Mas Suaidi and Pak Jayus of Trawas, Mojokerto, deserve a special mention for their loyal support over a period of eighteen months. Lastly, I offer my sincere gratitude to Stuart Robson for his encouragement and unswerving patience in the course of preparing the commentary, and without whose masterly translation this book could never had been written.

Hadi Sidomulyo
Tegallalang, Bali
May 2020

PART ONE

Tantu Panggĕlaran

Translation by Stuart Robson

Introduction

The Tantu Panggĕlaran (TP) is an Old Javanese prose text. The opening sentence tells us that it contains "tales of the island of Java from ancient times" (*kacarita nika nuṣa Jawa ring aśitkala*). These tales can be described as "myth and legend", as an indication of what their varied content covers. In a classic anthropological sense, the TP contains accounts of origins ("charters") relating to features of the natural world and the social order, culminating in its message of the continuity of religious institutions (*maṇḍala*), from divine actors to human ones. In this way it moves into quasi-history, conveying important themes for such communities located in the countryside of Java, especially on mountains. However, the TP is not history, and also not fiction, but intends to preserve and transmit aspects of life and belief for its audience, in the form of a literary work, stemming from a specific spiritual tradition, which can only be understood by reference to the geographical, social and historical setting of Java.

The TP was edited and translated into Dutch by Th. Pigeaud in 1924, as his dissertation at the University of Leiden (with Professor G.A.J. Hazeu as promotor). Pigeaud presented a critical edition. There is a large degree of variation among the manuscripts he used. Hence his choice to follow one manuscript in all details, including spelling, namely his A, although it was also necessary to use readings from B, in order to produce a usable text. Pigeaud says that thanks to the helpfulness of the archaeologist P.V. van Stein Callenfels[1] he was in a position to consult these two manuscripts from the latter's collection; these were *lontar* (palm leaf) manuscripts. He mentions their dimensions, but does not say where Van Stein Callenfels obtained them, or what became of them after he consulted them. They have not yet been identified in the Leiden or Jakarta manuscript collections. This is most unfortunate. Manuscript C is the Leiden Cod. Or 2212, while D and E are from the later Van der Tuuk Collection, also in the Leiden University Library, and are much less reliable, perhaps even representing a different redaction. All variants were faithfully listed in footnotes.

1. According to Amrit Gomperts, Pigeaud and Van Stein Callenfels were sharing a house in Noordwijk (near Leiden) in the period 1921–24, when they were writing their dissertations; Van Stein Callenfels was interested in topography, and may have encouraged Pigeaud to take the Tantu Panggĕlaran as his subject.

Pigeaud's text is attached as an appendix, so that the interested reader can consult it. Words can be searched in P.J. Zoetmulder's *Old Javanese-English Dictionary* (1982), bearing in mind that the citations found there bear references to page and line of Pigeaud's text.

Pigeaud's Dutch translation is clear and mostly reliable, although some corrections need to be made, allowing for advances in knowledge of Old Javanese since 1924, and there are a small number of other, typographical errors. The translation is also complete—not mere selections. The present translation is based directly on Pigeaud's Old Javanese text, also making use of the variants that he listed, and is the first to have been attempted into English. Pigeaud's Dutch translation was consulted, but was not followed in all instances, as can be seen from the footnotes.

The style of the original is simple, down-to-earth, even earthy, certainly not the product of the Hindu-Javanese court literary tradition. It is more likely to be derived from oral traditions circulating in the countryside, and the text betrays features of orality. So not surprisingly an author or a date are not mentioned, except for one colophon, with a date equivalent to AD 1635. One can speculate that the text was written in this form in the fifteenth century, somewhere in East Java.

Several of the religious establishments described are also listed in Canto 78.7 of the Deśawarṇana (1365), but the only *nagara* ("cities") to be mentioned by name are Daha and Galuh, leading to the possibility that the origins of the text should be sought in the Kaḍiri period, before the Singhasāri or Majapahit periods, that is to say, before 1222. Other place-names mentioned are Mĕḍang Kamulan, Mĕḍang Gaṇa and Mĕḍang Tañjung. Java is referred to by name, Yawaḍipa, as well as Jambuḍipa (India), several times, and even Cĕmpa (Champa), once. Many of the religious sites and mountains mentioned can be traced on the ground, and these will be described in detail in the chapters of the commentary compiled by Hadi Sidomulyo to be found below.

As far as language is concerned, the TP occupies a position by itself, as it contains a considerable number of words not found elsewhere. However, it is fairly close to other, similar, Old Javanese prose works, such as the Calon Arang (ed. Poerbatjaraka 1926) and Pararaton (ed. Brandes, 2nd ed. 1920). Pigeaud provides detailed summaries of contents of related but then unpublished Old Javanese texts that may be helpful for understanding the subject-matter; several have since been published.[2] Pigeaud's edition also contains extensive commentary, which is well worth consulting, but will

2. These titles are as follows: Dewaśāsana, Rajapatiguṇḍala, Pratasti-bhuwana, Wratiśasana, Ṛṣiśāsana, Śewaśāsana, Śilakrama, Sārasamuccaya, Ādipurāṇa, Brahmāṇḍapurāṇa, Anggastyaparwa, Caturpakṣopadeśa, Korawāśrama.

not be translated here. A Modern Javanese text that can be compared to the first part of the Tantu Panggĕlaran, on the origins of the island of Java, is the Sĕrat Manik Maya, found in a number of *macapat* verse versions.

When reading the translation, one should remember that various different names are often given to the same divine characters, and this may be confusing, but it was decided to follow the text exactly rather than attempt to regularize it. There is also much inconsistency in the spelling of the names, presumably deriving from the main manuscript, rather than being errors on the part of the editor; there is little point in reconstructing "correct" etymological spellings. The repetitions in the text have of course not been edited out. The square brackets indicate readings taken from manuscript B.

The footnotes are intended to draw attention to textual problems, such as unclear meanings, with alternatives and references to Zoetmulder's dictionary (Z followed by the page number). A continuing study of the text will probably offer progressively better solutions.

Further, it may be helpful to draw attention to some of the key terms, beginning with the title itself: Tantu Panggĕlaran.

tantu: this is a loanword from Sanskrit, where it means "a thread, cord, string, line, wire, warp (of a web) ... succession, line of descendants" (MW 436). This meaning seems to fit well in this Old Javanese text, where it refers to the process whereby religious establishments were set up by the gods and then were extended with new foundations, hence "line", or in some places "(holy) site" (Z 1933).

panggĕlaran: this noun refers to the process of extending or expanding (rolling out, deployment). Hence the suggested translation of the title, "Threads of the Unfolding Web".

maṇḍala: also derived from Sanskrit, this is the term for the religious establishments, specifically belonging to the tradition of the *rĕsi* (sages), the *karĕsyan*. This tradition is described in the Deśawarṇana, and existed alongside the Śaiwa and the Buddhist traditions. There were many distinct types, as mentioned by name in the text. The basic meaning of Sanskrit *maṇḍala* is "circle" (MW 775), extended to "district, territory ...; multitude, group, band". In Old Javanese it is "the abode of a religious community" (Z 1099). It is formed by a process of clearing land to make a new settlement, *taruka* and derived verbal forms (Z 1956).

dewaguru: the superior or head of a religious community (Z 396); not known in Sanskrit in this particular meaning. He has pupils (*śiṣya*), who can be male or female. He wears the insignia of headband, earrings and jacket.

wiku: this is the general term for a person who follows a religious life, and is supposed to conform with the rules pertaining to their specific sect. We cannot translate it with "monk", as it covers "nuns" as well, although there are other terms for female ascetics, such as *kili*.

pratiṣṭha: normally translated simply with "established", but probably a technical term relating to the establishment of a religious foundation, involving the performance of a ceremony of consecration or dedication, a meaning found in both Sanskrit and Old Javanese.

bhāwa: this word has a range of meanings, but here seems to refer specifically to a person's "way of living" (Z 226); Pigeaud translated it with Dutch *staat*, which means "state, condition", probably the status and way of life (or being) inherent in a certain religious position.

sangaskāra and derived verbal forms: "to perform the *sangaskāra* over", this being "purification, consecration, installation, initiation" (Z 1659), but here regularly translated with "ordination", as it applies to the change in status to that of *wiku*.

The interpretation of all these terms can be checked by comparing the various places in the text where they occur.

A note on the divisions of the text

Although the original Old Javanese text has no section breaks, Pigeaud (1924) tried to make it more manageable by dividing the work into seven "chapters", following roughly the changes in subject matter. He admitted, however, that these textual divisions were not entirely satisfactory. For the present edition we have followed Pigeaud's example in principle, but reduced the number of divisions to three. In the commentary to the translation, each chapter has been provided with its own separate heading. Herewith the three parts of the text, together with a list of the range of topics contained in each:

I – (Pigeaud 1–2)
- Descent of Bhaṭāra Jagatpramāṇa
- Creation of the first human beings on Mt Pawinihan
- Introduction of civilization/agriculture and the first dwellings at Mĕḍang-kamulan
- Rahyang Kaṇḍyawan and his family at Mĕḍang-gaṇa
- The origin of rice
- Creation of the mountain Hyang

- Succession of Wṛtti-kaṇḍayun at Mĕḍang-gaṇa
- Transport of the Mahāmeru to Java from Jambuḍipa
- Origin of the mountains of Java
- The Trinity of lords (Iśwara, Brahmā, Wiṣṇu) receive their vehicles (*wāhana*)
- Theft of the holy Kamaṇḍalu by the demons Rātmaja and Rātmaji
- The story of the demon Rāhu
- Creation of the mountains Wĕlahulu, Sañjaya, Walangbangan and Pamrihan

II – (Pigeaud 3–6)

- Establishment of the *katyāgan* at Bulon, Kupang, Huluwanwa and Pacira
- Bhaṭāra Guru at Maśin and the founding of the Manguyu order
- Birth of Kāmadewa and Smarī
- The hermitages of Bhaṭāra Guru and Dewī Umā on the Mahāmeru
- Birth of Gaṇa and Kumāra
- Origin of the place named Ḍingḍing
- Kāmadewa and Smarī at Mĕḍang-gaṇa
- Bhaṭāra Guru at Gĕgĕr-katyagan and Tandĕs, Dewī Umā at Maṇik
- Kumāra as Katu-katu
- Umā, Gaṇa and Kumāra, origin of the mountains Pilan, Tawungan, Ijo and Wija
- Riddle of Brahmā's five heads and the creation of the five *kuśika* deities
- Origin of Mt Sambadagni and the coconut palm
- Dewī Umā, Kumāra-gohphala and the precious stone Cintamaṇi
- The mountains Pasanggaman, Gulingaṇḍara, Marapi, Itip-ing-lĕmbu and Kĕdyangga
- Dewī Umā and her children: Kumāra-gimbal, Kumāra-siddhi and Kumāra-raray
- Further offspring of Dewī Umā: the *tabĕ-habĕt*, *ambaṇḍagiṇa anggoda* and *widu*
- Founding of the first *maṇḍala* at Sukayajña
- Ordination of Wṛhaspati, Soma, Buddha, Śukra, Raditya, Saneścara and Anggara
- Establishment of the second *maṇḍala* at Māyana
- Lord Wiṣṇu as *dewaguru* at Sukayajña, founding of the *maṇḍala* at Guruh
- Founding of the *maṇḍala* of Hahāh, Gĕrĕsik and Śūnyasagiri on the Mahāmeru
- Iśwara as *dewaguru* at Sukayajña; story of the brahman Tĕkĕn-wuwung (Sidḍayoga)
- Gagang-aking and Bubukṣa, the children of Mpu Sidḍayoga
- Lord Brahmā as *dewaguru* at Sarwasidḍa, the appearance of Bhagawān Karmaṇḍeya
- Origin of the *maṇḍala* of Kukub on Mt Mahāmeru
- The *maṇḍala* of the *trisamaya* (Iśwara, Brahmā, Wiṣṇu)
- Origin of the mountains Jaṭa, Kampil and Manuñjang
- Bhagawān Aśoṣṭi at Labdawara

- Origin of the *wasi*, *baru-baru* and *wiku ijo*
- Bhagawān Agaṣṭi on Mt Kawi
- The *rĕsi* Siddawangsitadewa and the trinity of Kāla
- Kāla and Anungkāla, the five Yakṣa and the Pañātūr-mukā on Mt Mahāmeru
- Origin of the names Triśrĕngga and Gaṇḍamaḍana for the Mahāmeru
- Lord Ḍarmarāja as the sage Taruṇa-tapa-yowana, *dewaguru* at Kukub
- Favours granted to Dewata-kaki by Baṭāra Guru
- Creation of the Tasik-lĕbu, Mt Phala and the lakes Wurung and Kombala
- Bhaṭāra Guru on Mt Pawitra and Mt Kumukus
- Dewī Umā on Mt Kampud; origin of the mountain Lĕbĕng
- Bhaṭāra Guru as the divine Analaga, and the mountain Gaḍa-wĕsi
- Kumāra as the demon Bṛnggiriṣṭi, Dewī Umā cursed as Durgādewī
- Bhaṭāra Guru as Kālarūdra on Mt Lawu

III – (Pigeaud 7)

- King Bhatati and the sage Mahāmpu Palyat
- Ordination of Mpu Kalotan and Mpu Waju-kuning
- Goddess Śrī as the widow Rāga-runting
- Mpu Barang (Śaiwa) and Mpu Waluh-bang (Sogata) at Anggirah
- The journey of Ki Kabhayan-panglayar in the eastern districts
- Foundation of the *maṇḍala* of Aṇḍawar, Talun and Waśaṇa
- Mpu Barang at Kalyasĕm, Mpu Waluh-bang at Warag
- Mpu Barang, King Taki and the Sogata brothers Tapa-wangkĕng and Tapa-palet
- Ki Kabhayan-panglayar and the foundation of the *maṇḍala* of Sāgara
- Mpu Barang, Tapa-wangkĕng and Tapa-palet in Jambuḍipa
- Mpu Barang, Tapa-wangkĕng and Tapa-palet on Mt Brahmā
- The goddess Smarī as Ibu-tĕngahan
- Mpu Barang, Mpu Waluh-bang and the first Kasturi *maṇḍala* at Bapa
- Ki Samĕgĕt-bagañjing prevents the sun from descending
- Mpu Tapa-palet, the wife of King Taki and the piebald cow
- The *maṇḍala* of Śelagraha-rong and the origin of the Kasturi Palet
- The husbands of Ibu-tĕngahan and the origin of the Kasturi Gĕnting
- The *maṇḍala* of Ḍupaka and Wariguh and the origin of the Kasturi Barang
- The *maṇḍala* of Bhulalak and the origin of the Kasturi Botahi
- Aji Uṇḍal and the *maṇḍala* of Ḍingḍing
- Ki Buyut Samaḍi and the *maṇḍala* of Ḍingḍing-Manuñjang
- Buyut Jala-Giri on Mt Wĕlahulu

- Tuhan Cañcurāja and the origin of the Kasturi Śrī-manggala
- The *walyan* Bugoleng and the origin of the Kasturi Lĕsung-burut
- The butcher Drĕwyānak and the origin of the Kasturi Arĕng
- Tuhan Galuh Śrī Wīratanu and her children Tṛṇawindu and Anggira
- The butcher Suka and the origin of the Sukayajña-pakṣa-Jiwaṇa
- Bhagawān Tṛṇawindu at Sukayajña, Anggira at Sarwasidḍa
- Bhagawān Anggira and the *maṇḍala* of Layu-watang

Translation

I

May there be no hindrance.

This is the holy Tantu Panggĕlaran. May your lordships pay close attention to it, all those who may wish to know about it. Come, enjoy listening to the tales of the island of Java in olden times. Human beings did not exist, and in particular the holy Mahāmeru[3] was not on the island of Java. However, it was located on the holy Maṇḍalagiri, a mountain great and high, which served as the centre of the world, and was situated in the land of Jambuḍipa.[4] For this reason the island of Java was unsteady, constantly moving up and down, as there was no Mandaraparwata, not to mention human beings. For this reason Lord Jagatpramāṇa[5] arose, and promptly performed yoga on the island of Yawaḍipa[6] together with Lady Parameśwarī.[7] For this reason we have what is called Ḍihyang[8] now, as a result of the Lord's yoga, the story goes.

The Lord performed yoga for a long time, and sent the gods Brahmā and Wiṣṇu to make human beings. Now the gods Brahmā and Wiṣṇu agreed, and made human beings. They kneaded lumps of clay and formed them into humans of perfect beauty, in appearance like the gods. The male human was the product of the god Brahmā's work, and the female was made by the god Wiṣṇu, both of perfect beauty. This

3. Synonyms for this holy mountain are: Maṇḍalagiri, Mandaragiri, Mandaraparwata, Niṣada, Ganḍamaḍana, Triśṛngga and so on.
4. The Indian subcontinent is intended.
5. Synonyms for this important figure are: Jagatnātha, Jagatwiśeṣa, Parameśwara, Mahākāraṇa, Guru, Mahāguru, Nandiguru, Nīlakaṇṭa, Nāmaśiwaya etc.
6. That is, the island of Java.
7. This is a reference to the goddess Umā or Parwatī.
8. Identifiable with the well known Dieng Plateau in central Java.

is the reason we have what is called Mount Pawinihan[9] now, a result of the gods Brahmā and Wiṣṇu making human beings, as the story goes.

The products of the gods Brahmā and Wiṣṇu making human beings were brought together, and they were joined in mutual love. They had children, grandchildren, great-grandchildren, great-great-grandchildren, *muning* and *anggas*.[10] Reproduction was the task of human beings. But they had no houses, male and female went naked in the forest, they broke sticks (by hand), as there was no other way to do it, and nothing to imitate. They had no loin-cloth, no lower garment, no shawl, no bathing cloth, no girdle, no crest and no scissors. They spoke but did not know what to say, as they did not understand language. They ate any leaves and fruits. Such is what people did in ancient times.

For this reason all the gods gathered and came together, and went to attend upon Lord Guru. Lord Jagatnātha directed the gods to establish order in Yawaḍipāntara. Lord Mahākaraṇa said:

"My son, the god Brahmā, go down to Yawaḍipa, sharpen the weapons (tools?) of men, such as arrows, chopping knives, chisels, cotton combs, axes, picks and all manner of human tools. You are called 'smith'; now because of your sharpening of weapons, there is a place (?) called Winduprakāśa. Your two big toes will hold and hammer (?), file (?) the iron with your *śarasantana*.[11] The weapons will be sharp because of your two big toes. For this reason your name as a smith will be Mpu Sujiwana [as your big toes sharpen iron, so you are called *mpu* (big toe) as a smith of iron] as your big toes are the means. Let such be my instructions to you, my son.

Also you, my son the divine Wiśwakarma, go down to Yawaḍipa, make a house to be imitated by humans, and hence your name will be 'carpenter' [You should be imitated by people in making a house, you will be called 'carpenter'].

As for you, divine Iśwara, go down to Yawaḍipa, teach people about the word, so that they understand about language, in particular the teaching of the ten kinds of good conduct and the five fields of learning. You shall be the teacher of village heads, and so your name will be Gurudeśa in Yawaḍipa.

And as for you, divine Wiṣṇu, go down to Yawaḍipa, and everything that you say should be obeyed by people, and they should imitate all that you do. You will be the teacher of human beings, and will rule over the world, my son.

9. From Old Javanese *winih*, "seed", or "seedling" (Z 2284).

10. Not clear how many generations removed.

11. Meaning unknown.

And as for you, divine Mahādewa, go down to Yawaḍipa, become a goldsmith and make the ornaments to be worn by people.

Lord Ciptagupta, you will make paintings, and will depict various artistic forms, every form that can be imagined, using as means your thumbs (*mpu tangan*), and so your name will be Mpu Ciptangkara when you paint".

Such were the instructions of Lord Guru to all the gods; they descended to Yawaḍipa. The god Brahmā became a smith and made use of the five elements, namely: earth, water, brightness, wind and sky. The earth served as his anvil, water as his tongs, brightness as his fire, the wind as his bellows and the sky as his hammer. This is the reason that there is a mountain called Brahmā now, as a result of the god Brahmā forging iron there in former times, it is told, up to the present time. Hammer and anvil are as big as a *tal* palm and the tongs as big as a *pucang* palm, the god Bāyu emerges from a cave, the god Agni is there day and night, as this is a result of the god Brahmā forging iron, the story goes.[12]

Lord Wiśwakarma descended as a carpenter and made a house, [and people imitated him when making houses], they also made houses. There is a village by the name of Mĕḍang-kamulan now, the origin (*mūla*) of people setting up houses in former times, the story goes.

The Lord Iśwara descended and taught beneficial words, in particular about the ten kinds of good conduct and the five fields of learning. He bore the title of Gurudeśa there.

Suddenly Lord Wiṣṇu descended with Lady Śrī, as rulers from the sky. *A* means "is not", *wa* means "high", and *hyang* means Lord, and so Rahyang Kaṇḍyawan was the name of Lord Wiṣṇu. Sang Kanyawan was the name of Lady Śrī at the court of Mĕḍang-gaṇa, as this was the origin of the kingdom, it is told, in former times, as she taught the people, and they knew how to spin and weave, to wear a loin-cloth, a lower garment and a scarf.

Lord Mahādewa descended and became a goldsmith, and Lord Ciptagupta descended and painted.

Let us tell of the divine Kaṇḍyawan, who had five sons. The eldest was Mangukuhan, Saṇḍang-garbha the second, Katung-malaras the middle one, Karung-kalah the second youngest, and Wṛtti-kaṇḍayun the youngest. Suddenly the vehicles of Lady Śrī arrived, birds four in number, namely: a turtle dove, a wood dove, a red dove and a black dove. The five sons hunted them, pursued them, and they alighted on a *warwang* tree,

---

12. The gods Bāyu and Agni represent the elements of wind and fire respectively.

and Wṛtti-kaṇḍayun hit them with a sling. The crops of the birds fell: the turtle dove contained white seed, the black dove contained black seed, the red dove contained red seed, and the wood dove contained yellow seed, spreading a fragrant perfume. The five sons were delighted and bit [the seed] till it was gone. This is why there is no yellow seed, even until now, as the five sons bit it all. Mangukuhan nurtured the seeds, white, [red] and black, and these became rice, even until today. But he buried the seed with a yellow peel and it turned into turmeric, so the seeds of four colours were complete, and have been so until today.

Let us tell how Lord Mahākāraṇa established order in Yawaḍipa, in order to leave behind sacred lines [*tantu hyang*], and these were arranged over the earth, stretching without breaking, extending without being wiped out, such was the procedure. However, the island of Java in the past was unsteady, constantly moving up and down, as there was nothing to hold it down. For this reason Lord Mahākāraṇa looked for a means of making it firm, in the past, future and present. Immediately Lord Guru performed yoga, and the deity stood facing east; he churned the water[13] and it turned into foam and turned into mountains. The reason there is a mountain Hyang even till now is the yoga of Lord Guru, as the story goes, in former times; and the earth at the Lord's feet turned into the mountain Limohan.

At the same time the island of Java was not steady, but was always moving up and down. Then Lord Parameśwara gave orders to the gods to finish putting the world in order and to return home, each to his own heaven. They all returned, and each left behind his yoga-child in order to take his place in all the doings of men.

Let us speak of the holy Kaṇḍyawan; he then left his five sons behind in order to replace him as king. But not a single one was willing. Finally he devised a draw of lots of *alang-alang* grass: the one who drew the wrapped one, he would replace him as king. The four of them drew one, but did not draw the wrapped one. Finally it came to Wṛtti-kaṇḍayun, and he drew the wrapped one. Wṛtti-kaṇḍayun was made king. Mangukuhan followed the career of a farmer, the source of what the king eats. Saṇḍang-garbha followed the career of a trader, the source of the king's money. Katung-malaras followed the career of a tapper, the source of the king's palm wine. Karung-kalah followed the career of a butcher, the source of the king's meat. As King Wṛtti-kaṇḍayun replaced his father. Lord Wiṣṇu returned home from where he was together with Lady Śrī. The people increased more and more.

13. The text has *taya*; read *toya*?

Let us speak of the host of gods paying homage to Lord Guru; all the gods, the sages, celestial women, *wiḍyādara* (fairies) and *ganḍarwa* (heavenly musicians) gathered the dust of the feet of Lord Mahākāraṇa. When they had made an obeisance, they sat down in orderly lines, attending on Lord Guru [who said:]

"Oh all you gods, sages, heavenly beings, *wiḍyādara* and *ganḍarwa*, go head for Jambuḍipa, all my sons, and move the holy Mahāmeru. Bring it to the island of Java [to serve as a weight], so that the island of Java will be firm and cease swaying, when the holy Mandaragiri has come here. Off you go, all my sons!"

Such were the words of the Lord to all the gods, the sages, heavenly beings, *wiḍyādara* and *ganḍarwa*. They all agreed and took leave to set off and go to Jambuḍipa, in order to work on the holy Mandaragiri together. They arrived at the mountain of Jambuḍipa, which was great and tall, reaching as far as the sky, one hundred thousand *yojana*[14] in height. The reason the distance between sky and earth was one hundred thousand *yojana*, was because formerly the holy Mahāmeru was one hundred thousand *yojana* high. But when it was moved to the island of Java, half of it was left behind in Jambuḍipa. So now the reason the holy Mahāmeru is only half the height of the sky is that it is the base of the holy Mahāmeru, and its peak has been moved to Java.

All the gods set to work on it together. Lord Wiṣṇu turned into a serpent of limitless size and length, and he served as the cord for turning the holy Mahāmeru. The god Brahmā turned into the king of turtles, of limitless size, and served as the foundation for turning the holy Mahāmeru. The serpent wrapped itself around the holy Mahāmeru, and together they all set to tearing out the holy Mahāmeru. There emerged a supernatural light as well as thunder and gusts of wind. Suddenly all the gods picked it up together, and the host of sages and divine beings uttered blessings and cheers. Lord Bāyu took the lead and placed it on the back of the turtle king, the holy Mandaragiri was turned by all the gods, and shouting "hurray" they carried the holy Mahāmeru away.

Now the people of Jambuḍipa saw the holy Mahāmeru moving along, but the gods were invisible to them. This is why they raised their voices, and all the brahmans praised the holy Mandaragiri: "quick, off you go!" such was the praise of all the brahmans.

Let us speak of all the gods: they were fatigued with turning the holy Mandaragiri, and each thirsted for water. There was water emerging from the holy Mahāmeru,

14. 1 yojana measures somewhere between 8 and 15 km in length, depending on the source consulted (cf. Z 2365).

called the poison Kālakūṭa. This served as the exudation of the mountain. Because of their exhaustion all the gods drank the poisonous Kālakūṭa water. Then all the gods died because of the power of the water called the Kālakūṭa poison. Lord Parameśwara saw this [and said:]

"Hey, all you gods have died! What is indeed the cause of your deaths? Hey, the mountain is dripping wet, perhaps you have drunk it, and this is why you have all died. Come, let me drink it!"

He drank the Kālakūṭa water, and the Lord's neck became black, looking like a birthmark. For this reason Lord Guru is called Lord Nīlakaṇṭa, because his neck is black like a birthmark. Lord Guru said:

"Hey, you are indeed very powerful. I am suffering pain because of this".

He looked closely at the Kālakūṭa poison, and it turned into the water of life Śiwāmba. This was used to fill the holy Kamaṇḍalu, and served as water for sprinkling on all the gods. Quick! The holy water of life Śiwāmba bathed all the gods, and they came to life, with the four Guardians of the World, the *wiḍyādara* and *ganḍarwa*, and all the gods paid homage to Lord Guru. Quickly Lord Parameśwara said:

"Come, turn the holy Mandaragiri once more, and let it come to the island of Java. Come on, my boys!"

Thus spoke the Lord to all the gods. They agreed. He was assisted by all the *detya*, *danawa* and *rākṣasa* in restoring all the gods. They turned the holy Mandaragiri, and in a moment it arrived on the island of Java at the western tip. Suddenly the holy Mahāmeru stopped, and the gods' footprints were smooth and shining.[15] For this reason the holy Mahāmeru is called Mount Kelāśa, as the gods' footprints were shining.

Oops! The west was low, and the east of the island of Java was high. Then the holy Mahāmeru was torn off and moved to the east. Its base stayed behind in the west; the reason there is a mountain called Kelāśa now, is that it was the stump of the holy Mahāmeru at one time, the story goes. Its peak was moved to the east, and was turned in a joint effort by all the gods. The holy Mahāmeru crumbled and fell. Now the first piece of the earth to fall turned into Mount Katong; the second piece of earth that fell turned into Mount Wilis; the third piece of earth that fell turned into Mount Kampud; the fourth piece of earth that fell turned into Mount Kawi; the fifth piece of earth that fell turned into Mount Arjuna; and the sixth piece of earth that fell turned into Mount Kumukus.

15. Text *makelah-kelah* (Z 859, this place only), meaning uncertain.

The lower side was missing a piece because of the crumbling of the holy Mahāmeru, and so it stood slanting toward the north, [its peak was broken and moved]. Then all the gods set the peak of the holy Mahāmeru upright. "Ah, pure and holy (*pawitra*)", said all the gods; and so now the peak of the holy Mahāmeru is called Pawitra, the old tale goes. However, the holy Mahāmeru was still not steady, and finally came to rest against Mount Brahmā, as plainly the holy Mahāmeru would have collapsed if it did not lean against Mount Brahmā, as it was missing a piece on the lower side. Because of the fact that it had the support of Mount Brahmā, suddenly the holy Mandaragiri stood firmly. This is the reason that the island of Java ceased moving up and down, and was seated firmly (*nisaḍa apagĕh*). And this is the reason that the holy Mahāmeru is called Mount Niṣaḍa.

Then Lord Parameśwara gave orders to all the gods to worship the holy Mandaragiri, so that they could make use of its contents. Then the Trinity of Lords were given the grant of a mount: a white bull served as the mount of Lord Iśwara; a white swan served as the mount of Lord Brahmā; and a white *garuḍa* served as the mount of Lord Wiṣṇu. When the Trinity of Lords had been given the grant of a mount, all the gods assembled in order to worship the holy Mahāmeru, king of mountains. This is now their nature, way of acting (*bhāwa*).

There was a jewelled pot, by the name of the holy Kamaṇḍalu, containing the holy water of life Śiwāmba, serving as the substance[16] of the holy Mandaragiri. This was then worshipped by all the gods. When they had finished doing this, they took the contents of the holy Mahāmeru, in the form of rubies, bezoars and diamonds; these they offered to Lord Parameśwara. They took no notice of the holy Kamaṇḍalu. Off went all the gods, and the holy jewelled pot was left behind.

There were demons two in number, by the name of Rātmaja and Rātmaji. They went on a pleasure trip to the holy Mandaragiri, wanting to pick up some gold, rubies, bezoars and diamonds, so they thought. But they did not get any gold, rubies, bezoars or diamonds; they found the holy Kamaṇḍalu. They picked it up and took it away (*wiring*),[17] thinking they would use it as a toy; they did not know what it was used for. [It looked truly glittering], and so they named the holy Kamaṇḍalu "Kĕtĕk-mĕlĕng". Off went Rātmaja and Rātmaji.

Let us speak of all the gods, who came to pay homage to Lord Guru. The Lord said:

---

16. For *hiji* or *iji*, see *wiji* (Z 2270).
17. Meaning unclear.

"Oh my sons all the gods, where is the essence of the holy Mahāmeru? [What have you done with it?] You have offered the gold, rubies, bezoars and diamonds, but where is the jewelled pot, the holy Kamaṇḍalu, which contains the water of life, Śiwāmba, which serves as the life of all the gods?"

This is what Lord Mahākāraṇa said. But none of the gods knew who had seized the holy Kamaṇḍalu: in particular the sages Nārada, Kapila, Ketu, Tumburu, [Sapaka and Wiśwakarma], no one knew who had taken the holy Kamaṇḍalu. The four World Guardians Indra, Yama, Baruṇa and Kowera, and the host of sages, celestial beings, *wiḍyādara* and *ganḍarwa*, did not know. All the gods were in a quandary, and finally questioned the gods Raditya (Sun) and Wulan (Moon). Raditya and Wulan said:

"There were demons, two in number, by the names of Rātmaja and Rātmaji. They seized the holy Kamaṇḍalu".

Such were the words of the gods Raditya and Wulan. Now Lords Brahmā and Wiṣṇu went to where Rātmaja and Rātmaji were. Quick! They reached the demons. Rātmaja and Rātmaji said:

"Oh, it is most unusual for the gods to come here. What is your lordships' intention?"

The gods Brahmā and Wiṣṇu said:

"Our intention in coming is [to ask]: What did you get from the Mandaragiri?"

The demons replied:

"Your lordships' servants did not find gold, rubies, bezoars or diamonds. What we got was Kĕtĕk-mĕlĕng".

The gods answered:

"What is this thing called Kĕtĕk-mĕlĕng? [What does it look like?]"

They showed them the jewelled pot. Then the gods asked for it, but the demons did not give it. They offered to buy it with gold and jewels, but the demons would not give it. Finally the demons asked:

"What kind of thing is the jewelled pot?"

The gods said:

"The jewelled pot is called the holy Kamaṇḍalu, and it contains the true nectar Śiwāmba, which serves as the life of the gods".

Quickly the demons grasped the jewelled pot, then put it away carefully and hid it. Now the gods Brahmā and Wiṣṇu were overcome with shame. From their understanding of what action to take, they adopted the appearance of beautiful women; now they were acting the part of these. They came to where Rātmaja and Rātmaji were and asked for the jewelled pot, and addressed them with seductive words. The demons were excited to see the beautiful women; and then they gave them the jewelled pot. Lord Wiṣṇu took firm hold of it. Quickly the gods Brahmā and Wiṣṇu ran away with it. Rātmaja and Rātmaji pursued them, but could not catch up with [the gods Brahmā and Wiṣṇu], as their speed was limitless. Rātmaja and Rātmaji were put to shame.

Let us speak of all the gods who were in attendance on Lord Parameśwara. Then they drank the true nectar Śiwāmba, the fruit of which is not to be affected by age and death; the leaves of the *wandira*[18] served as their drinking cups there. There was a demon by the name of Rāhu [his nature was to take on the appearance of the gods], who mixed with the gods when drinking the true nectar Śiwāmba; he used the leaf of the *awar-awar* as his drinking cup. The holy Sun and Moon caught sight of him and called out to the demon drinking the true nectar Śiwāmba. Lord Wiṣṇu threw his discus [at the demon]. [His neck was cut off] and his trunk died; the nectar was only held in his mouth and had not yet entered his body. For this reason Rāhu's head is alive. The holy Sun and Moon became the objects of his anger, and Rāhu has been a source of doubt and trouble to the holy Sun and Moon, even until now.

When the gods had finished drinking the true nectar Śiwāmba, Lord Śiwa promptly performed yoga: the mountain Wĕlahulu appeared. Lord Iśwara performed yoga, and Mount Sañjaya appeared. Lord Brahmā performed yoga, and Mount Walangbangan appeared. Lord Wiṣṇu performed yoga, and Mount Pamrihan appeared. From the time of the death of the boar Damalung it was called Mount Mawulusan, such is the story.

II

Let us tell of Lord Jagatpramāṇa, who formed the intention to withdraw from the world; for this reason there exists now the abode of ascetics Bulon, the first time that the Lord made a hermitage, according to the old story. The second time was at Kupang, the third time at Huluwanwa, and the fourth time at Pacira. There was a fierce serpent that wished to defeat the Lord. He hit it with his chopper; it died and grew up with leaves and flowers. So then it was named "*nagasari*", and hence Pacira was the first place where there were *nagasari* flowers. There was a chopper[19] left behind in the tree, and this turned into an animal called a *lutung* (black or grey long-tailed monkey), so the story goes.

The Lord proceeded from Pacira in a westerly direction to Maśin. He practised asceticism together with Lady Umā, building up goodness. Hence there are *manguyu*; they were followed in the way of the Manguyu order, creating an example to be

18. That is, the *waringin*, Ficus indica.

19. Text: *tuñci,* variant *tuḍḍi.* Meaning unknown, not listed in Z.

followed in the world. Lord Guru wished to have a handsome son; a son of the Lady was born. He was named the divine Kāmadewa, and was more handsome than any of the gods. His wife was named Lady Smarī. It happened that he was recalcitrant in eating; the Lady was grieved, and hurled the rice and buried it, and it grew up with long extended shoots. Hence there is what is called *gaḍung*; once it was rice, the story goes.

Ileru is a place of Lord Guru; Lady Umā with Lady Smarī went away and stayed in the gardens of Wanisari. Since then Wanisari has been a place of Lady Umā, and even up to now it is an established holy site (*tantu*) of Lady Umā.

Lord Guru left Maśin, and the god Kāmadewa and Lady Smarī stayed behind on Mount Kelāśa. Now Lord Guru came to the Mahāmeru with Lady Parameśwarī, and they both performed austerities. Lady Umā displayed (*umintonakĕn*) her nature, and after that the hermitage of Lady Umā was on Mount Pinton, separated by a gully from the hermitage of Lord Guru. Lady Umā arrived at Lord Guru's hermitage, and she stumbled on a sharp piece of wood like an iron spur (*taji*), and so the hermitage of Lord Guru came to be called Kayutaji. The Lady's foot was bleeding, and she wailed; her wailing turned into *pañcaśilah*,[20] her tears turned into the shoots[21] of bamboo, and her snot turned into the fungus of the *paḍali* (tree).

Lord Guru left Kayutaji, and changing into[22] the lake was his conduct (*bhāwa*), hence the hermitage of Lord Guru was called Ranubhawa. Lady Parameśwarī followed him, and the blood from the Lady's foot kept on spreading,[23] and hence Lady Umā's hermitage was called Kabyang. The Lady was in high spirits and adorned herself. Lord Guru saw the beauty of the Lady. Lord Parameśwara approached Lady Umā; they were joined, and Lady Umā conceived in her womb. He[24] left the hermitage and finally led the life of a *manguyu*; his place was in Pamanguyon-agung. He ate yams and taro; hence the Lord became a *lĕmbu-guntung*,[25] and was given the name Amanguyu-guntung.

20. A certain plant? (Z 1267, this place only).
21. Text as printed: *ktak* (Z 855, this place only); Pigeaud translates "shoot", but cf. Modern Javanese *(bung)kaṭèk*, (Pig.) "shoot from the stem (of sugar cane, bamboo)". It is not clear why the *paḍali* tree should be associated with fungus.
22. Text: *atma*, read *atĕmah*?
23. Text: *mabyang-byangan* (Z 284, this place only; to disperse, drip down?).
24. Gender not entirely clear.
25. A category of religious persons, see Z 556, and note in Pigeaud, p. 223.

The Lady's children were born, both male. Lord Guru said: "Formerly my followers[26] went to you, Lady, and so my sons will be called Gaṇa and Kumāra". Lady Umā was washing her menstrual cloths of *baruñjing*[27] in the stream of the holy Ranupuhan; hence it is now called Ḍingḍing. Her menstrual cloths were in rags,[28] and she abandoned them; they were surrounded by a cloud of loudly buzzing flies. They turned into a plant with leaves and vines, which was then named the *turuk-umung* ("buzzing-vulva").[29]

Let us speak of the god Kāmadewa and Lady Smarī, who went to Mount Kelāśa. The god Kāmadewa wished to have intercourse with Lady Smarī, but was afraid that Lord Guru would be angry with him. Lady Smarī divided her body in half; and so Lady Ratih became wife to the god Kāmadewa. Lady Ratih was incarnated in the deified ancestor (*hyangta*)[30] of Kaṇḍayun, and turned into Turuk-manis; [Kāmadewa was born and turned into Wĕngan, who became the husband of Turuk-manis]. For this reason Pinaleśawi[31] became the wife of Katiha; likewise Kuli-kuli in the land of Mĕḍang-gaṇa was the wife of Wawu-langit in the land of Mĕḍang-gaṇa.

Let us speak of Lord Guru and Lady Umā, who were in Pamanguyon-agung and had as sons Gaṇa and Kumāra. Finally Lady Umā went in search of the elder brother of Gaṇa and Kumāra; she went down to the plain[32] and carried petals and flowers with her. Lord Guru stayed behind to tend Gaṇa and Kumāra, and they were happy and enjoyed themselves. It is told that Lady Umā went begging alms.[33] Lady Umā was ashamed, and finally scattered the petals and flowers. Quick! Lady Umā returned home, and was greeted by Gaṇa and Kumāra. Suddenly she had a desire to eat; Lady Umā took salted food,[34] and mixed her rice with coconut fibre.

Let us tell of Lord Parameśwara, who left Lady Umā and Gaṇa and Kumāra. He had the plan to withdraw, and dwell on the mountain ridges (*gĕgĕr*); so the name of Lord Guru's hermitage was Gĕgĕr-katyāgan. Now Lady Umā set up house with Gaṇa

26. Text: *gaṇa* (Z 484, a follower of Śiwa).
27. Meaning unknown, this place only (Z 219–220).
28. Text: *amoh*, but perhaps read *mabo* "smelly" (Z 248)?
29. In Modern Javanese the word *turuk* is crude for "female genitals"; not listed in Z.
30. *hyangta* is probably the same as *rahyangta*, which is listed under *hyang* (Z 661).
31. Apparently a personal name, compare Noorduyn (1962, pp. 424–25) on the opening passage of the Carita Parahyangan.
32. Text: *ratha-ratha*, probably to be read *rata-ratā*, a level place, plain (Z 1519).
33. Text: *manangsi-nangsi*; probably from *tangsi* = *tasi* (cf. note 187 below).
34. Text: *apoyah* (Z 1376, "to eat" or "to talk"? this place only); any connection with *uyah* "salt"?

and Kumāra; she considered them both as her husband, and for this reason Gaṇa and Kumāra are the deities of the nun's girdle; a great sin is incurred by those who follow the way of life of a nun if they marry into a lower generation,[35] because of what Lady Umā once did, the story goes. Gaṇa followed Lord Guru; Lord Guru went off, and Gaṇa was left behind in Gĕgĕr-katyāgan. Lord Guru was penetrating (*tumaṇḍĕs*) in his thinking, and so Lord Guru's hermitage was called Taṇḍĕs.

Let us speak of Lady Umā, who left Pamanguyon-agung, and made a hermitage. "I am the jewel (*maṇik*) of the hills", she thought, and so Lady Umā's hermitage was called Mount Maṇik. Her style[36] was a crown, called Makuṭa. She wore a *basahan*[37] like the manner of the gods, and so the Lady's name was Kaki-dewata, even until now.

Now Kumāra followed Lord Guru, and was run off his feet.[38] "Hey, now I realize what it's really like to follow the Lord", he said. Then he was called Katu-katu. This is why Kumāra is the deity of the *katu-katu*,[39] and great is the sin incurred by those who follow the way of life of the *katu-katu*, if they marry a wife in a lower generation, because of what Lord Guru did, the story goes.[40] Kumāra was thirsty for milk, and went home to suckle with Lady Umā; when he had had enough, he returned to Lord Guru. He became thirsty again and was determined to go to the Lady, but Lady Umā saw Kumāra coming, and went into hiding. Kumāra noticed and followed the Lady, who turned into the *kalpataru*.[41] He squeezed the Lady's breasts, and then Kumāra saw that the *kalpataru* was moist, and this he sucked up. It tasted like the Lady's milk, and finally Kumāra understood that the tree was what Lady Umā had turned into. He finally addressed the tree with gentle words:

"I saw juice when I found the breast of mother as before". This is why there is what is called the *ano* (aren-palm) now; *duk* is the name of its fibre, and *dangu* is the name of its flower stalk.

This is what Kumāra said. Off went Lady Umā, heading in a westerly direction. Kumāra followed her, caught up with her, and looked at her closely;[42] this is why there

---

35. Text: *katurun alaki*; translation a guess.
36. Text: *bhāwa*; Pigeaud translates "ornaat".
37. Lower garment, *kampuh*, *wastra* (Z 221).
38. Text: *kaputangpati*, manuscript B *kapuntang-panting*; the translation is based on Modern Javanese *kepontang-panting* and Indonesian *terpontang-panting*, to be "flat out".
39. Perhaps the name of a tree, Z 823.
40. The intention of this passage is not clear.
41. The "wishing tree", or "tree of plenty" (Z 778).
42. Text: *pinipilan*; see Z 1365.

is a mountain called Pilan. Kumāra felt offended, and went to perform austerities on the mountain called Tawungan now, the former hermitage of Kumāra, the story goes.

The god Gaṇa came to Lady Umā, and it came about that he was of the very same appearance as Kumāra; this is why Gaṇa is green (*ijo*), and so Mount Ijo is the name of Lady Umā's mountain. Gaṇa was offended, and went to perform austerities; this is why there is now a mountain called Wija, formerly the hermitage of the god Gaṇa, the story goes.[43]

The Lord Guru granted Gaṇa the (power of) *mandi śwara* ("magically powerful voice"), and everything he said turned out to be true. The gods Brahmā and Wiṣṇu were doubtful when they saw Gaṇa's special power; for this reason they decided to set a riddle. The god Wiṣṇu came before Gaṇa [and Gaṇa said:]

"What is your business, divine Wiṣṇu?"

[The god Wiṣṇu spoke, saying:]

"Guess the answer to my riddle, Gaṇa".

"What is your riddle, divine Wiṣṇu?"

"What can be considered a fault of mine?"

"Ah, *brahmahatya* will serve as your fault".

"What does *brahmahatya* mean?"

"You keep killing your fellow gods".[44]

"No, I have never killed my fellow gods".

"Ah, you do kill your fellow gods—what if you do that sort of thing some time in the future (*kumĕlĕm*)?"[45]

Off went Lord Keśawa, and the god Brahmā came to set a riddle. The god Brahmā once had five heads; he hid the one in the centre, and four of his heads were visible. This was now his way of behaving (*bhāwa*). Off he went and came to where the god Gaṇa was.

"What is your business, divine Brahmā?"

Lord Pāwaka replied:

"Guess how many heads I have, Gaṇa".

"What will happen if I guess how many heads you have?"

"I will pay homage to you. And if you don't guess it, I will eat you, Gaṇa. [Come on, how many heads do you think I have, Gaṇa?]"

"You have four heads, divine Brahmā".

43. The intention of this passage is not entirely clear.

44. In fact "brahman-murderer" (Z 255); the TP has a somewhat different interpretation here.

45. A guess, based on the variant *hĕlĕm-hĕlĕm*.

"Ha, I'll kill you, Gaṇa, as I have five heads, Gaṇa".

Lord Parameśwara was watching [and said:] "Oh dear, my son will be killed by Lord Brahmā in a minute". For this reason Lord Guru cut off the god Brahmā's middle head with his left hand. Now the god Brahmā served as the right hand, and the god Wiṣṇu was the left; for this reason he ordered the god Wiṣṇu to seize the god Brahmā's head. It turned out that the god Gaṇa was proven right[46] regarding the god Wiṣṇu, that he was a *brahmahatya* (god-murderer).

Let us tell of the words of the god Brahmā with the god Gaṇa:

"Four is the number of your heads, divine Brahmā".

Oh no, five is the number of my heads, Gaṇa.

[Such were the god Brahmā's words.]

"Ah, I'll kill you, Gaṇa".

This is what the god Brahmā said; he was intending to bring his head out, when suddenly it was cut off by the Lord [and his blood spurted out]. Lord Brahmā was furious; for this reason he performed yoga over the blood, and it turned into great evil beings and demons, one hundred and eight in number, and he ordered these to kill Gaṇa. [The god Gaṇa ran away] and made an obeisance to Lord Guru, and Lord Parameśwara took him by the hand [and said:]

"Oh, I took away this Rājapati's head; you would already be dead if I had not taken away the head of the god Brahmā, as I sliced off[47] his middle head, and so you could see [only] four".

"Rājapati is furious now, my lord. And so he has made evil beings and demons one hundred and eight in number, which desire to kill your son now, my Lord, [and this] is why[48] your son is paying homage at your feet".

"Oh, do not be anxious, my son Gaṇa. If the god Brahmā creates demons, I shall create gods".

Quickly he performed yoga over his five fingernails; when he had done this, they turned into five deities, named Kuśika, Garga, Metri, Kuruṣya and Patañjala [such was their number]. He gave them orders to combat the demons; the five deities agreed. We need not speak of the battle of the five deities with the demons.

Let us speak of the god Brahmā's head; he cast it into the sea [the sea became dry]; laid it in the sky [the sky was scorched as if roasted]; he laid it on the earth, and it went straight through to the underworld. It fell on the head of the divine

46. Text: *kapacupi*; not in Z, but cf. Modern Javanese (Pig.) under *cup* and *ĕncup*, "to guess (a riddle)".
47. Text: *den tĕtakĕn*; a word *tĕtak* not listed in Z, but cf. Modern Javanese, "circumcise".
48. Text: *don*; see Z 413.

Anantabhoga, the serpent who serves as the foundation of the earth; his body was set in motion, and so the Lady Pṛthiwī (Earth) quaked and the holy Mahāmeru shook. Because of the power of the earthquake Lord Guru was afraid that the holy Mahāmeru would collapse; then he took the god Brahmā's head out of the depths of the underworld.

Let us speak of the great demons, already defeated and fearful of the five deities; for this reason the five deities came before Lord Guru [and asked for instruction]. The Lord did not permit Lady Umā to listen to the instruction; he then sent her far away, and ordered her to look for the milk of a virgin black cow. Lady Umā agreed, and off she went. The teaching of the five deities from Lord Guru went smoothly.

Now the Lord fixed his gaze on the god Brahmā's head, and finally buried it on Mount Kampud; for this reason Mount Sambadagni was in the end a name of Mount Kampud. The god Brahmā's head finally began to grow, and that is why there is now what is called the *nyu* (coconut palm), that the head [of the god Brahmā turned into], the old story goes.

Let us tell of Lady Umā, who wandered in the realms of heaven, searching for the milk of a virgin black cow; she went as far as the seven underworlds, but did not find the milk of a virgin black cow. She wandered into the middle realm, and it happened that she stumbled on a rock. Her left big toe was split open, and for this reason she walked with a stick. Lord Guru tempted her and tested Lady Umā's fidelity; for this reason Lord Guru turned into Kumāra-gohphala, a herds-boy of measureless handsomeness. [The white bull his mount] he allowed to become a virgin black cow, and this he tended. So this was his mode of action (*bhāwa*). It happened that Lady Umā came across Kumāra-gohphala while he was milking the milk of the virgin black cow. Lady Umā said:

"Hey, herds-boy, let me ask for some milk from you!"

"I will not give it".

"Ha, you won't give it; well, let me buy it with gold and jewels".

"Ha, I will not give it. What use would gold and jewels be to me?"

This is what they said. Finally Kumāra-gohphala asked her to have sex with him; Lady Umā was bewildered, and this is the form that her faithfulness took; so there is a mountain called Winihatya.[49] Lady Umā was longing for[50] the milk of a virgin

49. The variant of B is *winih satya* and of D and E *winasatya.*

50. Text: *matnge*, which looks like a typo for *matĕn* (Z 1987 under *tön*); Pigeaud translates "haakte naar" (longed for).

black cow, and for this reason she agreed to have sex with Kumāra-gohphala. She was even so[51] faithful to Lord Guru; when they had intercourse they were not joined in the private parts, but in the thighs, which she pressed together[52] to appear like private parts. Quickly they had intercourse (*asanggama*), and for this reason there is a mountain called Pasanggaman today. However, the union of the Lord and Lady turned into the precious stone[53] Cintamaṇi [having intercourse with the thighs] and so "*kasamputa*"[54] would be the name of Cintamaṇi. The *sĕmbung*[55] was made their pillow, the *apa-apa*[56] was made their mat, and that left Cintamaṇi, used as their bolster;[57] for this reason there is a mountain called Gulingaṇḍara now. His semen was spilt on the ground, and Lady Umā covered it over, and it turned into Mount Marapi. The split in the Lady's big toe was filled with the semen sprinkled by the Lord; for this reason the Lady's toe became swollen.

He gave Lady Umā some milk from the virgin black cow. Off flew Kumāra-gohphala and turned back into Lord Guru; and the bull also flew away, and was cursed by Lady Umā to fall to earth and be unable to get away. For this reason there is a mountain called Itip-ing-lĕmbu now. He accepted Lady Umā's curse, and she ordered him to perform austerities. The bull did this, and for this reason there is now a mountain called Kĕdyangga.

The milk that he poured out became a spring in the rock.

Let us tell of Lady Umā: her left big toe swelled up; it caused her trouble, she rubbed it, and there emerged blood, slime, and amniotic fluid. She rubbed it again, and there emerged three infants, and there emerged their afterbirth. For this reason Lady Umā was angry, quickly took hold of the weapons of the gods, and these were her state (*bhāwa*); it was her intention[58] to crush the children with them. Quickly the three boys paid homage to the Lady Parameśwarī; they said:

---

51. Text: *matapi*, probably a typo for *tamapi*; Pigeaud translates "toch" (even so).
52. Text: *dinĕngkulakĕn* (Z 389, this place only; but Pigeaud translates "bent", perhaps thinking of Modern Javanese *ḍĕngkul*, "knee").
53. Text: *komara*; probably *komala* is meant.
54. Is there any connection with *saput*, "cover"?
55. A particular plant, Conyza balsamifera, according to Z 1734. Many varieties, see De Clercq, no. 464.
56. Text: *papa*, probably the *apa-apa* (not listed in Z; De Clercq, no. 1552, Flemingia congesta, the dried leaves good for filling pillows).
57. Text: *kaguling-gulingan*; this form not in Z 551–2.
58. Text: *parya*, clearly *praya*, "intention", is meant.

"What should we do if we are to be killed by Parameśwari? Let us be acknowledged[59] as your sons, madam".

This is what the three boys said. Immediately Lady Umā's anger abated, and so finally the three boys were recognized:

"Oh my three sons, you emerged from my left big toe, and so the name of you three is Mpu Kuna. Now as for you, eldest, let me ordain[60] you; I shall rub your hair with oil;[61] and so your name is Kumāra-gimbal,[62] and now you are called a *wiku* Ṛṣi-angarĕmban. Let this be the gift I bestow on you: the weapon the holy Trikurungan. [Take good care of my gift].

Now as for you, middle one, let me initiate you: come, wear on your head my pubic hair, and then your name will be Kumāra-siddḍi. Serve the god Gaṇa, and so you will be called *wiku* Śewa[63] in the world. Instruct mankind in the knowledge[64] of letters, and you will be '*haṣṭapaḍāsari*'[65] in the world. *Bhuja* is a name for 'hand', *angga* is a name for 'body', and so your name will be Mpu Bhujangga. Come, let my gift to you be: what is called the weapon the holy Mṛṣa. Take good care of my gift.

Now as for you, youngest son, let me initiate you now: your name is Kumāra-raray. Look upon my private parts when you concentrate; your name in the world is *wiku* Boddḍa, become a visible form[66] of Lord Buddha in future. *Śo* is a name for 'hyang' (divine), *gata* means 'rĕm';[67] so you will be called Sogata in the world. Here, this is my gift to you: what is called the weapon the divine Guḍuha. Take good care of my gift.

And another boy, why are you looking for me?[68] Where do you come from?"

"By your leave, Lady, let your son be established, madam. Your child is what became of the boys' amniotic fluid".

59. Text: *prasidanĕn*, variant B *prasiḍākĕn*; see Z 1404, "to recognize as real, acknowledge as being indeed ..." for this place.
60. Text: *sangaskara* (Z 1659); we could also translate "initiate".
61. Text: *dak rarapusane*; Z 1510, from Pigeaud on the basis of Sasak = boreh; or to tie up? But *rapus* is not the same as *apus*.
62. The meaning of *gimbal* is "unkempt and sticking together (hair)" (Z 526).
63. Śaiwa is probably intended.
64. Text: *wijjāna*, but *wijñāna* is meant (Z 2272).
65. Meaning unknown.
66. Text: *pamiṇḍa*; note that this is an imperative with prefix *pa-*. The base-word is *piṇḍa* II (Z 1358–9).
67. Perhaps to be linked with *arĕm*, "quiet" (Z 124).
68. Text: *manglabĕt*; Z 949, "to look for, visit"; only this and one other place in Śrī Tañjung.

"Come, let me establish you. Perform austerities by the side of the road. Once you went in search of me, and so your name will be '*tabĕ-habĕt*'.[69] Here is my gift to you: the weapon called the holy Gora. Take good care of my gift.

Another child, why are you paying homage to me? Are you male or female?"

"By your leave, let your child be established, madam. Your child is what became of the boys' afterbirth, madam".

"Come, let me establish you. You must go around in the world; you must be a performer [let your condition (*bhāwa*) be like mine and your father's formerly], such will be your condition as a girl.

[And you boy child] let your condition be like your father when he tempted me; as sash you must wear a *ḍaḍung* (thick cord of vines), wear as bangle a *haḍa pinulir* (twisted midrib of leaf); and so your name in the world will be '*abaṇḍagiṇa anggoḍa*'. Such are my instructions to you.

Hey, animal, why are you paying homage to me?"

"By your leave, Lady, my name is the animal *lutung* (long-tailed monkey). Let your child be established".

"Come, let me establish you. [Here, the weapon called Gaḍa;] you must wear as *dodot* (lower garment) a *wiḍak*;[70] you must tell stories about the world, protect and praise the king; and so your name in the world will be *widu*.[71] These are my instructions to you".

Let us speak of Cintamaṇi, who was tended and nurtured by the gods. He (she?) asked about his mother and father, and the gods told him that he was a child of Lord Guru, with Lady Umā as mother. For this reason Cintamaṇi [went off] and came to Lord Parameśwara. Lord Guru did not acknowledge him as his child, and because of the teasing[72] by the Lord of Lady Umā she was ashamed to acknowledge him as

---

69. Perhaps to be read *tabĕh-abĕt*. This should be connected with the words *abĕt, pangabĕtan*, mentioned below, referring to "a community of religious persons" (Z 2), rather than *tabĕh*, "beating/striking a musical instrument" (Z 1892). The preceding lines are meant to "explain" the word in terms of either sound or sense, as these people once *manglabĕt* me (see note 68). Furthermore, the line above (text p. 80, line 8) commands "Perform austerities by the side of the road", perhaps intended to allude to *habĕt* (Z 568), in particular meaning 3, *angabĕt*, a very old term for "to commit armed robbery", indeed occurring on the side of the road.
70. Z 2261, meaning unknown; but note that a ceremonial cloth known as *bidak* is still known in the region of Lampung (South Sumatra).
71. Bard; actor.
72. Text: *pambeda*; see Z 238 under *bheda*, amongst other things "disuniting, sowing dissension"; Pigeaud translates "verleiding" (seduction), this meaning not listed as such in Z.

her son. Hence Cintamaṇi began to weep, and swiftly descended to the earth. The earth quaked, with thunder and gales; he caused a bright glow and supernatural signs as a result of his pain at not being acknowledged as a son by the Lord and Lady. Finally [the Lord felt pity], and so he finally received him and he was acknowledged as a son by the Lord and the Lady.

Let us tell the tale of how Lord Parameśwara continued the establishment of holy places (*tantu* [*praśiṣṭha*][73]) in Yawaḍipa. He founded the *maṇḍala*, wore a jacket and earrings, and was seated on a cushion[74] and a couch. Then he created the *dewaguru*, and filled all the hermitages, such as:[75] the *katyāgan*, *pangajaran*, *pangubwanan*, *pa[ma]nguyon*, *pangabĕtan*, *gurudeśa*, *anguṇḍahagi*, *angarĕmban*; he made all these. All the gods assembled and worked together to create a house only from[76] wood without fail, perfect in every way (*sarwasidḍa*), and hence the *maṇḍala* is now called Sarwasidḍa. They promptly made a house, and all the gods parted, wanting to make resting places; and so the mountain is now called Rĕrĕban, once the shelter of the gods according to the story. The happiness of all the gods was plain to see, and so the *maṇḍala* is now called Sukawela. The Lord made offerings happily, and so there is finally Sukayajña. Guru was the original one to clear the site, and Sukayajña was the first *maṇḍala* to exist.

Many people wished to become a *wiku* (follow the religious life) and were then ordained (*sangaskāra*) by Lord Guru. The first he ordained was the reverend Wṛhaspati, the second the reverend Soma, the third the reverend Budḍa, the fourth the reverend Śūkra, the fifth the reverend Raditya, the sixth the reverend Saneścara, and the seventh the reverend Anggara.[77] Such was the total number of Lord Guru's pupils at the time when he was in Sukayajña.

We need not mention how long it was, when he wished to go eastwards, [his intention] to come to the holy Mahāmeru. He then instructed Lord Wiṣṇu to take his place as *dewaguru*; but Lord Wiṣṇu did not wish to. Lord Parameśwara urged him strongly, and left the [parasol] earrings and jacket as a gift of the deity; finally Lord Wiṣṇu resigned himself. Off went Lord Guru, following the way of the hills; he kept an eye on what the divine Wiṣṇu was doing. The god Guru's feet were only

73. The same as *pratiṣṭha* according to Z 1404.
74. Text: *su[ra]ngga*; probably the same as *suraga* I (Z 1862).
75. Text: *kadyana*; probably the same as *kadyanggan* (Z 763).
76. Text: *sing*, presumably from *saking* (cf. note 101).
77. These seven are the names of the days of the week.

dimly visible, and so Māyana is a place of the god Guru; for this reason Sukayajña also follows the way of Māyana, the second of the *maṇḍala*.

Let us tell how Lord Wiṣṇu replaced the position of Lord Guru seated on the cushion and couch, but he had no companions. There were people wanting to follow the religious life, but he was unwilling to ordain them. Lord Guru saw this and then came to where the god Wiṣṇu was and spoke to him, saying:

"Hey, my son Wiṣṇu, what is the point of having no pupils? Many people wish to become a *wiku*, but I notice you have no companions.[78] Ordain them, my son!"

The god Wiṣṇu replied:

"Your lordship's son is unwilling to ordain them; it is a nuisance to have too many in the vicinity.[79] I prefer to do my observances by myself".

Lord Guru said:

"How can human beings then pass on from the five forms of suffering (Z 1264)? The aim of creating *maṇḍala* is to provide a means of gaining release from the sins of the forefathers.[80] The result of people taking ordination and desiring to be a *wiku* is: to perform *tapa* and rise[81] to become deities (*dewata*), deities rise to the level of gods (*hyang*), gods rise to become perfect sages (*siddhārṣi*), and perfect sages rise to become Lords (*bhaṭāra*). Apart from these there are also *wiku* whose observances take the wrong path; the result of this is that they are incarnated in the world and become a sovereign with power over the world, and fail to become a deity. The reason they fail to be a deity and are a world-sovereign is that they were a *wiku* whose observances went astray. For this reason, Wiṣṇu, ordain them!"

Lord Wiṣṇu replied sternly:

"Your Lordship's son will first ordain people, provided there are people split in half.[82] Only then will I ordain them".

"Oh, in that case you will ordain nobody, as there are no people who could be called 'cut in half'".

Off went Lord Guru; for this reason he took the form of half a person [with one arm, one leg, and an eye and a mouth on one side]. Quickly he arrived at where the god Wiṣṇu was [this was now his condition]. Lord Wiṣṇu saw him and laughed:

---

78. The text has *tan pamiśwa*; perhaps this is a typo for *tan pamitra* (found in variants).
79. Text: *mantara*; Pigeaud (p. 151) translates "met velen bij elkaar zijn" and comments that *antara* or *pantara* here seems to have the meaning of "surroundings". This meaning not in Z 84.
80. For a clarification of the word "sins" in this context, see Part 2, note 229.
81. Text: *sumambaha*, "to pay homage", but in view of the following this is probably an error for *sumĕngkaha* "rise, go up, ascend".
82. Text: *sasiwak*, Z 1793, "(split in) one half", this place only.

"Ha ha ha, I imagined that a person split in half did not exist; [hey, so there is a half person]. Well, what do you want coming here? I see that you are not whole;[83] what is your business coming hither?"

"Oh my reverend sir, my aim in coming is a wish to become a *wiku*; I desire to wear the state and marks of the Lord, sir".

"Oh, [due to] the great punishment decreed by the Lord,[84] I am not able to withdraw from my word".

Quick, when he had made the flower-offering (*puṣpa*), he worshipped as universal teacher[85] Lord Wiṣṇu; he did not wish to be denied.[86] He wore a *singhĕl* (headdress), the earrings and headband only;[87] having been ordained, he disappeared and flew away again. The praises of all the gods rang out loudly (*gumuruh*), and for this reason there is now a *maṇḍala* called Guruh.

Let us speak of Lord Parameśwara: he left Maśin[88] and headed east; Lady Parameśwarī followed. He stopped at Mount Wilis. The Lord said:

"If you please, Lady, stay behind here and take a rest".[89]

So then she was called Lady Kĕba-kĕba.

"I am going to go to the Mahāmeru; [when the decorations of the holy Mandaragiri are in good order, I will call you later. Don't come unless I call you!"

Such were the Lord's instructions to the Lady. Off went Lord Guru and approached the holy Mahāmeru; he made the *maṇḍala* of Hahāh, on the slope of the holy Mahāmeru] on the southeast. When he had cleared the *maṇḍala* of Hahāh, he made the *maṇḍala* of Gĕrĕsik, on the eastern slope of the holy Mahāmeru. When he had made the *maṇḍala* of Gĕrĕsik, he made a *maṇḍala* on the southern slope [of Mahāmeru]. *Śūnya sagiri* (the whole mountain was empty), there was no one doing *tapa*; and so the *maṇḍala* was called Śūnyasagiri.

Let us speak of Lord Wiṣṇu in Sukayajña; now when he already had many pupils, he came to the hermitage of Lord Iśwara, called Pangkeśwara. [Lord Wiṣṇu said:]

"Replace me wearing the *kurug*,[90] holy Iśwara; you will be *dewaguru* now".

83. Text: *sarosa*; this will be equivalent to *sarwasa*, and may mean "complete, whole" (Z 1702); but then a word *tan* (not) may have been omitted.
84. Text: *gung ri daṇḍa*; not very clear, Pigeaud says "possibly corrupt".
85. Text: *mamiśwaguru*, Z 2303, "to worship as universal teacher?" This place only.
86. Text: *kapapasa*, Z 1274 under *papas*, "go against, counter, oppose".
87. Text: *ḍawak*, Z 379, "self, by oneself, alone, own"; unclear.
88. The reading of the variants is Masin, while Pigeaud's text has Manis.
89. Text: *pakĕba-kĕba*, Z 833, this place only.
90. Text: *kuruwa*; P. 153 suggests *kuruga*, as *kurug* (Z 933) seems to be the same as *kalambi* (jacket).

He handed over the parasol, earrings and jacket to Lord Iśwara, and he replaced him as *dewaguru* at Sukayajña. Lord Wiṣṇu stayed at Māyan[a], and followed the way of the hills; Lord Iśwara was Sukayajña of the Rĕban path.[91]

There was a brahman from Jambuḍipa, called the holy Tĕkĕn-wuwung; he travelled through the air, following the course of the holy Mahāmeru. He saw a white glowing light: "That is a pure place of the deity", he said. He stayed high above the holy water flowing from Sukayajña; the god Iśwara saw him:[92]

"Fie, brahman" [said the god Iśwara], "do not stay high above this place. This water is unique,[93] you might possibly do something shameful,[94] and the water will be defiled.[95] Look for another place, you are putting yourself too high".

The brahman was firmly warned; but he just refused, went on being unashamed in the same way, and signs of his improper character appeared. He was contemptuous of the *paṇḍita*: he ate, threw garbage in the river,[96] and defecated[97] in the water:

"As if the *paṇḍita* will know [he said] that I have relieved myself in the river".

The brahman went home and sat by the fire; Lord Iśwara saw him [and said:]

"Oh, that brahman is unashamed, his faeces will soon[98] be carried downstream. Hey, go back, water [and go to the reverend Tĕkĕn-wuwung's yard!]"

[Immediately the water spread out and flowed uphill. The reverend Tĕkĕn-wuwung said:]

"Hey, the water is running into the yard, and my faeces and garbage,[99] that before were carried away, now are in[100] the yard. Hey, it's very odd for water to flow up and rise; this water is extraordinary, as the direction of the water is from[101] the valley. The *paṇḍita* is truly powerful!"

---

91. Unclear, perhaps *hanêng* is missing before Sukayajña.
92. Text: *tuminggal*, but the variant of B, *tuminghal* (see) is better.
93. Text: *tunggal*; unclear.
94. Text: *rinangkuṣa*; not as Z 1508, "to relieve oneself", but cf. Pigeaud's translation "ongegeneerd" (unashamed). The form is an obvious error for *nirangkuśa*, Z 1188, "lawless, unruly, wild, ill-mannered, rude".
95. Text: *acĕpĕl*; Z 322, "defiled", this place only.
96. Text: *swah*; the variant of B, *lwah* (river) is better.
97. The text has *angising*, "to shit", in this context, not a euphemism at all.
98. Text: *sĕne*; the variant of B, *mĕne*, is better.
99. Text: *ising mangan tajang*; Z 1901 under *tajang* says "faeces" (this place only), but this is already covered by *ising*. For *mangan* Pigeaud suggests *pangan*.
100. Text: *mungswing*, but the variant of B, *munggwing*, is better.
101. Text: *sing*, presumably from *saking*.

In a moment the reverend Tĕkĕn-wuwung came to where the god Iśwara was [and said:]

"Oh excuse your son, but what is the meaning of water running uphill, sir? It makes no sense for the water to come from the valley. I'm amazed at how water can run uphill. What does it mean?"

Lord Iśwara answered:

"Ah, it is very shameless indeed, to throw garbage and faeces in the river. I don't want that".

"Oh, how do you know [that I defecated in the river?]"

"I was at home, sitting there, and caught sight of you relieving yourself in the river. This is why I sent the water back".

"Oh, the *paṇḍita* is very powerful. Ah, what is this power of yours? Your son wishes to be taught it. There is plenty of gold in Jambuḍipa that I can provide as a gift[102] for you, sir".

"Well, if you, brahman, wish to be taught, [if you] do not adopt the wrong appearance; you should be of one and the same kind. Become a *wiku* with me, and wear the insignia of a Lord [and so you will be of one and the same kind]".

"In that case it is lucky, sir".

He agreed to accept[103] the marks of a *wiku*; quickly the brahman was ordained, and was ordered to perform the Śiwa ritual; he was given the name Mpu Siddḍayoga. Lord Iśwara instructed him in the teachings.

We tell how for some time Mpu Siddḍayoga conducted austerities, but was overwhelmed by the power of passion, and his bold efforts to defend himself were hurled to and fro by the Six Inner Enemies. For this reason he said humbly to his teacher:

"If you please, Lord, your son wishes to enter matrimony, sir. [I feel impelled to take a wife] I am not capable of living a single life".

"Come, be patient, Mpu Siddḍayoga, faithfully using vows as your support. Let there be perfect accomplishment, including the causes of going to heaven, until you should reach the realm of Parameśwara-śiwa, whatever you desire; there are no deities who are fully accomplished unless austerities and vows go ahead. You must make war on the battlefield, and anyone who is brave will be rewarded; seeking refuge in faithfulness and manliness, constantly endure in detachment,[104] and as if fighting in the

102. Text: *mangĕmbanga*; Z 845 under *kĕmbang*, "to worship with flowers".

103. Text: *wilaśa*, see Z 2279 under *wilasa* II, "to meet one's wishes, willing to help, sympathetic".

104. Text: *sĕpa-sĕpi*, see Z 1743–4 under *sĕpi*, "to free oneself from everything, abandon all".

midst of battle, you should not always be thinking about children and wife. Press on with what you are enduring; no matter how far it is to the end of the field, however wide it appears, if you go steadily you will be able to succeed.[105] [Do not retreat in the battle] the penalty is a fall in your estate. Later, when you have completed your austerities, share and choose (take) whatever you wish".

These were the words of the god Iśwara. He still wanted to take a wife, and preferred not to live a single life.

"Well, if you want to have a wife, there are princesses in Mĕḍang-gaṇa, by the names of Dewi Kasingi and Dewi Madumali, daughters of Mahārāja Wawu-langit. Take the elder one, called Dewi Kasingi".

Mpu Siddayoga set out[106] swiftly, as he was travelling through the air. Reaching the city, he asked for the royal princesses; Mahārāja Wawu-langit did not deny access. Mpu Siddayoga was ordered to choose; he chose the elder one. Mahārāja Wawu-langit said:

"How could[107] you, a scholar, possibly want my elder daughter, as she is blind, her eyes have no pupils and are cloudy, she does not see but gropes her way".

So said Mahārāja Wawu-langit. Back went Mpu Siddayoga, and arriving paid homage to his teacher, telling him that the elder princess was blind.

"Well, go back and take her; she will see and cease being blind. However, when you have married her, do not remain in the city. The work of a *manguyu* is what you must do".

So said Lord Iśwara. Mpu Siddayoga went on his way. Arriving in the city, he was married to Dewi Kasingi. When that had been done, he took leave to become a *manguyu*. He returned with her, and when they arrived he paid homage to his teacher:

"As you please, Lord, I am already married to Dewi Kasingi. Well, let the marks of our condition be the same".

Immediately Dewi Kasingi was ordained, and was given the name *wiku* Siddayogi.

"When you live with a female ascetic, you should have separate[108] houses; do not enter into a pupil-teacher relationship.[109] When you are overcome by the power of passion, then approach your female ascetic".

105. Text: *tan pabiṣa mamrih*; the translation follows the reading of variants D and E, *linonlon bisa mrih*.
106. Text: *mangkana*; read *mangkat ta* with B.
107. Text: *masi*; according to Pigeaud, the same as *masa*.
108. Text: *apadadwan*, but read *apadudwan*.
109. Text: *gulawĕṇṭah*; the only place in Old Javanese (Z 550); in Modern Javanese the meaning is "to raise, care for" (a child, especially the child of another). For comparison, see the Bujangga Manik, 849–867 (Noorduyn and Teeuw 2006, pp. 259–60). Translation tentative.

These were Lord Iśwara's instructions. Siddayogi lived on a ridge north of Māyana, separated by a river from Mpu Siddayoga. We need not tell how long it took, they had two children, both sons; the elder was Gagang-aking and Bubukṣa the younger. Both became a *wiku* at an early age, and both performed *tapa*.

Let us tell of the god Brahmā: he was the *dewaguru* at Sarwasidda, and followed the cult of the hills (*mapakṣa wukir*). There was a *paṇḍita* (scholar) from heaven, by the name of Bhagawān Karmaṇḍeya;[110] he had the appearance of an albino buffalo, and came to Mount Kelāśa. The Lord wanted to beat him, but he was fearful of being beaten; for this reason he changed his shape back into a scholar. Quickly he paid homage to Lord Iśwara. But Lord Iśwara wished to go to the holy Mahāmeru and to follow Lord Guru. Quickly he handed over the parasol, earrings and jacket to Bhagawān Karmaṇḍeya, and he replaced him as *dewaguru* dwelling on Mount Kelāśa. For this reason the *wiku* at Sukayajña do not eat albino buffaloes, as Bhagawān Karmaṇḍeya once had the form of an albino buffalo, according to the story.

Let us tell of the *trisamaya*, the Trinity of Lords, Iśwara, Brahmā and Wiṣṇu, who came to the holy Mahāmeru and followed Lord Guru. Off the three Lords went and arrived at the holy Mahāmeru. However, Lord Guru at the time was at the Śūnyagiri *maṇḍala*, manifesting himself as[111] the holy Astitijāti.[112] The gods Iśwara, Brahmā and Wiṣṇu paid homage to Lord Guru, and Lord Parameśwara said:

"Oh, you are welcome, my sons the Trinity; may you be my companions in making an established line (*tantu*) on the holy Mahāmeru. The world is without allotted tasks; you three will remove the impurities[113] adhering to the world; setting out offerings will be your task. However, gods Iśwara, Brahmā and Wiṣṇu, wash it clean, understand about *sisik-usung*,[114] you gods. You must each make sanctuaries, my three sons. Here are my gifts to you: the parasol, earrings and jackets of the teacher, as well as the book one fist in length, entwined with a serpent and bound like a girdle; its content am I. Come, pay close attention to my gifts again, divine Brahmā, Wiṣṇu and Iśwara".

Such was Lord Guru's gift to the three gods. The three of them made an obeisance. Off the three gods went, and each made a *maṇḍala*. However, the book

---

110. Presumably Mārkaṇḍeya is intended.

111. Text: *umawasakĕn*; Z 2213 under *wās*, *was*, suggests for this place "to manifest oneself as", otherwise "to make clear".

112. Perhaps *asthiti-jāti*; Z 1823 says *asthiti* = *sthiti* 3, "constant, firm, steadfast ..."; hence "changeless birth"? Unclear.

113. Text: *lĕka-lĕka*; Z 1003, "scale, impurity", this place only. Cf. Modern Javanese *lĕka*, "ketelsteen, tandsteen" (Pig.).

114. Meaning unknown; Z 1791, twice in the TP.

that the Lord had granted them was left behind unnoticed by the three gods; they only took the parasols, earrings and jackets. Lord Guru saw this:

"Oh, the Trinity of Lords have left the book behind; the three of them must have forgotten it".

Lord Guru took the book and carried it to the *pahoman* (place for offerings); he quickly covered it over (*kinukuban*) so that it could not be seen; for this reason Kukub was the name of the *maṇḍala* in the end, and Kukub was a sanctuary of Lord Guru.

Let us speak of the Trinity of Lords making *maṇḍala*: Lord Iśwara was the highest of the three,[115] and for this reason Tigāryanparwata was a sanctuary ...;[116] ... of Lord Brahmā; Nangka-parwata was the sanctuary of Lord Wiṣṇu. He had many *panasa* (jackfruit trees), and so the *maṇḍala* was called Panasagiri. Each was mindful of his own respective task.

Let us speak of Lord Guru while he was at Kukub: his twisted hair (*jaṭa*) was allowed to fall[117] in an easterly direction, and turned into Mount Jaṭa; this serves as the border of Taṇḍēs and Mount Maṇik. For this reason the earth is taboo and Mount Kampil may not be trodden on, as it was once the hair of the Lord, the story goes. Lord Guru said:

"My son, divine Gaṇa, prop up[118] my hairdo!"

The god Gaṇa agreed, and propped up the Lord's hair; so for that reason there is now a *maṇḍala* called Mount Manuñjang. It is the god Gaṇa who is established there.

There was a brahman who went to Java,[119] following the course of the holy Mahāmeru; his name was the reverend Kacuṇḍa, and he was a brahman of great supernatural power. He came to the holy Mandaragiri, and arrived at Kukub, paying homage to Lord Mahākāraṇa and asking to be granted the favour of the Lord's insignia. He was then ordained by the Lord in Kukub, was given the name reverend Aśoṣṭi, and the brahman took a number of[120] vows. After the ordination was complete, he left the *maṇḍala* of Kukub, in order to take service[121] with the intention of asking

115. Text: *pupus*; Z 1450 under *pupus* II.
116. There is apparently a gap in the text here. Brahmā's *maṇḍala* is mentioned below.
117. Text: *linolyakĕn*; Z 1046, "to cause to move, bring into motion"; but not as Pigeaud, "lette er niet op" (paid no heed to).
118. Text: *tuñjang*, not found in Z; see Sundanese "stutten, ondersteunen" (Eringa).
119. Text: *mangajawa*.
120. Text: *anusun*; Pig. "piled up".
121. Text: *naḍah amba*; translation suggested by Pigeaud, but unclear.

for land. Off went the reverend Aśoṣṭi, and arrived at the *maṇḍala* of Panasagiri. Lord Wiṣṇu said:

"It is lucky that you have come, brahman-sage. What is your intention in coming, and where are you heading for?"

The brahman-sage replied:

"I wish to go to Mĕḍang and look for a place that you advise".[122]

Lord Keśawa replied:

"If you wish for a place, then stay to the west of Kedman; it is lovely and close to the river and ravine".

The reverend Aśoṣṭi replied:

"Your kindness is most proper; if this is your advice, then the signs are that I will join you in making a settlement".

As soon as he had made a settlement, the reverend Aśoṣṭi informed Lord Guru in Kukub, and then asked to be granted the parasol, earrings and jacket, telling him that he had been given a place by the god Wiṣṇu. Lord Guru said:

"You have received a great favour (*labdawara dahat*), my son, being given a place by Lord Hari".

So said the Lord; then the *maṇḍala* was called Labdawara. Such is the story told of old.

There was an old spinster without a husband, who paid homage to Lord Guru, asking him to grant her a favour. She was ordained by the Lord, and allowed to wear the headband with hair plaited, to wear a *wiḍak* as her lower garment, and to wander the world; *kamawaśyahara*[123] was the sole thing she devoted herself to, and so she was called *mangawasi*. Such is the origin of there being people who become a *wasi* (ascetic).

There was a woman whose husband had died; she paid homage to the Lord and asked him to grant her a favour. She was ordained by the Lord, and then allowed to wear a girdle of *walatung* rattan, as a sign that she was faithful to her husband, and considered him as her final one. So then she would wear two belts (*hambulungan*) at the same time (*kalih-kalih*), and for this reason was called a *kili* (nun).[124] Such is the origin of the condition (*bhāwa*) of *kili*.

---

122. Text: *śwacara nira*; probably to be read as *gocara nira*; see Z 533, *gocara* 2. "discussion, conversation; advice, suggestion".
123. Skt. *kāmavasayin*, "eating foods that suppress desire" (MW).
124. On the *hambulungan*, see Wratiśāsana 28.2, quoted by Z 581.

There were a man and a woman who paid homage to Lord Guru and asked him to grant them a favour. They were ordained by Lord Jagatnātha, but not allowed to take permanent vows; they would wear the headband at the time of full moon (*pūrṇama*) and no moon (*tilĕm*); "when later on your tasks have been completed, you will be able to confirm your vows". So then their name was "*baru-baru*".

There was a young unmarried man, who paid homage to Lord Guru and asked to be granted the state of *wiku*. He was then ordained by Lord Guru, but he was not given a *singhĕl* (headdress) of *daluwang* (bark paper), but was given a *singhĕl* of the leaves of *alang-alang* grass; and so he was called a "*wiku ijo*" (green monk). Such is the origin of the *wiku ijo*.

Let us tell of the actions of Lord Jagatwiśeṣa: he performed yoga over his thumb,[125] burnt it to ash and sprinkled it with Śiwāmba holy water, performed yoga over it, and it turned into a deity in the form of a man.[126] This was named reverend Agaṣṭi, and he was granted *wiku*-ship by the Lord, and was ordered to perform *tapa* on Mount Kawi. And so after that he had Mount Kawi as his property, and this served as a sign of Lord Guru's instructions.

Again Lord Nandiguru performed yoga, and divided his knowledge in half, and Lord Ḍarmarāja emerged. Ordination was put on him, he was sprinkled with Śiwāmba holy water, and was named Sidḍawangsitadewa. He was granted *wiku*-hood, demarcated the holy freehold for ascetics,[127] and was ordered by the Lord to develop his *tapa*. The sage Sidḍawangsitadewa agreed, and developed his *tapa* tirelessly,[128] naked and observing silence[129] when overtaken[130] by night and day, without satisfying the need for food and sleep. This means: there was nothing he wished for, not the world, not heaven, not the Lord, not liberation, not release, not happiness, not unhappiness; there was nothing he praised, and nothing he despised. This is what can be called *tapa*. He was undeviating, moderate and just open, and the hermitage of the sage Sidḍawangsitadewa was named Sarjawa-Jambuḍipa. He was an incarnation of the one who formerly performed *tapa* on the mountain, Lord Ḍarmarāja.

While the sage Sidḍawangsitadewa was adhering to his immaculate concentration, the Lords Iśwara, Brahmā and Wiṣṇu saw his actions, adhering to immaculate

125. Text: *anggaṣṭa*; perhaps read *angguṣṭha* (Z 101, "thumb").
126. Text: *puruṣangkāra*; read *puruṣākāra* (Z 1457, "form, appearance of a man").
127. Text: *sima brata*; Z 1771.
128. Text: *malĕnggita*; the translation is a mere guess based on the context.
129. Text: *monaśrī tan*; Z 1148 reads *monāśritan*, "observing silence" (this place only).
130. Text: *kalangkahan*; see Z 982, perhaps an idiom.

concentration. "He is planning to destroy the world", the three Lords imagined, but they did not realize that it was Lord Ḍarmarāja who was doing the *tapa*; "he is just like all the other *paṇḍita*", they thought, "intending to destroy the world"—so the three gods thought. Their minds were troubled; and so for this reason the Trinity of Kāla appeared. The Kāla Lodra came out of Lord Brahmā, the Kāla Sambu came from Lord Wiṣṇu, and the Kāla Samaya came from Lord Iśwara; in a moment this was now their condition (*bhāwa*). These were ordered to put the sage Siddḍiwangsitadewa[131] to death. The three Kāla agreed.

Off went the Kāla and arrived where the sage Siddḍawangsitadewa was in the midst of adhering to his immaculate concentration. The Kāla came to fight him fiercely, and each one punched, kicked, beat, bit and kneed; the sage was undisturbed. The Kāla punched but their own companions were punched; they kicked but their own companions were kicked; they beat but their own companions were beaten; they bit but their own companions were bitten; they stabbed but their own companions were stabbed; the *paṇḍita* could not be overcome. The Kāla were ashamed that the sage Siddḍiwangsitadewa was not dead; off went the Kāla and took refuge with the gods Brahmā, Wiṣṇu and Iśwara, telling them frankly that they were not able to overcome the sage.

For this reason the Trinity of Lords went off intending to kill the sage. Immediately the god Brahmā took the body of Agni, intending to burn the sage, but the sage was unharmed. What is the reason that he was not killed by the god Brahmā? Because the god Ḍarma is not burnt by fire; for this reason the god Brahmā was fearful and frightened. Lord Wiṣṇu came forward, took on his wrathful form, with a thousand heads and two thousand arms. He took hold of all sorts of weapons and attempted to defeat the sage: he hurled the discus Suḍarṣana at him, beat him with the club Mandiki, stabbed at him with the dagger Nandaka, dazed him with the conch Pañcajanya; but the sage Siddḍiwangsitadewa was unharmed. And Lord Hari spun the discus Calakuṇḍa, the discus Tarĕnggabāhu and the discus Rĕbhawinuk, these he hurled at the ascetic. But the divine Ḍarmarāja was not overcome by a wrathful spirit; Lord Wiṣṇu was very fearful and frightened. Quickly Lord Iśwara took the form of Rudra, and violently attacked the ascetic sage; but the sage Siddḍiwangsitadewa was in the midst of adhering to his immaculate concentration, and remained firm and steadfast. He was not shocked, undisturbed, unhindered; buried with earth but not buried, firm

131. Here the spelling of Siddḍawangsitadewa suddenly becomes Siddḍiwangsitadewa.

and steadfast (*tunggĕng*) was he. For this reason there is a mountain called Tunggĕng. Flooded with water he is not washed away, not wetted.[132] What is the cause of this? It means: if the holy Ḍarma is buried it does not rot, if it is burned it is not scorched, if thrown in the water it is not washed away. Such is the perfect accomplishment of the sage Sidḍiwangsitadewa.

So the gods Brahmā, Wiṣṇu and Iśwara were fearful to see the ascetic sage's perfect accomplishment. Off the three Lords ran to the *maṇḍala* of Kukub. Even though the Lord was in the midst of giving audience to the four World Guardians, the three Lords came and made an obeisance before Lord Jagatnātha [saying:]

"If Your Lordship pleases, the aim of your sons in paying homage at your two feet is [this]: there is a *paṇḍita* carrying out asceticism, with the plan to destroy the world, such is our thinking. His power is exceedingly great, and even your three sons have been defeated by his might. The aim of your sons' homage is to ask for your assistance".

So said the three gods. Lord Guru replied:

"Oh, my sons, Brahmā, Wiṣṇu and Iśwara, did you imagine that the sage Sidḍiwangsitadewa was planning to destroy the world? No, it is not so, as the ascetic sage is Lord Ḍarmarāja. The reason he was not defeated by you, is that the ascetic sage is manifestly myself, as he is a division of my knowledge, and so you could not defeat him. However, you created demons, and plainly you are Kāla. For this reason there has been commotion in the world, as you are the same as those demons. Hence let those Kāla be killed by you!"

So said Lord Guru. The three gods said:

"As you please, the Kāla will not die, unless the sage Sidḍiwangsitadewa dies".

So said the three gods, and for this reason Lord Guru took[133] the life of the sage Sidḍawangsitadewa, as the Lord is his supreme ruler. He ordered the four Guardians of the world to lift the sage's body, as plainly the world would turn into one great sea if the body of the sage should fall on the earth. Then the four Guardians set off and came to where the sage did his asceticism. His life was plucked out by Lord Guru, and the ascetic sage died. His body was lifted up by the four Guardians. It was carried to the east, and that was called Puṇḍutan-śawa.[134] The body of the sage Sidḍiwangsitadewa was finally buried on the summit of the holy Mahāmeru; and so

132. Text: *tinĕtĕl*; read *tan tĕlĕs* with B.
133. Text: *umangsil*; probably the same as *umangsal*, but this form not in Z 106.
134. Literally, "picking up and carrying the dead body".

no one has the right to go higher than the summit of the holy Mahāmeru, as they buried Lord Ḍarmarāja there, the story goes. Clouds[135] and wind do not dare to go higher than the summit of the holy Mahāmeru, even the holy Sun and Moon do not go higher, and in particular human beings do not have the right to go higher than the summit of the holy Mahāmeru.

On Kelāśa-ground, perfect and high, is buried Lord Ḍarmarāja.

Kelāśa means "mountain", *bhumi* means "ground"; *sampūrṇawangan* means "lofty and high", and so Kelāśabhumisampūrṇawan [is a name of the holy Mahāmeru]. It is then considered as what is called the demarcation of the freehold of vows, taboo ground of the *lingga*-temple, which may not be dismantled; since then it serves to establish and demarcate the [vows] of the *wiku*-hood.

Let us tell of the gods Brahmā, Wiṣṇu and Iśwara killing the Trinity of Kāla: they directed the poison of their gaze at them and they were *bhasmibhūta*, turned to ash. The ashes of the three Kāla turned into Mount Wihanggamaya; [Mount Wihanggamaya] in Pangawān is the ashes of the three Kāla, the old story goes. After the three Kāla had died the Trinity of Lords returned home. Lord Iśwara went back to the *maṇḍala* of Tigapatra; Lord Brahmā went back to the *maṇḍala* of Jalaparwata; and Lord Wiṣṇu went back to the *maṇḍala* of Nangkaparwata.

Let us tell how the life and soul of the three Kāla turned into two demons, which emerged from Mount Wihanggamaya. These were called Kāla and Anungkāla. They paid homage to Lord Parameśwara and asked him to give them power over the world and human beings. Lord Guru said:

"My sons Kāla and Anungkāla, may you rule over the world and human beings. When the end of the age and the great destruction are nigh,[136] then you will be able to enjoy it; you should perform *tapa* first. Stand guard over the opening[137] of the holy Mahāmeru [on the west], there you will perform *tapa*. However, my instructions to you are: if there is at any time (anyone) who plunders[138] the property of the gods,[139] who seizes taboo ground, who destroys[140] the demarcations of the freeholds of the sages, who overthrows the establishment of the *wiku*-hood, you shall have these as

135. Text: *mogha*; but variant B has *megha*.

136. Text *tĕngĕta*, which does not seem to make sense; prefer the reading of D and E, *ḍatĕngeng*.

137. Text: *babahan*; Z 182, "door, gate, entrance, opening, aperture", and also orifice.

138. Text: *mangrampa*; read *mangrampad* (Z 1498, "to rob, plunder, take by force").

139. Text: *dṛwyaśwa*; read *dewaswa* (Z 398, "property of the gods").

140. Text: *lumbur*; not in Z, translation a guess. Any connection with *lĕbur* (Z 1001, "destroyed, annihilated ...")?

your possession, in particular every kind of *sisik-usung*[141] and all that is plundered—you shall have all of that as your possession. However, if one ruins the holy [establishment] of the *wiku*-hood, may he fall into the great Rorawa-hell, and not come to heaven. Well, take good notice of all my instructions".

So said Lord Guru. Kāla and Anungkāla stood guard at the western opening of the holy Mahāmeru; Pangawān was the name of the opening [so there is a village of Pangawān, the opening of the holy Mahāmeru]. Kāla and Anungkāla were established to be offered devotion at Pangawān; Kāla and Anungkāla carried out yoga: their voices became thunder, their blinks became lightning, and their tusks and teeth became thunderbolts. Their nails turned into the five Yakṣa, called Lumanglang, Lumangling, Lumangut, Mangdulur and Manginte. These warn if there are wrong deeds or wrong words, according to the story.

The god Gaṇa was ordered to guard taboo grounds and to keep watch at the opening of the holy Mahāmeru facing east; for this reason there is a village called Pūrṇajiwa now, the opening of the holy Mahāmeru facing east. The god Gaṇa was established to be offered devotion at Pūrṇajiwa.

Now the sage Agaṣṭi was ordered to guard taboo grounds and to keep watch at the opening of the holy Mahāmeru facing south; for this reason there is now a village called Paḍang, the [southern][142] opening of the holy Mahāmeru. The sage Agaṣṭi is offered devotion in Paḍang.

Now the goddess Ghorī was ordered to guard taboo grounds, and to keep watch over the opening of the holy Mahāmeru facing north. For this reason there is now a village called Gantěn, the opening of the holy Mahāmeru facing north; Lady Ghorī is established as being offered devotion in Gantěn.

The four openings of the holy Mahāmeru are called by the name Pañātūr-mukā.

Let us tell of Lord Ḍarmarāja, who emerged from the peak of the holy Mahāmeru. Its summit split [into three parts; this is why the holy Mahāmeru has three summits] even until now. From then Mount Triśṛngga has been the name of the holy Mahāmeru, as it has three peaks. The perfume [of Lord Ḍarmarāja when he emerged from the peak of the holy Mahāmeru] spread its fragrance; so this is the reason the holy Mahāmeru was called Mount Ganḍamaḍana in the end. Lady Earth quaked, as if the holy Mahāmeru would collapse, the ends of the earth[143] bowed

141. See note 114.

142. Apparently omitted in the text.

143. Text: *bhumiwaśaṇa*; Z 272, "the earthly abode"? This place only; *waśaṇa* uncertain.

low, the waters of the sea surged, and Lord Parameśwara was anxious [lest the holy Mahāmeru should collapse].

This is why Lord Guru approached and went to the peak [he travelled through the air with the divine bull]. Swiftly he arrived at the peak of the holy Mandaragiri, and caught sight of Lord Ḍarmarāja emerging from the crack in the holy Mahāmeru. He had three eyes and four arms, just the same as the appearance of Lord Guru. Straight away Lord Ḍarmarāja stood on the hump of the bull-god;[144] he pushed him away, and it seemed the bull-god would die from the push. Then Lord Ḍarmarāja was taken on Lord Guru's lap and taken to the *maṇḍala* of Kukub. He was seated on a jewelled lotus and sprinkled with holy water. *Kaluku* served as bath for the bull-god, and so the bull-god was pleased. Again Lord Ḍarmarāja was endowed with initiation, was given the name sage Taruṇa-tapa-yowana, and was granted the favour of *wiku*-hood by the Lord, demarcating the freehold of the holy freehold of vows. The sage Taruṇa-tapa-yowana was instructed to be kindly disposed to the whole world; the property of the gods was handed to him. *Śo* means a deity; and so the property of the gods was the holy Mahāmeru, which is called the taboo ground of the Lord, and serves as the *ṣima* marker (*susuk-ṣima*) of the sage(s); it served as a copper-plate charter (*tambrapuraṇa*), which is considered what is called a *mantra* without writing.

Again Lord Guru gave the bull-god to the sage Tapa-taruṇa-yowana, to be used as a means for protecting the world. Again he handed over the parasol, earrings and jacket; he succeeded as *dewaguru* of the *maṇḍala* of Kukub. This is why if there is a youthful sage, doing *tapa* in his early years, emerging from a split in the holy Mahāmeru, without father and without mother, without family and without cousins, he should be taken to serve as the *lingga*[145] of the holy Mahāmeru and should dwell in the *maṇḍala* of Kukub; his name will be the sage Ḍarma-ūtpṭi.[146]

Again there was a deity bound to the earth who could not escape, at one time struck by a curse of the sage Siddiwangsitadewa, the story goes. He paid homage to Lord Parameśwara, asking to be sent back to heaven. Lord Guru replied:

"Oh my son *dewata kĕna sapa* (deity-struck-by-curse), may you return to heaven; when the sage Tapa-yowana returns to heaven you will not be left behind. However, my instructions to you are: perform *tapa* first. Here are the favours I grant you:

144. There follows an insertion from B and C, not in the text but in Pigeaud's translation, down to "*kaluku* served as a bath for the bull-god". What *kaluku* is, is unknown.

145. Perhaps *lingga* here has the meaning of "centre, pivot" (Z 1034).

146. As Pigeaud (p. 166) suggests, probably to be read as Ḍarmotpati, "born of the line of Ḍarma".

the parasol, earrings and jacket. But you will be without ordination, and from now on Dewata-kaki (Grandfather-deity) will be your title in the world, and you should consider heaven (*swarga*) as your hermitage".

Such were Lord Guru's instructions; and so there is now [a place] called Swarga, such is the story. Again Kāla and Anungkāla were instructed by Lord Guru to protect the sage Taruṇa-tapa-yowana: "When he goes to heaven, you should not be left behind". So said Lord Guru.

Let us speak of the actions of Lord Guru in order to complete his work establishing [the world]. He performed yoga on the peak of the holy Mahāmeru, focusing on the tip of his nose facing west; this is why the front of a sanctuary is west, as it was west the Lord was facing when he did yoga. He bowed his head and looked down, and all he saw below turned into the Tasik-lĕbu (Sea of Dust); such is the story. He did yoga again, with as fruit (*phala*) the welfare of the whole world; for this reason there is a hill called Phala. "But there is no water for purification", he thought; he made a lake as his place of purification.

Let us tell about Lady Umā: she was on Mount Wilis for a long time; she was impatient for the Lord to call her. The Lady could not bear it, and then set off to go to Mahāmeru. When the Lord was in the midst of making a lake, Lady Umā arrived, and Lord Guru said:

"Ah, Lady, what is the reason for coming? Did I not make an agreement with you, 'I will call you later on, when the adornments of the holy Mahāmeru have been made beautiful?'. This is what I said".

Immediately Lady Umā was enraged; the Lord's making the lake did not go ahead (*wurung*), and for this reason there is now a lake called Wurung. Off went Lady Umā, and went to Mount Arjuna. But Lord Guru continued with making a lake; he washed his jacket (*kombala*), and for this reason it was called Kombala, and up to the present it is the pool of the holy Mahāmeru.

The Lord's course took him from Mahāmeru to Mount Pawitra. The Lord performed the *trisādhya*[147] observances: he bathed three times a day and three times a night. His outflow reached Warunggama, and so there is no[148] water on Mount Pawitra, as it was used up for the Lord's bathwater, as the story goes. He proceeded

147. Text: *atrisadyabrata*; under *trisādhya* Z 2040 gives "the three objects to be accomplished? Three kinds of purificatory bathings seem to be meant". However, *trisandhyā* may be better, referring to the morning, noon and evening ritual observances (Z 2040).

148. Read *tan* with B.

from Pawitra, and did yoga on the peak of Mount Kumukus. Lord Guru felt like urinating, and it smoked and became sulphur,[149] even until now.

Let us tell of Lady Umā: she left Mount Arjuna, came to Mount Kawi, and then went on to Kampud. In a fit of rage the Lady tore off the summit of Mount Kampud and hurled it to the southwest; this is why there is a mountain called Lĕbĕng[150] now, the summit of Mount Kampud as the story goes. She kicked what was left of Mount Kampud, and a split opened as far as the Southern Ocean [to Rĕnĕb, because of Lady Umā's anger], and so the water of Mount Kampud flowed and killed human beings. "Master, Noble Lord, Highness!" all the world wailed. Lord Guru was in the midst of doing yoga on Mount Kumukus, and heard the weeping of the whole world. When he glanced to the south he could see the stump of the summit of Mount Kampud; he knew that it was the Lady's mood.[151] He said:

"Oh, what will become of the whole world if I do not take pity on it? I shall put it right".

He took the form of a handsome prince, and then was given the name Dewaputra, and restored the whole world. He dammed up the Lady's fury, and it collected and formed a pond,[152] and became the lake on Mount Kampud; then the Lord was called the divine Analaga. He remained calmly on Mount Kampud, raised his iron club, so big and high that it reached the sky. Off went Lady Umā, and her fury subsided. Lord Guru said:

"Formerly when I was the teacher of the whole world, my name was Lord Guru. But now that I have put the whole world right, 'Tuhan, Rahadyan, Pangeran (Master, Noble Lord, Highness)' is what the suffering people said when they cried out to me. Hence my name is Lord Tuhan, I am Lord Pangeran, I am offered devotion by mankind, and I fill the world completely; hence another name for me is Lord Anungkurāt. I pervade the whole world, I am the object of the offerings of all the world; indeed any persons who approach Mount Kampud without bringing offerings will become deaf".

So said Lord Tuhan; then the people approaching Mount Kampud each had offerings; the offerings of the whole world on Mount Kampud face west. But Lord Tuhan formerly had his human birth in Kumāra.

---

149. Text: *warirang*; variant of B, *walirang.* This alludes to Mount Welirang.

150. Variant of B: Sĕbĕng.

151. The text has *ambĕk* (Z 60–61); perhaps the sense of "outburst of bad temper".

152. Text: *analaga*; from *talaga* (Z 1907); nothing to do with *salaga*, a "bloemkelk" (calyx), as Pigeaud (p. 168) would have it.

However, the iron club turned into a *silādri*, a mountain of stone reaching[153] as far as the sky. But when the holy Śiwa-raditya (Sun) sank in the west, the holy Mahāmeru was not illuminated by the holy Sun, as it was screened[154] by the mountain Gaḍa-wĕsi. He then seized Mount Gaḍa-wĕsi and dropped it in the ocean, where it became coral. The remnants were laid on the earth, but were unstable (*anggang-anggang*); so there is a Mount Anggang-anggang now.

Let us speak of Lady Umā: she took refuge on Mount Ganḍamaḍana. Kumāra came and paid homage to Lord Iśwara, in order to ask about Lord Guru. Lady Umā replied:

"What are you asking about the Lord? As I don't know where he is".

Kumāra answered:

"Your son desires to pay homage at the feet of the Lord, as the Lord is the origin of your son, and you are only an intermediary,[155] a way for your son".

So said Kumāra. Lady Umā was furious at how she was called a go-between by Kumāra. So she took Kumāra and seized his blood, body hair and marrow. Then he was cursed by Lady Umā to turn into a demon (*wil*) in the form of Kumāra, and so he turned into Bṛnggiriṣṭi. While this was being done to Kumāra by Lady Umā, Lord Guru came; he could see Lady Umā treating Kumāra like this. Lord Guru was furious and cursed Lady Umā:

"Fie, Lady Umā! What sin has your son committed toward you, that you cause him to turn into a demon, and then take away his blood, marrow and body hair? You are very horrible (*durga*), Lady Umā, and I shudder to see your appearance".

So said Lord Guru to Lady Umā. No different from a bamboo spear striking mud [as the proverb has it], without fail the Lord's words to Lady Umā hit home. [For this reason she suddenly changed form[156]] Lady Umā took the form of a female demon, she was stinking and smelly,[157] and then her name was Lady Durgādewī. Off went Lady Durgā from Mandaragiri, carrying Kumāra on her hip (*indit*), and then went off and buried Kumāra's body hair, marrow and blood. *Wala* is a name for child, so then Walanḍita was the name of the mountain where the blood, body hair

153. Text: *kumutug*; but plainly this should be *tumutug*.
154. Text: *katingkĕran*; Z 2017 says "screened, hidden (behind)" for this place; but note also Sundanese (Eringa 1984, p. 783), "omsluiten, insluiten, isoleren" (enclosed).
155. Text: *panĕlangan*; this meaning not given in Z 1730–1. Pigeaud translates "tussenschakel" (link).
156. Text: *rūpajuti*; not in Z. A guess.
157. Text: *mangi*; see Z 586 under *hangi*.

and marrow of Kumāra were buried, so the story goes. Off she went to the graveyard *kisidul palayasara.*[158]

However, Lord Guru had never been overcome by fury before [but now he was overcome by fury]; he cursed himself and turned into a demon (*rākṣasa*). [Suddenly Lord Guru had the form of a demon] with three eyes and four arms; and so his name became the divine Kālarudra. All the gods were terrified, in particular the whole world, on seeing Lord Kālarudra's appearance; he desired to eat everything in the world.

In a moment the Lords Iśwara, Brahmā and Wiṣṇu blocked Lord Kālarudra's eating; [they descended to the middle world to perform *wayang*], telling the true story of the Lord and the Lady in the world. They had a stage and a screen, chiselled leather served as their puppets, and they described them with beautiful[159] songs.[160] Lord Iśwara was the *hudipan,*[161] protected by the gods Brahmā and Wiṣṇu. They roamed the world practising the art (*giṇa*) of *wayang* performance, [so they were called *abaṇḍagiṇa awayang*]; such is their origin according to the story.

Again as a means of blocking Lord Kāla used by the Lords Iśwara, Brahmā and Wiṣṇu, they would roam the world and depict Lord Kāla, as *ijo-ijo*[162] they moved in the *bale*, and they spread comfort and cheer (*lumawu-lawu*).[163] The god Iśwara became the *śwari*, the god Brahmā became the *pederat*, and the god Wiṣṇu became the *tĕkĕs*;[164] they went around singing and performing [and so were called *baṇḍagiṇa menmen*]. Such is the origin of the *abaṇḍagiṇa menmen.*

However, the Lord Guru spread comfort and cheer with his body; and hence there is now a mountain called Lawu, once the hermitage of Lord Kālarudra as the story goes. For a long time Lord Kāla practised *tapa*, and returned to his original form as Lord Guru. Lady Dūrga requested an end to the curse from Lord Parameśwara; she was ordered to practise *tapa*. She did *tapa* in the underworld; for a long time she did *tapa*, and returned to her original form as Lady Umādewī. She emerged from the underworld, and so there is now a mountain called Bret, the path taken by Lady

158. Pigeaud says "corrupt"; no meaning found.

159. Text: *langon-langon*; this form not found in Z, but apparently based on *langö*.

160. Text: *pañjang*; Z 1270 under *pañjang* II, "the singing of *kakawin*-fragments (esp. in the *wayang*?)".

161. This term occurs only here (Z 646); it is assumed that it refers to the *dalang*.

162. A particular type of performance (Z 624).

163. Text: *lumawu-lawu*; Z 995. Cf. *anglalawu sarira* in Malat, and *anglawĕ-lawö*; the idea seems to be to spread comfort and cheer, but not clear how. See a second place four lines further down.

164. These three are apparently fixed roles; also found in Deśawarṇana 91.5, in the context of a performance.

Umā from the underworld, the story goes. As for Kumāra Bṛnggiriṣṭi, he requested an end to his curse from Lady Umā; he was ordered to practise *tapa*, and returned to his original form as Kumāra.

III

Let us tell of Lord Guru: he continued with his work of creating lines (*tantu*) in Yawaḍipa; he left[165] a line of continuity (*atantu*) like the track of a flying heron, stretching on unbroken, in a line unobscured, was the whole track of Lord Guru. He had the appearance of a *wiku*, he was a *bhujangga* of the Śaiwa order, and his name was Lord Mahāmpu Palyat. He betook himself to the cemetery of Kalyasĕm, and made the cemetery his hermitage, to the southeast of Paguhan. As for his method of *tapa*, he practised according to the Bhairawa order, eating the corpses [of people]; he kept them cool and damp, and in the middle of the night he ate them.

After a full [*dwidaśa*] twelve years the king of Galuh, by the name of Mahārāja Bhatati, heard that the *wiku* was in[166] the Brahmāloka; he would summon the group of *wiku*, and would hold a sacrifice. All the dignitaries[167] were invited to come, and Mahāmpu Palyat was [also] invited. Before long the due time[168] of the royal ceremony arrived, on the fifteenth of the bright half of the ninth month; all the people from the south of Galuh came, and from the west of Galuh. Mahāmpu Palyat set out together with the guardian of the cemetery, and they carried excellent meat. The skull of people they used as drinking cup, and bowls[169] five in number, these served as their containers for keeping the corpses cool and damp.[170] Mahāmpu Palyat arrived [at the shelter]; King Bhatati asked the *pangambehan*,[171] saying:

"Mpu Waju-kuning, Mpu Kalotan, where is the *wiku* Palyat sitting? What does he look like?"

---

165. Text: *matilĕl*; read *matinggal* with B.
166. A word such as *ring* ("in") may be missing in the text.
167. Text: *gowantĕn* (Z 540); this place only. The translation is a guess.
168. Text: *tanggung*; this meaning not found in Z 1940.
169. Text: *kaṇṭora*; Z 793, three places in this text only; cf. Sanskrit and Hindi *kaṭora*, a metal bowl for food.
170. Text: *angayĕm*; cf. Modern Javanese (GR "vochtig of koel maken of houden, bv. tabak in pisang bladeren").
171. Meaning unknown, not found in Z; a variant has *pangabehan*.

"See there, sir, he is the one sitting on the west".

"Hey, how could I see him? He is popping up here and there[172] with the appearance of a layman.[173] I had imagined he would have a water jar and be wearing a headband and the jacket of a teacher [with a parasol and earrings], and be escorted by his disciples, a hundred or two hundred of them".

So said the Mahārāja. Mpu Kalotan replied:

"No, sir, as he is a *bhujangga* of the Śaiwa sect, this is the reason he does not have a headband".

"Ah, that's how it is. But what is that in front of him?"

"The skulls of people and what is called a *kaṇṭora* (bowl), sir".

"What are the skulls for?"

"They serve as drinking cups, sir".

"What is the bowl for?"

"It is his container for keeping people's dead bodies cool and damp, sir".

(Retching sound) the Mahārāja vomited: "Hey, betel man, give me a betel quid".

"Well, Mahāmpu Palyat eats people then? A *wiku* like that looks like a case of what is called *brahmālokasanghāra*, destruction of the realm of Brahmā. Remove him from the island of Java, throw him into the ocean, so that there is no longer any such action".

King Bhatati was angry; Mahāmpu Palyat went home, knowing that the king was angry. He laughed: "Ha, ha, ha!" and went back to his hermitage in Kalyasĕm.

In the morning Mpu Kalotan and Mpu Waju-kuning went there with orders to do away with[174] the *paṇḍita*. Off the emissaries went and arrived in Kalyasĕm. Mpu Kalotan and Mpu Waju-kuning bowed low and paid homage, informing him that they had been sent by the king to throw the *paṇḍita* into the ocean.

"So be it, I resign myself, my friends; I realize that the king is angry".

Mpu Kalotan and Mpu Waju-kuning bustled about[175] and seized him together, bound him with rattan, and then Mahāmpu Palyat was thrown into the ocean. Having done this, off they went and informed Mahārāja [Bhatati] that Mahāmpu Palyat had already been thrown into the ocean. The next day Mpu Kalotan and Mpu Waju-kuning

172. Text: *purungul-purungul*; the translation is a mere guess. The form suggests plurality or repetition.

173. Text: *dayaka*; Z 382 under *dāyaka*, "benefactor, patron; lay benefactor not belonging to the community of monks?"

174. Text: *tumilangakĕna*; but read with B *humilangakĕna.*

175. Text: *wusungan*; see Z 656 under *husung.*

went, sent by the king, to go and check on Mahāmpu Palyat. Off the emissaries went and found Mahāmpu Palyat resting quietly. [They bowed low, and Mahāmpu Palyat said:] "I am not dead. Go and look for a stone a man's height in length and as big as a lontar palm".

Then they bound him to the stone and threw him into the ocean; in the morning they were sent again,[176] and found Mahāmpu Palyat there. Finally he was burnt, and his ashes thrown into the ocean; in the morning they went again and found Mahāmpu Palyat sitting cross-legged on the ground. Mpu Kalotan and Mpu Waju-kuning were silent with amazement[177] to see the *paṇḍita's* supernatural power; then Mpu Kalotan and Mpu Waju-kuning embraced the sage's feet. Forthwith they licked the *paṇḍita's* feet [and said]:

"We did not succeed in killing you, sir".

Mahāmpu Palyat replied, saying:

"Mpu Kalotan [and Mpu Waju-kuning], let me depart from here, as I was only enjoying myself making a trip to the island of Java, as my country is on what is called the island (*nūṣa*) of Kambangan; [my *maṇḍala kabhujanggan* is there]. But now the king of Galuh is angry, so I shall return to my *maṇḍala* on the island of Kambangan".

"Lord, your grandsons will follow you, and will constantly be at your feet, sir".

"So be it, what should I say in that case? Let me look for a stone ten fathoms long, to serve as a boat for me to sail on".

He displayed the power of his words;[178] Mpu Kalotan and Mpu Waju-kuning followed him. They found a red lotus in the midst of the sea, with leaves of silver[179] and with flowers of gold. He arrived at the island of Kambangan, was greeted by his pupils, such beautiful people with ornaments, one hundred and eighty in number. They approached and paid homage; Mpu Kalotan and Mpu Waju-kuning asked:

"What people are these, so beautiful with ornaments?"

"Ah, they are what became of[180] the people I ate when I was on the island of Java".

"So that's how it is, sir".

176. The text may not be in order here, but the meaning is clear.
177. The text has *kawongan*, but read *kawĕngan* (Z 2244) with B.
178. Text: *kawakyan*; translation follows Pigeaud, but not listed in Z 2176 under *wākya*.
179. Text: *sakala[nga]n*; read *salaka*, "silver". This may allude to the famed Wijayakusuma flower, said to grow on the island of Nusakambangan.
180. Text: *dedening*; read *dadening*. See Z 347 under *dadi, dadyan*.

Mahāmpu Palyat was hospitably entertained by all his pupils. When that had been done Mpu Kalotan and Mpu Waju-kuning were ordained; Mpu Janaḍipa was the title of Mpu Kalotan, and Mpu Narajñāna was the title of Mpu Waju-kuning, as they were of clear mind.[181] When this had been done Mpu Janaḍipa and Mpu Narajñāna made a flower offering in order to take leave to return to the island of Java. After they had left the island of Kambangan, they arrived back on the island of Java, and betook themselves to the king of Galuh. They informed the Mahārāja of everything that had happened to them;[182] then King Bhatati took Mpu Janaḍipa as his teacher, and Mpu Narajñāna as his court priest.

Let us tell of Lady Śrī: she lived as a widow,[183] and so she was given the name Widow Rāga-runting. She spun in the shade[184] of a *tañjung* tree at her house, and this is why there is now a village by the name of Mĕḍang-tañjung. There was a merchant by the name of Parijñana, and he was a very greedy[185] man; [the widow Rāga-runting did not wish to be acquainted with a greedy man]. He was struck by her broom and swept aside[186] in an easterly direction as far as Mount Bañcak; [so there is a mountain called Karurungan now].[187] She kept herself at a distance[188] from the merchant Parijñana; and so there is now a mountain called Kĕṇḍĕng.

Let us tell about Mahāmpu Palyat: he returned to the island of Java. He divided his body into two, and it became a Śaiwa and a Sogata (Buddhist), with the names Mpu Barang and Mpu Waluh-bang. Mpu Barang was of the Śaiwa sect, and Mpu Waluh-bang of the Sogata sect. Off they went and arrived in Java; they headed for Girah,[189] and set up a hermitage at Anggirah.

Let us tell about the divine elder of Kukuh, the sage Taruṇa-tapa-yowana, by the name of Lord Mahāguru. Many were his pupils, so he arranged them by their tasks, such as: *pangadyan*, *ulu-kĕmbang-pakalpan*, *pomah*, *pajanan*, *atanĕk*, *abrih*, *akarapa*, *juru-amañjang-amañjing*, *kabhayan-panglayar*, *kabhayan-maṇḍala*, *mahawanĕtha*,

181. Text: *buddhi kṛta*; unclear.
182. Text: *sasokrama nira*; see Z 1882 under *swakrama*.
183. Text: *mangraṇḍa-raṇḍa*; Z 1502, this place only.
184. Read *ĕb ning*, following variant B.
185. Text: *dibyaloba*.
186. Text: *manglaru*; read *manglurung*, Z 1067, "... go aside, give way".
187. The base-word *rurung* may be connected with *lurung* as above. Note also the reading of D and E, *tkeng gunung Karungrangan aranya*.
188. Text: *makĕṇḍang-kaṇḍang*; read with B *makĕṇḍung-kĕṇḍung*. Meaning uncertain.
189. Manuscripts D and E add: on the mountain Hyang.

bahudĕṇḍa, but-wiśeṣa, asaṇḍing-among, kabhayan-pamĕkas. Such were the kinds of their tasks.

Now Lord Mahāguru held a banquet; the celebration would be held for the whole of the month of Aśuji (September–October). Ki Kabhayan-panglayar was ordered to go asking for contributions;[190] he followed a course in an easterly direction asking for contributions. Soon the month of Aśuji arrived, and all the Lord's pupils came, as well as the Trio of Lords; all of his pupils paid homage to Lord Guru; only the old Kabhayan-panglayar had not yet come. The Lord's celebration was over, all of his pupils returned home, as well as the Trio of lords,[191] who returned to their respective *maṇḍala*.

Just at that moment Ki Kabhayan-panglayar arrived. Let us tell of his journey from the east: impeded,[192] with difficulty and in trouble. Many were the items he brought with him: *guci* (pots), *krĕci*,[193] *mata lĕmbu* (cow eyes) and in particular *gĕrang kĕbo* (dried buffalo meat), buffaloes, cows, dogs, pigs, ducks, chickens and especially male and female people wanting to become *wiku* and asking to be presented to Lord Mahāguru. Ki Kabhayan-panglayar's progress was held up, but his tracks from the east were: at Ragḍang is where he left *gĕrang asu* (dried dog meat), at Tambangan is where he left *gĕrang kĕbo* (dried buffalo meat), at Pacelengan is where he fed[194] the pigs, at Untehan is where he twisted cord,[195] at Kuḍampilan is where he made cuts of beef,[196] at Cangcangan is where he tied up a sow,[197] at Bakar is the place where he did some roasting, at Duk is the place where he looked for palm fibre, and at Payaman is the place where he left some chickens behind.

Now when he reached as far as Kukub, he asked the *kabhayan-wiśeṣa* to kindly bring him into the presence of Lord Mahāguru. He knew that he would be blamed by Lord Mahāguru. Promptly the *kabhayan-wiśeṣa* spoke to Lord Mahāguru, and told him [frankly] that Ki Kabhayan-panglayar had come. The divine Mahāguru spoke, saying:

---

190. Text: *manangsi-nangsi*; not listed in Z, but obviously the same as *manasi-nasi* (see Z 1958 under *tasi*, "to beg").
191. The text has *maṇḍala* here, which seems to be an error.
192. Text: *kabĕlat*; read *kabĕlĕt* with B (Z 234).
193. Possibly Modern Javanese *krecek*, dried buffalo skin.
194. Text: *makan*; probably not "eat". Cf. variant *nangcang*, "tie up".
195. Text: *angunte-unte*; or "made *unte*", in Malay "rasped coconut and sugar" (Wilk).
196. Pigeaud suggests a link with Modern Javanese *sampil*, a cut of rump.
197. Text: *pagor*; prefer reading of B, *bagor* (Z 186).

"Don't let that Panglayar approach me; his offence is that he came too late for the celebration. Tell him to go back!"

So said the divine Mahāguru. The *wiśeṣa* went back and informed Ki Kabhayan-panglayar that he was not approved[198] by the Mahāguru; his offence was coming too late for the ceremony. Finally Ki Kabhayan-panglayar ordered the *but-wiśeṣa* to go back and get all the things he had brought and were left in the mountain gullies of the south, and to present them to Lord Mahāguru. But Ki Kabhayan-panglayar (himself) set off to the east, with as cord his tears,[199] and with as sunshade his lament;[200] off went the reverend Panglayar.

Let us tell about the officials:[201] arriving in the southern gullies, they fetched what Ki Kabhayan-panglayar had collected: the pots, *krĕci*, even the dried buffalo meat, cows,[202] dogs, pigs. The officials arrived in Kukub; the dried meat was left in Payaman, and did not pass the River Sarayu; that served as the limit.[203]

Let us tell about Ki Kabhayan-panglayar: he wanted to found a *maṇḍala* on the saddle between the holy Mahāmeru and the holy Brahmā, and he took shelter among the *aṇḍawar* palms;[204] and so the *maṇḍala* was called Aṇḍawar. There was a gift from Lord Mahāguru, called the holy key Sandijñāna;[205] this he shot at the world, and for this reason the whole world was drawn[206] to pay him homage. Men and women equally wanted to become a *wiku*, but he did not ordain them, as he had not yet received this favour from Lord Mahāguru. Hence they were (only) allowed to wear strips (*babakan*) of bark as their *singhĕl*, and then were called Bakal.

"Later I will ordain you, when I have been granted the favour of Lord Nāmaśiwaya".[207]

So he said; they knew that he was subject to the rules of the elder of Kukub. He left Aṇḍawar and came to the mountain of Hyang, and asked for land from the headmen of Bĕsar. He asked for abandoned gardens (*talun*), and the heads of Bĕsar did not withhold them, but gave him the gardens; this was called the *maṇḍala* of Talun.

---

198. Text: *kasatmata*, but *kasanmata* is intended.
199. Text: *talingis*; prefer variant of B, *tangis*.
200. Text: *sampĕt*, but Pigeaud suggests the variant of D and E, *sambat*, "lament".
201. Text: *kang masĕrĕhan*, lit. "those with assigned duties".
202. Text: *sami*; read *sampi*, following variant B.
203. Text: *makahangan*; read *makahingan* with B.
204. Text: *ngaṇḍawar-haṇḍawar*; see variant of B, *umĕgil ta sireng ngandawar.* Z 584, this place only, but cf. Sundanese *hanjawar*, a kind of pinang palm (Eringa 1984, p. 282).
205. "Esoteric knowledge", according to Z 1650.
206. Text: *kerut*; lit. "caught" (see Z 701 under *irut*, "overwhelmed, captivated").
207. Following the reading of D and E, Pigeaud (p. 117, note) thinks this is used as another name for Guru.

There was a demon (*rākṣasa*) there, who did not permit it to be made into a *maṇḍala*. He opposed him with yoga and *samāḍi*, and the demon was defeated, finally exposed undefended; he shot the key Sandijñāna, and it drew the whole world to him.

He proceeded from Talun, in order to found a *maṇḍala* in Waśaṇa.[208] There was a demon there, who did not allow his house to be made a *maṇḍala*; he opposed him with yoga, and the demon was defeated by him. There was a stone called Ubhusan, and this served as the offering to the teacher, and is there now. Again he shot the key Sandijñāna, and it drew the whole world to him; many men and women wanted to become *wiku*, but he did not ordain them.

Let us speak of Mpu Barang and Mpu Waluh-bang, who were looking for a sect to follow. Mpu Waluh-bang went westwards, in order to found a settlement in Warag, and Mpu Barang went east and created the visitation of cemeteries. There was a cemetery on Mount Hyang, at (a place) called the peak of Kalyasĕm, a communal cemetery[209] where people gathered to carry out funerary rites. People from east of Mount Hyang and from the north of Mount Hyang equally conducted their funerals at Kalyasĕm. That was a place for gathering many dead bodies, and this served Mpu Barang as his hermitage; he was of the Bhairawa sect, and ate the dead bodies of people.

There was a king who reigned in Daha, the elder son of King Bhatati, called Mahārāja Taki. He was ruling in Daha, and heard that there was a *bhujangga* following the way of the Bhairawa and doing *tapa* in the cemetery on the peak of Kalyasĕm, and that he ate the dead bodies of people. The Mahārāja was appalled to hear this, and sent the two Sogata brothers, by the names of Mpu Tapa-wangkĕng and Mpu Tapa-palet. These two were sent by the king to put Mpu Barang to death.

The emissaries agreed; they set off travelling through the air, equally powerful, as they were incarnations of Lords Brahmā and Wiṣṇu; the god Brahmā became Tapa-wangkĕng, and the god Wiṣṇu became Tapa-palet. Off the two Sogatas went to put the unclean *bhujangga* to death; this was their action (*bhāwa*). They soon arrived at Mount Hyang and headed for the cemetery of Kalyasĕm; they found Mpu Barang sitting facing a bowl with excellent meat,[210] the skulls of people his drinking cups, and the bodies of people as his food. Mpu Tapa-wangkĕng and Tapa-palet arrived and told him that they had been sent by the king; Mpu Barang just resigned himself. Together they seized him, and then he was bound with rattan, and now Mpu Barang

208. Variant of B: *Pathanā*.

209. Text: *sĕma bandung*, probably to be read *baṇḍung* (Z 203, this place only).

210. Text: *mahāmangsa*; Z 1082, "excellent food (meat)". Also found in RY 26.24b.

was thrown into the ocean. Having returned, they informed the Mahārāja of Daha that Mpu Barang had been thrown into the ocean.

In the morning the king sent the two *bhujangga* brothers to go and check on the unclean *bhujangga*. They agreed, and soon arrived at Kalyasĕm, where they found Mpu Barang. They seized him again, bound him with rattan, entwined him with raw iron,[211] and threw him in the ocean. The emissaries went straight back.

The next morning they were sent again, and found Mpu Barang there again. Finally they burnt him, and when Mpu Barang had become ash,[212] the two Sogata returned and informed the king that Mpu Barang had already become ash.

In the morning the king sent them to check on the unclean *bhujangga*; the emissaries agreed. They travelled quickly as they went through the air; arriving in Kalyasĕm, they found Mpu Barang there again. They burnt Mpu Barang again, and they threw his ashes into the ocean; the two Sogata brothers returned and told the Mahārāja that they had spread Mpu Barang's ashes in the five directions.

The next morning again the king sent them to check on the unclean *bhujangga*. The two agreed, and shortly arrived at the peak of Kalyasĕm, where they found Mpu Barang again. At that time Mpu Tapa-wangkĕng and Mpu Tapa-palet paid homage to Mpu Barang; they knew that he was Lord Parameśwara. Then Mpu Barang wished to leave Mount Hyang, and intended to go to the country of Jambuḍipa. He made what was called the book Aḍidarwa,[213] with a jacket; then he left the book with the jacket behind in the shrine. Off he went to Jambuḍipa, and Mpu Tapa-wangkĕng and Mpu Tapa-palet followed him; they all travelled through the air.

Now let us tell of Ki Kabhayan-panglayar: he betook himself from the *maṇḍala* of Waśaṇa, and came to the peak of Kalyasĕm, escorted by demons by the names of Ki Maranak and Ki Lĕmah-bang. They were intending to come to Mpu Barang, but it happened that he had already gone away; finally they discovered the book and the jacket in the shrine. They unwrapped the book, and it contained the Aḍidarwa, Mpu Barang's spiritual legacy. This they considered as a favour from Lord Guru. Finally the cemetery was cleared and made into a *maṇḍala*, and then they placed[214] the jacket in the shrine, and so the *maṇḍala* was called Sanggara.[215]

211. Text: *kaṭe*, probably to be read *kati* (Z 821).

212. Text: *hasṭi*; see Z 146, *asthi*, *asti*, "bone; ash (in later texts)", variants *(h)awu*.

213. Mentioned again below, with the spelling *Adidrawa* in the text, and with the variants *Adidarwa* and *Adiparwa*.

214. Text: *anurud*; see Z 1867, "to ask, receive or take as a *surudan*", i.e. something left over by someone of high rank to be consumed or used by others.

215. Variant of B: *Sanggar*.

Again the two demons asked for a favour; he was able to ordain (them?) wearing the jacket in the shrine, and so they were called "*wiku sanggara*". Again he shot the Sandijñāna, and all the world was drawn to him; there came men and women to pay homage to him, and they offered all their possessions. The number of pupils grew, and the number of the pupils and property was as incomparable as the ocean (*sāgara*); for this reason the *maṇḍala* was finally called Sāgara. He ceased having the name Kabhayan-panglayar, and finally all the world referred to him as Lord Guru. He was the original founder of the Sāgara *maṇḍala*, and he spoke familiarly to his children and pupils:

"You should not address me as 'son' (*tanaya*)—let your terms for addressing me be 'grandson' (*putu*) or 'great-grandson' (*buyut*)".[216]

Such was his familiar speech to his children and pupils; for this reason the familiar term for addressing him was: the *buyut* of Sāgara. Again the *dewaguru* of Sāgara did not wear a jacket with needlework,[217] no more than a *dodot* with decorative hem,[218] as he had not yet received the favour from the god Guru, *buyut* of Kukub.

"Only later on, when the favour has been granted by the holy *buyut* of Kukub, will you have a right to wear a jacket with needlework, be able to use the term '*tanaya*', and so you are allies of Sāgara[219] (unclear). Do not fail to remember that Kukub was the origin; come, take good notice of what I tell you. Now if you don't remember what I have instructed, may you be struck by misfortune".

Such is what Ki Kabayan-panglayar said; he was the founder of Sāgara, and he made the trio of *maṇḍala* on Mount Hyang.

Let us tell of Lord Mpu Barang: he arrived in the country of Jambuḍipa; there he found some brahmans in the midst of worshipping the god Haricaṇḍana, about a thousand brahmans in number. Mpu Barang came and remained standing; the brahmans said:

"Fie! Why are you just standing there, and not paying homage to Lord Haricaṇḍana? We are brahmans of pure birth, so we pay homage to the Lord, don't we,[220] as it is he who made the three worlds".

Mpu Barang replied:

"I refuse to pay homage, as I am a Javanese brahman".

216. This instruction is somewhat confusing, although the grammar of the sentence seems clear enough.

217. Text: *adomdoman*; this form not in Z 423.

218. Text: *sinalusur*; see Z 1619, under *salusur* II.

219. Translated according to the variant of B.

220. Text: *mayan*; see Z 1130, "you are ... aren't you" etc.

"You're a brahman anyway; come on, pay homage, Javanese brahman!"

"I refuse to pay homage".

They seized him first, then took hold of his hands, and forced him to make an obeisance to Lord Haricaṇḍana. He had just fallen to his knees when Lady Pṛthiwī quaked, and the image[221] of Lord Haricaṇḍana split, as it is till now. Then the brahmans were astounded to see Mpu Barang's supernatural power; and then all the brahmans worshipped Mpu Barang. Finally the brahmans gave him gold, rubies, bezoars and diamonds; but Mpu Barang did not want them. He asked to exchange ash-marks, the mark of Mpu Barang was *ganḍa*,[222] and the mark of the brahmans was *rātnadwada*.[223] They exchanged ash-marks; in the end *rātnadwada* was Mpu Barang's mark, and Mpu Barang's *ganḍa* served as the mark of the brahmans.

When they had finished exchanging ash-marks, the king of Jambuḍipa, called Mahārāja Cakrawarti, arrived and paid homage to Mpu Barang, offering him fine garments, gold, rubies and diamonds fit for a king. But Mpu Barang did not accept them; he asked for what was revered by the king. It was not withheld, and he was given the golden image in the form of Lord Wiṣṇu which is revered in Jambuḍipa. This was given to Mpu Barang, but he did not take it, although he imitated its form; this is what he took back with him to Java.

Mpu Barang set out accompanied by Mpu Tapa-wangkĕng and Mpu Tapa-palet, each travelling through the air. Arriving in Java, they headed for Mount Brahmā, the site (*tantu*) where the god Brahmā had once worked as a smith. There Mpu Barang recited the text[224] Tigarahaṣya, Mpu Tapa-wangkĕng recited the text Tigalana, and Mpu Tapa-palet recited the text Tigatĕpĕt. As for Mpu Barang, he made gold and turned it into a golden image shaped in the form of Lord Wiṣṇu; it was carved by Mpu Tapa-palet and Mpu Tapa-wangkĕng. The shavings[225] from the carving (chiselling, sculpting) scattered like water, and then turned into jet,[226] even until now.

When the holy golden image was perfectly finished, it was placed as pinnacle on Mount Suṇḍawiṇi. The king of Daha, Mahārāja Taki, heard that there was a holy golden image on Mount Suṇḍawiṇi; then the Mahārāja sent a messenger to call Mpu Barang as well as Mpu Tapa-wangkĕng and Tapa-palet. The messenger agreed, set off and swiftly arrived; he paid homage to Mpu Barang, saying:

221. Text: *arca*, but oddly enough Pigeaud translates with "heiligdom" (sanctuary).
222. Meaning unclear; surely not "perfume". Sandal?
223. Meaning unknown.
224. *Mangaji* (Z 34).
225. Text: *taha-taha ning*, variant B *tahi-tahi ning*; possibly to be emended to *tatah-tatahan ing*.
226. *kṛṣṇa* (Z 895, *watu kṛṣṇa*).

"Your child [that is, I] has been sent by the king of Daha, in order to invite you to come to the city, sir".

"So be it", [said Mpu Barang], "I have no objection".

Mpu Barang set off accompanied by Mpu Tapa-wangkĕng and Tapa-palet, and soon the threesome arrived in Daha, and went to King Taki. The king asked for the golden image; he did not withhold it, Mpu Barang gave it. This is the reason the holy golden image is revered by the kings of Daha, even until now.

Let us speak of Lady Smarī: she took the form of a human being, a girl of limitless beauty; her name was Ibu-tĕngahan. She followed her father in the person of Lord Mpu Barang, and did *tapa* divided by a gorge from her father; her state (way of life, *bhāwa*) was *tapi-tapi* (female ascetic). And so there is a ridge called Tapi now.

Let us speak of Lord Waluh-bang: he joined the sect of the Ṛṣi-mabadḍa ("sage-with-headband") and left the sect of the Buddhists. He separated from Warag, and came to Tigāryan. He just stood there without paying homage to Lord Iśwara; Lord Iśwara said to his pupils:

"I wonder why the *wiku* Waluh-bang is just standing there without paying homage to me".

His pupils replied:

"His knees are stiff, sir".

After that he was called the "*wiku kasture*". Then Lord Iśwara handed over[227] the parasol, earrings and jacket to Lord Waluh-bang; he replaced him as *dewaguru* of Tigāryan, and served as head of the Kasturi sect.[228] Lord Iśwara returned to his heaven.

Let us speak of Mpu Barang: he came to Tigāryan and went to Lord Waluh-bang. Lord Waluh-bang said:

"Come, let us both wear the *kurug*, Mpu Barang, the result of being one with you".

Immediately he handed over the parasol, earrings and jacket [and said:]

"You are a *dewaguru*, old chap, and your *maṇḍala* will be the first of the Kasturi law".

This is what Lord Waluh-bang said; Mpu Barang agreed, and cleared a *maṇḍala*, which was then called the first of the Kasturi law, called Bapa.[229] He followed the

227. Text: *supranāthakĕnira*; translated according to variant B, *sumrahakĕnira*.

228. See Pigeaud's note on this, p. 32 ff.

229. Text: *Antabapa*; variant B and E, *aran ta Bapa*.

way of life of the Bhairawa, and ate anything without passing it over. The village heads (*rāma-rāma*) offered him their ears of rice;[230] by magic he turned these into white cooked rice, soft and thick.[231] The heads returned from offering the ears (*atur ūryan*), and so the village was called Tūryan, and served as the first of the Kasturi *maṇḍala* at Bapa.

Let us tell about Mpu Tapa-wangkĕng and Tapa-palet: while they were both in Daha, Mpu Tapa-wangkĕng was called Ki Samĕgĕt-bagañjing. He had a debt of 10,000, and promised to repay it after midday. He had nothing to repay it with; he held the holy Śiwa-aditya (Sun) back, so that it remained at midday and did not move down. The king had taken a vow for invincibility,[232] and would not break it if the sun had not yet gone down. He was hungry but did not break his fast, as it was not yet afternoon; the king said:

"I wonder why the Sun is taking so long to go down. I'm hungry now".

He sent a messenger to Ki Samĕgĕt-bagañjing in order to ask what it could mean that the holy Sun was taking so long to go down. The emissary agreed, and went to Ki Samĕgĕt-bagañjing [and said]:

"Your grandson [I], sir, has been sent by the king: what is the cause that the holy Sun has not gone down after so long?"

Ki Samĕgĕt-bagañjing answered:

"I am ashamed to tell you, old chap; if I do not inform you, perhaps the king will be angry. I have a debt of 10,000, old chap, and promised after midday, but I have nothing to pay it with. This is why I have held the holy Sun back".

"Ah, so that's how it is. I shall tell the king".

Off he went and informed the king how it was with Ki Samĕgĕt-bagañjing. The king gave the money, and it was used to repay the debt; suddenly the holy Sun set.

Let us tell of Mpu Tapa-palet: he was having an illicit affair with the noble wife of the king. The queen became pregnant;[233] the king knew that it was not his, and that the unborn child of the king's wife was not legitimate. The king said to the queen:

"You have been unfaithful to me. That unborn child of yours is not mine".

The noble king's wife replied:

230. Text: *(h)uryan*; not found in Z; Pigeaud translates "aren" (ears), probably Modern Javanese *wulen.*

231. Text: *apulĕn*; Z 1436, this place only; Modern Javanese *pulĕn*, "firm, soft and tasty (cooked rice, cooled)".

232. Text: *angajaya*; not listed in Z.

233. Text *udwita*; see Z 2102, apparently this place only. Variants B *udita* and E *uddita.*

"By your leave, would I not be faithful to you, the king?"

"Well, if you have been faithful to me, let the child be born perfectly good looking—if that unborn child of yours is mine. However, if it is not mine, and you have been unfaithful, may it be born misshapen".

So said King Taki. Then a cow was born with black and white spots.[234] At that time the queen was driven away by the king. Off she went, and turned back into Lady Śrī. She said when about to leave:

"If in future there is a powerful woman who arises in Daha, known by the name Queen Nini, that am I". She went away, and reigned as queen in Cĕmpa.

The piebald cow, however, was raised by Ki Samĕgĕt-bagañjing. Tapa-palet realized that he would be done away with, and then left Daha. Off he went, making his way eastwards. Also the troops of King Taki spread out looking for Mpu Tapa-palet; some went east, some went west, some went south, some went north. They found him running away and taking shelter in a cave; Mpu Tapa-palet said:

"Don't kill me. I have a skill that I transfer to you, the skill of making temples, and the holy images located within them, carved and lowered into position.[235] Also the skill of making a block for pounding rice, and the skill of making caves".

They said:

"As for the cave, this will be our place, and such will be our life as *jalagrahā*".

"*Jala*" is a term for water, and "*graha*" is a term for cave, and so they were called "*jalagrahā*". They gave up the idea of killing him, as he had given them the skill for doing such things—the first *jalagrahā*.[236]

As for Tapa-palet, he wore the headband and the *sampĕt* (sash) and adhered to the sect of the Ṛṣi; he abandoned the sect of the Buddhists. He asked for the favour of the jacket in the holy *maṇḍala pūrwa-ḍarma* in Bapa; then he was called the *dewaguru* of the holy Kasturi *maṇḍala* of Śelagraha-rong. It was he who was the original founder, and so his name was Kasturi Palet; such is the story of the Kasturi Palet.

Let us tell of Mpu Barang's daughter, who was called Ibu-tĕngahan: she requested to have an ascetic as husband; she was allowed to marry an ascetic. She was sick of being married to him, so she left the ascetic. But the ascetic was unwilling to be separated from her, and she threw a palm sheath at him; and so this is why ascetics are inseparable from the betel-tray and betel-bag.

234. The term is *bulalak* (Z 270, "piebald"); KBW *blalak.*

235. Text: *ingĕṇḍĕk-ĕṇḍĕk*; translation uncertain, see Z 456; Pigeaud, "with bas-reliefs".

236. Text: *jalagraga*; clearly a typo.

Again she asked to marry a spiritual teacher; when she had had enough, she left him. The teacher was unwilling to be divorced from her, and she threw (*gutuk*) a stone at him; and so there is now a stone called Gutuk, to the south of Tūryan.

She asked to marry a *widu*, and was allowed. When she had had enough of being married, she left the *widu*. The *widu* was annoyed with her, and so cut her head off, and off went the *widu*. Only the head was left alive, and her head said:

"Fie! Herds-boy, put me in place with my body!"

"Hmph, I don't feel like it".

"Ah, come on then".

"I don't feel like it; my cow has gone I don't know where".

"Well, when you find her she'll have a calf".

"Ah, but my cow's a male".

"Well, anyway[237] you'll find him with a calf".

Right away the body was joined with the head, she was complete again, and returned to her father. The herds-boy found his two cows. As for the *widu*, he took refuge in the *maṇḍala* of Śelagraha-rong, and asked to be made a *wiku*. He was ordained and given the name Buyut Gĕnting, and founded *maṇḍala* on Mount Kawi; the names of his foundations were: Braja-hning, Arga-maṇik, Jangkanang, Bhamana, and Gumantar. Such was the number of the *maṇḍala* he founded; these were known by the name Kasturi Gĕnting.

As for Mpu Barang, he left the *maṇḍala* of Bapa, and took himself to the west, and founded the *maṇḍala* of Ḍupaka. He then followed the Bhairawa sect, ate anything without exception, abandoned wife and children, and turned his mind to renunciation; for this reason the *dewaguru* of the sect are called "*tyāga*". He was the first of the *dewaguru* of the Tyāga sect of the holy Kasturi *maṇḍala* of Ḍupaka. Again he founded a *maṇḍala* at Wariguh on the northern slope of Lord[238] Wilis, he was there in the bright half of the month, and these[239] were called by the name Kasturi Barang; such is the old story.

Let us tell of Ki Samĕgĕt-bagañjing: he wore the headband (*mabadḍa*) and followed the sect of the Ṛṣi. He left Daha, and founded a *maṇḍala* by the side of the road, and dry palm leaves[240] and rice straw served as his shelter. He was given

237. Text: *parandene*, as in Modern Javanese; not listed in Z.

238. The text has *bhaṭāra*, remarkable for a mountain.

239. The text has *loka*, but should be read as *yeka*, as Pigeaud notes, although this is not found in the manuscripts.

240. Text: *bhararak*; Modern Javanese *blarak*.

faeces and urine by people passing by on the road; and this is why their title for him was Kaki Botahi (Grandpa Smell-of-faeces). Right away the buildings came down from high in the sky, together with banks and walls. Then the people were amazed to see Kaki Botahi's supernatural powers. The piebald cow was still in his care; and this is why it was finally called the *maṇḍala* of Bhulalak.

The cow became pregnant, and he cared for her by the side of the road; she gave birth to a beautiful young girl. He took his child home and gave her to the rice-cook [saying:]

"There were people separating and they left their child on the road".

So said Kaki Botahi. When the child had grown up, she was exceedingly beautiful in appearance. King Taki did not have a wife; he took Kaki Botahi's daughter, who had a cow as mother. She was made his queen. Such is the story of the *maṇḍala* of Bhulalak, and they were called the Kasturi Botahi.

He instructed his pupils:

"If later there is someone of the Śaiwa sect by the name of Tapa-wangkĕng, knowledgeable,[241] powerful and skilled at reciting texts, not far from Daha, do not fail to be attentive; I am he, coming back again to my *maṇḍala* of Bhulalak".

Such were Kaki Botahi's instructions.

There was a king, also of Daha, called Aji Uṇḍal. He was engaged in a fight with King Taki; Aji Uṇḍal was beaten. He was not faithful in battle, frightened of dying, did not wash[242] and hid himself away. There were some slaves of his, two *pujut*[243] and one *walyan*,[244] and these followed him constantly.

He took refuge on Mount Kawi, and set up a camp there to hide in. He made a well, and so it is now called Uṇḍal, and the well still exists till now. He took a piece of bark cloth on a rack [thinking:], "How would it be if I become a *wiku* (*mandar lamun wikuha*)!" And so there is [a place] called Lamunwiku now, on the slopes of the holy Kawi facing east. He came to the holy Mahāmeru, wanting to settle at Taṇḍĕs. When questioned about the place where he had been ordained, he told them he had taken the bark cloth from a rack; he was not allowed to advance,[245] as he was not yet a *wiku*.

241. Text: *kawi*; read *kawih* (Z 828).

242. Text: *mambolot*; Z 251 gives only *bolotĕn*, "dirty, muddy, unclean, unwashed".

243. The *pujut* are described by Z 1434 as "a particular group of people (dark-skinned, Negrito?)"; they are often mentioned alongside *jĕnggi* (possibly East Africans), as in e.g. Sumanasāntaka 112.8c.

244. Glossed by Z 2189 as "physician, healer, *ḍukun*"; listed in inscriptions among the *watĕk i jro* (group of the interior). Cf. Balinese *balian*.

245. Text: *mangśu*; Z 107 under *angsu* links this with *angsö*, "to advance?" This place only.

He descended from Taṇḍĕs, and set up camp in the ravine of Śiṇḍo. He sent his slaves off to Kukub, in order to pay homage to Lord Mahāguru, and to ask for the favour of ordination. He was unwilling to be looked down on, [that was] his aim in sending a messenger. Away went the slave named Kajar together with the *walyan* named Bugoleng; the *pujut* named Tĕnggĕk stayed behind to keep an eye on him, together with one male dog.

Now the ones named Kajar and Bugoleng arrived at Kukub, paid homage to Lord Mahāguru, and told him that they were sent by Aji Uṇḍal. Then Lord Ḍarmarāja sent the *ulu-kĕmbang-pakalpan* (an official) to go to Aji Uṇḍal, and to send him the cloth of ordination; then he brought the parasol, earrings and jacket, so that the Mahārāja could become *dewaguru* in Gĕrĕsik.

Without demur the *ulu-kĕmbang-pakalpan* set off, but was not allowed to take too long; two nights was agreed. Quickly he came to Śindo, but it happened that he did not find King Uṇḍal, as just then he was out to amuse himself. Having waited a long time and he did not come, the *ulu-kĕmbang-pakalpan* went home, leaving the ordination cloth on a rock, the rock where Lady Umā had washed her menstrual cloths, the story goes.

Off went the *ulu-kĕmbang-pakalpan*; after he was gone, the Mahārāja arrived; he bound the ordination cloth around himself, and donned the parasol, earrings and jacket. The rock was given the name Ki Ulu-kĕmbang-pakalpan, and is still there now, the place where Lady Umā washed her menstrual cloths, the story goes; and so the name of the *maṇḍala* has been Ḍingḍing[246] till now. For this reason the *maṇḍala* at Ḍingḍing does not recognize the higher rank[247] of Kukub, till now: the king was unwilling to be looked down on, the story goes.

There was a pupil to the Lord of Ḍingḍing, by the name of Ki Buyut Samaḍi. He served the Ḍarma; after he had done flower-worship in the night, he was given the favour of *wiku*-hood. He (the Lord) was whispering untroubled with Buyut Samaḍi; however, Kajar, Tĕnggĕk, Bugoleng as well as the black dog were sleeping in the space below, and heard what they were whispering. They had no trouble hearing about the holy *wiku*-hood, [even though] they did not know about the holy Ḍarma.

When Ki Buyut Samaḍi had been given the favour of holy *wiku*-hood, he was given the parasol, earrings and jacket, and was ordered to be *dewaguru* in Manuñjang,

246. Listed in Modern Javanese in the meaning of "screen".

247. Text: *marĕk.*

once a foundation of the holy Gaṇa; so then its name was Ḍingḍing-Manuñjang. Such is the story.

Now let us tell of Kajar and Tĕnggĕk, who heard the whispers of the Lord to Ki Buyut Samaḍi. Kajar spoke up, saying:

"Goodness, Tĕnggĕk, did you hear that?"

"Yes, I heard it".

"What I heard was plain; now I know the meaning of *wiku*; now I'm able to be a *wiku* without having a teacher".

So the two of them said. There was a piece of folded bark-cloth of the king, and this they both used to bind around themselves. They said:

"*Wiku* is the term for the two of us. Kajar, what is your name as a *wiku* now?"

"Buyut Jala is my name now. And you, Tĕnggĕk, what is your name as a *wiku*?"

"Buyut Giri is my name now. And so Buyut Jala-Giri is the name of us both. Buyut Jala, pay homage to me!"

"I don't feel like it. Both knees are stiff for you. Buyut Giri, pay homage to me!"

"Ah, I don't feel like it. Both my knees are stiff".

For this reason "*wiku kasturi*" was the name of them both. Off they both went, and came to Mount Wĕlahulu in order to perform *tapa*; for this reason there is now a place called Arga-kleṣa,[248] the hermitage of Buyut Jala-Giri. Such is the story of the Kasturi of Jala-Giri.

There was a prince who was driven[249] from the kingdom of Galuh, by the name of Tuhan Cañcurāja. He went into hiding, and came to Buyut Jala-Giri, asking them to save his life. Buyut Jala-Giri said:

"Come, you prince, if you want to live, become a *wiku* to us".

Tuhan Cañcurāja said:

"I don't feel inclined to become a *wiku* to you, as I am a prince".

"Well then, go back to the capital, if you're unwilling to be made a *wiku*".

This is what Buyut Jala-Giri said. Finally the prince resigned himself, was ordained by the *pujut*, and was named Buyut Śrī-manggala. He was instructed by Buyut Jala-Giri:

"Do not become familiar with other *wiku*—that is a great sin for a *wiku*. On the contrary, do whatever you want; do not[250] pass up anything eatable; take a wife; use all your possessions. You are allowed to ordain wife and children, allowed not to

248. Variant of B: *Arga Kelaśa*.

249. Text: *hinilangakĕn*; lit. "caused to disappear, removed".

250. Text: *tajana*; variant of B, *hajāna*, probably *aja ana*.

make offerings, allowed not to worship or fast, allowed not to know the scriptures, allowed not to[251] be taught about anything. Think of yourself as just the Lord".

Such were the instructions of Buyut Jala-Giri to Buyut Śrī-manggala. Off went Buyut Śrī-manggala, and founded *maṇḍala* on the shore of the Southern Ocean. The names of his foundations were: Rājamaṇik, Panimbangan, Gilingan, and Wungkal-ibĕk; this was the number of the *maṇḍala* he founded, and these were termed Kasturi Śrī-manggala. Such is the old story.

Let us tell about the *walyan* by the name of Bugoleng: he knew that Kajar and Tĕnggĕk had gone away. He had had no trouble hearing all about the holy *wiku*-hood, so off went Bugoleng; he came across a dead *wiku*, so he gathered up the bark-cloth and headpiece and made a robe to wear.[252] He went off begging for alms and called in at a palm wine tapper's place; the tapper was called Lulumpang-burut. He gave him palm wine to drink, while they laughed together; after that Lulumpang-burut mentioned becoming a *wiku*. Bugoleng said:

"If you like, let me ordain you, if you want be be a *wiku*".

Immediately he ordained him, and then they drank palm wine and laughed together, and he taught him about the holy *wiku*-hood. He was named Buyut Lĕsung-burut. Off he went into a forest area, and founded the *maṇḍala* of Arga-tilas. He proceeded eastwards, and founded the *maṇḍala* of Jawa,[253] thence northwards and founded the *maṇḍala* of Rĕbhālas,[254] at the foot of Mount Suṇḍawiṇi. He asked for the jacket in Tigāryan, and these are the Kasturi of Lĕsung-burut. Such is the old story.

Let us tell about the black dog, who had had no trouble hearing about the holy *wiku*-hood, and he knew and had heard about the holy Ḍarma. He saw that Kajar and Tĕnggĕk had gone away, so he went as well. There was a butcher by the name of Drĕwyānak, who had a lot of pigs with him; he found the dog. He spoke, saying:

"Hey, now I've found my dog. He went away for a long time, when I hit him before. His fault was that he couldn't be trained[255] to obey, so he went away. A stroke of luck!"[256]

This is what the butcher said; the dog said:

---

251. Text: *hanājāna*; variant of B, *hajāna*.
252. Text: *baddha rañjing-rañjingan*; Pigeaud (p. 192) guesses that this may be an alternative term for *rasukan*.
253. Variant of B and E, Jiwa.
254. Variant of B and E, Rĕgālas.
255. Text: *hoṣanya tanpasara*; read with B, *doṣanya tan paśarama* (see Z 1813 under śrama, sarama).
256. Text: *atutuku anĕmu*; an idiom, "go out to buy, and find it anyway".

"Fie! Rich as you are you ask (for free) what is for sale,[257] thinking I'm your dog. How much money do you have? May your pigs die".

This is what the dog said; the pigs died. The butcher said:

"Oh dear, you're an extraordinary sort of dog: you know how to talk like a human, and you're very powerful. All my pigs are dead now; you must be an incarnation of the Lord".

Straight away Drĕwyānak paid homage to the dog, and asked to be granted a favour; the black dog said:

"Well, let me make you a *wiku*; but I have instructions to you: use ash as your mark; you are allowed not to worship or take vows; you should eat anything without exception; have a wife and children; you are allowed not to know the scriptures; you are allowed not to recite formulas and *mantra*. Let there be nothing considered as knowledge, only the Lord is how you should think of yourself, and you may ordain your children and wife. Do not become familiar with other *wiku*, as this is a great sin and crime for the *wiku*. Let such be my instructions to you".

After he had ordained Drĕwyanak, Buyut Arĕng was his name as *wiku*. Off he went and came to Wĕlahulu. Buyut Arĕng founded *maṇḍala*, and the names of his foundations were: Anaman, Andrala, Kĕpuh-rĕbah, and Jun-maṇik; such was the number of the *maṇḍala* he founded. He paid homage to the Lord in Tigāryan, and asked to be granted the favour of the jacket; and this is the reason they are called the Kasturi of Arĕng.

Let us tell again about the princess from Daha, by the name of Tuhan Galuh Śrī Wīratanu, a daughter to Mahārāja Taki. She was expelled from her city at the time when Tapa-palet was removed from Daha and the queen was driven out. The noble princess was bewildered; then the princess left Daha and sought refuge in the *maṇḍala* of Labdawara with the reverend Aśoṣṭi. There is no need to tell how long she was there, the reverend Aśoṣṭi felt he could not bear to look upon the beauty of the noble princess; he then got together with Rakryān Galuh Śrī Wīratanu. She conceived[258] and became pregnant; she was ashamed to give birth in Labdawara, so she set off and came to Mount Kawi. She gave birth to boy twins, of perfect good looks. She understood that the children might be an embarrassment, and abandoned the boys in the forest. Off she went to go back to her city.

---

257. The intention here is not entirely clear.
258. Text: *kāwaran*; perhaps to be read *kaworan*.

Left there the boys wept and wailed.[259] The reverend Agaṣṭi saw them, and felt pity at seeing the pathetic condition[260] of the boys left behind by their mother. He took them, then bathed and fed them, and raised them with yoga and *samāḍi*. Finally the boys were grown up, and he took them westward to Maśin, and they came to the peak of Kelāśa, to the *maṇḍala* of the reverend Mārkaṇḍeya, who was about to return to his heaven. He then handed over the parasol, earrings and jacket to the reverend Agaṣṭi, who would replace him as *dewaguru* keeping watch over the peak of Kelāśa, taking the place of the reverend Mārkaṇḍeya. The reverend Agaṣṭi was *dewaguru* of Sukayajña. As for the two boys, they were endowed with ordination, and given the names reverend Tṛṇawindu and reverend Anggira; they were granted the holy *wiku*-hood by the reverend Agaṣṭi.

Let us tell about the reverend Mārkaṇḍeya: he left the peak of Kelāśa, and roamed the world, living the life of a religious mendicant.[261] He called in at the house of a butcher;[262] Suka was the name of the butcher. When the reverend Mārkaṇḍeya saw the bones, ribs and[263] skins, he realized that it was the house of an outcast (*caṇḍala*). Off he went; Suka followed him and said:

"Oh, come back, scholar, sir, partake of all the sorts of fruits and roots of a sage, sir. What is the meaning of not looking back?"

The reverend Mārkaṇḍeya did not reply but went straight on. He betook himself eastwards along the southern foot of the holy Mahāmeru; all the time the butcher was following behind. Suddenly they stopped to rest in a forest, Suka was feeling weak and tired, as he had trouble in keeping up with the scholar; and so he now went to sleep. While Suka was fast asleep, the reverend Mārkaṇḍeya set off to the east; he left his *sampĕt* behind on the stump of a jackfruit tree. Without delay he carried out vows and concentration (*samāḍi*) on the holy Mahāmeru, lasting seven days and seven nights, in order to free himself of the impure *caṇḍala*. When he had finished doing this he returned to his heaven.

Let us tell about Suka: when he awoke the scholar was nowhere to be seen, all he could see was his bark garment left behind on the stump of the jackfruit tree. He took the bark cloth and wrapped it around himself; he paid homage to the stump,

259. Text: *makanang-kanangan*; Z 789, a rare word, only here and two places in Nawaruci.

260. Text: *kasesi*; read as *kasyasih*.

261. Text: *amrabhajita*; Pigeaud derives this from *prawrajita*, but cf. Z 1415 under *prawrajyā*, "wandering about (as a religious mendicant)".

262. Text: *abhelawa*; Z 239 says, "butcher, seller of meat". However, see *wallawa, ballawa* (Z 2186), "cook".

263. Text: *igulan*; read *igā lan*?

thinking of it as the scholar. He cleared the forest as a *maṇḍala*; "*waṇa*" is a term for forest, and he was looking for the "*ajī*" (spell), so now the name of the *maṇḍala* is Jiwaṇa. He paid homage to the Lord of Sukayajña, asking for a favour from the reverend Agaṣṭi; after he had been given the favour of the jacket, he founded *maṇḍala* at the foot of Lady Wilis.[264] The names of the foundations were: Bhāṇa, Talutug and Aribhāṇa; such is the number of the *maṇḍala* founded. These are called the Sukayajña-pakṣa-Jiwaṇa.[265] Such is the tale of old.

As for the reverend Agaṣṭi, he returned to his heaven; the parasol, earrings and jacket were handed over to the reverend Tṛṇawindu, who replaced him as *dewaguru* of Sukayajña and dwelt on the peak of Kelāśa. As for the reverend Anggira, he was given the favour of the parasol, earrings and jacket by the reverend Tṛṇawindu, and was ordered to become the *dewaguru* of Sarwasidḍa, of the sect of the hills. The reverend Anggira was auspicious (*manggalya*), as he was not *sukāwaśa*-eating;[266] so then he was called Sukayajña-pakṣa-manggalya.

He founded a *maṇḍala*, drained the water in the river, and caught[267] its fish; so then it was called the *maṇḍala* of Panatmaku.[268] He had many pupils, he went to Mount Burukah to regulate the flow,[269] made a plank bridge over[270] the river, and used[271] thin[272] pieces of wood. After he had finished chopping the wood, the water-manager returned; the wood did not want to be made into a bridge, and in the night the poles ran away and went down into the river. In the morning the water-manager came, but did not find the poles; the stumps and *guntur*[273] had turned into stone, and are there till now. He followed the trail of their flight down into the river; and so the *maṇḍala* was called Layu-watang, and ceased being called Panatan.

264. *Bhaṭārī*; but above (note 236) it was the Lord (*bhaṭāra*).
265. Presumably the Jiwaṇa branch of the Sukayajña order.
266. Text: *anghāraka*; Z 591, "to eat", perhaps "especially edible roots and fruit?" *Sukāwaśa* unclear.
267. Text: *winet*, an error for *pinet*.
268. Variant D has *ring Panatan* here, probably alluding to "draining" the water; see Z 1709 under *sat*.
269. Text: *anguñjang-añjing*; meaning unclear, these places only, but see KBW I 373, *nganjingang*, "het water doen afloopen door een kekalen" (to drain the water through a channel).
270. Text: *malaring*; read *malari ing*.
271. Text: *artha*; unclear.
272. Text: *mali*; read *malit* with variant E.
273. Meaning unknown; not "flood" (Z 556); variant E, *tungtung*, "tip".

Colophon

MS D (only): Such is the Tantu Panggĕlaran, to be held in possession by those practising religion, the *kabuyutan* of the island of Java, the four *pakandan* (divisions?), the four sects and the *kabuyutan* of the Nangga mountain. And it is without date, it is the beginnings of people in Java, when the holy Mahāmeru had not yet come to Java and after it had arrived; such is the reason it is without date, because it was so in the beginning.

The holy Tantu Panggĕlaran has been copied in the compound of the *kabhujanggan* of Kutri-tusan,[274] on the day Umanis, Budha, in Maḍangsiya, in the first month of *rah* 7, tĕnggĕk 5, *ṛṣi panḍawa buta tunggal*: 1557 [AD 1635].

274. Kutri is a village in Gianyar, Bali, where a famous image of Durgā is preserved in a temple.

Mt Semeru (3,676 m), Java's highest peak, viewed from the village of Ledokombo in the Tengger highlands. *Photo by Hadi Sidomulyo, 2018.*

PART TWO

Commentary on the text by Hadi Sidomulyo

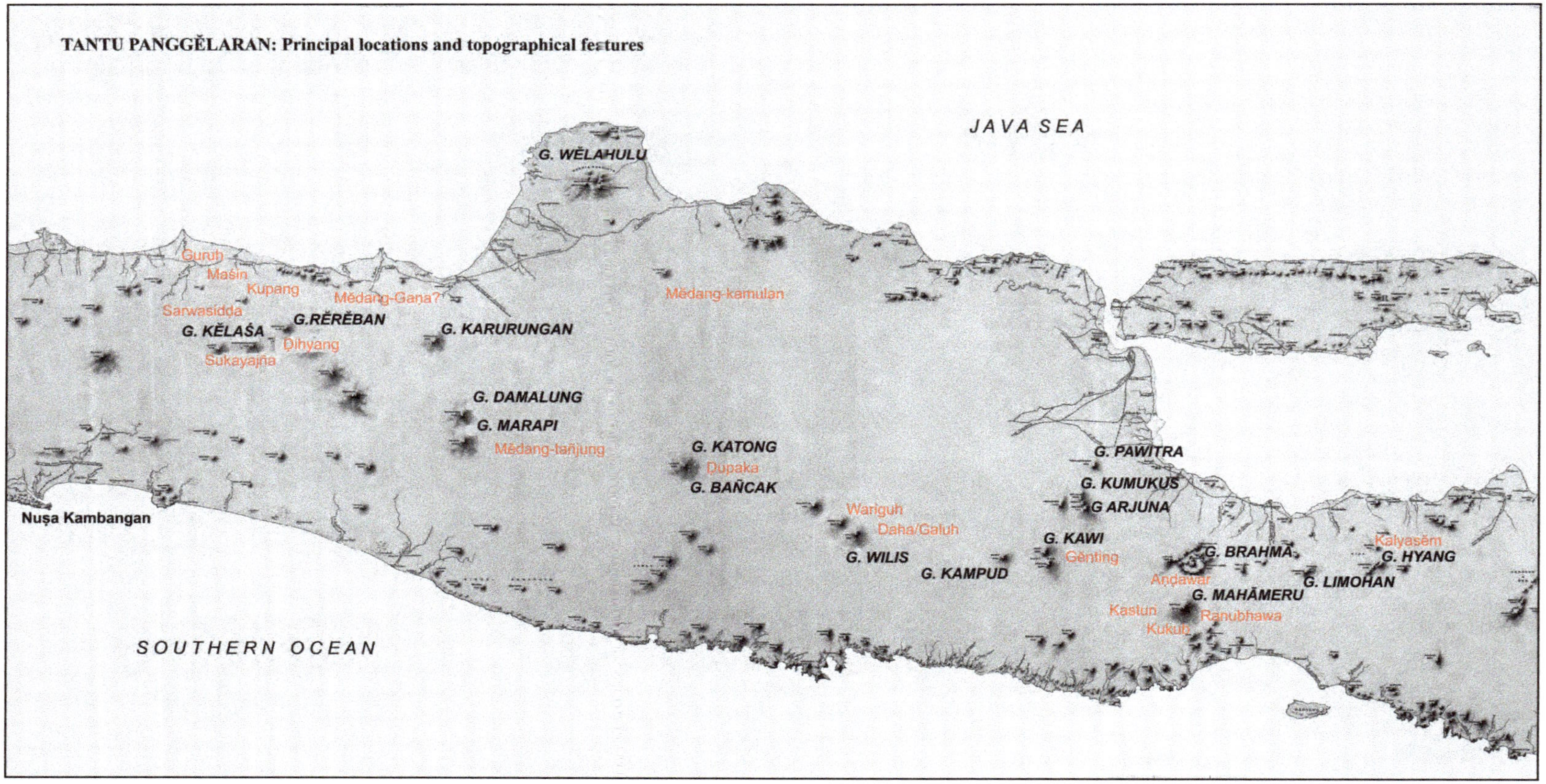

Figure 1 Map of central and eastern Java, showing principal locations and topographical features mentioned in the TP.
Adapted from: Name: 08955; Scale: 1: 1,000,000; Type: Nautical chart; Year: 1915

Introduction

The text introduced here belongs to a category of prose literature composed during the so-called "age of transition" in Javanese history, spanning roughly the fifteenth and sixteenth centuries. This was a time which saw the decline and collapse of the island's last and greatest Hindu-Buddhist kingdom, with its capital at Majapahit, and the rise to power of a confederacy of Muslim coastal states under the leadership of Demak. In marked contrast to the preceding era, which has left us a rich legacy in the form of royal edicts preserved on stone and metal, as well as a substantial body of classical literature, this transition period is remarkable for its scarcity of reliable historical data. The literary work under discussion is thus especially valuable for its ability to shed some light on this poorly documented age, and thereby help to strengthen the bonds linking the past to the present. The text is further unusual for its subject matter, which comprises principally an account of the origin and development of the Śaiwa cult on the island of Java, with a focus on the numerous ascetic communities scattered throughout the countryside. As such, it provides a rare glimpse of life outside the court environment during the pre-Islamic period.

The essential message, as well as the author's intent, are already encapsulated in the title of the work, Tantu Panggĕlaran, introduced immediately following the invocation. This has been very aptly translated by Stuart Robson as "Threads of the unfolding web". As already explained in the introduction to the text, the web refers here to the network of Śiwaite institutions, while the threads (*tantu*) may be viewed as its manifold permutations, whether in the form of sacred sites, holy orders, or established "lines" of continuity. In the commentary to follow an attempt will be made to disentangle some of these threads and clear a path, as it were, through what one writer once described as an "encyclopedic jungle of Śivaitic traditions".[1]

The narrative itself is made up of a series of episodes, beginning with the creation of the first human beings, the origins of civilization and transport of the holy Mount Mahāmeru from the Himalaya, followed by the gradual establishment of the institutions supporting the ascetic community. These are described in various terms, from simple hermitages generally referred to as *patapan*, to the more complex

1. Van der Meulen (1977), p. 96.

maṇḍala establishments, which were presided over by a spiritual guide (*dewaguru*). The storyline is interspersed with legendary tales explaining the origin of numerous sacred domains and natural landmarks referred to in the text, usually connected in some way with the activities of the gods and holy sages. Inasmuch as these events unfold against a landscape which is in many cases still recognizable today, the line separating myth and reality is not always clear cut. As the narrative progresses, however, the historical foundation is strengthened and the text brought down to earth through an ongoing dialogue between the legendary founders of the *maṇḍala* and the Javanese court. Although the royal palace itself is referred to alternatively as Galuh and Daha, it is quite evident that both names represent the same kingdom, i.e. that of Kaḍiri in the twelfth and thirteenth centuries.[2]

As already observed by Th. Pigeaud, the ascetic communities described in the TP probably lay for the most part outside the sphere of court influence and had little interest in royalty.[3] Since they appear to have represented a variety of initiatory traditions, moreover, it is unlikely that much can be learned about their inner workings from written documents. Even so, the text of the TP provides a few clues. It is mentioned, for instance, that the *patapan*, or "abodes of ascetics", comprised several categories. Some of these are self-evident, such as the *pangajaran*, *pangubwanan* and *anguṇḍahagi*, referring respectively to places of men of learning (*ajar*), female hermits (*ubwan*) and craftsmen engaged in the art of wood-working (*uṇḍahagi*).[4] Others are less certain. An example is the term *manguyu*, which P.J. Zoetmulder defined rather vaguely as a "category of male religious persons (ascetic, hermit?)".[5] The text of the TP, however, rather suggests that the way of the *manguyu* was open to householders, a probability supported by the name Pamanguyon-agung attached to the "family residence" of Bhaṭāra Guru and Dewī Umā on Mt Mahāmeru. It can be noted further that it was only after the *wiku* Mpu Siddayoga had married that he adopted the life of a

2. Inscriptional and literary records indicate that Daha was the name of both the palace and capital city of the land of Kaḍiri, a name which is itself synonymous with the Galuh of later Javanese tradition. The legendary princess of Kediri named Candra Kirana or Dewi Sekartaji, well known from the popular stories of Pañji, consistently bears the additional title of Raden Galuh. Likewise, in the TP, the daughter of Mahārāja Taki of Daha is known by the name of Tuhan Galuh Śrī Wīratanu (Part 1, p. 65).

3. Pigeaud (1960–63), vol. IV, p. 247.

4. This indicates that the ascetic communities were not averse to engaging in mundane activities. Another term encountered in the TP is *bhaṇḍagiṇa*, which points to an active interest in the performing arts (cf. Zoetmulder 1982, p. 202).

5. Zoetmulder (1982), p. 1114.

manguyu.[6] By contrast, there are indications that *tyāga* ascetic practice was more severe, and that the hermitages of this category, known as *katyāgan*, did not admit female members.[7] Finally, concerning the term *angarĕmban*, D. Weatherbee has made some useful comments in his discussion of the early fourteenth century charter of Mariñci, which refers to a religious (probably agricultural) community known as *pangarĕmban.*[8]

One group comprising four hermitages, apparently founded very early on, was the so-called *katyāgan* of the *caturāśrama*. These establishments are also mentioned by Prapañca in the fourteenth century *kakawin* Deśawarṇana and will be described more fully in section II of the commentary to follow. Prapañca makes further reference to the *caturbhasma*, or four principal *maṇḍala* of Sāgara, Kukub, Sukayajña and Kasturi. The TP explains in some detail how each of these parent communities came into existence. Sukayajña was apparently the oldest, being described as "the first *maṇḍala* to exist".[9] As will be demonstrated, this revered institution was formerly located in the vicinity of the Dieng Plateau in central Java. The renowned sages Mārkaṇḍeya, Agaṣṭi (Agastya) and Tṛṇawindu are listed among its succession of *dewaguru*. The other three *maṇḍala* were situated in the eastern part of the island. Of these, Kukub was regarded as the most senior, located on the Mahāmeru, while the founder of Sāgara on Mount Hyang was heir to the spiritual legacy of the sage Mpu Barang, an honoured preceptor of the Bhairawa sect. Finally, the *maṇḍala* of Kasturi was another centre of Bhairawa worship, presided over by Mpu Barang himself at Tūryan.[10] The TP lists numerous branches of the Kasturi order, established throughout the eastern districts.

Much as it would be desirable, an exhaustive study of these diverse communities, the nature of the various orders and their relationship to one another, as well as their distinguishing features, extend beyond both the bounds of this publication and the competence of the present writer. Discussion will thus be confined to some general points of interest, aimed principally at opening some avenues of research for those more qualified in the specialized fields of Old Javanese language, literature and religion.

6. Part 1, p. 33. See also Pigeaud (1924, p. 221), who likewise considered the *manguyu* to have included married couples.
7. This assumption is supported by an episode in the TP (Part 1, p. 60), which depicts the sage Mpu Barang "abandoning wife and children" to found the Tyāga branch of the Kasturi order.
8. Weatherbee (1985), p. 350. For the meaning of the word *ārĕmbha*, see Zoetmulder (1982), p. 124.
9. In the light of this statement in the TP (Part 1, p. 28), it is difficult to understand how Pigeaud (1960–63, vol. IV, p. 247) came to regard Sukayajña and Kasturi as the two "younger" members of the *caturbhasma*.
10. Identifiable with the present town of Turen in the regency of Malang.

Although the highlands of Ḍihyang (Dieng) and Mt Kelaśa[11] were acknowledged as the origin of the Śaiwa cult in Java, it is evident that during the later East Javanese period the spiritual centre of the island had moved to Mt Semeru in the Tengger Massif, and in particular the *maṇḍala* of Kukub, which lay on the mountain's southern slope (see Figure 1). The story in the TP of the transport of the holy Mt Mahāmeru from Jambuḍipa, itself a local adaptation of the well known Indian legend Samudramanthana, is perhaps an allusion to this shift in orientation. It was on the Mahāmeru, after all, that the gods had together partaken of the "water of life" (Śiwāmba) and the Trinity of Lords, Iśwara, Brahmā and Wiṣṇu, received their vehicles. Kukub, moreover, preserved the "contents" of the Supreme Lord in a special book, "entwined with a serpent and bound like a girdle".[12] The *maṇḍala* was presided over by a manifestation of Bhaṭāra Guru himself, who upon his first appearance on the mountain as a *wiku* is portrayed in the following way: "naked and observing silence ... without satisfying the need for food or sleep. Adhering to immaculate concentration", there was "nothing he wished for, not the world, not heaven, not liberation, not release, not happiness, not unhappiness; there was nothing he praised, and nothing he despised". Such, the author tells us, was his state of *tapa*.[13]

The above description is sufficient to demonstrate that the main purpose of the *maṇḍala* was to provide a means for the aspiring *wiku* to gain release from the cycle of existence. Those receiving ordination were expected to adhere to ascetic disciplines (*tapa*), through which they could realize the highest stage of being, rising through the realms of gods (*dewata, hyang*) and perfect sages (*siddārṣi*) to the exalted state of *bhaṭāra*. Conversely, those *wiku* who went astray and failed to reach the level of *dewata* would remain tied to the earthly plane, destined to be reborn as world-sovereigns (*cakrawarti*).[14]

The text of the TP makes it abundantly clear that both the structure and organization of the *maṇḍala* communities were founded on a well-established tradition. The opening of a *maṇḍala* belonging to the Kasturi order, for example, required the sanction of the *dewaguru* at either Tūryan or Tigāryan, while in other cases approval was granted directly by the lord of Kukub. Ordination of a *wiku* could only be conducted by a *dewaguru*, who in turn received his office from the highest spiritual authority. As the guardians of an esoteric doctrine, it is understandable that the *dewaguru* did not pass

11. Variant Kailāśa. According to Hindu tradition, the abode of Lord Śiwa and his spouse Umā.
12. Part 1, p. 34.
13. Part 1, p. 37.
14. Part 1, p. 29.

on their knowledge indiscriminately, and were only prepared to ordain individuals who met the required standards.

There were, however, exceptions. An episode towards the end of the text recounts the story of a certain Aji Uṇḍal of Daha, who was installed as a *dewaguru* by the lord of Kukub, but later refused to acknowledge the latter's authority. One night he proceeded to confer ordination upon a deserving pupil, unaware that the space below his room was occupied by a group of slaves, accompanied by a black dog. Overhearing the teacher's words, the uninvited guests automatically gained possession of the key to *wiku*-hood, effectively allowing each of them, including the dog, to become a *dewaguru* and establish his own *maṇḍala*.[15] The result was that the four newly ordained *wiku* left the service of their master and proceeded to attract disciples indiscriminately, imparting the message: "Do whatever you want; eat anything without exception; take a wife; there is no necessity to make offerings, to worship or fast, to know the scriptures or to be taught about anything, just think of yourself as the Lord".

The inclusion of this episode in the TP points to the presence of a heterodox current, which ran counter to accepted norms and probably aroused a measure of disapproval from the Hindu-Javanese religious establishment. Of interest is the fact that the blatant contempt for authority displayed by these renegade *wiku* finds a parallel in the activities of the controversial sixteenth century Islamic saint known as Seh Lĕmah Abang, or Siti Jenar, whose radical teachings were actively opposed by the court of Demak. Considering the strong Indian influence on the philosophy expounded by Siti Jenar,[16] it is hardly surprising that his message, albeit presented within an Islamic framework, should not differ essentially from that of the *wiku* referred to above. Noteworthy too is the fact that Siti Jenar, like his counterparts in the TP, is said to have been subject to an unauthorized, or "accidental" initiation, being transformed from the state of a lowly worm upon inadvertently gaining access to the "Great Mystery of the Supreme Being".[17] In short, all of these threads of information help

15. Part 1, p. 62. This accords with the tenets of the Kāpālika sect of Bhairawa worshippers, which hold that "by merely entering on the initiatory ceremony a man becomes a Brāhmaṇa at once", and "by undertaking the *kāpāla* rite a man becomes at once an ascetic" (cf. Gopinath Rao 1971, vol. II, p. 26).
16. Discussed in Zoetmulder (1990), pp. 352–67.
17. Cf. Rinkes (1996), pp. 173–75. This event is said to have occurred during the ordination conferred upon Sunan Kalijaga by the *wali* Sunan Bonang. In order to prevent anyone from overhearing, the latter had chosen to impart the secret doctrine to his disciple in the middle of a lake. The boat in which they travelled, however, turned out to contain a leak, which was subsequently blocked with a lump of clay in which a worm was hiding. As acknowledged by Sunan Bonang himself, the mere presence of the worm during the "Revelation of the deepest Truth" caused the creature to assume human form.

us to establish a line of continuity, linking the age of the Hindu-Javanese *maṇḍala* with that of the early Islamic period.[18]

In this connection, it is interesting to consult the journal of the early Portuguese traveller Tomé Pires, who visited the north coastal region of Java in the years 1512–13. Pires mentions the community of hermits, or "*tapas*", adding that "there are about fifty thousand of these in Java", comprising "three or four orders",[19] an image reminiscent of Prapañca's description of the *caturbhasma*. The fact that Pires himself was quite probably a contemporary of the author of the TP makes his report all the more significant. Of further interest is the observation that "these men are also worshipped by the Moors, and they believe in them greatly; they give them alms; they rejoice when such men come to their houses".[20] This account of wandering holy men, revered both by Hindus and Muslims, clearly invites a separate discussion into which we will not venture at this point. Suffice it to say that Pires appears to provide us with an eyewitness account of the inhabitants of the various *patapan* and *maṇḍala* described in the TP. Although now no more than a vague memory, these same communities were doubtless instrumental in transmitting and preserving for posterity the rich legacy of an ancient tradition, which continues to find expression today in a variety of cultural forms, the most notable being the Javanese *wayang*, or "shadow play".

Before turning to the main part of the commentary, it would seem worthwhile to try and narrow the margins for the age in which the text of the TP achieved its present form. As already noted by Stuart Robson in his introduction to the translation, the text displays linguistic similarities to other literary works attributed to roughly the same period, among them the Calon Arang and Pararaton. The contents of the latter in particular display some remarkable parallels with the TP, especially those relating to the early life of the semi-legendary founder of the Rājasa dynasty, known as Ken Angrok. Yet these similarities do not in themselves enable us to determine precisely when either of these literary works was composed. In his thesis of 1924, Pigeaud attempted to arrive at more certainty, but was unable to reach any firm conclusions.[21] Comparison of the language with other works of literature proved indecisive, while the narrative itself contained few elements which could be used to help date the manuscript. In short, Pigeaud could do little more than suggest that the work was

18. For an interesting discussion of the Islamization of a Hindu-Javanese *maṇḍala*, see Guillot (2002), pp. 154–59.
19. Cortesão (1944), p. 177.
20. Ibid.
21. Pigeaud (1924), pp. 48–51.

probably committed to writing at some time after the year 1500, but before 1635, a date found in the colophon attached to one of the manuscripts.[22]

One clue which Pigeaud apparently overlooked was the story concerning a golden image of the god Wiṣṇu, said to have been fashioned by the sage Mpu Barang upon his return from Jambuḍipa and subsequently presented to the ruler of Daha. The episode concludes with the statement: "This is the reason the holy golden image is revered by the kings of Daha, even until now".[23] The implication, of course, is that there was a king residing at Daha when the TP was being composed, and that the author himself might even have set eyes on the same golden image.

This calls for some reflection. Since it is more or less unanimously agreed that our text can, on linguistic grounds, be dated to the closing years of the Majapahit era, if not somewhat later, there must have been a king of Daha paying reverence to the Wiṣṇu image at that time. Although the identity of this ruler is unknown, it is hard to imagine that he or she was still reigning, or that the image had remained intact, after the city had been overrun by the forces of a Muslim alliance under the leadership of Sunan Kudus in the year 1527.[24] This date can therefore be regarded as a *terminus ante quem* for the composition of the TP.

It might even be possible to advance a step further by enquiring as to why the name Majapahit is nowhere mentioned in the text. The answer is surely that, in the author's time, the city had already been abandoned and the royal court shifted southward to the relative safety of Daha, in the present region of Kediri. This suggestion finds accordance with the journal of Tomé Pires, mentioned earlier, which states that the "heathen" king of Java resided at "Dayo", or "Daha".[25]

It remains now to consider the year in which this exodus occurred. According to the Pararaton, the last king of Majapahit died in his palace in the Śaka year 1400

---

22. It should be added here that the rather long-winded arguments advanced by Pigeaud for the dating of the TP do not inspire much confidence, being founded principally upon a rather tenuous connection between a *ratu ring* Cĕmpa occurring in the text, and the well known *putri* Cĕmpa of later Javanese tradition.
23. Part 1, p. 57. Pigeaud (1924), p. 117. "*Yata matangnyan sang hyang pratima hmās kinabhaktenira de sang prabhū ring Dahā, katamapi katkaning mangke*".
24. The reliability of this date, preserved in the Babad ing Sangkala, has been acknowledged in the publications of such notable scholars as de Graaf and Pigeaud (1986), as well as Guillot and Kalus (2003).
25. Cortesão (1944), pp. 175, 190. It can be added that Pires likewise made no reference to Majapahit, indicating that the place was no longer recognized as a political centre of any importance in the second decade of the sixteenth century.

(AD 1478–9).[26] The same date is preserved in the later Javanese tradition, being the year in which the royal palace was overrun by the forces of Demak.[27] It therefore seems likely, in the absence of further data, that the evacuation of the city occurred at around that time, allowing us to place the composition of the TP between the years 1478 and 1527.[28]

26. Par. 32: 24–25 (Brandes 1920, p. 40). This event is marked by the chronogram: *śunya nora yuganing wong*.
27. It is remarkable that the inscriptional record from the district of Trowulan (Mojokerto), site of the Majapahit royal palace, ends abruptly in the year 1475, just three years before the date recording the fall of the capital in the traditional sources.
28. Although the stone inscriptions issued by Śrī Girindrawardhana dyah Raṇawijaya seem to indicate that there was a king in residence at Majapahit in the year 1486, the lack of supporting documentary evidence gives reason for caution. For the time being we prefer to leave the matter undecided. The figure of Śrī Girindrawardhana has been discussed at some length by Noorduyn (1978, pp. 244–53).

I
PROLOGUE

Descent of Lord Jagatpramāṇa

Rahyang Kaṇḍyawan and his descendants

Mĕḍang-gaṇa and Mĕḍang-kamulan

Transport of the Mahāmeru from Jambuḍipa

Mt Kelāśa

The mountains Wĕlahulu, Sañjaya, Walangbangan and Pamrihan

Descent of Lord Jagatpramāṇa

It is told that in former times the island of Java (Yawaḍipa) was an unstable land mass, without mountains or inhabitants; a condition which prompted the Supreme Lord Jagatpramāṇa (Bhaṭāra Guru) to descend to earth, together with his consort Bhaṭārī Umā. Setting up an initial residence at Ḍihyang, the divine couple proceeded to perform yoga. The gods Brahmā and Wiṣṇu were then instructed to create human beings. Kneading lumps of clay, Lord Brahmā created the male and Lord Wiṣṇu the female,[29] an act which is said to have taken place on the mountain named Pawinihan.[30]

As already observed, the name Ḍihyang refers to the misty heights of the Dieng Plateau in central Java (see Figure 2). The fact that this region preserves some of the island's earliest surviving Hindu-Javanese temple remains can hardly be regarded as accidental, but rather indicates that the author of the TP acknowledged the antiquity

Figure 2 The highland village of Dieng, viewed from the summit of Mt Prahu. The mountain Pawinian forms the highest point on the horizon (right).
Photo by Hadi Sidomulyo, 2019.

29. This is in accordance with the conception of the deities Brahmā and Wiṣṇu as the "right" and "left" hands of Lord Śiwa, as illustrated in the well known myth of the origin of the *lingga* (cf. Swellengrebel 1936, p. 46; Zimmer 1946, pp. 128–30; Gopinath Rao 1971, vol. II, pp. 106–7).
30. See Part 1, p. 11 (note 9). Identifiable with present day Mt Pawinian, a steep, forest-covered peak lying not far to the southwest of Dieng in the district of Karangkobar (Banjarnegara Regency).

of Ḍihyang, both as a "senior" religious centre and cradle of the Śaiwa cult in Java.[31] This in turn implies that an ancient network of ascetic communities maintained an unbroken dialogue throughout the Hindu-Javanese period, impervious to the shifting of the royal courts and accompanying political turmoil. Both the inscriptional and literary records provide evidence of such a continuity. In the region of Dieng itself, R.D.M. Verbeek already noted the existence of a rock inscription displaying the Śaka date 1132 (AD 1210–11), and a stone image of Wiṣṇu dated Śaka 1216 (AD 1294–5) was reported by N.W. Hoepermans.[32] More recently, S. Satari has proposed a fourteenth or fifteenth century dating for an important *yoni* pedestal preserved in the district of Petungkriyono (discussed below).[33] Further indication of an ongoing tradition is provided by the Old Sundanese poem recounting the journey of Bujangga Manik. Composed in around the year 1500, this work is of particular interest for its reference to quite a number of religious institutions mentioned in the TP, several of which were situated in central Java.[34] There is, in addition, a collection of *lontar* manuscripts popularly known as the Merapi-Merbabu corpus, preserved in the National Library at Jakarta. As yet little studied, these valuable documents give us reason to believe that a literary tradition continued to flourish in the mountain retreats of central Java until quite recent times.[35]

Returning now to the text of the TP, following the appearance of the first inhabitants, more gods and holy sages were summoned to aid in the development of civilization. Lord Iśwara, serving as *gurudeśa* (teacher of village headmen), was instructed to establish the various branches of learning, including language and ethics. The divine architect Wiśwakarma was responsible for the art of carpentry, Lord Mahādewa for that of the goldsmith, while the skills of the painter were introduced

31. As noted pertinently by van der Meulen (1977, p. 100, note 51), "... the text's East Javanese author would scarcely have placed the sacred origins of Śivaism in Central Java without any basis in fact".
32. Verbeek (1891), p. 124, no. 54 (report by F. Junghuhn); Hoepermans (1913), p. 88. See also Krom (1914), p. 124, no. 379.
33. See note 76.
34. Noorduyn and Teeuw (2006), pp. 254, 257–58, 264–65. That these centres were still flourishing during Majapahit's later years is supported by the statement: "... I just came from the mountains, just arrived from the east, came from Mt Damalung, arrived from Mt Pamrihan, from the district of the religious schools" (BM 593–597). As will be seen, the names Damalung and Pamrihan refer to the central Javanese mountain Merbabu.
35. For a summary of the Merapi-Merbabu corpus, see Setyawati, Wiryamartana and van der Molen (2002). Although the bulk of the collection does indeed originate from the vicinity of the mountains Merapi and Merbabu, the listing in the National Library Catalogue includes a number of manuscripts from other highland areas, among them Mt Lawu and Mt Wilis. The documents bearing dates, which so far number about sixty, span a period of 230 years, from 1443 until 1673 of the Javanese calendar.

by Mpu Ciptangkara, an incarnation of the sage Bhagawān Ciptagupta. Lord Brahmā, in the meantime, became the metal smith Mpu Sujiwana, entrusted with the task of forging tools and weapons in the crater of Mt Brahmā.[36] Lastly, Bhaṭāra Wiṣṇu took on the role of world ruler, descending to earth with his heavenly consort, the goddess Śrī. The latter is credited with the introduction of agriculture, as well as the arts of spinning and weaving. In this way, it is said, the first civilized communities were established on Java.[37]

Rahyang Kaṇḍyawan and his descendants

In his role of world ruler, Lord Wiṣṇu became incarnate in the figure of Rahyang Kaṇḍyawan, who reigned at Mĕḍang-gaṇa with his queen Sang Kanyawan, herself an incarnation of the goddess Śrī. This union produced five sons. The eldest, named Mangukuhan, took charge of agriculture, while the second, Saṇḍang-garbha, organized the kingdom's trade. The third son, Katung-malaras, engaged in the production of palm-wine, working as a tapper, and the fourth, Karung-kalah, was a butcher. The youngest, named Wṛtti-kaṇḍayun, succeeded his father as ruler of Mĕḍang-gaṇa.[38]

The legend of Kaṇḍyawan and his five sons is apparently an ancient one. Javanese literature of a later period preserves several variants of the story, in particular those surrounding the figure of Aji Saka and his descendants at Mĕḍang-kamulan.[39] A comparative study of these sources would doubtless be instructive, but will not be attempted here. Pigeaud already drew attention to some of the complexities involved.[40]

One version of the Kaṇḍyawan legend which should be mentioned, however, is that found in the Old Sundanese Carita Parahyangan, a text apparently overlooked by Pigeaud but later discussed at length by Noorduyn.[41] Although displaying some

36. Identifiable with Mt Bromo, an active volcano in the Tengger highlands of eastern Java.
37. Part 1, p. 12.
38. Part 1, pp. 12–13.
39. In these accounts Kaṇḍyawan is named alternatively Ardiwijaya, Sawela Cala, or Sri Mahapunggung. Compare, for example, the versions offered in the Sĕrat Kanda (Brandes 1904a, pp. cxvii–cxxxi) and Babad Kadhiri (Suyami et al. 1999, pp. 27, 32, 79, 83–84). It can be added that Kaṇḍyawan's eldest son, Mangukuhan, plays a major role as the reigning king of Mĕḍang-kamulan in the eighteenth century Manik Maya (Prijohoetomo 1937, pp. 1–47). To this day, the grave of Ki Makukuhan (*sic*)/Sri Mahapunggung at Kedu in northern central Java remains a revered place of pilgrimage.
40. Pigeaud (1924), pp. 202–9.
41. For a transcription and discussion of the relevant passages, see Noorduyn (1962), pp. 405–32.

remarkable parallels to the TP, the account differs sharply in certain details.[42] The storyline, moreover, is in general more elaborate. On the basis of these observations, it could be argued that the Carita Parahyangan dates from a slightly later period. As to how the Kaṇḍyawan legend made its way to the royal court of western Java, it is not hard to imagine a pilgrim such as Bujangga Manik carrying home a *lontar* manuscript on his return from the "district of religious schools" in the east.[43]

Mĕḍang-gaṇa and Mĕḍang-kamulan

The TP places the earliest sites of habitation in Java at Mĕḍang-gaṇa and Mĕḍang-kamulan. The former, as already explained, was the place where Wiṣṇu and Śrī first incarnated as Rahyang Kaṇḍyawan and his queen Sang Kanyawan. Mĕḍang-kamulan, on the other hand, is described as the site of the first dwellings constructed by the sage Wiśwakarma.

Legendary tales surrounding the famed kingdom of Mĕḍang-kamulan survive in the traditional *babad* literature, as well as in the stories of Pañji, but the historical foundation for these accounts is not so widely known or appreciated. Given the available data, we can be quite sure that Mĕḍang-kamulan was an historical reality, as will be argued below. The name Mĕḍang-gaṇa, on the other hand, seems not to have survived in the later records, making its placement more problematic. It could be that it is identifiable with one of the other places named Mĕḍang which are known to tradition.[44] Whatever the case, we find no good reason to doubt its existence.

Discussing the site of Mĕḍang-gaṇa more than forty years ago, van der Meulen argued persuasively in favour of a location not far from the Dieng Plateau.[45] Starting from the premise that Gaṇa was a shortened version of the name of the elephant-headed god Gaṇeśa, he remarked that the Gaṇeśa cult "seems to have been practiced with extraordinary devotion in the environs of the Dieng", and that the same region "may indeed have been the cradle of the cults of both Śiva and Gaṇeśa". In support of his thesis the same writer drew attention to W.F. Stutterheim's comments on the

42. An example is to be found in the opening verses, where the sons of Kaṇḍyawan are equated with the *pañca kuśika*, or "five deities", named Kuśika, Garga, Metri, Kuruṣya and Prātañjala (Noorduyn 1962b, p. 406). The TP, by contrast, introduces the latter in an entirely separate context (see Part 1, p. 23).
43. See note 34 above.
44. Among these places we can mention Mĕḍang-kamulan, Mĕḍang-kumuwung, Mĕḍang-tamtu, Mĕḍang-agung and Mĕḍang-gowong, all of which occur in the popular legend of Śrī Sĕdana/Mahapunggung (cf. Rassers 1982, pp. 10–12).
45. Van der Meulen (1977), pp. 98–100.

large number of Gaṇeśa statues from the Dieng area which were housed in the National Museum at Jakarta. Van der Meulen himself estimated that some 30 per cent of stone images recovered from the neighbourhood of Dieng were representations of Gaṇeśa, with a peak of 45 per cent at Boja (Kendal). On the basis of the number of Gaṇeśa images recorded in the area lying between the Dieng Plateau and Mt Ungaran, he concluded that the elephant-headed god was "two to three times as popular as Śiva himself, and about five times as popular as any other god". As such, the name Mĕḍang-gaṇa was "extremely fitting for this region, perhaps more so than for any other".

Considering now a more precise location for the site of Mĕḍang-gaṇa, we find several occurrences of the toponym "Gono" (Gaṇa) in the regency of Kendal (see Figure 3). One of these is the village of Gonoharjo, which occupies the northwestern slope of Mt Ungaran in the district of Limbangan. Significant archaeological remains discovered in this area, notably near the settlements of Nglimut, Segono and Gonoriti, help to strengthen the identification.[46] Another village name that invites attention is Rambutgono, indicating a "sacred place of Gaṇa".[47] This fertile settlement on the northern bank of the river Turen at Patean still preserves the "grave" of a certain Sri-wedari, possibly identifiable with the legendary Dewi Rengganis.[48] A stone Gaṇeśa image has been found near the village.[49]

Although the exact position of Mĕḍang-gaṇa must for the time being remain conjectural, a proposed location somewhere in the regency of Kendal becomes more convincing as the story of the TP unfolds. We read later, for instance, of the descent from Mt Kelāśa of the divine couple Kāmadewa and Smarī, who took up earthly incarnations at Mĕḍang-gaṇa. Another episode recounts the marriage of the princess Dewi Kasingi of Mĕḍang-gaṇa to the sage Mpu Siddayoga, who resided with Bhaṭāra Iśwara at Sukayajña. As will be demonstrated, both Kelāśa and Sukayajña were situated in the vicinity of the Dieng Plateau, forming a geographical configuration that accords well with our proposed location of Mĕḍang-gaṇa.

Turning now to Mĕḍang-kamulan, we can begin with T.S. Raffles, who visited the site in 1815 and published the following description in his History of Java:[50]

46. I note in particular the temple remains named Candi Argokusuma, first described by Friederich (1870, pp. 512–15). See also Tjahjono, Indrajaya and Degroot (2015), pp. 337–38 and figures 9–12.

47. Probably derived from Old Javanese *rabut*, "sacred place" (Zoetmulder 1982, p. 1471), rather than *rambut*, meaning "hair".

48. See notes 71 and 272.

49. Tjahjono, Indrajaya and Degroot (2015), p. 347, no. 34. Other Gaṇeśa images have been found further upstream on the river Turen, notably at Ngargo and Surugajah (cf. Brumund 1868, p. 145; Hoepermans 1913, p. 215).

50. Raffles (1817), vol. II, p. 53.

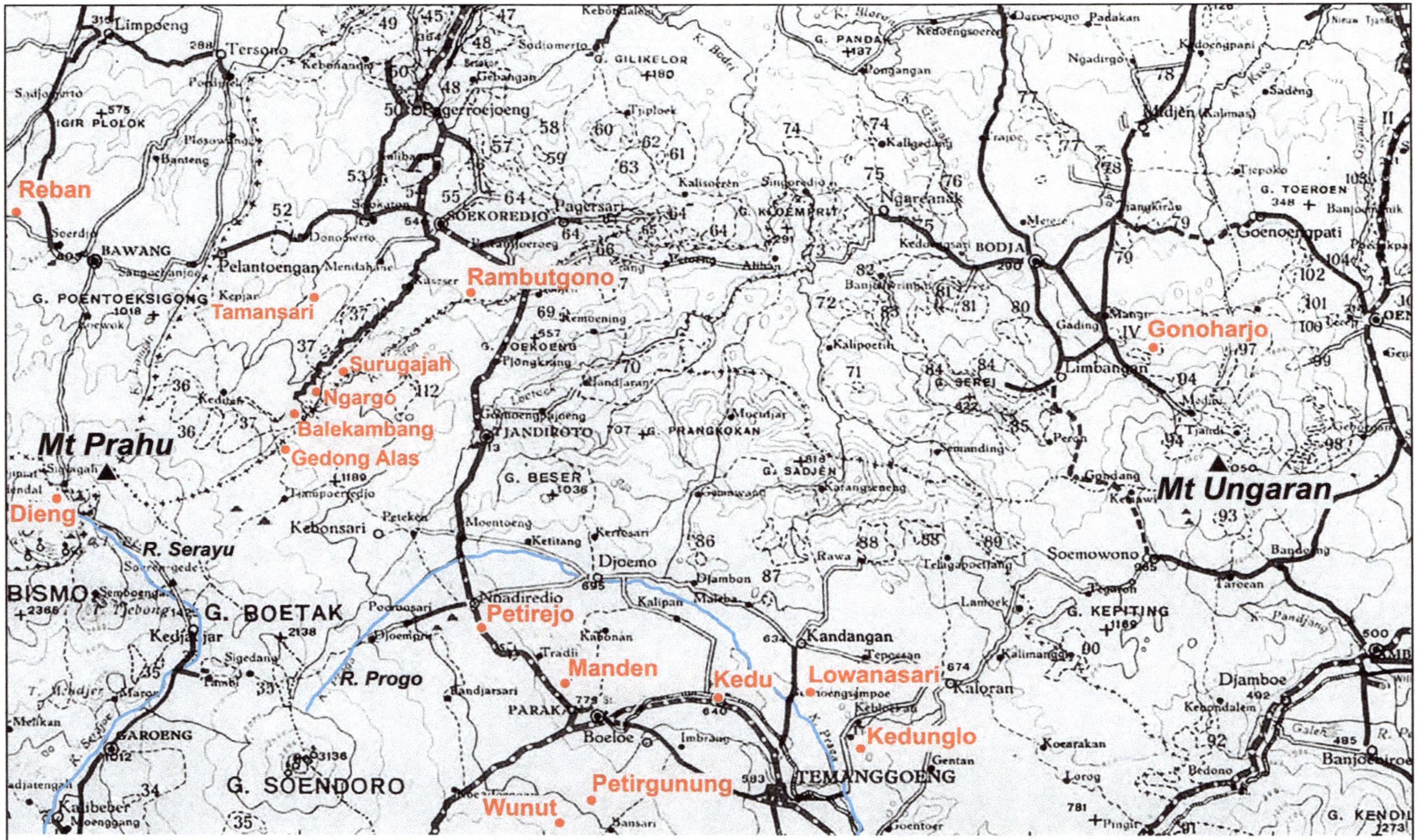

Adapted from the Dutch Topographical Map Series, 1943 (1:250,000), Sheet III

Figure 3 Map showing the regions of Temanggung and Kendal, to the east and northeast of Dieng. *Adapted from: Name: 05271-03; Scale: 1: 250,000; Type: Topographic map; Year: 1943*

> *Medang Kamulan* was situated in the district of *Wirasaba*,[51] where in the centre of an extensive forest is pointed out the site of the *Setingel*, distinguished by heaps of stones and bricks; and at no great distance from it are the walls and excavation of an extensive tank, several hundred feet in length and breadth. These ruins, of which little more can be said than that they are clearly discernible, are situated between *Penwadado*[52] and the most eastern of the volcanic wells alluded to in a former part of this work.[53]

Raffles' placement of Mĕḍang-kamulan in the present regency of Grobogan (Central Java) finds correspondence in the Sĕrat Centhini, a Javanese work of literature dating from roughly the same period. Although the Centhini is a work of fiction, the detailed descriptions of topographical features and archaeological remains encountered were quite clearly based on eyewitness reports, either by the authors themselves or at least by reliable informants. Thus we learn that, on his journey westward from the site of Kayangan Api in the forest of Dander (Bojonegoro), the wandering prince of Giri named Jayengresmi sojourned for a while at Kasongo as a guest of one Ki Jatipitutur, who was well versed in the local tradition. From his host Jayengresmi heard the legend of the serpent Joko Linglung, before being taken on a guided tour of the major places of interest, which included the villages of Crewek and Mendikil, the pool named Sendang Ramesan, the natural phenomenon known as "Bledug" at Kuwu, and the remains of the palace of Mĕḍang-kamulan.[54] This last mentioned site was described as an extensive, raised area of land covered in forest.

The description in the Centhini allows us to identify the former site of Mĕḍang-kamulan with the settlement of that name in the district of Gabus, at the eastern extremity of the regency of Grobogan, where a river (*kali*) Medang is still known (see Figure 4). Archaeological research conducted by E.W. van Orsoy de Flines in the early 1940s, followed up by recent excavations in the present hamlet of Medang Kamulan itself, provide further support for the identification.[55]

The location of Mĕḍang-kamulan as described in the story of Bujangga Manik is not at variance with the sources referred to above. In this case, however, Bujangga

51. This appears to be a typing error. Clearly the district of Wirosari (Grobogan Regency) was intended.
52. Purwodados on Raffles' appended map, identifiable with modern day Purwodadi.
53. This is a reference to T. Horsfield's description of the "salt wells" extending eastward from Grobogan as far as Blora (Raffles 1817, vol. I, pp. 23–24).
54. Darusuprapta et al. (1991), vol. I, pp. 65–76.
55. Orsoy de Flines (1941–47), pp. 66–69, 80–84. Investigations conducted a few years ago by staff from the Balai Arkeologi, Yogyakarta, revealed a foundation of ancient large-size bricks near the site of the former "palace". This was followed up by a spate of unofficial excavations by the local inhabitants, which yielded a great quantity of ceramic shards, coins, tools and ornaments of metal, pointing to intensive and continuous settlement (cf. Tribunjateng.com, 17 October 2015).

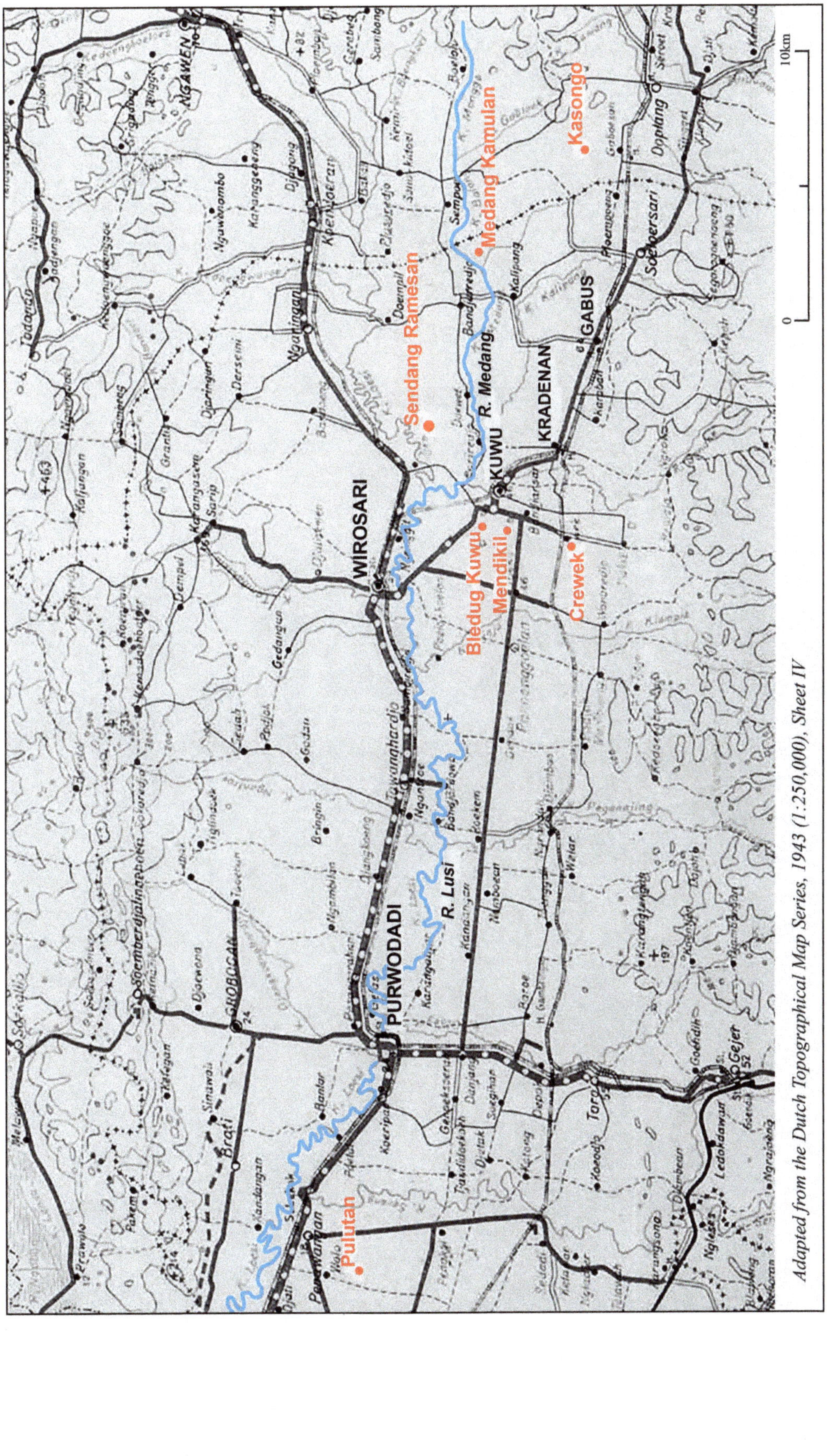

Adapted from the Dutch Topographical Map Series, 1943 (1:250,000), Sheet IV

Figure 4 Map of the regency of Grobogan, showing the position of Mĕḍang-kamulan, as well as places mentioned in the Bujangga Manik and Sĕrat Centhini.

Adapted from: Name: 05271-04; Scale: 1: 250,000; Type: Topographic map; Year: 1943

Manik was travelling in an easterly direction and arrived at the historic site after passing through the village of Pulutan, on the western side of Purwodadi. Despite its brevity this reference is extremely valuable, for it shows, as Noorduyn remarked, that Mĕḍang-kamulan was "a reality in the fifteenth century".[56] Further supporting evidence, however, is unfortunately hard to find. One written source of possible relevance is an inscription from the temple complex named Candi Sukuh, on the slopes of Mt Lawu to the south of Grobogan (see Figures 5 and 6). M. Muusses already observed that this document, dated Śaka 1363 (AD 1441–2), records the defeat of a place named Rajĕgwĕsi by the people of Mĕḍang.[57] If we accept Noorduyn's placement of Rajĕgwĕsi in the present regency of Bojonegoro, which lies not far to the east of Grobogan,

Figure 5 Candi Sukuh, on the western slope of Mt Lawu, Karanganyar Regency, Central Java. *Photo by Hadi Sidomulyo, 2020.*

56. Noorduyn and Teeuw (2006), pp. 447–48.
57. Muusses (1923b), p. 501 (no. 3), 507–9. See also Noorduyn (1978), p. 262, note 8.

Figure 6 Candi Sukuh; inscription dated Śaka 1363.
Photo by Hadi Sidomulyo, 2020.

there would seem to be good reason to associate the Mĕḍang of the inscription with Mĕḍang-kamulan, for whose inhabitants the terraced sanctuaries on Mt Lawu were perhaps important places of pilgrimage.[58]

Transport of the Mahāmeru from Jambuḍipa

Despite the intervention of the gods, the island of Java remained unstable and continued to sway back and forth. For this reason, it is said, Bhaṭāra Guru turned to the east and performed yoga once again, creating the mountain Hyang. The earth at his feet, in the meantime, turned into Mt Limohan.[59] There is no doubt that this is a reference to the Hyang Massif, a mountain range crowned by the summit of Argopura at the far eastern end of Java. We can thus safely assume that Limohan is an old name for present Mt Lemongan, which forms a prominent appendage at the western end of the

58. For a discussion of the location of Rajĕgwĕsi, see Noorduyn (1968), pp. 477–78.
59. Part 1, p. 13.

range (see Figure 7). The fact that the creation of Mt Hyang took place before the arrival of the Mahāmeru from India would seem to indicate that the author of the TP recognized the antiquity of this region, perhaps regarding it as a second ancestral seat after Ḍihyang. As will be seen, Mt Hyang was the site of an ancient hermitage, which spawned a number of prominent *maṇḍala* establishments.

Returning to the narrative, the island of Java continued to move up and down. In order to overcome the problem, the Supreme Lord summoned all the gods and other heavenly beings, instructing them to remove the holy mountain Mahāmeru from the Himalaya and bring it to Java, where it would serve to fix the island in place.[60] The delegation duly departed, but upon arrival in Jambuḍipa (India) soon discovered that the mountain was too large to be taken intact. After some deliberation, a decision was made to take only the summit and leave the lower half behind. Led by the deities Brahmā and Wiṣṇu, who devised an efficient method of transport, the celestial host succeeded in removing the top of the Mahāmeru and began the homeward journey.

A setback occurred when the gods and their retinue quenched their thirst with the water flowing from the mountain, which turned out to be deadly poisonous. Through

Figure 7 The Hyang Massif and Mt Lemongan (foreground), viewed from Ledokombo, Tengger highlands. *Photo by Hadi Sidomulyo, 2018.*

60. Part 1, p. 14 ff.

the intervention of Bhaṭāra Guru, however, the poison, known as Kalakuṭa, became transformed into the "water of life" (Śiwāmba), which served as an antidote. The journey was then resumed and the Mahāmeru finally reached Java, where it was set down at the western end of the island.

The gods were now confronted with a new problem. The weight of the mountain was so great that the land in the west began to sink, while in the east it rose. There was no alternative but to remove the upper half once again and carry it eastward to restore the balance. As it travelled through the air, however, the Mahāmeru began to crumble and fall to earth, forming the mountains Katong, Wilis, Kampud, Kawi, Arjuna and Kumukus.[61] The result was that, upon reaching its final destination, the mass that remained was no longer able to stand freely, having lost a good part of its lower section. The matter was resolved by placing the Mahāmeru alongside Mt Brahmā, which served as a support. The topmost peak in the meantime became detached to form the holy Mt Pawitra.

The mountains listed above are all situated in eastern Java. The names of some of them, such as Wilis, Kawi and Arjuna, remain unaltered to this day, making their identification self-evident. Others require some explanation. Starting from the premise that the Mahāmeru followed a course from west to east, we can with some confidence associate the mountain Katong with present day Mt Lawu, which lies to the west of Mt Wilis on the provincial boundary of Central and East Java. The name is undoubtedly preserved in the semi-legendary figure of Betoro Katong, identifiable as the Sunan Lawu of Javanese tradition, and at the same time can probably be associated with the thirteenth century king Jayakatyĕng (variant Jayakatong), of Gĕlang-gĕlang.[62] As to the names Kampud and Kumukus, both are mentioned in Prapañca's Deśawarṇana and undoubtedly refer to the present mountains Kelud and Welirang. Mt Brahmā is of course identifiable with the crater of Mt Bromo in the Tengger highlands, which

---

61. See Figure 1. An interesting variant of this episode is to be found in the manuscript numbered Cod. 5056 in the Leiden University Library. The relevant passage lists a great many mountains, some of which still need to be identified, among them Bajwa-langit, Katingalan, Maṇḍalikā, Suji, Kambe, Puṣpa, Balangbhangan and Tatar (cf. Pigeaud 1924, p. 214). Another version of more recent origin is preserved in the Manik Maya. This version includes not only the peaks of western Java, but also a number of hilltop sanctuaries which to this day continue to attract pilgrims, such as Pandan, Bancak and Sokarini.
62. Sidomulyo (2010), p. 92. The 1255 charter of Mūla-Malurung provides the clearest evidence of Śrī Jayaktyĕng's seat of government at Gĕlang-gĕlang, which is described as the "capital city" (*nagara*) of the land (*bhūmi*) of Wurawan. As to its geographical position, we have enough inscriptional data, backed up by literary sources such as the Sĕrat Kanda, Babad Tanah Jawi and the stories of Pañji, to place Gĕlang-gĕlang (variant Gĕgĕlang) with certainty in the region of Madiun-Ponorogo, on the eastern side of Mt Lawu.

lies adjacent to Semeru, Java's highest peak. Finally, the detached top section known as Pawitra is none other than the mountain known today as Penanggungan, whose unique form displaying a symmetrical arrangement of five summits has apparently been associated with the Mahāmeru since at least the tenth century (see Figures 8 and 9).[63]

The above narrative is a local rendering of the well known Indian legend named Samudramanthana, or "Churning of the Milky Ocean", recorded in the epic Mahābhārata as well as the Viṣṇu and Matsya Puraṇa.[64] The story is also found in an Old Javanese version of the Ādiparwa, composed during the last decade of the tenth

Figure 8 Mt Penanggungan, viewed from the hill town of Trawas, Mojokerto Regency. *Photo by Hadi Sidomulyo, 2013.*

63. Concrete evidence of this connection is the bathing place of Jolotundo at Trawas, completed in Śaka 899 (AD 977–8), the central terrace of which was once crowned by a top piece displaying a symmetrical configuration of nine cylindrical stone columns in the coils of a serpent, symbolizing both the mythical Mahāmeru and the mountain Penanggungan itself. For a detailed discussion, see Stutterheim (1937b). With regard to the textual sources, the earliest known reference to Pawitra is preserved on the stele of Cunggrang, located on the eastern foot of Mt Penanggungan and dating from Śaka 851 (AD 929). Transcription in Stutterheim (1925), pp. 208–81.
64. Zimmer (1946), pp. 17–18, 105, 176.

Figure 9 Top piece from the bathing place of Jolotundo at Trawas.
Photo by Hadi Sidomulyo, 2013.

century.[65] Although the version presented in the TP makes drastic revisions to the central theme, it nonetheless retains many important details of the original narrative. Thus, for example, we find the function of the Mandara mountain as churning stick replaced by the transport of the mountain itself to Java, while the episodes concerning the theft of the holy Kamaṇḍalu, the fate of the demon Rāhu, as well as the origin of Lord Śiwa's name Nīlakaṇṭa, are all faithfully preserved.

Mt Kelāśa

According to the TP, the base of the Mahāmeru left behind at the western end of Java became known as Kelāśa. As noted by both R. Ng. Poerbatjaraka and W.J. van

65. Now preserved at the University of Leiden. For the text, see Juynboll (1906), pp. 31–33. It is noteworthy that the date of this manuscript (discussed in Zoetmulder 1983, pp. 109–13) coincides almost precisely with that of the remains at Jolotundo mentioned above (note 63).

der Meulen, the "western end" referred to here need not be interpreted literally.[66] The fact that the first piece of earth to fall from the Mahāmeru on its journey eastward became the central Javanese mountain Lawu is already an indication that the author's conception of "Java" was confined to the lands occupied by the native speaking Javanese.[67] There is thus no conflict in placing Kelāśa somewhere in the region of Ḍihyang (Dieng), a suggestion which finds support from the epigraphical data.

Among the early sources pertaining to this highland region, three late ninth century charters are of particular importance. The first, inscribed on a single copper plate, mentions the presence of a *juru i Ḍihyang* and *pitāmaha i Kailāśa* as key witnesses to an edict transferring the obligations of the residents of Kapuhunan from Pintang Mas to Mangulihi.[68] This last-mentioned village is the subject of a separate stone inscription discovered at Dieng early in the last century.[69] The fact that the *pitāmaha* of Kailāśa in the Kapuhunan charter bears the additional title of *samgat* Mangulihi establishes this figure's close connection with Ḍihyang, as well his probable residence nearby.

Further support comes from a third inscription, known as Er Hangat, which refers to a *guru hyang ing Kelāśa*.[70]

These combined data would seem sufficient to allow an association of the historical Kelāśa with one of the peaks surrounding the Dieng Plateau. As to which one, an immediate choice is the mountain known today as Prahu, which overlooks the village of Dieng at the northeastern end of the plateau (see Figure 10). Named after its flat, elongated summit, resembling the upturned hull of a ship (*prahu*), the same form could in earlier times have been regarded as the truncated base of the Mahāmeru. The identification is strengthened by the discovery of significant archaeological remains

---

66. Poerbatjaraka (1992), pp. 97–98, note 14; van der Meulen (1977), pp. 96–97.
67. For the author of the TP, the land of Sunda apparently lay outside the Javanese realm. It is only in the later Manik Maya, described (perhaps rather unfairly) by Poerbatjaraka as a "confused copy" of the TP, that the mountains of west Java gain a place in the story. For this reason it is difficult to accept an identification of Kelāśa with Mt Pulosari in the region of Banten, as proposed by Guillot, Nurhakim and Wibisono (1996, pp. 99–100).
68. This plate is preserved in the Library of the University of Leiden. For transcriptions, see Poerbatjaraka (1992), pp. 94–97 (Indonesian translation); Sarkar (1971–72), vol. I, pp. 203–7, no. xxxvii (English translation).
69. Known as Mangulihi A and B, current whereabouts uncertain. Krom (1913c, pp. 93–94) noted the precise discovery site as *Fundamen* L, referring to a number of archaeological diagrams whose present location is (regrettably) unknown to me. Partial transcriptions in Damais (1955), pp. 104, 206–7.
70. See note 94 below.

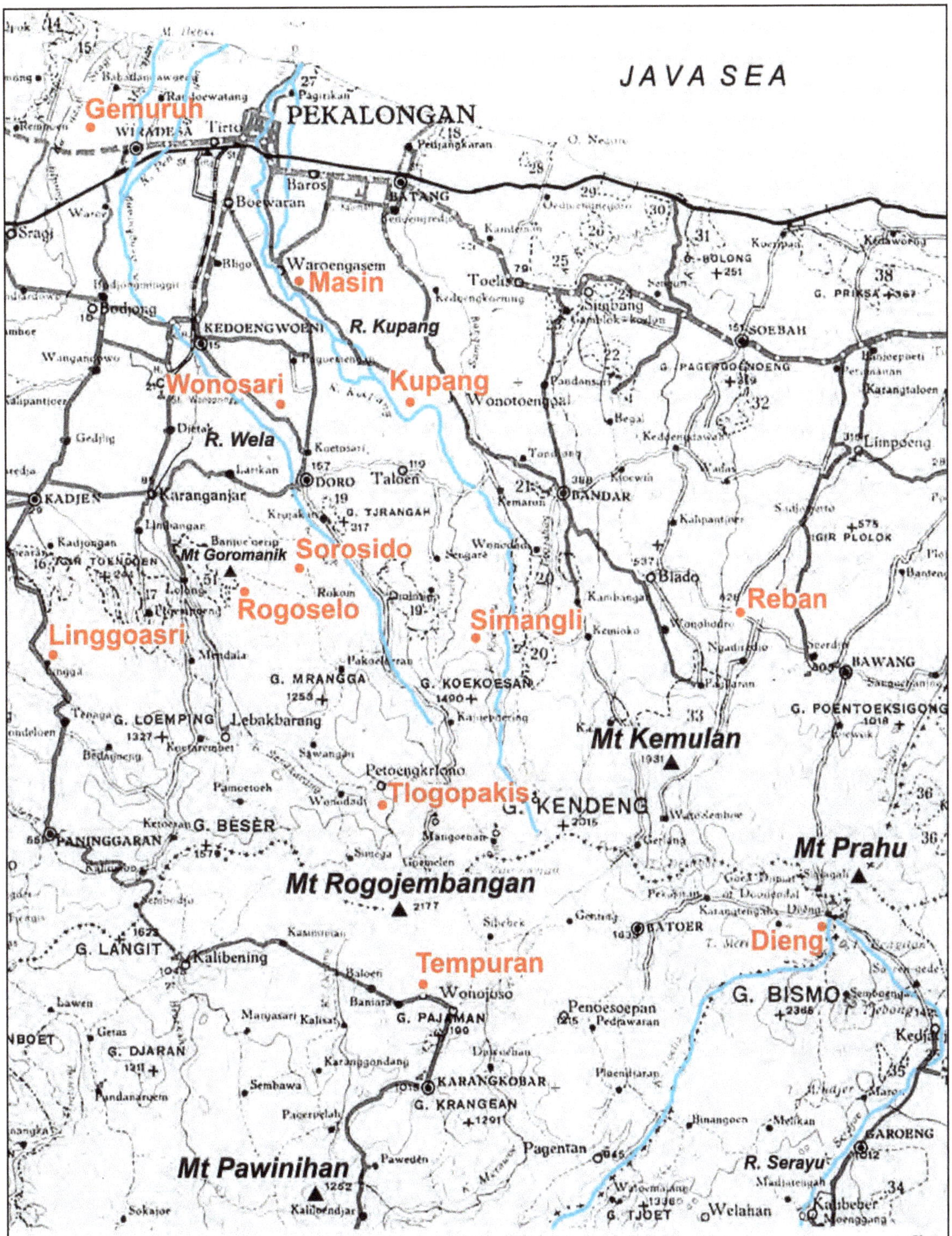

Adapted from the Dutch Topographical Map Series, 1943 (1: 250,000), Sheet No. III

Figure 10 Map showing the highlands of Dieng and the northern plains of Batang and Pekalongan. *Adapted from: Name: 05271-03; Scale: 1: 250,000; Type: Topographic map; Year: 1943*

on the mountain's northeastern slope.[71] Worth mentioning too is a nineteenth century report by Friederich, who observed the remnants of a circular stone structure on the western summit of Mt Prahu.[72]

On the other hand, it is curious that the name Kelāśa does not occur in the text of the Bujangga Manik. The pilgrim, after all, supplies us with a detailed list of the mountains visible in the south from the town of Semarang, among them Merapi, Merbabu, Ungaran, Sumbing and Sindoro, as well as a peak named Rahung, described as lying "to the west of Mt Diheng" (*sic*).[73] As noted by Noorduyn, this could well be a reference to Mt Prahu. Doubts thus arise concerning an identification with the Kelāśa of the TP, leading us to consider alternatives.

And so we turn to the mountain Rogojembangan, whose summit overlooks the northern plains of Batang and Pekalongan, some 20 km west of Dieng (see Figure 10). Of particular interest here is a curious configuration of archaeological sites, which can hardly be dismissed as accidental. Starting on the northern side of the mountain, the highland district of Petungkriyono preserves a *yoni* pedestal known as "Naga Pertala" (or Pratala),[74] located in the ricefields at Tlogopakis (see Figures 11 and 12). First reported by C. den Hamer in 1893, the site was visited a few years later by E.A. Sell, who observed the pedestal, along with a few weathered statues, on a cleared area measuring about 30 square metres.[75] The ornamental features of the *yoni* are particularly impressive, and appear to function in unison as a symbol of the Samudramanthana. The base has been fashioned to resemble a turtle, above

71. See Figure 3 above. Of particular importance here are the sites in the district of Sukorejo (Kendal). Although in a fragmentary state today, they provide evidence of concentrated building activity in early times. For a useful introduction to these remains, see the report by Brumund (1868, pp. 143–47), who connects them with the legendary female ascetic named Dewi Rengganis (mentioned further in note 272). Rengganis is said to have settled at Sukorejo, where she constructed a residence, complete with sacred place of worship, bathing pool and pleasure garden. These places are identifiable with the sites of Ngargo, Surugajah, Tamansari and Balekambang (Kentengsari), as well as the remains of Candi Argopura on the hill Gedong Alas. For further details, see Krom (1914), pp. 184–86 (nos. 576–586), 301 (no. 989), as well as Tjahjono, Indrajaya and Degroot (2015).

It can be added that the identification of Mt Prahu with the former Kelāśa raises the possibility that one of these sites represents a memorial to the king Rakai Warak dyah Manara (r. 803–827), who is known to have borne the epithet *lumāh i Kelāśa* in Balitung's 908 charter of Wanua Tĕngah III (Pl. Ib: 5). For a transcription and discussion of this document, see Kusen (1988).

72. Friederich (1876), pp. 49–50. Although in a collapsed state, this structure appears to have included a pillar formed from stones of receding size, as well as two boulders, one of which displayed the clear impression of a footprint.

73. Noorduyn and Teeuw (2006), pp. 257–58, 446–47.

74. From Modern Javanese *pratala*, meaning "earth", "ground", referring to the legendary god of snakes, Antaboga.

75. Den Hamer (1893), pp. cxxi–cxxii; Sell (1912), pp. 163–65.

Figure 11 The *yoni* Naga Pertala at Tlogopakis
Photo by Hadi Sidomulyo, 2019.

Figure 12 Naga Pertala (detail)
Photo by Hadi Sidomulyo, 2019.

which the *nāga* Basuki, portrayed here with jaws wide open, bears the *yoni*, the holy Mahāmeru, in its coils. According to Satari, the *nāga* is of "East Javanese type" and datable to the Majapahit period.[76]

Having noted one unusual artefact on the northern slope of Mt Rogojembangan, it is curious to learn of a second *yoni*, likewise named Naga Pertala, situated on the opposite side of the mountain in the hamlet of Tempuran (Wanayasa, Banjarnegara), at almost precisely the same distance from the summit as its counterpart at Tlogopakis.[77] Equally curious is the complete absence of a single published description of this object (at least as far as I am aware), proof of its existence being limited to a number of early Dutch topographical maps.[78]

It was thus an unexpected surprise to discover, upon visiting the area in July 2019, that the site of this second Naga Pertala was still well known to the local

76. Satari et al. (1977), pp. 5, 14; Satari (1978), p. 8.

77. A rough calculation indicates that the two pedestals lie 4.5 km from the summit of Rogojembangan, aligned on a north-south axis.

78. To my knowledge, the earliest reference to the Naga Pertala at Tempuran is to be found on a topographical map of the regency of Banjarnegara dated 1903 (sheet XIVm; scale 1: 25,000).

inhabitants. Sadly, however, there was no opportunity for field documentation, as it turned out that the *yoni* had been carried off by treasure hunters a few years ago. A small prominence in the ricefields was the sole remaining testimony to its former presence. Even so, the visit was not without its reward, as the villagers were able to explain, entirely unprompted, how the Naga Pertala of Tempuran and Tlogopakis were in fact a married couple (husband and wife respectively). Whatever the origin of this tradition, it is hard to argue against the almost perfectly symmetrical placement of the *yoni* pedestals. At the very least, the presence on the mountain of these two serpent guardians, one clearly preserving an image of the Samudramanthana, is in our view sufficient to allow a tentative identification of Mt Rogojembangan with the Kelāśa of the TP.

The mountains Wĕlahulu, Sañjaya, Walangbangan and Pamrihan

Having partaken of the nectar of immortality (Śiwāmba) on the slopes of the Mahāmeru, the four deities Śiwa (Guru), Iśwara, Brahmā and Wiṣṇu returned briefly to central Java, where they created respectively the mountains Wĕlahulu, Sañjaya, Walangbangan and Pamrihan.[79] This brief episode brings the first part of the TP to a close.

The identification of Mt Wĕlahulu has been problematic. In his topographical notes on the story of Bujangga Manik's journey in 1982, Noorduyn already drew a connection between the Wĕlahulu that passed by the pilgrim near the town of Semarang and the mountain of that name in the TP. He observed further that the only mountain of any significance in the area was Mt Muria, whose form matched the meaning of the word *wĕlahulu*, "split head". The problem was that Mt Muria was located north of Bujangga Manik's position, whereas according to the text Wĕlahulu lay to the east.[80]

Looking again at the passage in question, it seems as if the words *ti wétan na Wĕlahulu* were the cause of Noorduyn's uncertainty. In the published text of 2006, however, the complete phrase translates, "... to my left was the territory of Demak, to the east of Mount Wĕlahulu".[81] This would seem to mean that Bujangga Manik was pointing out the plains of Pati and Juwana, which not only lie to the east of Mt Muria, but at that time could well have been referred to as the "territory" of Demak. If this explanation is acceptable, there need no longer be any hesitation about equating Mt Muria with the Wĕlahulu of both the Bujangga Manik and the TP.

Mt Sañjaya is not mentioned in any other source known to me, thus making it difficult to locate. The name of the mountain points to a connection with the founder

79. Part 1, p. 18.

80. Noorduyn (1982), p. 424.

81. Noorduyn and Teeuw (2006), p. 258 (BM 780–781).

of the ancient kingdom of Mataram, which in turn suggests that it was situated in central Java. More than that not much can be said. Important archaeological remains were observed near the source of the river Senjoyo at Tingkir (Salatiga) in the nineteenth century.[82] This might allow us to identify Sañjaya with one of the summits of Merbabu, or perhaps with Mt Telomoyo, which lies not far to the west.

The mountain Walangbangan is likewise hard to locate. The name probably does not refer to the kingdom of Blambangan at the far eastern end of Java, but should rather be sought in the centre of the island. Walambangan is mentioned alongside a number of central Javanese mountains, among them Ḍihyang (Dieng), Marapwi (Merapi), Sumbing and Susuṇḍara (Sindoro), in the imprecation attached to the copper plate inscription of Kuṭi, which dates back to the central Javanese period.[83] There is today a village named Blambangan on the southern bank of the river Serayu, not far west of the town of Banjarnegara. This might indicate the former existence of a summit of that name in the vicinity, either in the highlands of Dieng or the Serayu range of mountains to the south.

Finally, with regard to Pamrihan, the TP informs us that the mountain was known also as Damalung or Mawulusan. This finds confirmation in the story of Bujangga Manik, where Damalung and Pamrihan are mentioned together.[84] The Merapi-Merbabu manuscripts, moreover, make it clear that these two names, while possibly indicating separate summits, refer to present day Mt Merbabu.[85] Further support comes from a stone inscription discovered at Ngadoman on the eastern slope of the same mountain, the text of which mentions *wukir hadi umalung* in connection with a bathing place (*patirtan*) at Palĕmaran.[86] The name Umalung, which appears to be a misreading of Damalung, is also found in the imprecation section of the Kuṭi inscription referred to above.[87]

---

82. Reports by Hoepermans (1913), pp. 208–10; Friederich (1876), pp. 72–73. See also Stutterheim (1937a), p. 18 and figure 14; 1940, pp. 16, 35 and figure 29.
83. Transcription in Boechari (1985–86), pp. 16–21, pl. VIIIb, line 4. Although scholars have tended to dismiss this inscription as a confused conflation of separate edicts, there seems no reason to doubt the reliability of the toponyms.
84. See note 34 above.
85. Examining the colophons to the manuscripts listed in the catalogue prepared by Setyawati, Wiryamartana and van der Molen (2002), we find twenty-six references to Pamrihan and thirty-seven to Damalung. Among the villages where these documents are said to have been composed or copied, the names Gandariya, Tajuk, Patĕmon, Wanalaba and Samagawe are still identifiable in the vicinity of Mt Merbabu.
86. Transcription in Cohen Stuart (1875), p. 36 (no. xxvii). The stele of Palĕmaran, dated Śaka 1371, is preserved in the Volkenkunde Museum at Leiden (Juynboll 1909, p. 229, no. 1620).
87. Boechari (1985–86), pp. 16–21, pl. VIIIb, line 3. For further discussion of Umalung/Damalung, see Noorduyn and Teeuw (2006), p. 462, note 4.

II
THE HEAVENLY REALM — TALES OF THE GODS

The hermitages of Bulon, Kupang, Huluwanwa and Pacira

Bhaṭāra Guru at Maśin

Kāmadewa and Smarī at Mĕḍang-gaṇa

The first hermitages on the Mahāmeru

The Sukayajña order and its offshoots

Mt Goromanik and the maṇḍala of Sarwwasidḍa

The maṇḍala on the Mahāmeru

The hermitages of Bulon, Kupang, Huluwanwa and Pacira

Having fixed the Mahāmeru firmly on Java, Bhaṭāra Guru next proceeded to establish four principal hermitages (*katyāgan*) at Bulon, Kupang, Huluwanwa and Pacira.[88] These same places (though in a different order) are mentioned in canto 78: 7 of Prapañca's Deśawarṇana, where they are described as the *katyāgan* of the *caturāśrama*.[89] In the same way that the *maṇḍala* network in Java was derived from four sects (*caturbhasma*), so the *katyāgan*, or "places of recluses", were apparently identified with four parent communities.[90]

The hermitage of Bulon must for the time being remain a mystery, as the name is not mentioned in any other inscriptional or literary source known to me, and Prapañca's brief description offers no further clue. The site of Kupang, however, can almost certainly be associated with the present river Kupang, and specifically the settlement of that name on its western bank at Brokoh, a village lying 10 km south of the coastal town of Batang in central Java.[91]

The archaeological site at Kupang reveals the remnants of a terraced sanctuary beside the river, aligned to the mountains in the south. Although the original structure is barely visible today, a surviving statue known as Watu Gajah ("elephant stone") is of particular interest. Formerly consisting of two parts, one of which has disappeared, the stone is thought to depict the Karivarada (or Varadaraja), the "deliverance of the elephant Gajendra by the god Wiṣṇu", as related in the Bhagavata Purāṇa (see Figure 13).[92]

This evidence allows us to take a step further and identify these remains with the Kupang mentioned by the pilgrim Bujangga Manik on his journey eastward through central Java.[93] It might even be possible to connect the site with a village named

88. Part 1, p. 18.

89. Pigeaud (1960–63), vol. I, p. 60.

90. The Sanskrit word *caturāśrama* is commonly associated with the four stages in the life of a brahmin. In this case, however, the term seems to refer to a particular category of religious persons, or, to use Pigeaud's words, a "quadripartite classification of popular anchorites". For further discussion, see Pigeaud (1960–63), vol. IV, pp. 193–95, 248–49, 258–59; Zoetmulder (1982), p. 313.

91. See Figure 10 above.

92. Gopinath Rao (1971), vol. I, pp. 266–69; Zimmer (1946), p. 77. This identification was first proposed by Satari (1978, pp. 5–8). If correct, as the same writer observed, the Watu Gajah of Kupang would be the single known representation of the Karivarada in Indonesia.

93. Noorduyn and Teeuw (2006), pp. 257, 446 (BM 749–751). The passage reads: "... the territory of Arĕga Sela, of Kupang and Batang. To the left was Pakalongan" (*sic*). The position of present day Kupang is in complete accordance with this description, lying to the south of Batang and Pekalongan and to the east of the village of Rogoselo (Arĕga Sela).

Figure 13 Watu Gajah ("Elephant stone") at Kupang (Brokoh), Batang Regency.
Photo by Hadi Sidomulyo, 2019.

Kupang recorded in the late ninth century charter of Er Hangat (Ratanira), issued by the king Dyah Tagwas Śrī Jayakirtiwardhana (r. 885).[94] This inscription refers to a community named Salud Mangli, a *guru hyang* from Kelāśa, as well as the heads of neighbouring villages (*rāma tpi siring*), among them Kupang and Nuṣa. It seems not impossible that we have here a reference to the settlement of Kupang at Brokoh, while Salud Mangli and Nuṣa could be identifiable with the nearby hamlets of Simangli and

94. The two copper plates comprising the inscription of Er Hangat (Ratanira) were discovered in the central Javanese regency of Banjarnegara, west of the Dieng Plateau. Transcription in Boechari (1985–86), pp. 53–56. For a tentative English translation, see Wisseman Christie (2002), no. 124.

Adinusa, located respectively at Silurah and Reban. Significant archaeological remains have been found in all of these districts (see Figure 14).[95]

Whatever the case, the available data, both topographical and archaeological, allow the association of present day Kupang with the second of the hermitages established by Bhaṭāra Guru. It can be added that Kupang lies just 6 km upstream from the village of Masin, itself probably identifiable with the Maśin of the TP, as will be argued below.

The place name Huluwanwa is recorded in a number of central Javanese inscriptions dating from the ninth and early tenth centuries, among them Tru i Tĕpussan II, Wanua Tĕngah III, as well as Taji Gunung.[96] All point to a location in the present regency of Temanggung, on the eastern side of the Dieng plateau.[97] In one of them, a village chief (*rāma*) of Huluwanwa is listed among the guests in attendance at the founding ceremony of a *sīma* at Tru i Tĕpussan. The fact that this figure is mentioned along with representatives from places which are still known today in the Temanggung region makes it likely that Huluwanwa was located somewhere nearby.[98]

Examining the Dutch topographical maps, it turns out that a hamlet named Lowanasari used to exist at Wadas, some 3 km east of Kedu.[99] A field survey in 2019 revealed that the settlement once occupied the foot of a forest-covered hill, on the

95. Notable is the large seated Gaṇeśa image beside the river at Simangli, as well as the ninth century stele of Indrokilo from Reban, discussed below.

96. See Sarkar (1971–72), vol. I, pp. 102–11, no. XIV (Tru i Tĕpussan II, Śaka 764); Kusen (1988) (Wanua Tĕngah III, Śaka 830); Sarkar (1971–72), vol. II, pp. 123–24, no. LXXX (Taji Gunung, Sañjaya 194 = Śaka 832).

97. According to early reports (Verbeek 1891, p. 149, no. 276; Krom 1914, p. 212, no. 679), the precise origin of the two inscribed stones named Tru i Tĕpusan I and II could not be determined. An investigation by Stein Callenfels (1924, p. 24), however, revealed that these items had almost certainly been recovered from a place named Candipetung, located in the sub-district of Manden (under Jetis) in the regency of Temanggung. Although the name Candipetung is no longer known, the village of Manden (now Mandisari) can still be found on the northwestern outskirts of the town of Parakan (see Figure 3 above). This established, it becomes possible to accord roughly the same provenance to the stele of Taji Gunung, which preserves a number of toponyms found in the charter of Tru i Tĕpusan. As to the two copper plates comprising the inscription of Wanua Tĕngah III, their discovery site at Gandulan, to the northeast of Temanggung, supports the assumption that the contents of the charter pertain to this same region.

98. Among the toponyms immediately recognizable is Kḍu, identifiable with the village and district of Kedu, as well as Wunut and Ptir (now Petirgunung) in the district of Bulu, on the western side of Temanggung. Another village, named Petirejo, can be found to the northwest of Parakan at Ngadirejo (see Figure 3 above).

99. See Figure 3 above. According to local residents, the settlement was abandoned about fifty years ago. The name Lowanasari can be traced back to Lowano, a variant of Huluwanwa in the TP.

Figure 14 Gaṇeśa at Simangli (Silurah), Batang Regency.
Photo by Hadi Sidomulyo, 2019.

summit of which can be found a scattering of temple remains.[100] Noteworthy too is the fact that Lowanasari lies not far north of the hamlet of Kedunglo at Gandulan, where the Wanua Tĕngah III inscription was unearthed in 1983. This position accords well with the charter's description of Huluwanwa as one of the neighbouring communities (*tpi siring*), whose leading officials were presented with gifts at the time of the restoration of the *sīma* at Wanua Tĕngah.[101]

Finally, the location of the fourth hermitage at Pacira can be determined with the help of the story of Bujangga Manik, which describes a section of the pilgrim's homeward journey as follows: "… went past Mount Hiang, and came to Pacira. The slopes of Mount Mahameru I passed on the southern side". These directions make it clear that Pacira was located near the southeastern foot of Mt Semeru and may be identified today with the district of Pasirian, whose position conforms with the route described in the Bujangga Manik. This same route is followed today by travellers journeying from Lumajang to Malang. The road first leads south to the village of Tempeh, before turning westward and climbing into the foothills of Mt Semeru by way of Pasirian and Candipuro. Substantial archaeological remains have been discovered in this region over the years.[102]

Bhaṭāra Guru at Maśin

Having established the last of the *caturāśrama* hermitages, Bhaṭāra Guru is described as heading westward to Maśin, the location of which can be determined from an episode in the closing section of the text.[103] The story tells of the adoption of two orphans (later the sages Tṛṇawindu and Anggira) on Mt Kawi by the reverend Agaṣṭi, who "took them westward to Maśin, and they came to the peak of Kelaśa, to the *maṇḍala* of the reverend Mārkaṇḍeya ...". The *maṇḍala* in this case was that of Sukayajña, established by Bhaṭāra Guru himself when he was residing at Maśin.[104]

100. Some of these temple stones have been transferred to an adjacent *pertapan* (hermitage) of more recent construction. In this connection it is worth noting the report by Hoepermans (1913, pp. 174–75) of a rectangular stone box, recovered from a "bathing-place" at Lowanasari.

101. Wanua Tĕngah III, Pl. IIb: 5–8 (transcription in Kusen 1988).

102. For a summary of the remains at Candipuro, see Muusses (1923b, pp. 91–92). These include a variety of stone images and a *yoni* pedestal, as well as the remnants of two structures, known as Candi Gedung Putri. A collection of bronze ritual items from Penanggal (Candipuro) is currently preserved in the National Museum, Jakarta (Inv. nos. 6078, 7354–7359). For further details, see Appendix 2.

103. Part 1, p. 66.

104. It can be added that Maśin was the birth place of Kāmadewa and Smarī, who subsequently "stayed behind on Mount Kelāśa" when their parents returned to eastern Java.

This is a clear indication that Maśin lay at no great distance from Mt Kelaśa, whose position has already been established in the highlands of Dieng. We thus find it quite acceptable to place Maśin on the banks of the river Kupang at modern day Masin, to the south of Pekalongan. This site has yielded at least one item of archaeological interest, thereby attesting to its antiquity.[105] Of further interest is the revered grave of a certain Syekh Ghono (Gaṇa?), who is associated by tradition with the ancient kingdom of Mo-ho-sin.[106] According to the caretaker of the grave, the original entrance to the site of Mo-ho-sin was located about 1.5 km downstream, in what is now the village of Gapura.[107]

The TP informs us that Bhaṭāra Guru and Dewī Umā resided at Maśin on two occasions. During the first visit, the divine couple devoted themselves to asceticism, founding the order known as Manguyu.[108] Not long afterwards they had a son named Kāmadewa, who was married to the goddess Smarī. The text then mentions two places named Ileru and Wanisari, associated respectively with Lord Guru and his spouse. Although presumably situated not far from Maśin, these places are nonetheless hard to identify. The toponym Ileru does not appear to correspond with any known reference, thus making its location impossible to determine. Wanasari (or Wonosari), by contrast, is such a common place name that it forces us to juggle alternatives. One possibility is the village of Wonosari at Karanganyar, 12 km southwest of Masin, where archaeological discoveries include a collection of about one hundred inscribed *lontar* leaves, formerly preserved at a *kabuyutan*, or ancestral site, at Prendengan.[109] There is also a Wanasari at Sragi (Siwalan), itself an historic district on the western side of Pekalongan. The village of "Sranggi" features prominently in the Sĕrat Cĕnthini.[110] Yet another village named Wonosari can be found in the foothills of Mt Prahu at Bawang, some 30 km to the southeast, but this location seems rather remote in the

105. See NBG 53 (1915): 54, 74, for the report of a golden ear ornament from Masin, now preserved in the National Museum, Jakarta, Inv. no. 5608. Although insignificant today, the village of Masin formerly controlled an extensive region to the south of Batang and Pekalongan, holding the status of a district (Veth 1869, vol. II, p. 458).

106. It is unclear as to how and when this tradition originated. The identification of Masin near Pekalongan with the Mo-ho-sin reported by the monk I-tsing in the seventh century was already suggested as a possibility by L.C. Damais. For further discussion, see van der Meulen (1977), p. 105.

107. For a report on archaeological remains at Gapura (Warungasem), see Indrajaya and Degroot (2012–13), p. 373.

108. Part 1, p. 18.

109. NBG 19 (1881): 86.

110. Darusuprapta et al. (1991), p. 288.

context.[111] All things considered, a likely match is the village of Wonosari at Doro, which lies just 5 km south of Masin on the banks of the river Wela, not far from the historic site of Rogoselo (discussed below).[112]

The second period of residence at Maśin coincided with the foundation of the earliest *maṇḍala* communities, and will be mentioned in connection with the site of Sukayajña.

Kāmadewa and Smarī at Mĕḍang-gaṇa

Following their initial sojourn on the plains of north central Java, Bhaṭāra Guru and the goddess Umā travelled eastward to the Mahāmeru, leaving their offspring, Kāmadewa and Smarī, behind on Mt Kelaśa. Although not specifically stated, the text implies that the young couple were brother and sister. For this reason they were reluctant to consummate their marriage, for fear of arousing their father's anger. Instead, they chose to adopt human form in the land of Mĕḍang-gaṇa, becoming incarnate in the descendants of Rahyang Kaṇḍyawan.[113] Herewith the relevant passage, following the transformation of Smarī into the goddess Ratih:

> Lady Ratih was incarnated in the deified ancestor (*hyangta*) of Kaṇḍayun,[114] and turned into Turuk-manis; Kāmadewa was born and turned into Wĕngan, who became the husband of Turuk-manis. For this reason Pinaleśawi became the wife of Katiha; likewise Kulikuli in the land of Mĕḍang-gaṇa was the wife of Wawu-langit in the land of Mĕḍang-gaṇa.

In his commentary on this passage, Pigeaud chose to accept the word *pinaleśawi* as a proper name, noting its resemblance to Pileku-sewu, a grandson and successor of Hyang Kaṇḍawan according to the manuscript Pratasti Bhūwanā.[115] The association of Pinaleśawi with Pileku-sewu finds further correspondence in the Carita Parahyangan, where we find the names Mepeles-awi, Rawunglangit and Kulikuli among the descendants of Sang Kandiawan.[116] This image of a dynastic line presumably influenced Pigeaud's choice of the variant *makānak*, "to have a child", over *mangkana*, "likewise", thereby

111. For an archaeological report, see Sell (1912), p. 175.
112. See Figure 10 above.
113. Part 1, p. 20.
114. Perhaps Kaṇḍyawan was intended. If not, the text is referring to the former king's youngest son and successor, Wṛtti-kaṇḍayun.
115. Pigeaud (1924), p. 141, note 6. For the relevant section of the Pratasti Bhūwanā, see p. 203 of the same volume.
116. Noorduyn (1962), pp. 424–25.

acknowledging Kulikuli as the daughter of Katiha and Pinaleśawi.[117] The text of the TP does in fact infer as much. Unfortunately, the precise relationship between the three married couples, namely Wĕngan + Turuk-manis, Pinaleśawi + Katiha and Kulikuli + Wawu-langit, is not sufficiently explained. We can assume, however, that Wawu-langit was a successor of Wṛtti-kaṇḍayun, as he is specifically referred to as the king of Mĕdang-gana later on in the text.[118]

Herewith a diagram showing the descendants of Kaṇḍyawan according to three different sources (see Figure 15). In the Pratasti Bhūwanā Hyang Kaṇḍawan heads the list of kings who ruled during *kṛtayuga*, the first of the four world "ages" according to Hindu tradition.[119] The TP and Carita Parahyangan, on the other hand, identify Kaṇḍyawan respectively with the lands of Mĕdang-gana and Mĕdang-jati, the latter associated with the kingdom of Galuh in west Java. Viewed together, these three sources appear to conserve the fragments of an original Kaṇḍyawan myth, which might yet survive on a manuscript waiting to be discovered.

Rahyang Kaṇḍyawan and his successors, according to three different sources

Pratasti Bhūwanā	*Tantu Panggĕlaran*	*Carita Parahyangan*
Hyang Kaṇḍawan	Rahyang Kaṇḍyawan	Sang Kandiawan
Kṛthi-kaṇḍahyun	Wṛtti-kaṇḍayun	Writi-kandayun
Pileku-sewu	Wĕngan + Turuk-manis	Rahyangta Kulikuli
Wṛkaṇḍila	Katiha + Pinaleśawi	Rahyangta Surawulan
Kulikuli	Wawu-langit + Kulikuli	Rahyangta Mepeles-awi
?	?	Rahyangta Rawung-langit

Figure 15 Rahyang Kaṇḍyawan and his successors.
Diagram by Hadi Sidomulyo, 2019.

The first hermitages on the Mahāmeru

Upon reaching the holy Mahāmeru, Bhaṭāra Guru and the goddess Umā proceeded to set up a series of hermitages.[120] Dewī Umā began by establishing a residence on the mountain (*arga*) Pinton, while her husband stayed nearby at Kayutaji. These two

117. Pigeaud (1924), pp. 71, 141–42.
118. Part 1, p. 33. The Pratasti Bhūwanā likewise mentions a king Wawanglungid of Mĕdang-kana (Pigeaud 1924, p. 294).
119. Known collectively as the *caturyuga*, the other three are named *tretā*, *dwāpara* and *kali*.
120. Part 1, pp. 19–21.

locations are said to have been "separated by a ravine". Bhaṭāra Guru subsequently moved to a new dwelling named Ranubhawa, upon which Umā followed him, residing at Kabyang. Then, following the birth of their children Gaṇa and Kumāra, the divine couple shared a hermitage known as Pamanguyon-agung. Some time later Lord Guru left the family residence and withdrew to an isolated location on the mountain ridges (*gĕgĕr*), appropriately named Gĕgĕr-katyāgan. From there he moved again to a new residence at Tandĕs, placing Gĕgĕr-katyāgan in the charge of his son Gaṇa. Goddess Umā likewise departed from Pamanguyon-agung and set up her own separate hermitage on Mt Maṇik.

The text goes on to mention a few other locations, associated for the most part with the legendary activities of Bhaṭārī Umā and her children. Among them are the mountains named Pilan, Ijo, Wija and Tawungan, the last two described as the hermitages of Gaṇa and Kumāra respectively. Finally, there is a curious episode explaining the origin of a place named Ḍingḍing, which lay on the sacred stream (*tūsan*) Sang Hyang Ranupuhan.

In his commentary on the TP, Pigeaud was only able to offer a few vague suggestions concerning the geographical positions of the places mentioned above.[121] The text, admittedly, offers little to help us identify them. In 1982, however, J. Noorduyn published his topographical notes on the Old Sundanese Bujangga Manik, which contains some important comparative data.[122] These will serve as the foundation for the discussion to follow.

The greater part of the story of Bujangga Manik recounts a journey from one end of Java to the other. Beginning at the court of Pakuan in the west, the pilgrim travelled through the island's northern districts as far as Blambangan, crossed over to Bali, and later returned by way of the southern coast. The mountain Mahāmeru was thus passed on two occasions. On the outward journey the text reads:

> … walking to the eastward. The slopes of the Mount Mahameru, I passed at the north side. I came at Mount Brahma, arrived at Kadiran, at Tandes, at Ranobawa. Walking northeastward, I arrived at Dingding, that is the seat (*hulu*) of a prior (*dewaguru*).[123]

Then, on the return journey:

> ... I walked southwestward, came to the district of Kenep, arrived at Lamajang Kidul, went past Mount Hiang, and came to Pacira. The slopes of Mount Mahameru I passed on the southern side. After coming to Ranobawa, I went past Kayu Taji.[124]

121. Pigeaud (1924), pp. 222–29.
122. Noorduyn (1982), pp. 411–42 (republished in Noorduyn and Teeuw 2006, pp. 437–65).
123. Noorduyn and Teeuw (2006), pp. 258–59 (BM 815–823).
124. Ibid., p. 263 (BM 1035–1043).

The two short passages quoted above confirm the former existence of no less than five religious establishments mentioned in the TP, namely Tandĕs, Ranubhawa, Ḍingḍing, Pacira and Kayutaji. The fact that they are mentioned in a sequence along the route followed by the pilgrim, moreover, provides an opportunity to place them in a firmer geographical setting.[125] Determining their locations, even approximately, will in turn bring other parts of the TP text into focus, as well as allow us to make use of the relevant archaeological data (see Figure 16).

We can begin by observing that on both his outward and return journeys Bujangga Manik visited Ranobawa.[126] This place must have occupied a strategic position on the eastern side of Mt Semeru, from where travellers heading west had the option of passing the mountain by way of a northern or southern route. Bujangga Manik himself had, on the first occasion, passed north of Semeru by way of Mt Brahma (Bromo), thence to Kadiran, Tandes and Ranobawa, before turning northeast towards Dingding. On his return journey along the south coast he once again passed through Ranobawa, before continuing along the southern foot of Mt Semeru towards Kukub by way of Kayu Taji. It therefore seems quite evident that the former site of Ranobawa was located somewhere in the foothills of the Tengger range above the town of Lumajang, most probably in the present district of Senduro.

In fact we can narrow the field still further by following the path taken by Bujangga Manik through the Tengger highlands, which doubtless crossed the "sand sea" of Mt Bromo to either Wonokerso or Ledokombo on the eastern rim of the caldera, from where it probably descended along the course of the river Menjangan to the village of Kandangan.[127] This route has for long served as the principal access to Mt Bromo from the region of Senduro.

Writing almost a century ago, J.E. Jasper reported the presence of local Tengger priests (*dukun*) in no less than twelve villages on the eastern side of Mt Semeru.[128] Although that number has decreased somewhat since then, the district of Senduro remains home to a sizeable Tengger community, whose members acknowledge the village of Kandangan, and in particular the sacred terraced sanctuary of "Wadung

125. This possibility was already noticed by Noorduyn (1982, pp. 429–30), but he limited his comments to some general observations and did not explore the matter in depth.

126. Ranubhawa in the TP.

127. Compare the journal of the botanist F.W. Junghuhn (1854, vol. IV, pp. 873–74), who travelled this same route in 1844.

128. Jasper (1927), p. 217.

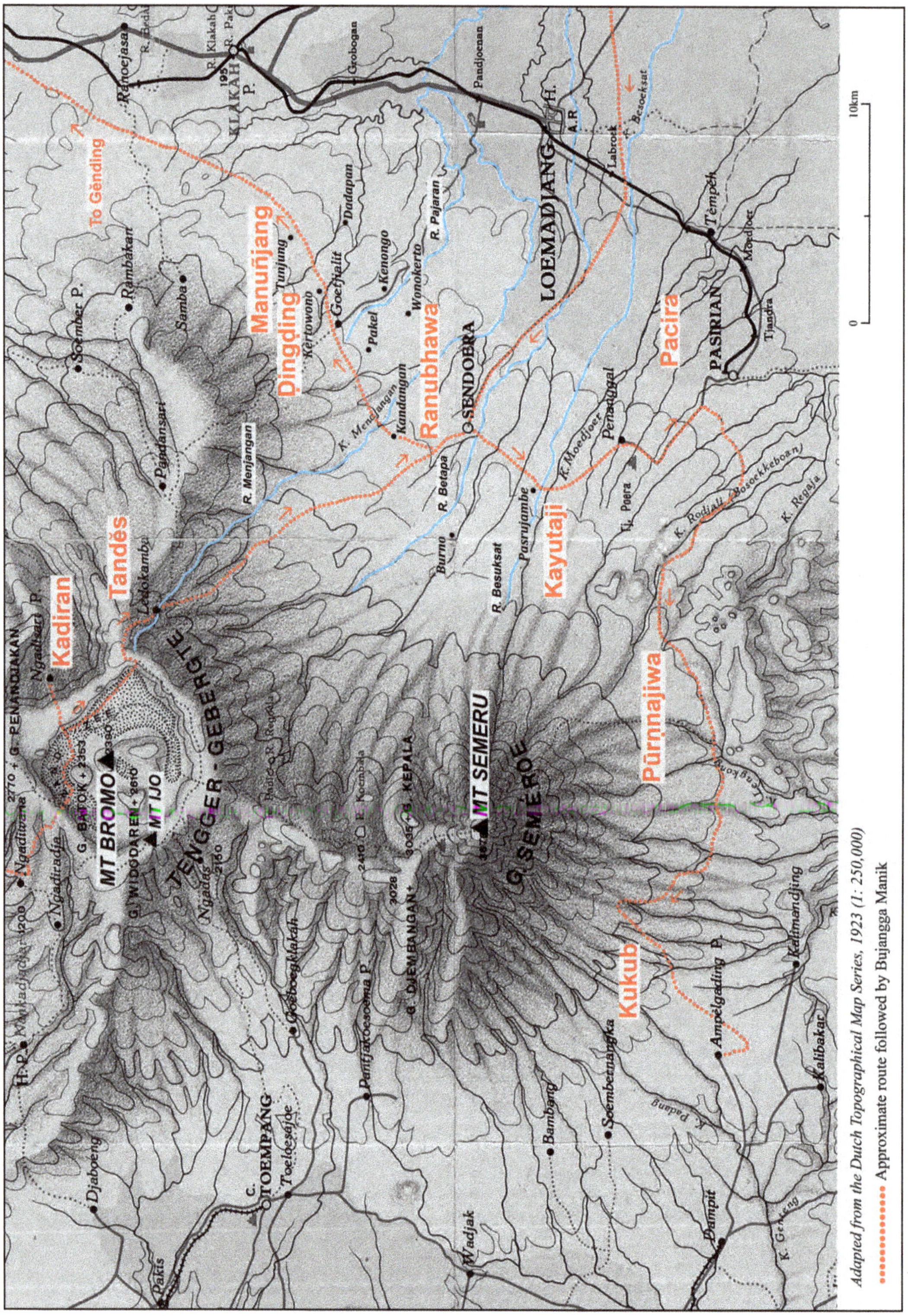

Figure 16 Bujangga Manik's journeys in the region of Mt Semeru.
Adapted from: Name: 05077; Scale: 1: 250,000; Type: Topographic map; Year: 1923

Prabhu", as an important ancestral seat (see Figure 17).[129] The cultural significance of Kandangan in former times is further attested in the well known Sĕrat Centhini, which gives an account of Jayangsari and Rancangkapti's brief sojourn in the village as guests of one Syekh Amongbudi.[130] The association of this village with the former site of Ranobawa would thus seem not at all improbable.

Returning to Bujangga Manik's route, the next step is to identify the places named Tandes and Dingding, which were passed immediately before and after Ranobawa. For this it is first necessary to consult the text of the TP. An episode towards the end of

Figure 17 The menhir Wadung Prabhu at Kandangan (Senduro), Lumajang Regency. *Photo by Hadi Sidomulyo, 2018.*

---

129. Despite the founding of the Hindu-Balinese *pura* Mandara Giri Semeru Agung at Senduro in 1992, the local Tengger community continues to recognize the "seniority" of the Wadung Prabhu site, regarding it as the leading authority in matters pertaining to ritual and ceremony. This fact was confirmed emphatically by the resident *dukun* at Kandangan during a discussion with the present writer in September 2018. It can be added that Jasper (1927, p. 304), in his discussion of an important Tengger festival known as *Unan-unan*, referred to the sanctuary of Wadung Prabhu as the "*sanggar sejati*, or renowned forest hermitage".

130. Darusuprapta et al. (1991), vol. I, pp. 244–50.

the narrative relates how a certain king of Daha, named Aji Uṇḍal, travelled to the Mahāmeru and resided temporarily at Tandĕs.[131] Desiring to devote his life to religion, he sent a messenger to the spiritual lord of Kukub, requesting ordination as an ascetic (*wiku*). While awaiting a reply, he descended from Tandĕs and camped in the ravine named Śiṇḍo. It was not long before the request was granted by the *dewaguru*, who ordered an official to present the cloth and other symbols of ordination to Aji Uṇḍal. Upon arrival at Śiṇḍo, however, the official found no sign of the king and so ended up leaving the ordination cloth on a rock. It is said that this same rock marked the original location of Ḍingḍing, which was subsequently established as a *maṇḍala* under the authority of Aji Uṇḍal.

If the topographical details from this episode are extracted and combined with the data provided by the Bujangga Manik, it can be concluded that Ḍingḍing lay to the northeast of Ranubhawa in the vicinity of a ravine, below the hermitage at Tandĕs and close to a sacred stream named Ranupuhan. Although there is no mention of distance, the overall context strongly suggests that the *maṇḍala* was located not far from Kandangan, and thus quite probably in the neighbouring district of Gucialit. If such was indeed the case, we can proceed to identify Tandĕs with one of the highland villages mentioned above, namely Ledokombo or Wonokerso, which are directly accessible from both Senduro and Gucialit. Of these, the most likely choice is Wonokerso, whose antiquity is firmly acknowledged by the local community (see Figure 18).

Finally, with regard to Kadiran, which according to Bujangga Manik lay close to Mt Bromo, this toponym would seem to be recognizable in present day Ngadisari, a prominent Tengger settlement on the northern rim of the caldera. It can be added that the village of Ngadisari features along with Kandangan in the Sĕrat Centhini.[132]

Having just about exhausted the information contained in the Bujangga Manik, it remains to offer a few comments on some of the other places mentioned at the beginning of this section. The hermitages Gĕgĕr-katyāgan and Pamanguyon-agung are to my knowledge no longer known in the region of Mt Semeru. The former suggests a remote location on the mountain ridges (*gĕgĕr*), and as such is extremely difficult to identify. The same can be said for Pamanguyon-agung, which means literally an "abode of *manguyu* ascetics". On the other hand, the mountain named Ijo, associated with Bhaṭārī Umā in the TP, is probably identifiable with present day Mt Ijo on the western perimeter of Mt Bromo's sand sea. Likewise, the hermitage of the god Kumāra

131. Part 1, pp. 61–62.
132. Darusuprapta et al. (1991), vol. I, pp. 214–38.

Figure 18 A menhir marking the altar of the Tengger village temple at Wonokerso, Probolinggo Regency. *Photo by Hadi Sidomulyo, 2018.*

on Mt Tawungan can with some confidence be placed on the hill of Penawungan, which is situated to the northeast of the Tengger massif in the district of Ranuyoso (Lumajang).[133] The fact that Penawungan lies directly alongside another hill named Penyancangan, presumably the Cangcangan of the TP (discussed below), provides further support for this identification.

Turning now to the archaeological evidence from the eastern foothills of the Tengger range, we can begin by noting that the predominance of ritual objects, mostly of bronze, supports the presence of religious communities in the past. The distribution of these items, moreover, is not at variance with the conclusions reached above.[134] With regard to historic sites, the sanctuary named Wadung Prabhu at Kandangan has already been mentioned. This monument, comprising a hierarchy of menhirs arranged on a number of ascending terraces, reflects a merging of Hindu-Buddhist

133. See Figure 40, as well as the map on p. 220.

134. See Appendix 2.

and ancient Javanese beliefs, and as such could well trace its origins to one of the hermitages referred to in the TP. As to which one, we have already found reasons for an identification with Ranubhawa.

To the northeast, in the district of Gucialit, a river named *kali* Pajaran (from Old Javanese *pājaran* = hermitage)[135] flows down towards the town of Lumajang from the villages of Pakel and Wonokerto.[136] As suggested above, the former foundation at Ḍingḍing could well have been situated in this region. One site displaying clear signs of early human settlement is the graveyard named Sentono Kates at Kertowono. Among the items of interest here are several stone *lumpang*, a pillar support dated Śaka 1330 (see Figure 19), and a quantity of ceramic shards.[137] To the northeast of

Figure 19 Dated stone pillar support at Sentono Kates, Gucialit.
Photo by Hadi Sidomulyo, 2018.

135. Zoetmulder (1982, p. 31) defines *pājaran* more specifically as a "dwelling place of *ajars*".
136. Archaeological remains have been found at both of these places (see Appendix 2).
137. According to Nawawi (1990, p. 17), the pillar support displays an additional inscription which reads: [illegible]= *akuṭa rajaśa*. As to the ceramics, Nitihaminoto (1990, p. 15) reports that the earliest are datable to the twelfth century.

Kertowono, an impressive waterfall known as Antrukan Pawon cascades into a natural cavern enclosed by a ravine, while to the west a revered ancestral grave crowns the summit of a hill named Jenggolo-manik.

Viewed as a whole, there is no denying a configuration which bears an uncanny resemblance to the image portrayed in the TP. Assuming that the account preserved in the text is describing actual places, as well as prominent landmarks, it is not difficult to connect Antrukan Pawon with the legendary Sang Hyang Ranupuhan, while the position of Jenggolo-manik allows an identification with Mt Maṇik, the hermitage of Bhaṭārī Umā mentioned earlier. In short, the surviving evidence, albeit fragmentary, seems sufficient to place the former site of Ḍingḍing in the vicinity of present day Kertowono at Gucialit.

It remains now to identify the location of Kayutaji, which is listed first among the hermitages established by Bhaṭāra Guru on Mt Mahāmeru. If we follow Bujangga Manik's directions, it lay somewhere on the route leading westward from Ranobawa to the *maṇḍala* of Kukub. As will be demonstrated below, the position of Kukub can be fixed on the southwestern slope of Mt Semeru, probably near Ampelgading, indicating that Kayutaji must have been located further to the east. More than that, however, the textual sources are of little help, making it necessary to search for direct evidence in the field.

Reports of archaeological discoveries to the south of Mt Semeru are few and far between. The village of Pronojiwo, which will be discussed later in connection with the four "openings" (*pañātūr-mukā*) of the Mahāmeru, has yielded a few items of stone and bronze, helping to strengthen the identification with the Pūrṇnajiwa of the TP. Further fragmentary remains, among them a Gaṇeśa statue, have been reported from the coastal district of Tempursari.[138] This region, however, seems an unlikely location for Bhaṭāra Guru's first hermitage on the holy mountain. The ruined brick monument at Candipuro, located further east, is likewise difficult to connect with the site of Kayutaji, as it appears to represent a monument to a deified royal ancestor.[139] We thus find ourselves back on the eastern foot of Mt Semeru, where a substantial quantity of archaeological remains still require a context.

138. Nastiti et al. (1994/1995), p. 18.

139. Known as Candi Gedung Putri, this site was completely destroyed during the eruption of Mt Semeru in 1895. Fortunately, the monument was described in sufficient detail by nineteenth century observers to allow the conclusion that it once served as a royal mortuary shrine dating from the Majapahit period. For further discussion, see Verbeek (1891), pp. 310–11 (nos. 632, 633); Krom (1916), pp. 422–24; Knebel (1904), pp. 120–22; Lunsingh Scheurleer (2008), pp. 329–31. See also note 102 above.

The village of Pasrujambe, to the southwest of Senduro, has seen some remarkable discoveries over the years, among them a four-armed statue of the goddess Umā/ Parwatī, now preserved in the National Museum, Jakarta, as well as a substantial horde of bronze ritual items.[140] This is not to mention some twenty-five inscribed stones, displaying for the most part brief invocations, but including diagrams (*yantra*) and at least one aphorism which seems to pertain to an ascetic community. Three of the stones date from the Śaka year 1381 (see Figure 20).[141]

The remains at Pasrujambe originate for the most part from Munggir, Jabon and Tulungrejo, three settlements lying on the northern bank of the river Besuksat, which flows down from the upper slopes of Mt Semeru. To the south, on the opposite bank, another collection of bronze items was recovered from the village of Penanggal at the

Figure 20 Inscribed stone dated Śaka 1381, from Pasrujambe, Lumajang Regency. *Photo by Hadi Sidomulyo, 2011.*

140. Knebel (1904), p. 123; TBG LXV (AV 1925): 747, no. 5870; JBG VI (AV 1938): 100, nos. 6432–6435; JBG VII (AV 1939): 94, nos. 6976–6978. Nastiti et al. (1994–95), pp. 10–11.

141. Sukarto Kartoatmodjo (1990), pp. 16–19; Nastiti et al. (1994–95), pp. 6–10, 29–36. Sixteen of these inscriptions are now preserved in the Mpu Tantular Museum at Sidoarjo, while others can be found in the regional Museum of Lumajang.

beginning of the last century.[142] Still in the same region, the hamlet of Tesirejo has yielded the earliest known document yet recovered from the area lying to the east of the Tengger highlands. An inscribed stone displaying the Śaka year 1113, expressed in the chronogram *kaya bhūmi śaśi iku*, coincides almost precisely with the accession of Sarweśwara II (Śṛnggalañcana), last of the kings who reigned supreme in the land of Kaḍiri during the twelfth and early thirteenth centuries.[143]

Taken together, this rich concentration of archaeological remains invites further enquiry. To begin with, the bronze items and stone inscriptions clearly point to the former existence of religious settlements. The recovered dates, moreover, suggest continuous habitation in the region for close to three centuries. Noteworthy, too, are the respective positions of Pasrujambe and Penanggal on the northern and southern banks of a substantial river, calling to mind the description in the TP of the first hermitages established by Bhaṭāra Guru and Dewī Umā on the Mahāmeru, which were likewise "separated by a ravine". Coupled with the fact that these two villages lie on the road leading westward from Kandangan along the southern foot of Mt Semeru, and that this same route was in all probability followed by Bujangga Manik on his homeward journey, it would seem not unreasonable to identify them, at least tentatively, with the former sites of Mt Pinton and Kayutaji.

To conclude this discussion, we will turn our attention to the original site of Kabyang, which together with Ranubhawa comprised the second pair of "twin hermitages" founded by Bhaṭāra Guru and the goddess Umā.[144] Judging by the archaeological evidence, a possible location is the present village of Burno, which lies just 3 km southwest of Kandangan. Discoveries here include a *yoni* pedestal, as well as two stone images representing Brahmā (*caturmukha*) and Wiṣṇu, all formerly situated close to the river Betapa.[145]

The Sukayajña order and its offshoots

The setting now shifts back to Maśin on the northern plains of central Java, where Bhaṭāra Guru presided over the foundation of the first *maṇḍala* at Sukayajña, located

142. See note 102 above, as well as Appendix 2.

143. Sukarto Kartoatmodjo (1990), pp. 13–15. The stone is preserved in the Mpu Tantular Museum.

144. Pigeaud (1924, p. 222, note 3) offers an interesting rationale for this configuration of "twin hermitages".

145. Nawawi (1990), p. 8. The statues are now preserved in the Mpu Tantular Museum, while the *yoni* is reportedly still *in situ*. The name of the river Betapa could well be a corruption or variant spelling of modern *petapa*, meaning "hermit", itself derived from the Old Javanese *tapa*, "penance, asceticism" (Zoetmulder 1982, p. 1945).

on the slopes of Mt Kelaśa.[146] Prapañca lists Sukayajña along with Sāgara, Kukub and Kasturi in his Deśawarṇana, referring to this group as the *caturbhasma*, or "four ashmarks". The same places feature prominently in the TP. Whereas Sāgara, Kukub and Kasturi traced their origins to the Tengger and Hyang mountains in eastern Java, the *maṇḍala* of Sukayajña appears to have developed independently in the vicinity of Ḍihyang, its sphere of influence confined for the most part to the island's central districts. It is not until the closing section of the TP that we learn how the Sukayajña tradition was carried eastward by the retired *dewaguru* Bhagawān Mārkaṇḍeya.[147] This last-mentioned figure is said to have succeeded Bhaṭāra Iśwara as lord of the *maṇḍala*, later passing on his office to Bhagawān Agaṣṭi. The significance of the succession of spiritual lords at Sukayajña requires a closer study (see Figure 21).[148]

The TP goes on to describe several other *maṇḍala* established at the time when Bhaṭāra Guru returned to Maśin from eastern Java. Unfortunately the chronology is not very clear. According to the text, the "second of the *maṇḍala*" was at Māyana, a place to where the Supreme Lord retired after appointing the god Wiṣṇu as his successor at Sukayajña, while the third was at Guruh. There is further mention of two places named Sukawela and Sarwasidḍa, apparently founded in conjunction with Sukayajña. Attributed to the combined effort of the gods, these communities are said to have been closely associated with a mountain named Rĕrĕban.[149]

The position of Māyana is uncertain, unless it is identifiable with the hill of Moyanang, which lies close to the village of Lingga (now Linggoasri) at Kajen, 25 km southwest of Pekalongan (see Figure 22).[150] The presence of a settlement named Mendala in the immediate vicinity, along with a river Wisnu, helps to strengthen the identification.

With regard to Guruh, this *maṇḍala* is said to have been named after the "resounding praises" (*gumuruh*) of the gods. On the basis of the toponym there is reason to place it at present day Gumuruh in the district of Siwalan, which lies not far from the sea to the north of Kajen.[151] This proposed location finds support from

146. Part 1, p. 28.
147. Part 1, p. 66.
148. We are assuming here, with Poerbatjaraka (1992, p. 98, note 14), that the TP preserves an allegorical account of the history of Śiwaism in Java.
149. Part 1, p. 28.
150. Linggoasri derives its name from a former terraced sanctuary preserving a number of stone *lingga* (menhirs), one of which is still held in reverence by the local inhabitants.
151. See Figure 10 above.

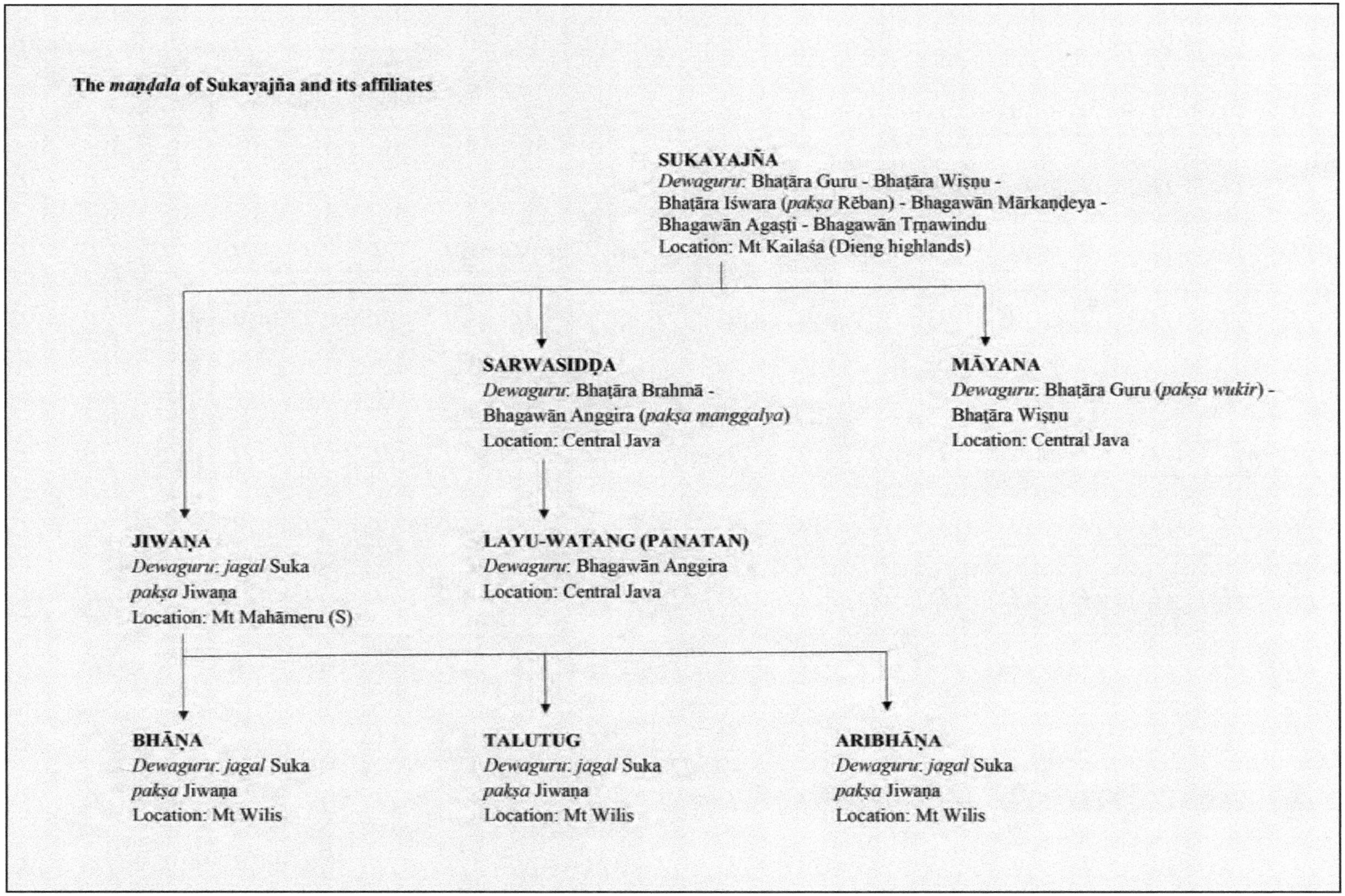

Figure 21 The *maṇḍala* of Sukayajña and its affiliates.
Diagram by Hadi Sidomulyo, 2019.

Figure 22 Menhir at Linggoasri (Kajen), Pekalongan Regency.
Photo by Hadi Sidomulyo, 2019.

the discovery of an early bronze standing figure at Siwalan,[152] as well as the presence of submerged brick foundations at Nglorok, a neighbouring hamlet preserving the last of the *siwalan* trees from which the district received its name. In view of the value of the *siwalan*, which would have been exploited to full advantage by a religious community, it could be that the presence of the trees influenced the original choice of Gumuruh for the site of a *maṇḍala*.[153]

152. Now preserved in the National Museum, Jakarta, Inv. no. 6035. Report in JBG I (AV 1930–1932): 220. According to an elderly resident of Siwalan, encountered during a field survey in July 2019, this object (or perhaps a similar one) was recovered from the village graveyard at Gumuruh.
153. The *siwalan* palm (Borassus flabellifer) formerly served multiple purposes, the leaves providing the material for *lontar* manuscripts, fibre for the roofs of sacred structures, and fruit for the production of palm wine. Growing in abundance in eastern Java, the tree is much less common in the central districts.

Despite the arguments presented above, however, the possibility that the original *maṇḍala* of Guruh was located further south in the vicinity of the holy Mt Kelāśa should not be entirely ruled out. The National Museum in Jakarta preserves an important collection of gold and silver items, among them images of Śiwa and Parwatī, recovered from the hamlet of Gemuruh at Banyukembar (Wonosobo) in the early years of the twentieth century.[154]

According to the TP, Bhagawān Mārkaṇḍeya relinquished his position as *dewaguru* at Sukayajña upon the arrival at Kelaśa of the sage Agaṣṭi and the latter's adopted twin sons, Anggira and Tṛṇawindu, from Mt Kawi.[155] Bhagawān Agaṣṭi then headed the *maṇḍala*, to be succeeded in turn by Tṛṇawindu, while Anggira served as *dewaguru* at Sarwasidḍa. Mārkaṇḍeya, in the meantime, travelled eastward to the Mahāmeru, where his spiritual legacy was perpetuated by a butcher named Suka. This unlikely candidate for *wiku*-hood is said to have founded the sect known as Sukayajña-*pakṣa*-Jiwaṇa, the name Jiwaṇa representing the forest area cleared for the site of a *maṇḍala* on the southern foot of the mountain. Further branches of the sect were subsequently established at Bhāṇa, Talutug and Aribhāṇa, in the region of Mt Wilis.

With regard to the precise location of Jiwaṇa there is little direct evidence, but it is perhaps noteworthy that a village named Sumberurip is still to be found in the district of Tirtoyudo (Malang Regency), on the southwestern foot of Mt Semeru.[156] As will be seen, this region is quite rich in archaeological remains. As to the respective positions of the three branches of the *maṇḍala* established near Mt Wilis, there is little that can be said, except to note a possible identification of Bhāṇa with present day Bono, which lies on the mountain's eastern foot to the south of Tulungagung. The adjacent villages of Kendalbulur and Boyolangu preserve evidence of early settlements, among them the site named Candi Gayatri.[157]

Mt Goromanik and the maṇḍala of Sarwasidḍa

The name Rogoselo has already been mentioned in connection with Arĕga Sela, a place passed by the pilgrim Bujangga Manik on his eastward journey through Java. The original site of Arĕga Sela is quite probably represented today by the remains

154. Cat/Inv. nos. 486a/4568, 497a/4569, 498a/4572, 514b/4573, 517b/4565, 517c/4566, 517d/4567, 519a/4570, 519b/4571. For a discussion of these items, see Brandes (1904b), pp. 552–77.

155. Part 1, pp. 66–67.

156. The Old Javanese words *hurip* and *jīwana*, "life", are synonymous (cf. Zoetmulder 1982, pp. 654, 745).

157. For a report on archaeological discoveries in the villages of Kendalbulur and Boyolangu, see Bosch (1915a), pp. 288–89 (nos. 1936, 1937).

preserved on Mt Goromanik, located some 18 km south of the coastal town of Pekalongan.[158]

The principal object of interest here is a former terraced hill sanctuary, at the foot of which stand two imposing guardian figures (*dwārapāla*) among a group of menhirs.[159] At the top of the monument can be found a few stone remnants, among them a damaged *yoni* and a statue pedestal (*padmāsana*).[160] More isolated objects and fragments lie further down the hill. Van der Meulen associated this site with a "cult of Rāhu", equating the name Goromanik with the jewelled pot (*kuṇḍi maṇik*) of the TP (see Figure 23).[161]

The village of Rogoselo has in the past yielded stone images depicting a four-armed deity carved in relief, popularly identified as "Pañji", and a female spout figure known as "Perawan-sunti".[162] In addition, the National Museum at Jakarta preserves a very late stone inscription recovered from Rogoselo in the nineteenth century.[163] Significant discoveries in the neighbouring villages of Rokom and Sinutug, as well as the remnants of the so-called *kraton* of Miroloyo at Suroloyo, suggest that this area was once an important centre of religious activity.[164]

Considering the above, we find no difficulty in placing the *maṇḍala* of Sarwasidḍa near the present hamlet of Sorosido, which lies just 2 km northwest of Mt Goromanik.[165] As at Kupang, Sorosido shares its name with that of the nearby river, pointing to the antiquity of the settlement.[166] Field observations reveal that Arĕga Sela and Sarwasidḍa

158. See Figure 10 above.
159. The site is known locally as "Baron Sekeber".
160. For an early description of these remains, see den Hamer (1893), p. cxx.
161. Van der Meulen (1977), pp. 107–10. Observing that the *dwārapāla* were depicted "clasping their *kuṇḍi* to their breasts as if to defend them", the same writer even suggested that these guardian figures represented Rātmaja and Rātmaji, the *rākṣasa* who by chance stumbled upon the holy Kamaṇḍalu and later caused a problem for the gods by refusing to give it up.
162. Satari et al. (1977), pp. 3, 24 and photo no. 3.
163. Inv. no. D.24. First reported in 1861, this document was described a few years later by Hoepermans (1913, pp. 82–83) and the contents discussed by Brandes (1904c, pp. 458–59). The inscription is dated the Śaka year 1571 (AD 1649–50).
164. For a summary of these finds, see Krom (1914), pp. 132–33 (nos. 396–401). Among the items recovered were several articles of gold, notably a gold *lingga* on a silver dish.
165. See Figure 10 above. In this connection it is worth pointing out an expanse of forest above Sorosido, where four "graves" (*punden*) aligned with the cardinal points mark the boundaries of an area of land measuring about 20 ha. The purpose and significance of these four *punden* is unclear.
166. The river has its source in the hills to the south, above Pakuluran, from where it flows northwards for about 15 km, passing the villages of Rokom, Suroloyo and Sorosida,

Figure 23 *Dwārapāla* at the site of Baron Sekeber on Mt Goromanik, Pekalongan Regency. *Photo by Hadi Sidomulyo, 2019.*

were close neighbours, connected by an efficient network of mountain trails. An archaeological survey might help to shed more light on the relationship between these two communities in the past.

Before leaving this region, it is worth drawing attention to a number of revered Muslim graves at Rogoselo, among them Kyai Atas Angin, Pangeran Jipan and Pangeran Slingsingan.[167] This last-mentioned name invites attention, as it recalls the village of Salingsingan referred to in a number of central Javanese inscriptions from the ninth century.[168] It is difficult, however, to connect these charters directly with the hill of Goromanik. On the other hand, an inscription discovered in more recent times near

167. Sell (1912), pp. 161–62.

168. I note here the charters of Salingsingan (Boechari 1985–86, pp. 34–37), Kurambitan (Boechari 2012a, pp. 331–40) and Śrī Manggala II (Sarkar 1971–72, vol. I, pp. 194–96, no. xxxii).

the village of Reban, just 20 km east of Rogoselo, offers more certainty.[169] Known as the stele of Indrokilo and dating from Śaka 804, the charter records the purchase of farmland at Salingsingan for the benefit of a *sang hyang dharma* at Ḍihyang.[170] Since it is clear that Ḍihyang refers to the highlands of Dieng, and the district of Reban commands the northern access to the plateau, it seems likely that Salingsingan lay close to the discovery site of the inscription. The grave of Pangeran Slingsingan might thus preserve an ancient memory of historical ties between Rogoselo and Reban.

The name Reban itself is found in an early manuscript recording the bestowal of the sacred text Śewaśāsana upon a certain *mpungkwing* Rĕban by a king of Mĕḍang.[171] In the TP, Rĕban refers both to the ascetic path (*pakṣa*) established by Lord Iśwara at Sukayajña, as well as the mountain Rĕrĕban, described as the "shelter of the gods". Probably all of these variants converge in modern day Reban, which like Rogoselo shows evidence of having once been an important religious centre.[172] The remains of an ancient settlement still exist in the hills to the southwest of the village.[173] As for the mountain Rĕrĕban, it could well be identifiable with the peak known today as Kemulan, which lies a further 5 km to the southwest.

The maṇḍala on the Mahāmeru

Having established the first group of *maṇḍala* in northern central Java, Bhaṭāra Guru turned his attention once more to the Mahāmeru. Departing from Maśin for the second time, he left Sukayajña in the care of the god Wiṣṇu, while instructing Dewī Umā to remain behind on Mt Wilis until summoned.[174]

Reaching the slopes of the holy mountain, the Supreme Lord began with the foundation of a *maṇḍala* named Hahāh, said to have been located in the southeast.

169. Satari (1978), p. 2.

170. For a provisional transcription and English translation, see Wisseman Christie (2002), no. 117.

171. Pigeaud (1924), p. 301.

172. For a summary of archaeological discoveries in the vicinity of Reban, see Indrajaya and Degroot (2012–2013), p. 373. Worth mentioning too is an inscribed bronze temple bell dating from the early tenth century, apparently dedicated to a certain *bhaṭāra ing Rabwān*. In view of the fact that this item was unearthed near the site of the Naga Pertala at Tlogopakis, discussed earlier, there would seem good reason to associate the name *Rabwān* with modern Reban, which lies just 20 km distant. For further discussion, see Boechari (2012b, pp. 347–48), who already made the same observation.

173. This historic site is currently in the process of being transformed into an Islamic place of pilgrimage, the few visible remnants having been recycled to mark the "grave" of Syekh Maulana Mahribi, a figure well known to Javanese tradition from a more recent period.

174. Part 1, p. 30.

This places it theoretically somewhere in the present districts of either Pronojiwo or Candipuro in the regency of Lumajang. Unfortunately, a lack of supporting data makes it impossible to be more precise. The name is not listed among the places passed by Bujangga Manik on his journey along the southern foot of Mt Semeru, and the existing toponyms in the region appear to offer no further clues. We are thus for the most part reliant on the archaeological record, which still requires further study.

With the completion of Hahāh a second *maṇḍala* was established at Gĕrĕsik, on the eastern side of the Mahāmeru. This place is mentioned further on in the text in connection with the site of Ḍingḍing, discussed earlier. It is said that, upon receiving a request for ordination from Aji Uṇḍal, the spiritual lord of Kukub intended to raise the king's status to that of *dewaguru* at Gĕrĕsik. As will be recalled, however, the official sent to convey the message to king Uṇḍal ended up leaving the ordination cloth and other symbols of office on a rock in the Śiṇḍo ravine, with the result that the latter proceeded to establish his own independent community at Ḍingḍing.

This legendary account is instructive inasmuch as it establishes a link between the *maṇḍala* of Gĕrĕsik and Ḍingḍing, thereby confirming once again that the events described took place on the eastern side of the Tengger range. As a matter of fact, a hamlet named Gresik can still be found in the vicinity, about 10 km north of Gucialit (see Figure 24).[175] A field survey at the location in September 2018 revealed a variety of early ceramic items unearthed by local villagers, confirming the antiquity of the site. Considering further the position of Gresik at the foot of Mt Duk, a place which features in a later part of the narrative, an identification with the *maṇḍala* of Gĕrĕsik would seem quite likely.

The third *maṇḍala*, Śūnyasagiri, was to become the centre of a network of religious establishments scattered throughout eastern Java. The text explains how Lord Guru received the gods Iśwara, Brahmā and Wiṣṇu at Śūnyasagiri, instructing each to open his own *maṇḍala*, at the same time presenting them with a book "entwined with a serpent".[176] The Trinity of lords (*trisamaya*) duly accepted their symbols of office and departed, but ended up forgetting to take the book with them.[177] Seeing that the three

175. This settlement can be found at Cepoko in the district of Sumber (Probolinggo). The fact that it is situated to the northeast of present day Mt Semeru need not overly concern us, as the Mahāmeru of the TP apparently referred to the Tengger Massif as a whole.

176. Part 1, pp. 34–35.

177. It is noteworthy that this case of absent-mindedness on the part of the gods appears to be a repeat of an earlier incident, in which the holy Kamaṇḍalu, container of the elixir of immortality, was carelessly left behind on Mt Mahāmeru and allowed to fall into the hands of the demons Rātmaja and Rātmaji.

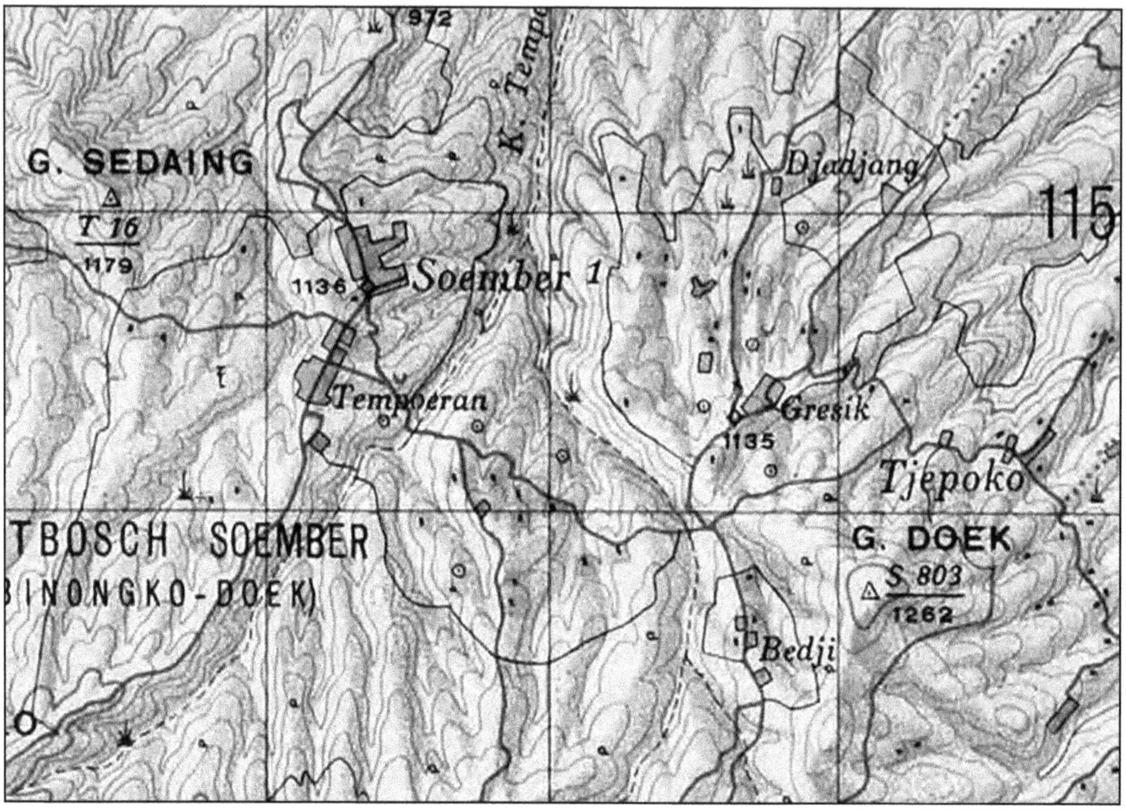

Figure 24 Detail of a Dutch topographical map from 1938 (scale 1: 50,000), showing the position of the settlement of Gresik at Cepoko, Probolinggo Regency.
Adapted from: Name: 05120-391-B; Scale: 1: 50,000; Type: Topographic map; Year: 1938

gods had left his gift behind, Bhaṭāra Guru covered (*kinukuban*) the book and placed it on an altar. From then on the *maṇḍala* of Śūnyasagiri became known as Kukub. The book served as the foundation of the establishment, its contents inseparable from the Supreme Lord himself.

The *maṇḍala* of Kukub has already been mentioned together with Sāgara, Sukayajña and Kasturi in connection with the *caturbhasma* of Prapañca's Deśawarṇana. A third source, representing an extract from the manuscript labelled Cod. 5056 in the Leiden University Library, describes the union of Kukub, Sāgara and Kasturi as inseparable, "one and equal from the beginning: with Kukub as the head, Sāgara as the belly, and Kasturi causing them all to multiply".[178] This image finds accordance with the TP, which describes in great detail the numerous branches of the Kasturi order, while acknowledging Kukub as the firm centre and origin of the *maṇḍala* network in eastern

178. Pigeaud (1924), p. 33. Translation by Stuart Robson.

Java (see Figure 25). Notable, however, is the absence in the Leiden extract of the name Sukayajña, the fourth member of the *caturbhasma*. As observed earlier, this central Javanese *maṇḍala* was apparently not widely represented in the eastern districts.

Further references to Kukub can be found in the Bujangga Manik and *kidung* Pañji Margasmara, which together supply enough useful topographical data to establish the approximate position of the *maṇḍala*.[179] Noorduyn already drew attention to the importance of these references in his well known article of 1982, using them to show that the place named Sagara Dalĕm, passed by Bujangga Manik, was not the same as the *wanāśrama* Sāgara described by Prapañca.[180] With regard to Kukub, however, he chose not to investigate further, simply noting that the place must have been located "on the southern or western side" of Mt Semeru.

Comparing the two sources once again, the relevant passage in the Bujangga Manik describes the pilgrim's western progress along the southern foot of the Mahāmeru, passing Ranobawa, Kayu Taji and Kukub, before arriving at Kasturi.[181] Since we know from the TP that the first Kasturi *maṇḍala* was located at Tūryan, identifiable with modern Turen in the regency of Malang, it is very likely that this is the same Kasturi referred to in the Bujangga Manik. The village of Turen, after all, lies directly west of Mt Semeru and thus almost certainly on the route travelled by the pilgrim.[182] It follows then that Kukub, which was passed before reaching Kasturi, lay at some distance to the east, probably in the southwestern foothills of the mountain.

Turning now to the Pañji Margasmara, an episode in the story recounts the abortive attempt by the *adipati* of Singhasāri to secure the marriage of his daughter, Ken Candrasari, to a certain Jaran Warida; an event scheduled to take place at the *maṇḍala* of Kukub, with the *dewaguru* presiding.[183] An account of the journey to Kukub follows, in which the bride and her retinue are pictured departing from the *kadipaten* and travelling in procession by way of Kiḍal, the "ravine of Lamajang"

179. Noorduyn and Teeuw (2006), p. 263 (BM 1040–1046); Robson (1979), p. 309. Worth mentioning also is a mid-fourteenth century copper plate inscription, which is unfortunately not as helpful as it could be, as its exact provenance is uncertain. Known as the charter of Manah i Manuk, this legal document (*jayapatra*) mentions a donation of ancestral lands to the maṇḍala of Kukub. For a transcription, see Boechari (1985–86), pp. 97–100.

180. Noorduyn (1982), pp. 429–30.

181. See Figure 16 above.

182. For further discussion of this section of Bujangga Manik's journey, see Sidomulyo (2007), pp. 102–3, note 139.

183. Since the Pañji Margasmara can be dated to the Śaka year 1380 (AD 1458–9), based on the chronogram *dwiradānahut sitangsu* (Robson 1979, p. 307), this extract provides a valuable insight into the relationship between the royal court and the *maṇḍala* communities in the mid-fifteenth century.

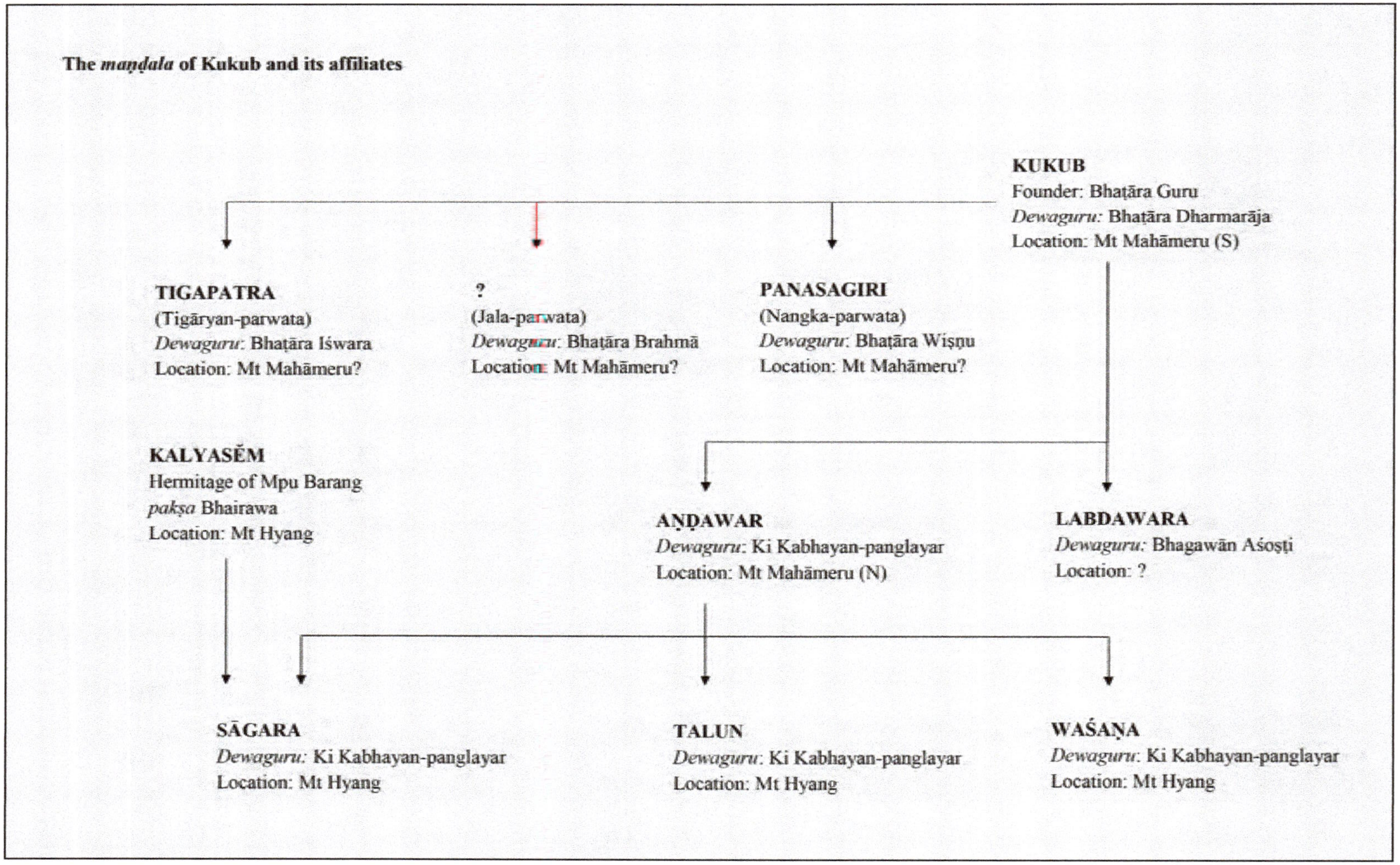

Figure 25 The *maṇḍala* of Kukub and its affiliates.
Diagram by Hadi Sidomulyo, 2019.

and Paḍang, before reaching their destination.[184] The first place mentioned is clearly recognizable in the modern village of Kidal, on the eastern side of the city of Malang, while the ravine of Lamajang almost certainly corresponds with the valley of the river Pamotan at Majang Tengah,[185] located 20 km south of Kidal near the town of Dampit (see Figure 26). This allows us to fix the position of Paḍang at present day Kalipadang, a settlement lying on the bank of the river (*kali*) Padang, 4 km east of Dampit and 12 km southeast of Turen. The *maṇḍala* of Kukub must therefore have been situated not far from Kalipadang, most probably somewhere to the northeast, in the districts of Ampelgading or Tirtoyudo. Further precision is difficult, but an examination of the archaeological record for this region can perhaps help to narrow the field.

The earliest report of antiquities on the southwestern slope of Mt Semeru is that of C.F. Clignett, who in 1836 encountered a number of stone items on a hill in the vicinity of "Utan Sungi Petung", among them the remnants of a temple entrance, a rectangular basin with a lid displaying a pair of intertwining serpents (*nāga*), two inscriptions and a standing Gaṇeśa image (see Figures 27 and 28).[186] Although the directions provided by Clignett are somewhat obscure, it is possible to identify the hill described with the place known today as *kramat* Lemahduwur at Simojayan (Ampelgading). This site lies very close to the hamlet of Petungombo, where additional discoveries were reported later in the nineteenth century (see Figure 29).[187] Still in the immediate vicinity, a small bronze container, together with several items of gold and silver jewellery from Ampelgading, entered the National Museum at Jakarta in 1939.[188]

184. Regardless of whether or not this text refers to actual historical events, there seems no reason to doubt the reliability of the topographical data. As noted in a previous publication (Sidomulyo 2014, p. 106), the author of the *kidung* displays an intimate knowledge of the local geography, making it likely that he was a native of Singhasāri.

185. Formerly Lamajang Tengah (cf. Veth 1869, vol. II, p. 312). The deep gorge formed by the river Pamotan at Majang Tengah was already noted by the botanist Franz Junghuhn (1849, vol. I, p. 118) in his account of an expedition to Mt Semeru.

186. Clignett (1844), pp. 159–60; Juynboll (1909), p. 21 (no. 1759). Krom (1916), pp. 450–51; Muusses (1923b), pp. 52–53 (no. 2338). As noted by Muusses, the Gaṇeśa image is probably the same one that has been preserved for many years in the Volkenkunde Museum, Leiden (see also Junghuhn 1849, vol. I, p. 137). The whereabouts of the remaining items are unknown, with the exception of the lid from the basin, which can be found today at the bathing place of Banyubiru near Winongan (Pasuruan), East Java.

187. Muusses (1923b), pp. 53–54 (no. 2339). These include a statue identified as Hanuman, now preserved in the National Museum, Jakarta (no. 3398), as well as two stones bearing the Śaka dates 1360 and 1362.

188. JBG VII (AV 1939): 91 (nos. 6918–6939).

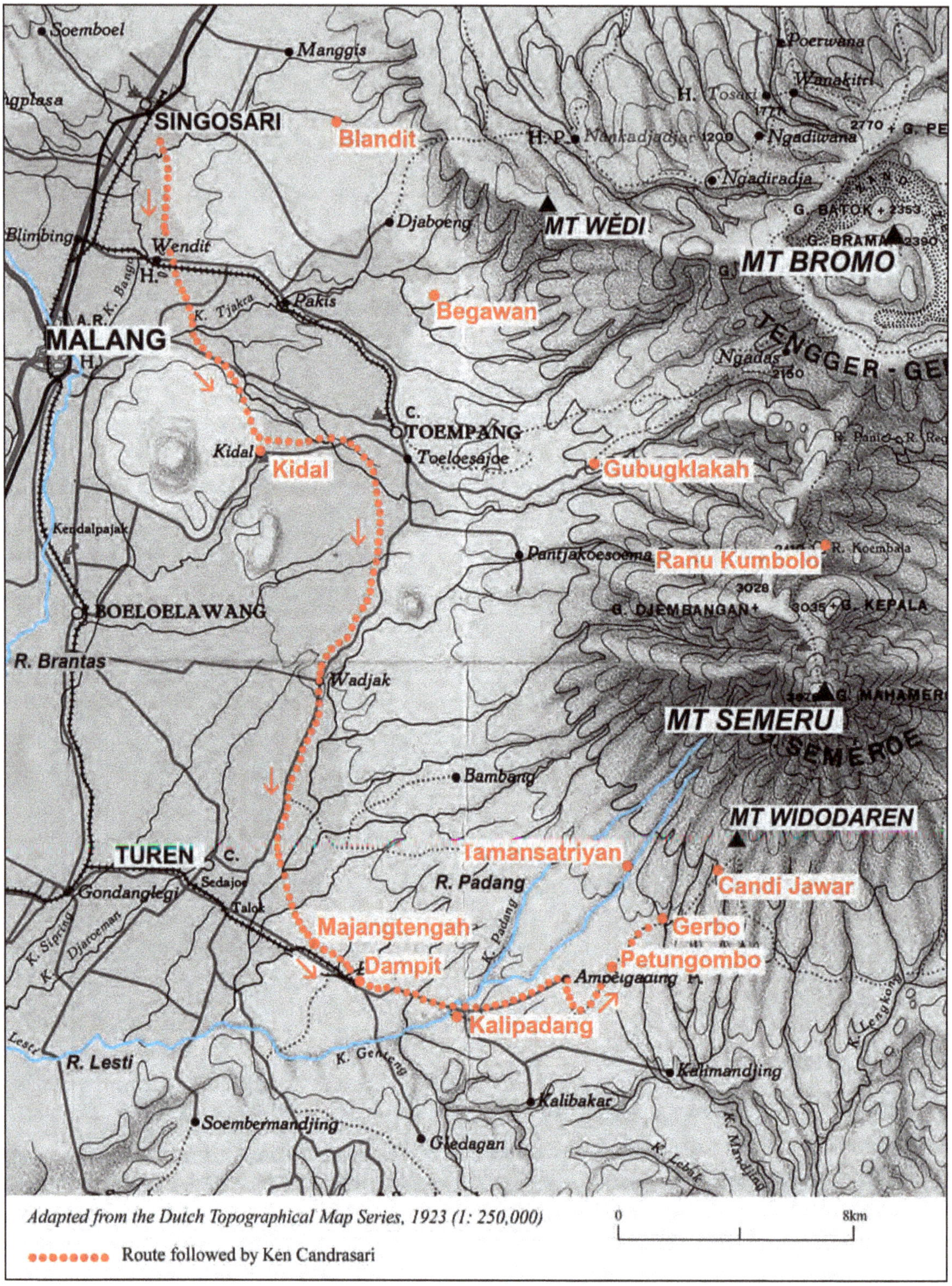

Figure 26 Reconstruction of the journey of Ken Candrasari from the court of Singhasāri to the *maṇḍala* of Kukub, as described in the *kidung* Pañji Margasmara.
Adapted from: Name: 05077; Scale: 1: 250,000; Type: Topographic map; Year: 1923

Figure 27 Standing Gaṇeśa from "Utan Sungi Petung", collection Volkenkunde Museum, Leiden. *Photo courtesy of the Volkenkunde Museum, Leiden.*

Figure 28 A *nāga* from the lid of the basin seen by C.F. Clignett at "Utan Sungi Petung" in 1836, now preserved at the bathing place of Banyubiru (Winongan), Pasuruan Regency. *Photo by Hadi Sidomulyo, 2018.*

Figure 29 Statue representing Hanuman (?), from Petungombo (Ampelgading), Malang Regency. Collection National Museum, Jakarta. *Photo reproduced from ROC 1912, plate 8.*

Moving further up the mountain slope, three inscribed stones were observed in the former plantation of Supiturang in 1889.[189] Not long afterwards, a *lingga* from the same location was donated to the Volkenkunde Museum in Leiden.[190] Still more discoveries in recent years include the remains of a monument constructed from limestone in the village of Tamansatriyan at Tirtoyudo (see Figure 30), as well as a site known as Candi Jawar at Mulyosari (Ampelgading).[191] Concerning the former, it is regrettable that the location had already been disturbed when the Archaeological Service first learned of its existence in 1969, with the result that only a small part of the building was recovered. Nonetheless, a reconstruction of the surviving components revealed a representation of the Samudramanthana (see Figure 31). As for Candi Jawar, the site displays the typical features of Javanese mountain sanctuaries dating from the fourteenth and fifteenth centuries.

Lastly, we should mention an inscribed stone currently preserved in the Tugu Hotel at Malang (see Figure 32).[192] Despite the absence of an official report, the close similarity of this inscription to those from Supiturang and Pasrujambe supports the commonly held belief that it originates from the hill named Widodaren, to the northeast of Candi Jawar.[193] The opening phrase, *lĕmah kasturi*, is particularly significant, as it recalls the Kasturi order of ascetics referred to so frequently in the TP.

To sum up, both the nature and distribution of the archaeological remains described above allow us to envisage a concentrated network of hermitages, shrines and terraced sanctuaries, all attached in one way or another to the religious centre at Kukub. As to which one of these sites represented the central *maṇḍala* is of course difficult to say. If, however, as the historical record seems to indicate, the influence and prestige of the *ṛṣi* communities tended to increase during the fourteenth and fifteenth centuries,

189. Verbeek (1891), p. 293 (no. 612). Identifiable today with the village of Gerbo (Ampelgading). In view of the similarities between these inscriptions and the examples from Pasrujambe discussed above (note 141), it is evident that they are likewise the products of a *maṇḍala*-type establishment. According to Brandes (1889, pp. 73–74), the language points to a date posterior to the fourteenth Śaka century, thus raising the interesting question of just how long these ascetic communities continued to survive in the more isolated districts of Java.

190. Juynboll (1909), p. 40 (no. 3190).

191. Wibowo (1975), pp. 48–61; Rangkuti (2000), pp. 16–17.

192. Listed in Wahyuni and Galeswangi (2011), p. 81, with an accompanying transcription and provisional translation.

193. See Figure 26 above. Widodaren lies close to the tree line on Mt Semeru's southwestern slope, at an altitude approaching 2,000 m (nowadays about as far as is safe to ascend the mountain from this direction). The hill of Widodaren was described by Clignett (1844, pp. 160–61), as well as Junghuhn (1849, pp. 117–21), in the course of expeditions to Semeru in the nineteenth century.

Figure 30 Miniature limestone temple from Tamansatriyan (Tirtoyudo), Malang Regency. Collection Trowulan Museum.
Photo by Hadi Sidomulyo, 2019.

Figure 31 A scene from the Samudramanthana, depicting the rescue of the holy Kamaṇḍalu by the gods Brahmā and Wiṣṇu (detail of Figure 30).
Photo by Hadi Sidomulyo, 2019.

Figure 32 The Widodaren inscription, preserved in the Tugu Hotel, Malang.
Photo courtesy of Arlo Griffiths.

it would not be surprising to find them commissioning monuments and sculpture of a high standard, perhaps under royal patronage. Given this possibility, one could consider placing Kukub at present day Simojayan in the district of Ampelgading, where the most substantial collection of stone images and inscriptions has been observed in the past.[194] It can be added that this village lies just 6 km northeast of Kalipadang, which accords well with the topographical data provided by both the *kidung* Pañji Margasmara and the Bujangga Manik.

As to precisely when the *maṇḍala* of Kukub was founded, one can do no more than conjecture. Despite the fact that the place is not mentioned in any official record until around the year 1350, the reference to its "ancient order" in Prapañca's Deśawarṇana at least indicates that the community was already well established long before the age of Majapahit.[195] If it is assumed, moreover, that the earliest events recorded in section III of the TP occurred during the twelfth century, it follows that the foundation of Kukub must date from a still earlier period. This leads us to suspect that the *maṇḍala* was opened not long after the shift of the seat of royal power from central to eastern Java, at which time the "taboo ground" (*lĕmah larangan*) of the holy Mahāmeru was demarcated and the Pañātūr-mukā established, together with their guardian deities.[196] The mountain itself thus became the preeminent *lingga*-temple. As the TP records, Lord Guru completed the work by performing yoga on the summit of the Mahāmeru, "focusing on the tip of his nose facing west", thereby determining the orientation of the temple sanctuaries of eastern Java.[197]

With regard to the Pañātūr-mukā, the TP informs us that two demons (*rākṣasa*) named Kāla and Anungkāla were appointed by Bhaṭāra Guru to serve as guardians of the western entrance to the Mahāmeru, which was situated at Pangawān. The *rākṣasa* are said to have emerged from Mt Wihanggamaya, itself formed from the ashes of a trinity of wrathful emanations of the gods Brahmā, Wiṣṇu and Iśwara.[198] Curiously, this legendary episode finds an echo in Pu Siṇḍok's charter of Gulung-gulung (line 6 *recto*), which attributes the origin of the *kahyangan* at Pangawān to

194. As mentioned above, the settlements of both Petungombo and Lemahduwur belong to Simojayan, whose eastern boundary is formed by the river Manjing. For the precise locations, see Peta Rupabumi Digital Indonesia (1: 25,000), Sheet 1607–441, Tlogosari. BAKOSURTANAL, 2001.

195. DW 78: 7 (Robson 1995, p. 81). See also note 179 above.

196. Part 1, p. 41. The TP lists the Pañātūr-mukā as Pangawān (west), Pūrṇajiwa (east), Paḍang (south) and Gantĕn (north), their respective deities being Kāla and Anungkāla, Gaṇa, Agaṣṭi and Ghorī. Note that the same configuration applies to the images placed in Javanese Śaiwa shrines, i.e. Mahākāla and Nandiśwara, Gaṇa, Agaṣṭi and Durgā-Mahiṣāsura-mārdinī.

197. Part 1, p. 43.

198. Part 1, pp. 40–41.

a mountain known as Wangkḍi.[199] I am thus inclined to identify Pangawān with the present hamlet of Begawan at Pandansari Lor, which lies on the western foot of the Tengger highlands in the district of Jabung (Malang), not far from a mountain peak named Wĕdi (perhaps formerly Wangkḍi).[200]

It is further noteworthy that the ancient site of Pangawān is mentioned in several early tenth century royal charters from the regency of Malang, specifically in connection with two other sacred sites, namely Himad and Walaṇḍit. The earliest reference to Himad is found in a copper plate inscription bearing a date equivalent to 10 October 905, issued by the king Dyah Balitung.[201] The document records the granting of *sīma* status to some tracts of farmland at Kubukubu and Samuḍung for the benefit of the holy sanctuary at Himad. More information is provided by the inscription of Gulung-gulung, dating from 20 April 929 (the very beginning of Pu Siṇḍok's reign), which indicates that Himad was a major centre of worship, possessing both a tower temple (*sang hyang prāsāda*) and presiding deity (*bhaṭāra*), supported by a network of *sīma* communities.[202] Yet another royal charter, issued just over a year later on 26 May 930, records the establishment of an additional *sīma* territory at Jĕru-jĕru, once again for the benefit of the sacred foundation (*sang hyang śāla*) at Himad.[203]

Lying in close proximity to the Himad sanctuary was a second religious centre named Walaṇḍit, which possessed its own *bhaṭāra*. A certain *dewata kaki* Sang Śiwarāśi of Walaṇḍit is listed among the attending guests of honour in the inscriptions of Gulung-gulung and Jĕru-jĕru mentioned above,[204] and a separate edict of Pu Siṇḍok dated 3 September 929 records the foundation of a *sīma punpunan* at Linggasuntan, dedicated to the *bhaṭāra* at Walaṇḍit.[205]

Of additional interest is the fact that one of these tenth century royal charters became the determining factor in a legal dispute between the communities of Himad

199. Dated Śaka 851 (20 April 929), the stele of Gulung-gulung originates from the region of Singosari (transcription in Krom 1913a, OJO 34). The antiquity of Pangawān is attested further in the imprecation section of the copper plate inscription of Kuṭi, parts of which appear to date back to the ninth century (Boechari 1985–86, pp. 16–21, plate IXa: 1–2). Prapañca (DW 78: 5c–d) describes Pangawān as one of the foremost independent districts of the *mḍang hulun hyang*, "exempt since former times" (Robson 1995, pp. 81, 137).

200. See Figure 26 above. The mountain named Wĕdi is marked clearly on a 1918 Dutch topographical map of the Pasuruan Residency (scale 1: 50,000), Sheet 12.

201. Damais (1955), p. 45; Boechari (1985–86), pp. 155–59.

202. Krom (1913a), OJO 38; Damais (1955), pp. 104–5.

203. Krom (1913a), OJO 43; Damais (1955), p. 180.

204. OJO 38, line 30 (*verso*); OJO 43, line 20 (*verso*).

205. Krom (1913a), OJO 39; Damais (1955), p. 56.

and Walaṇḍit more than four hundred years later. A copper plate inscription issued during the reign of the queen Tribhuwana Wijayottunggadewī of Majapahit refers specifically to a *praśasti* of Siṇḍok in connection with Walaṇḍit's claim for autonomy.[206] This privileged status is reaffirmed yet again in a charter drawn up on the order of king Rājasanagara in 1381–82, which portrays the inhabitants of Walaṇḍit as spiritual guardians (*hulun hyang*) of the holy mountain Brahmā (Bromo) in the Tengger highlands.[207]

As to the original location of Walaṇḍit, the inscription of Linggasuntan itself provides a sufficiently clear indication. The stone was reportedly discovered in the village of Lawajati (now Lowokjati), which lies to the east of the archaeological remains at Singosari and just 4 km northwest of a settlement which is still known as Blandit (see Figure 33). A village named Manggis is also to be found in the immediate vicinity, reminiscent of the Mamanggis-lili referred to in Rājasanagara's charter of Walaṇḍit (line 2 *recto*).

According to the TP, Walaṇḍita was the name of a mountain where the goddess Umā buried the mortal remains of her son Kumāra, after cursing him to become the demon Bṛnggiriṣṭi.[208] This act of cruelty aroused the fury of her husband, Bhaṭāra Guru, who in turn laid a curse on the goddess, forcing her to undergo a period of penance in the wrathful form of Durgā. After completing the sentence, she is said to have returned to her original state, emerging from the underworld on the mountain named Bret. Now it is curious that the village of Lowokjati, already associated with the ancient site of Walaṇḍit, is located at the foot of Mt Gondomayi, a name reminiscent of Umā's place of penance as Ra Nini in the *kidung* Sudamala.[209] Of further interest is the fact that a hill situated just over 1 km north of Gondomayi is known to this day as Mt Bret, making it possible to connect the legendary accounts of Umā's penance, either as Ra Nini or Durgādewī, with actual places situated near the former religious centres of Himad and Walaṇḍit. It can be added that an "old woman of Gandamayi" plays an important role in the *kidung* Pañji Margasmara, which is set in the former court of Singhasāri. In view of Robson's dating of the *kidung*, we can thus conclude that the mountain at Walaṇḍit was already associated with the goddess Durgā in the fifteenth century. Today the site of Mt Gondomayi continues to command respect from the local community, and is considered to be haunted.

206. M. Yamin (1962), vol. II, pp. 83–84.
207. Boechari (1985–86), pp. 87–88.
208. Part 1, pp. 45–46.
209. Zoetmulder (1983), p. 540.

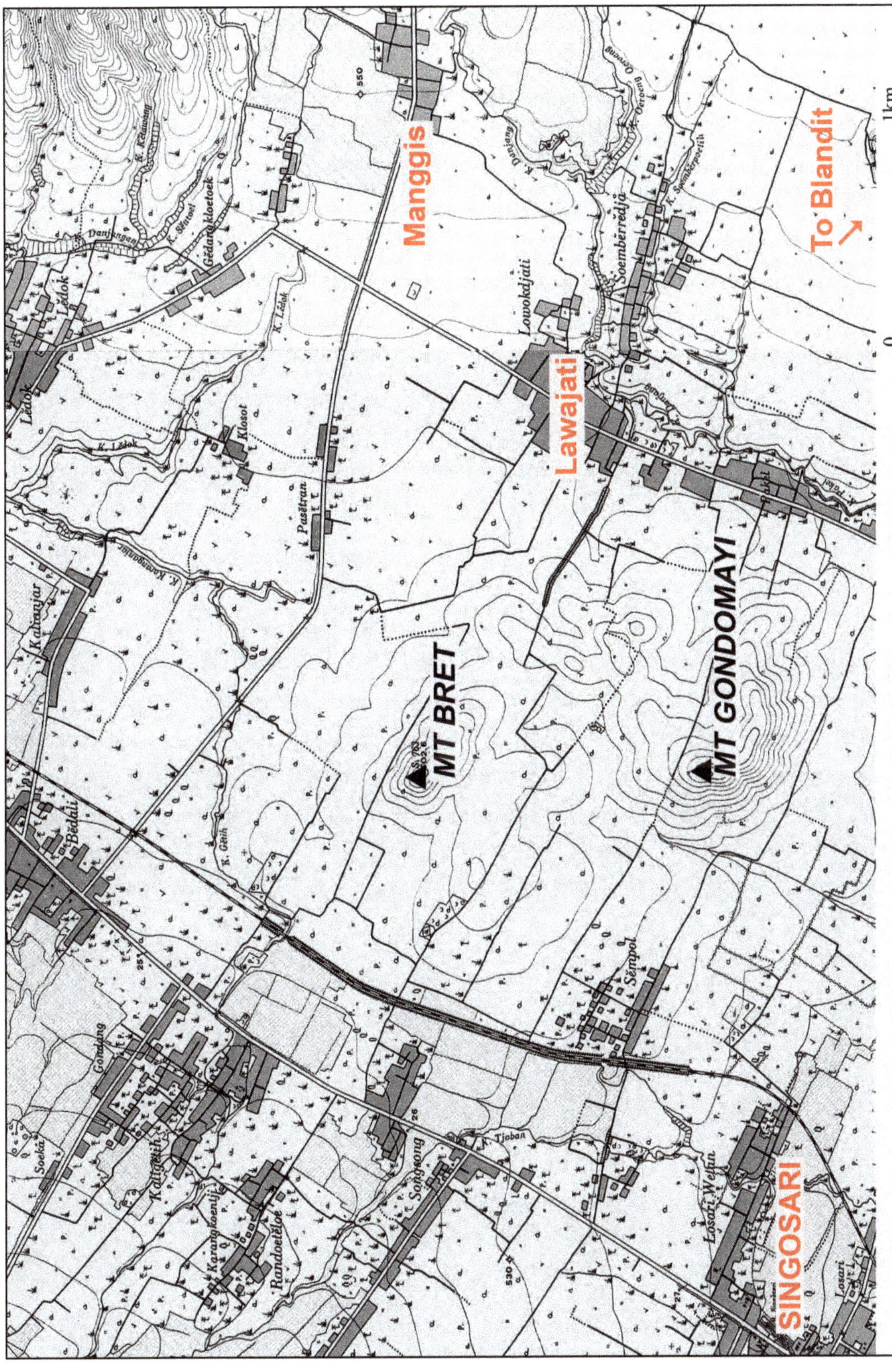

Adapted from the Dutch Topographical Map Series, 1914 (1: 20,000), Sheets KVIII, LVIII

Figure 33 Map showing the former location of Linggasuntan.
Adapted from: Name: 04894-024, 04894-025; Scale: 1: 20,000; Type: Topographic map; Year: 1914

Following the legendary account of the origin of the *kahyangan* at Pangawān, the TP names three more sacred foundations whose function was to protect the "taboo grounds" of the holy Mt Mahāmeru, namely Pūrṇajiwa, Gantĕn and Paḍang.[210] Mention has already been made of antiquities discovered in the village of Pronojiwo, on the southeastern foot of Mt Semeru, allowing a probable identification with the Pūrṇnajiwa of the TP. With regard to Gantĕn, one could suggest a connection with the village of that name mentioned by Prapañca in his Deśawarṇana, but the location seems rather far from the Mahāmeru.[211] More certainty surrounds the site of Paḍang, which has already been mentioned in connection with the journey of Ken Candrasari, as recounted in the *kidung* Pañji Margasmara. In all probability the place was located near the present settlement of Kalipadang at Amadanom, on the eastern side of the village of Dampit.[212]

It was not until Bhaṭāra Guru had founded the *maṇḍala* of Śūnyasagiri (later Kukub) that the Trinity of lords (*trisamaya*), Brahmā, Wiṣṇu and Iśwara, came to the Mahāmeru to pay homage, at which time each of them was instructed to establish his own religious centre (*kahyangan*). Bhaṭāra Iśwara, as the most senior, opened the *maṇḍala* of Tigapatra on Mt Tigaryan (Tigaryan-parwata), while Brahmā and Wiṣṇu occupied the mountains Jala-parwata and Nangka-parwata respectively.[213]

Although not specifically stated, the text of the TP seems to imply that the *maṇḍala* of the Trinity of lords were situated in the vicinity of the Mahāmeru. Whether or not this was in fact the case, these places remain elusive. Pigeaud was inclined to identify the Nangka mountain with the ancestral seat of Bañak-wiḍe (Wiraraja), as recorded in the Pararaton,[214] a suggestion which certainly finds support from the prevalence of the toponym Nongko on the western side of the Tengger range.[215] This region, after

210. See note 196.

211. DW 20: 1–2 (Robson 1995, p. 40). Gantĕn is listed among the eleven Buddhist communities which welcomed king Rājasanagara's arrival at Madakaripura during the royal progress of 1359. Its position on the northern side of the Tengger Massif accords roughly with the description in the TP.

212. The site of Kalipadang today consists primarily of an extensive graveyard, attesting to a more prominent role in the not so distant past. The river (*kali*) Padang, on whose banks it lies, is marked clearly on nineteenth century Dutch topographical maps (cf. Kaart van de Residentie Pasoeroean, 1858, sheet no. 21 of the Atlas van Nederlandsch Indië).

213. Part 1, p. 35.

214. Pigeaud (1924), p. 246; Brandes (1920), p. 24.

215. A group of settlements named Nongkosewu, Nongkorejo, Nongkopait, Nongkosongo and Karangnongko can be found at Poncokusumo and neighbouring Tumpang in the regency of Malang, while Nongkojajar lies somewhat further afield in the district of Tutur (Pasuruan Regency).

all, is situated not far east of the former court of Singhasāri, where Bañak-wiḍe was in service. It is possible, then, that the remains of the *maṇḍala* of Nangka-parwata, known also as Panasagiri, lie somewhere near the mountain village of Gubugklakah (Poncokusumo), where terracotta remains have been reported and a fourteenth century copper plate inscription discovered in 1909.[216]

The creation of a *maṇḍala* on the mountain Manuñjang is attributed to the god Gaṇa. From the text of the TP we know that it was closely connected with the mountains Kampil/Pilan and Jaṭa, the latter forming "the border of Tandĕs and Mt Maṇik".[217] Since the positions of these two last mentioned places have already been fixed on the eastern side of the Mahāmeru, it follows that Manuñjang was located in the same region. Further support for this assumption comes from the fact that the *maṇḍala* was later inherited by one Buyut Samaḍi, a pupil of the *dewaguru* at Ḍingḍing, at which time it became known as Ḍingḍing-Manuñjang (see Figure 34). One can thus conjecture that the original site of Manuñjang, like that of Ḍingḍing, was situated in the district of Gucialit (Lumajang) and might even be recognizable in the present village of Tunjung,[218] which has in the past yielded various items of bronze, silver and copper, among them a bronze zodiac beaker (*prasen*).[219] To this day, a number of stone menhirs can still be found at the grave sites of Lamdaur and Danyangan.[220]

The TP refers to the *maṇḍala* of Labdawara immediately after that of Manuñjang. The founder and first *dewaguru* is described as an Indian brahmin named Ḍang Hyang Kacuṇḍa, who after receiving ordination at Kukub became known as Bhagawān Aśoṣṭi. Although the precise location of Labdawara is not mentioned in the text, the fact that the site was chosen on the advice of the god Wiṣṇu at Panasagiri, and the foundation sanctioned by the lord of Kukub, suggests that the *maṇḍala* was situated in the vicinity of the Mahāmeru.

Finally, we should mention the *maṇḍala* of Aṇḍawar, first of four religious establishments founded by Ki Kabhayan-panglayar, a functionary serving under the

216. NBG 47 (1909): 190–91. Transcription in Boechari (1985–86), pp. 110–11, no. E.48. It is not clear to me how Krom (1913b, pp. 257–58) read the Śaka date 1463. The abbreviated formula at the end of the inscription is typical of that found on several copper plate charters issued during the early years of the fourteenth Śaka century, and as such would seem to indicate the year 1303, equivalent to AD 1381. For the position of Gubugklakah, see Figure 26 above.

217. Part 1, p. 35.

218. See Figure 16 above.

219. These objects are preserved in the National Museum, Jakarta. See JBG IX (AV 1942): 103, nos. 7660–7666.

220. Nitihaminoto (1990), p. 24.

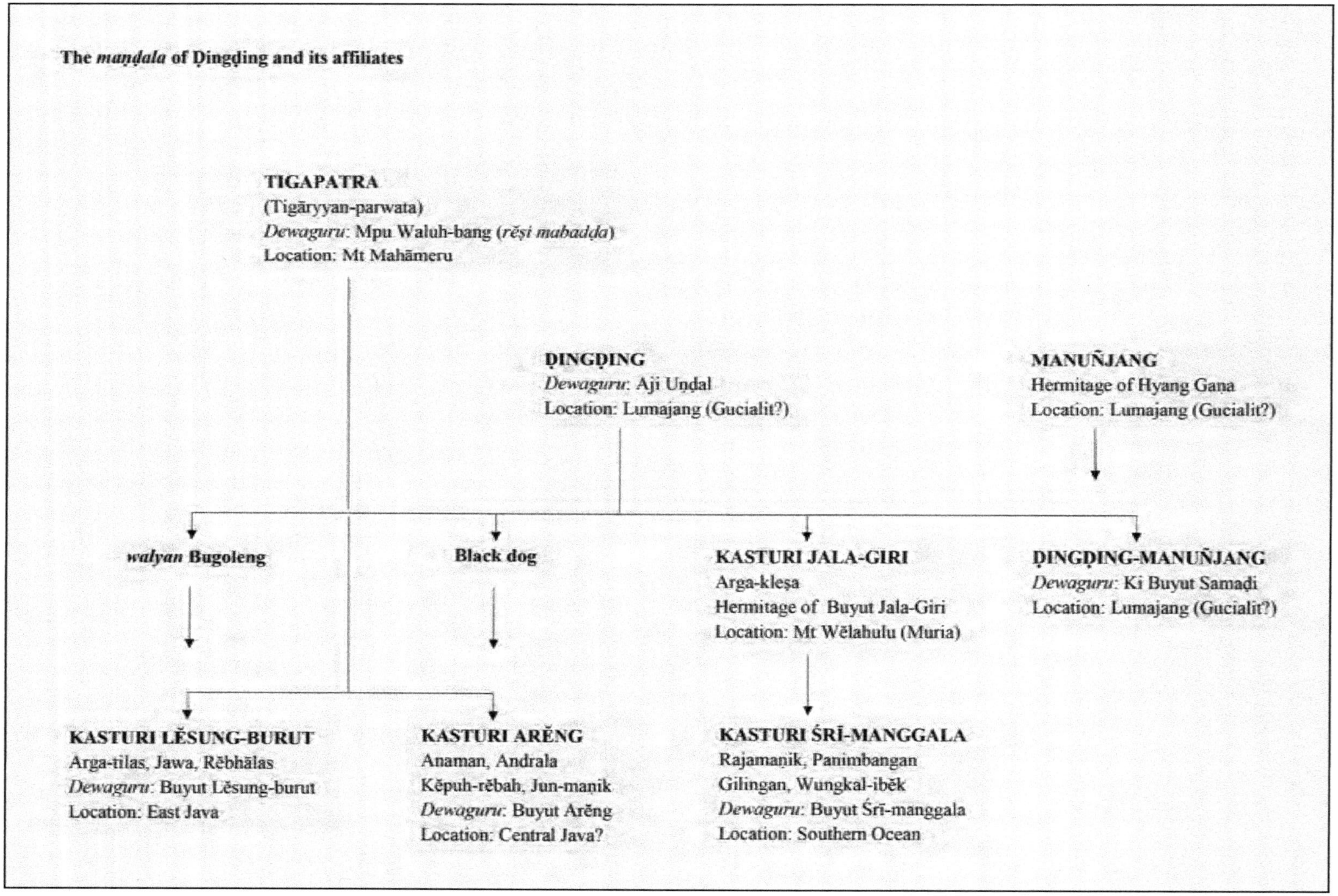

Figure 34 The *maṇḍala* of Ḍingḍing and its affiliates.
Diagram by Hadi Sidomulyo, 2019.

dewaguru at Kukub. Aṇḍawar is described as lying on the saddle between Mt Brahmā and the Mahāmeru. This allows a possible identification with present day Ranupane, where a local village priest (*dukun*) still presides over a traditional Tengger community. Alternatively, the *maṇḍala* might in former times have been situated in the vicinity of the lake named Ranu Kumbolo, which preserves a rock inscription commemorating the pilgrimage of a certain Mpu Kāmeśwara, possibly in the Śaka year 1232 (see Figure 35).[221] The site of Aṇḍawar will receive further attention when following the adventures of Ki Kabhayan-panglayar.

Figure 35 The rock inscription of Ranu Kumbolo.
Photo by Hadi Sidomulyo, 2018.

221. Bosch (1920), pp. 100–101; Bosch (1926a), p. 33. The inscription reads: *mpu kāmeśwarā tīrthayatra.*

III
THE EARTHLY REALM —
TALES OF MEN

Mahāmpu Palyat and the Bhairawa cult in Java

The widow Rāga-runting at Mĕḍang-tañjung

Mpu Barang, Mpu Waluhbang and the founding of the Kasturi order

Ki Kabhayan-panglayar and the maṇḍala trisamaya

Further historical and topographical aspects

Afterword

Mahāmpu Palyat and the Bhairawa cult in Java

It is told that Lord Guru became manifest in the form of Mahāmpu Palyat, a *bhujangga* of the Śaiwa denomination who practised austerities in a cemetery on Mt Hyang, following the rites of the Bhairawa order.[222] Upon learning that there was an unusual ascetic residing in the realm of Brahmāloka,[223] the reigning king at Galuh,[224] named Mahārāja Bhatati, desired to meet him, and to that end summoned the entire community of *wiku* to participate in a royal ceremony. When, however, the king caught sight of Mahāmpu Palyat, whose attributes included a drinking cup in the form of a skull, as well as a bowl (*kaṇṭora*) containing human flesh, he was outraged and immediately ordered for the renegade *wiku* to be put to death. The two officials appointed to the task, Mpu Kalotan and Mpu Waju-kuning, went straight to Mahāmpu Palyat's hermitage on the following morning and carried out the king's orders, binding the ascetic with rattan and throwing him into the sea, before reporting back to the palace. When they returned the next day, however, they were surprised to discover the *wiku* sitting calmly in his hermitage as usual, as if nothing had happened. Twice more they attempted to kill the holy man, weighting him down with stones in the ocean and even burning him to ashes, but to no avail. Realizing that Mahāmpu Palyat was none other than the Supreme Lord Parameśwara himself, the two emissaries bowed low at the sage's feet and requested to become his disciples. After receiving ordination as Mpu Janaḍipa and Mpu Narajñāna, they returned to the capital, where they were installed respectively as teacher and court priest to Mahārāja Bhatati.

Leaving aside the more fantastic elements, it is noteworthy that both the historical and geographical setting of the above account are in accordance with the inscriptional record. As far as I am aware, the earliest dated reference to the worship of Bhairawa in eastern Java is to be found in the charter of Hantang, issued by the Kaḍiri king Mapañji Jayabhaya in the year 1135.[225] It is remarkable that the same document refers specifically to the king's "teacher" (*pangajyan*), described as "a master proficient in

222. Part 1, p. 47.

223. According to Hindu conception, Brahmāloka represents the highest stage of creation, beyond the summit of Mt Mahāmeru. Zimmer (1952, pp. 142–43) describes it as "the realm of formless being and purely spiritual bliss".

224. As already noted, the name Galuh in this context should be understood as a reference to the court of twelfth century Kaḍiri.

225. In fact, the origin of Bhairawa worship in Java appears to be traceable to a still earlier period. As noted by Reichle (2007, p. 33), the term *kapālikabrata* is already found in the Old Javanese Udyogaparwa (Zoetmulder 1982, p. 797; Zoetmulder 1983, pp. 111–12). For the relationship of the god Bhairawa with the Indian Kāpālika sect, see Gopinath Rao (1971), vol. II, pp. 26–29.

yoga through the Bhairawa way".[226] This lends credibility to the story of Mahāmpu Palyat, and perhaps tells us something about how the Bhairawa doctrine came to be embraced by Javanese royalty. At the very least, these combined data provide a reason to regard the court of Kaḍiri as the cradle of the Bhairawa cult in eastern Java (see Figure 36).[227]

Figure 36 The *candrakapāla*, symbol of Bhairawa and official emblem of king Jayabhaya's predecessor, Śrī Bāmeśwara (c. 1117–35). Depiction on the stele of Gĕnĕng at Brumbung (Kepung), Kediri Regency. *Photo by Hadi Sidomulyo, 2011.*

226. For further details, see Sedyawati (1994), p. 211.

227. The Bhairawa sect subsequently grew in popularity. Although the data are fragmentary, it can be noted that the 1255 charter of Mūla-malurung (Pl. IIIb, 3–5), issued by king Wiṣṇuwardhana of Singhasāri, records at least two prominent religious officials of the Bhairawa *pakṣa*. The first, entitled *mpungkwing* Kapulungan, was a chief priest (*sthāpaka ring kabhairawan*), while the second, named Sang Apañji Pati-pati, is described posthumously as a *bhujangga śiwapakṣa bhairawabrata* in the 1296 inscription of Sukamṛta (Pl. VIIIa, 2–3). It can be noted further that adherents of the *bhairawapakṣa* were predominant among the Śiwaite "interpreters of the *dharma*" (*dharmopapatti*) listed in royal inscriptions dating from mid-fourteenth century Majapahit (cf. Santiko 1995, p. 58).

This naturally raises the question of whether the graphic descriptions in the TP of skull cups and *kaṇtora* used for the preservation of human flesh should be taken literally. In India, these ritual items are usually associated with the Śaiwa sect known as Pāśupata, whose branches included the Kālāmukha and Kāpālika, the latter acknowledging Bhairawa as the Supreme Lord. Although it is hard to know the extent to which the gruesome rites attributed to these orders were actually performed in Java, it is at least clear that the author of the TP understood their symbolic value.

It is related, for example, that upon arrival at Mahāmpu Palyat's residence on the island (*nuṣa*) of Kambangan, Mpu Kalotan and Mpu Waju-kuning were surprised by the appearance of one hundred and eighty of their teacher's pupils, and enquired, "What people are these, so beautiful with ornaments?"; to which the *wiku* replied casually, "Ah, they are what became of the people I ate when I was on the island of Java".[228] This is in accordance with the specific nature of Bhairawa, who is said to "swallow the sins of his devotees".[229] We find the same essential message contained in the well known story of the two ascetic brothers, Bubukṣa and Gagang-aking. Upon being rebuked by Kālawijaya, an envoy of Bhaṭāra Guru, for eating everything without discrimination, including humans, Bubukṣah explains that by doing so he is in fact helping the victims attain to a higher status in the next life.[230]

The widow Rāga-runting at Mĕḍang-tañjung

The storyline is interrupted briefly at this point by a curious episode describing the early history of Mĕḍang-tañjung, third of the "lands of origin" referred to in the TP.[231] It is said that Mĕḍang-tañjung was formerly the residence of a widow (*raṇḍa*) named Rāga-runting, an incarnation of the goddess Śrī, who spent her days spinning thread in the shade of a *tañjung* tree.[232] Disturbed by the presence of a greedy merchant named Parijñana, Rāga-runting took evasive action by using her broom to "sweep

228. Part 1, p. 49.
229. Gopinath Rao (1971), vol. II, pp. 175–76. Note that "sins" in this context should be understood in the sense of *karma* (actions, deeds).
230. Rassers (1982), p. 82.
231. The other two, Mĕḍang-gaṇa and Mĕḍang-kamulan, have already been discussed. Without losing sight of the fact that the term Mĕḍang itself came, over the course of time, to represent a "concept" (see van der Meulen 1977, p. 99, note 45), I find no reason to doubt that our text is referring here to an actual geographical location.
232. Part 1, p. 50. The *tanjung* tree (Mimusops elengi) is known for its fragrant flowers, traditionally used by Javanese women as a hair ornament.

him away to the east" as far as Mt Bañcak, after which she is said to have "kept her distance from him" on a mountain named Kĕṇḍĕng. This at least is what the text seems to imply, although the author's intention is somewhat obscured by a number of variants in the available manuscripts.[233] Fortunately, new data acquired in the course of a recent field survey in central Java allow us to carry the discussion a little further.

In July 2019, while visiting a settlement named Tanjung in the district of Klego (Boyolali Regency), it was curious to discover that a prominent hill nearby was named Rogo-runting, upon the summit of which could be found a wooden enclosure housing the grave of a certain Eyang ("grandfather") Rogo-runting (see Figure 37).[234]

Figure 37 The grave of Eyang Rogo-runting at Tanjung (Klego), Boyolali. *Photo by Hadi Sidomulyo, 2019.*

233. See notes 186–188 to the translation.

234. With regard to the identity of this figure, I note that Pigeaud (1967, pp. 68–69, 75) lists two religious texts featuring a holy man entitled Mpu Raga-runting, namely the Drawa Puruṣa Prameya and Guwar-gawir. The Balinese Babad Pasek likewise lists Mpu Raga-runting among the seven sons of Hyang Genijaya (cf. Sugriwa 1956, p. 19).

According to local legend, this revered figure was the founding father of the community at Tanjung, whose name derived from a large *tanjung* tree which formerly shaded an ancient well in the centre of the village.[235] Considering the remarkable correspondence with the story in the TP, there would seem good reason to associate the village of Tanjung at Boyolali with the historical Mĕḍang-tañjung, and at the same time identify Mt Kĕṇḍĕng with the hill of that name lying some 9 km to the north at Wonosegoro (see Figure 38). This established, it follows that the mountain named Bañcak in the text can be none other than the well known Mt Bancak in the regency of Magetan, which does indeed lie directly "to the east" of Boyolali.[236]

We are of course still left with the problem of identifying the mountain Karurungan, which in Pigeaud's manuscripts A and B is found in parenthesis immediately after Mt Bañcak, whereas in D and E it actually takes the place of Mt Bañcak. One could of course suggest that these are alternative names for the same mountain, were it not for the fact that Noorduyn already identified Karungrungan (and its variants Karurungan and Karungrangan) with Mt Ungaran, which lies some 40 km northwest of Boyolali![237] It looks as if this apparent contradiction will have to remain unsolved, at least for the time being.

Mpu Barang, Mpu Waluhbang and the founding of the Kasturi order

Returning now to eastern Java, it appears that the god Śiwa as Bhairawa occupied a preeminent position for the *wiku* community. According to the TP, Mahāmpu Palyat subsequently divided his body into two, becoming a Śaiwa and a Sogata (Buddhist).[238] These two denominations were represented respectively by the sages Mpu Barang and Mpu Waluh-bang. The former is said to have returned to Mahāmpu Palyat's

235. The original tree no longer exists, but the well survives to this day.

236. Mt Bañcak forms a prominence near the southeastern foot of Mt Lawu, in the district of Kawedenan. Verbeek (1891, p. 210, no. 404) already noted the existence of archaeological remains on the mountain's summit, and a few years later Knebel (1905–6, pp. 60–63) described in some detail the sacred enclosure housing the grave of Ratu Maduretna (d. 1809). Today a few *candi* stones can still be encountered, and traces of early stone terracing are visible on the northern side of the hill. An aging and weathered *dwārapāla*, apparently *in situ*, guards the entrance to the grave site.

237. Noorduyn (1982), p. 424. I note that Mt Ungaran appears as Noengroengan on a Dutch topographical map dating from 1860 (scale 1: 100,000).

238. Part 1, p. 50.

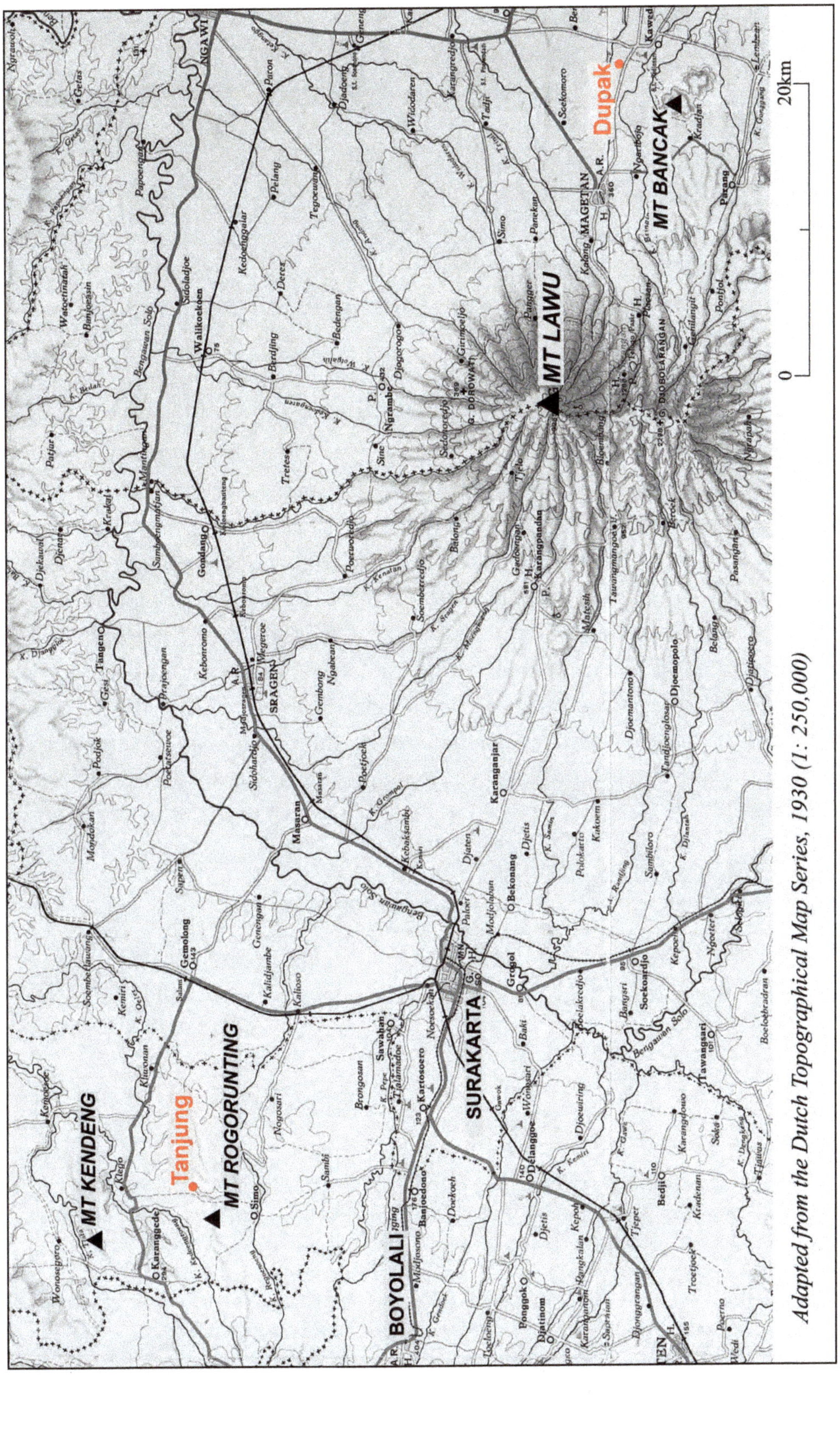

Adapted from the Dutch Topographical Map Series, 1930 (1: 250,000)

Figure 38 Geographical reconstruction of the story of the widow Rāga-runting.
Adapted from: Name: 04910-1; Scale: 1: 250,000; Type: Topographic map; Year: 1930

hermitage on Mt Hyang, where he continued to perform the Bhairawa rites, while the latter established a settlement at a place named Warag, the location of which remains unidentified.[239] Some time later, however, during the reign of king Bhatati's successor, Mpu Waluh-bang abandoned the Sogata sect to become a Ṛṣi-mabaḍḍa, or "sage-with-headband", succeeding Lord Iśwara as *dewaguru* at the *maṇḍala* of Tigāryan. Once settled, he joined forces again with his counterpart Mpu Barang, and together these two emanations of Mahāmpu Palyat opened a new *maṇḍala* at Tūryan (Turen). Established as the "first of the Kasturi law" (*pūrwa-ḍarma-kasturi*), this community was presided over by Mpu Barang, who continued to follow the way (*pakṣa*) of the Bhairawa.[240]

The Kasturi sect was apparently widespread and attracted numerous adherents (see Figure 39). One of these was a figure known as Buyut Gĕnting, who upon receiving ordination went on to found no less than five *maṇḍala* on the slopes of Mt Kawi (see Figure 40).[241] With regard to the name Gĕnting, there is good reason to connect it with the settlement of Genting at Merjosari, now a part of the city of Malang, on the eastern foot of the Kawi range. The National Museum in Jakarta possesses a substantial collection of bronze ritual items from Genting, and extensive archaeological remains were reported in the vicinity of Merjosari by E.W. Maurenbrecher in 1923.[242] One item of special interest is an inscribed stone, which records the founding of a *maṇḍala* in the Śaka year 1138 (see Figure 41).[243] Although there is no specific mention of the name Kasturi, this document at least provides some concrete support for the tradition surrounding the figure of Buyut Gĕnting, as preserved in the TP.

Ki Kabhayan-panglayar and the maṇḍala trisamaya

The TP describes a group of *maṇḍala* occupying the Hyang Massif at the far eastern end of Java. Their foundation is attributed to a religious official known as

239. Part 1, p. 53.

240. Part 1, pp. 57–58.

241. Part 1, p. 60. The names of these *maṇḍala*, as listed in the TP, are Brajahning, Argha-maṇik, Jangkanang, Bhamana and Gumantar. Although their former locations remain for the most part unidentified, it is possible that at least some of them can be connected with the terraced sanctuaries on Mt Kekep and Mt Butak, described by Maurenbrecher (1923a, pp. 89–90) early in the last century.

242. Maurenbrecher (1923b), pp. 178–79. For the items from Genting, see NBG 42 (1904): 7 and bijl. XX, nos. 807a, 808b, 816d, 824b, 836b, 892u, 936a, 942d, 943c, 944a, 952c, 1078b, 1747c.

243. Transcription by Crucq (1929), p. 279. See also Damais (1949), pp. 11–12.

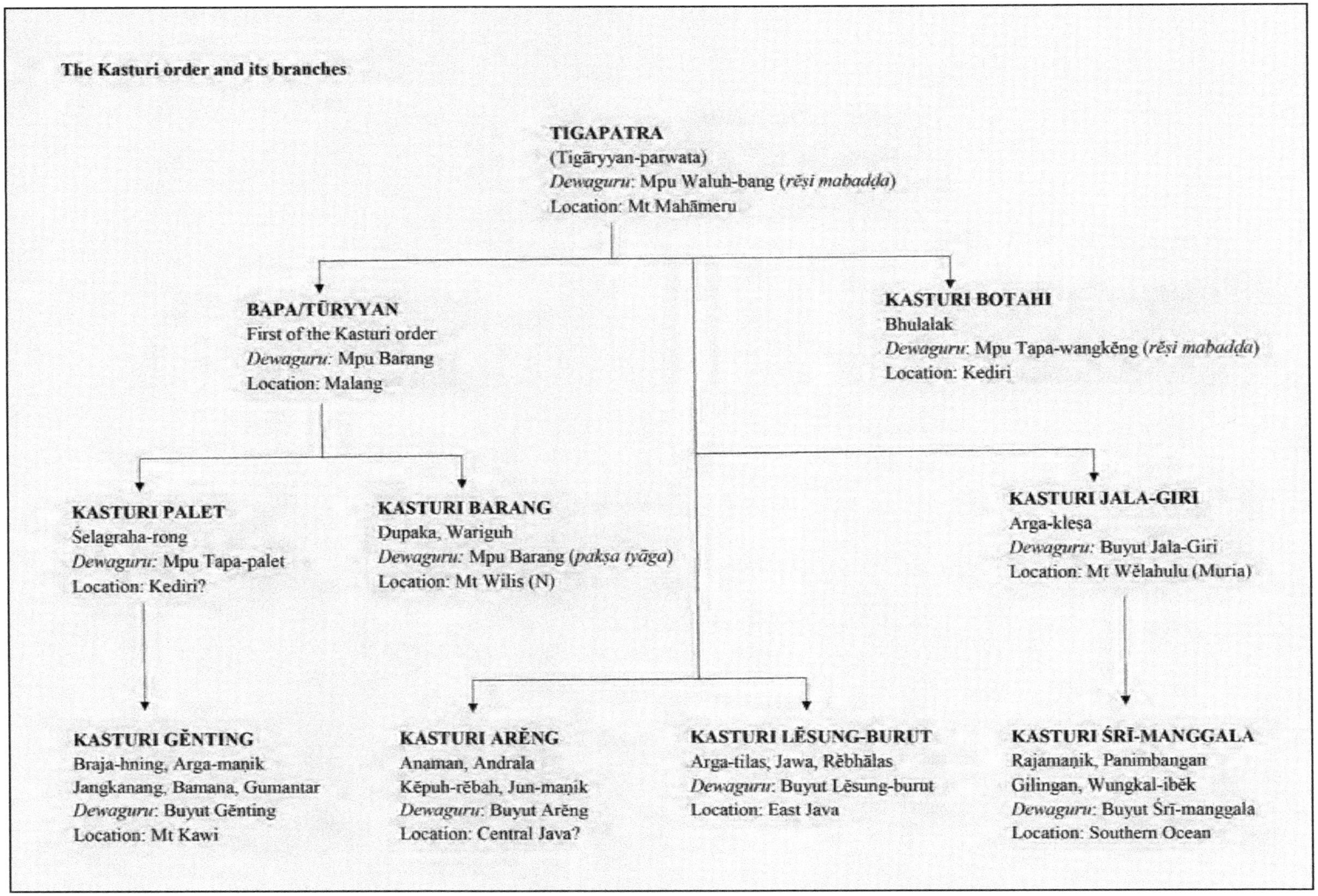

Figure 39 The Kasturi order and its branches.
Diagram by Hadi Sidomulyo, 2019.

Figure 40 Inscribed stone at Selobrojo (Ngantang), on the northwestern slope of Mt Kawi, possibly identifiable with the *maṇḍala* of Brajahning, founded by Buyut Gĕnting.
Photo by Hadi Sidomulyo, 2003.

Figure 41 The stele of Merjosari. National Museum, Jakarta, No. D.179.
Photo by Hadi Sidomulyo, 1988.

Ki Kabhayan-panglayar,[244] who was employed in the service of the spiritual lord of Kukub. The story goes that Bhaṭāra Guru, in the role of the *dewaguru* Taruṇa-tapa-yowana, was preparing a festival at Kukub in the month of Asuji (September–October), and ordered Ki Kabhayan-panglayar to collect contributions from the districts lying to the east of the Mahāmeru. The latter duly set off, and before long had gathered a substantial quantity of supplies, as well as attracted numerous followers wishing to be introduced to the lord of Kukub. Progress on the return journey, however, was impeded by the attempt to transport an excessive amount of goods, with the result that Ki Kabhayan-panglayar arrived late for the celebrations, much to the anger of the *dewaguru*.[245]

This curious episode, though probably apocryphal, is nonetheless a valuable source of topographical data. On his return journey to Kukub from the eastern districts, Ki Kabhayan-panglayar is said to have stopped at several places whose names are directly associated with the various items, particularly livestock, which he was forced to leave behind. Listed (presumably) in order from east to west, they are: Ragḍang, Tambangan, Pacelengan, Untehan, Kuḍampilan, Cangcangan, Bakar, Duk and Payaman. Although for the most part obscure and difficult to identify, these toponyms together provide sufficient data for at least a partial reconstruction of the route followed (see Figure 42).

We can begin by noting the position of the mountain Duk,[246] mentioned earlier in connection with the *maṇḍala* of Gĕrĕsik. The fact that this prominent landmark lies roughly 8 km west of a hill named Penyancangan accords well with the relative

---

244. The term *kabhayan-panglayar*, which would seem more fitting in a nautical context (*layar* = sail) than that of a remote mountain sanctuary, is just one of a number of obscure offices introduced at this point in the text. Presumably these titles formed a hierarchy under the *dewaguru*.

245. Part 1, p. 51.

246. According to the Sĕrat Kanda, Mt Duk was at one time the residence of a certain Raden Juru, the younger brother of Patih Udara of Majapahit. Upon the death of his wife (the daughter of a vanquished ruler of Probolinggo), Raden Juru retired to the mountain with his daughter, where he spent the remainder of his life as a hermit. Curiously, the daughter is said to have given birth later to Jaka Sangara (king Andayaningrat of Pengging), following an amorous encounter with the crocodile Bajul Semanggi (cf. Brandes 1920, pp. 218–19; de Graaf and Pigeaud 1986, pp. 260–61, note 304).

We can add that an interview with the resident caretaker on Mt Duk in November 2018 revealed that local tradition still preserves the memory of a hermitage on the mountain. Unfortunately, the construction of a radio tower on the summit some decades ago has left little hope for an archaeological survey.

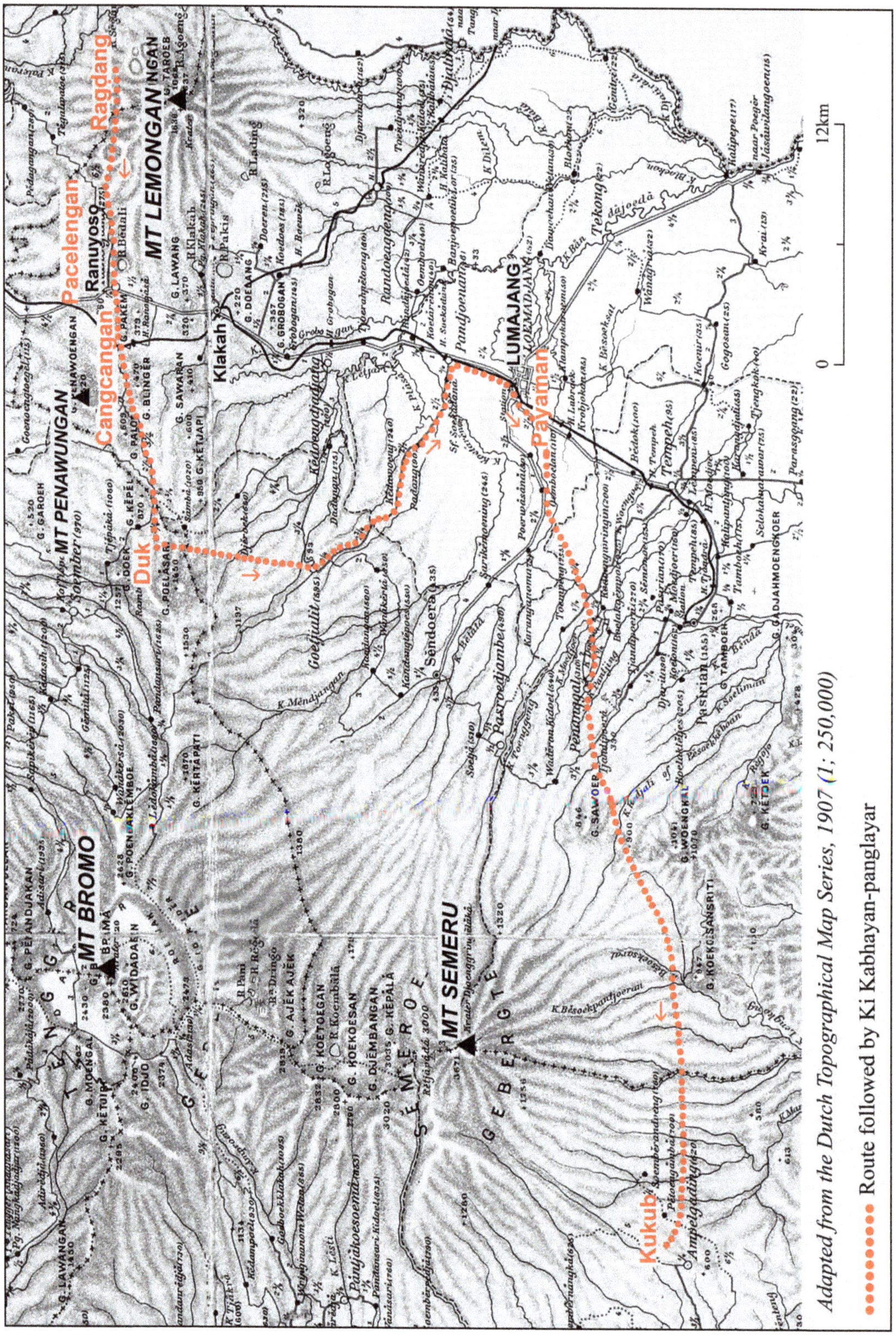

Figure 42 Map showing the journey of Ki Kabhayan-panglayar in the eastern districts.
Adapted from: Name: 05082; Scale: 1: 250,000; Type: Topographic map; Year: 1907

positions of Duk and Cangcangan[247] as described in the TP. There is thus reason to place a section of the Kabhayan-panglayar's journey in the districts of Sumber (Probolinggo) and Ranuyoso (Lumajang), to the northeast of the Tengger Massif. This established, it becomes possible to extend the route eastward to the foothills of the Hyang Plateau, allowing an identification of Ragḍang with present day Ranugedang, located near the mountain village of Tiris. Further west, the toponym Pacelengan could well be a variant of Pawijungan, a place passed by king Rājasanagara of Majapahit during his eastern progress of 1359, and almost certainly situated near Ranuyoso.[248]

Continuing onwards from Duk, Ki Kabhayan-panglayar travelled to Payaman, the last village mentioned before reaching Kukub. This name can be connected with another place visited by king Rājasanagara in 1359, identifiable with present day Bayeman on the southwestern outskirts of the town of Lumajang.[249] Ancient brick remains are still to be found in the immediate vicinity, notably at the grave sites of Srangin and "Mbah Ratmojo".[250]

To recapitulate, having journeyed as far as the eastern end of the Hyang Massif, Ki Kabhayan-panglayar apparently returned by way of a route which skirted the northern foot of Mt Lemongan, passing through the "lake district" of Ranuyoso and Klakah as far as Mt Duk. From there the path turned southward to Lumajang, before heading west once more along the southern slope of the Mahāmeru towards Kukub.

It seems that the Supreme Lord's anger was quick to subside, for not long afterwards Ki Kabhayan-panglayar was granted a divine favour in the form of the

247. From Old Javanese *cangcang*, meaning to bind or tie up (Zoetmulder 1982, p. 301). According to local inhabitants interviewed by the present writer in November 2018, the hill of Penyancangan features in a legend concerning the harnessing of horses. This is not so far removed from the explanation of the name Cangcangan in the TP, as the place where the Kabhayan-panglayar tied up a sow (*nangcang bagor*).

248. DW 21: 1d (Robson 1995, p. 40); Sidomulyo (2007), pp. 51, 94 (note 72). Both *celeng* and *wijung* mean "wild boar" (Zoetmulder 1982, pp. 323, 2272).

249. DW 21: 2c (Robson 1995, p. 41); Sidomulyo (2007), p. 52. If this identification is correct, it follows that the river Sarayu, referred to rather cryptically in connection with the site of Payaman in the TP, must be the former name of the present river Paruk, on whose southern bank the hamlet of Bayeman is situated.

250. Nawawi (1990), p. 5. One is tempted here to connect Mbah Ratmojo with the demon Rātmaja, who together with his colleague Rātmaji stole the jewelled pot Kamaṇḍalu (container of the water of life) from the gods, as recounted in the TP. It seems more likely, however, that the name is a variant of Repatmojo, a character featuring in the popular legend of Dewi Rengganis (see note 272 below).

holy Sandhijñāna, the "key" to esoteric knowledge, which allowed him to open the *maṇḍala* of Aṇḍawar on the saddle between Mt Bromo and the Mahāmeru, mentioned earlier.[251] This was the first of four religious establishments founded by Ki Kabhayan-panglayar. The remaining three, named Talun, Waśaṇa and Sāgara, were located on Mt Hyang and are referred to in the TP as the *maṇḍala trisamaya*. It is to these foundations that attention will now be turned.

Fortunately, we have access to at least two important comparative sources, which enable us to place this trio of *maṇḍala* in a fairly certain geographical setting. Before consulting them, however, it is useful to review the relevant section of the TP itself, which runs as follows: Having set up the community at Aṇḍawar, Ki Kabhayan-panglayar journeyed eastward to Mt Hyang, where he was granted a tract of land by the elders of a place named Běsar, consisting of gardens (*talun-talun*) no longer in use. Hence the *maṇḍala* was named Talun. A second establishment was founded shortly afterwards at Waśaṇa, connected with a curious stone known as Ubhusan. On both occasions Ki Kabhayan-panglayar's skills in yoga and *samaḍi* were put to the test in combat with a fierce guardian spirit.[252]

As to the origin of Sāgara, it is said that Ki Kabhayan-panglayar left Waśaṇa and travelled to Kalyasěm, the site of an ancient graveyard and renowned hermitage of Mpu Barang. Upon arrival, however, he discovered that the great sage had since vacated the premises, leaving behind his jacket and a book of teachings. Mpu Barang's spiritual legacy (*palupuynirā*) thus passed to Ki Kabhayan-panglayar, who proceeded to establish a *maṇḍala* on the spot. It is said that the community flourished, attracting countless pupils, and so in the end became known as Sāgara (= ocean).[253]

Turning now to the comparative sources mentioned above, the listing of Sāgara among the *caturbhasma* in Prapañca's Deśawarṇana has already been noted. The same text goes on to provide an account of king Rājasanagara's journey to a forest hermitage (*wanāśrama*) named Sāgara in 1359.[254] The route followed is said to have led southward into the hills from the coastal town of Pajarakan (east of present day Probolinggo), thus making it certain that the place visited was situated on the saddle of Mt Lemongan and the Hyang Plateau. Looking further, we find good reason to locate the hermitage of Sāgara near the present lake of Segaran in the mountain district of Tiris, 25 km south of Pajarakan. This identification has for long received

251. Part 1, p. 52.
252. Part 1, pp. 52–53.
253. Part 1, pp. 54–55.
254. DW 32: 2–34: 2 (Robson 1995, pp. 46–48).

general acceptance among scholars, despite the objections raised by P.V. van Stein Callenfels.[255]

Another valuable source which can help us achieve further precision is a fragmentary copper plate inscription preserved in the National Museum at Jakarta.[256] This incomplete document forms part of a collection of items recovered from the northern foothills of the Hyang Massif early in the last century.[257] Despite the absence of a date, Krom showed conclusively on the basis of internal evidence that the inscription was issued by the Majapahit queen Tribhuwana Wijayottunggadewī between the years 1334 and 1350.[258] Popularly known as the charter of Batur, after the name of the village where the plates were discovered, the contents concern regulations pertaining to a number of *maṇḍala*, among them Kaṇḍawa, Talun, Wasana and Sāgara, as well as the sacred ancestral seat (*kabuyutan*) of Kalyasĕm. Inasmuch as the names of these religious foundations correspond closely with those occurring in the story of Ki Kabhayan-panglayar, the Batur charter confirms the accuracy of this section of the TP, thereby strengthening our faith in the reliability of the work as a whole. It now remains to see how far the combined data can help us identify the places which they describe.

As already noted, the first *maṇḍala* founded by Ki Kabhayan-panglayar was at Aṇḍawar, located on the saddle of the mountains Brahmā and Mahāmeru. This was followed by the establishment of three more communities at Talun, Waśaṇa and Sāgara,

255. Cf. Stein Callenfels (1918), pp. 9–12; Kern (1927), p. 621; Pigeaud (1960–63), vol. IV, p. 93; Robson (1995), p. 115. It was the seeming absence of significant archaeological remains at Segaran that led Stein Callenfels to reconsider the possibility of connecting Sāgara with the site of Candi Kedaton, which is located further south at Andungbiru. This identification itself, however, is no less problematic. To begin with, it is hard to ignore the fact that the principal structure at Kedaton displays the Śaka date 1292 (AD 1370), carved in relief beside the entrance steps. In other words, the building did not yet exist at the time of king Rājasanagara's visit to Sāgara. Furthermore, close examination of the text of the Deśawarṇana reveals that the landscape at Kedaton does not match Prapañca's description of the king's journey. Lastly, there are in fact signs of an ancient settlement on the northern side of Ranu (lake) Segaran, specifically in the adjacent village of Jangkang (cf. Sidomulyo 2007, p. 72 and notes 145–147).

256. No. E.50 a–c. Transcription in Boechari (1985–86), pp. 112–14.

257. According to Bosch (1915b), pp. 105–6, the inscription comprised three copper plates, two of which were fragments. Other items recovered included two bronze bells, two sets of scales, and a further single engraved copper plate, apparently representing a separate, barely legible inscription (National Museum, Jakarta, nos. 5629–5632, E.51). For the last mentioned item, see Boechari (1985–86), p. 114.

258. Krom (1919), pp. 161–68. For some unknown reason, Pigeaud (1960–63, vol. IV, p. 412) chose to attribute this inscription to the reign of king Hayam Wuruk (Rājasanagara).

referred to as the *maṇḍala trisamaya* on Mt Hyang. Now it is interesting to observe that, if the name Aṇḍawar (or Ngaṇḍawar) is accepted as a variant of Kaṇḍawa, these same four *maṇḍala* are to be found listed in precisely the same order on plate 2a: 4 of the Batur charter.[259] Although the contents of the latter do not help much to determine their geographical positions, the discovery site of the inscription provides a clue. Pigeaud already observed that the name Batur was probably connected with an ancient religious community, and suggested that it might even refer to the original *batur i* Talun mentioned in the charter.[260] Before jumping to conclusions, however, it is advisable to take a closer look at the available data.

The present village of Batur lies on the northern foot of the Hyang Massif, 18 km southeast of Pajarakan in the district of Gading, Probolinggo Regency (see Figure 43). Archaeological reports from the nineteenth and twentieth centuries list a number of significant discoveries in this region, among them several stone images displaying Śiwaite attributes, at least three of which originate from Batur.[261] To this day the remains of various ancient structures can be found scattered throughout the surrounding hills, pointing to the former existence of religious communities of the type described in the TP. Among the surviving evidence I note an inscribed rock displaying a chronogram at Wangkal (see Figure 44), a hilltop sanctuary and adjacent *punden* named "Mbah Guru" at Sumergo, as well as the remnants of two foundations known as Telogo Indro and Bujuk Santi in the mountain village of Plaosan.[262]

There are in addition two literary sources which can help to provide a context for these archaeological remains, namely the Calon Arang and the Bujangga Manik. The former specifically mentions the village of Gaḍing as a place passed by the sage Mpu Bharāda on his journey eastward from Lĕmah-tulis to Bali in the eleventh century.[263] Judging by the course followed on this section of the route, to wit Pajarakan – Lesan

259. Curiously, Pigeaud (1960–63, vol. IV, p. 415) failed to comment on this remarkable correspondence, drawing instead a rather unlikely parallel with the *caturbhasma* of DW 78: 7. On the name Kaṇḍawa and its identification with the mythical Khaṇḍawa forest, see Robson (1995), p. 124 (note to DW 50: 3d).

260. Pigeaud (1960–63), vol. IV, pp. 414–15. The word *batur* is generally understood to refer to a stone terrace or foundation, such as the *batur patawuran* (platform for offerings to the demons) of DW 8: 4b, or the *sang hyang batur pājaran* (sacred terrace of the abode of ascetics) mentioned in an inscription from Gubugklakah (note 216 above). Further examples are cited in Zoetmulder (1982), p. 225.

261. Knebel (1904), p. 111; Krom (1916), pp. 426–27.

262. The remains at Sumergo and Plaosan were already reported by J. Hageman (published in Krom 1916, pp. 427, 430–31). For the rock inscription at Wangkal, see Knebel (1904), pp. 111–12.

263. Poerbatjaraka (1926), p. 138.

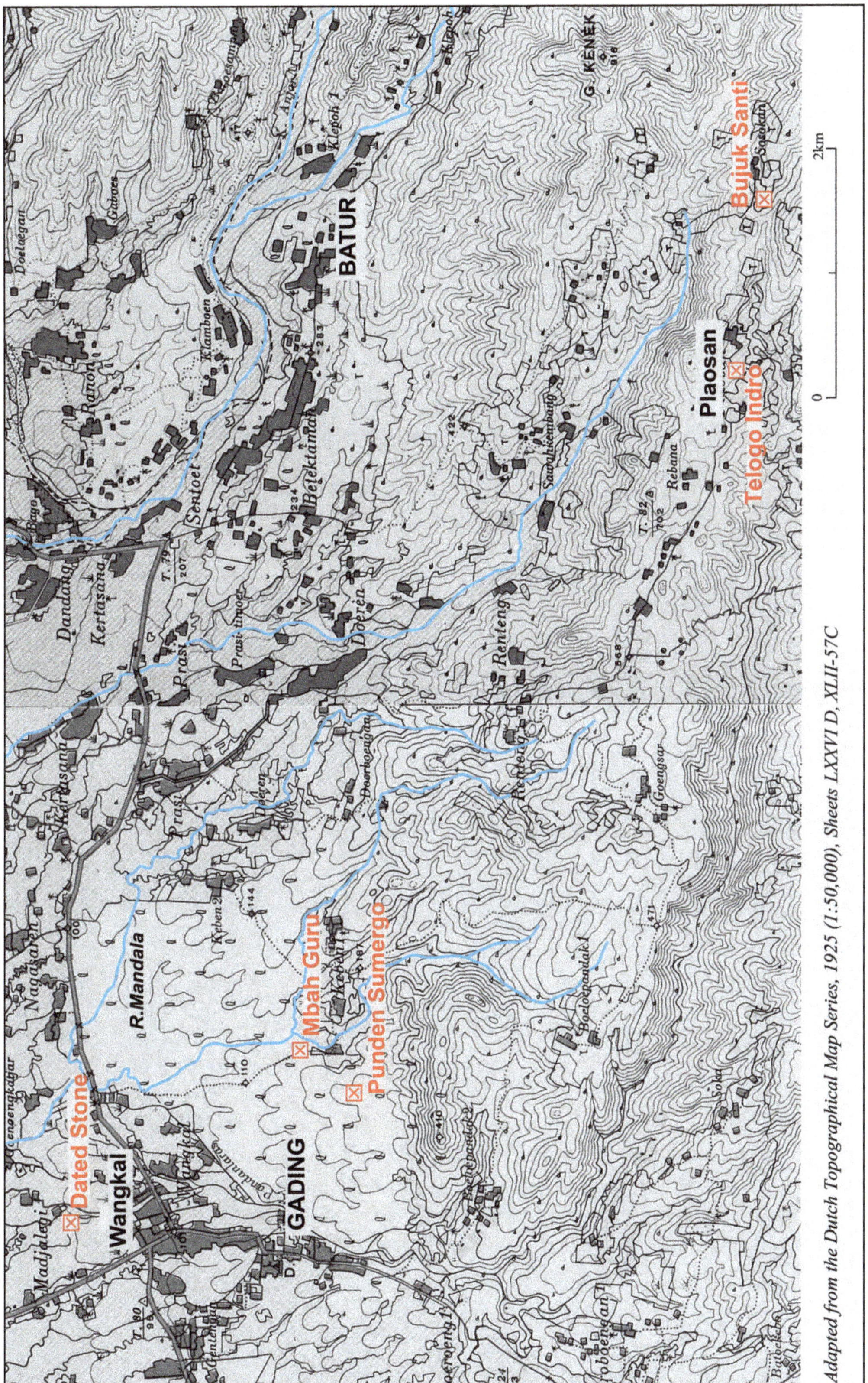

Adapted from the Dutch Topographical Map Series, 1925 (1:50,000), Sheets LXXVI D, XLII-57C

Figure 43 Map showing archaeological sites in the vicinity of Batur (1).
Adapted from: Name: 05120-406, 05120-420; Scale: 1: 50,000; Type: Topographic map; Year: 1926, 1925

Figure 44 Rock inscription at Wangkal (Gading), Probolinggo Regency.
Photo by Hadi Sidomulyo, 2018.

– Sĕkar-rawi – Gaḍing – Momorong,[264] it seems clear that Bharāda made an intentional detour inland, probably for the purpose of visiting a religious community.[265] The same can be said of Bujangga Manik, who on his outward journey turned southeast at Lesan towards the foothills of Mt Hyang, passing through a place named Kaman-kuning on the way.[266]

Batur itself occupies a strategic position at the entrance to two valleys enclosed by steep hills, extending eastward into the heart of the mountain range for about 12 km (see Figure 45). Through these valleys flow two sparkling rivers, the Anyar and

264. Concerning these toponyms, the hamlet of Lesan can still be found on the eastern side of Pajarakan in the village of Rondokuning (district Kraksaan). A place named Sĕkar-rawi is no longer known, but it probably lay close to present day Krejengan, between Lesan and Gading (for a discussion of Sĕkar-rawi and its connection with the Kambang-rawi of DW 31: 5, see Sidomulyo 2007, p. 70, note 136). As to Momorong, this name can be recognized in the settlement of Morong at Triwungan (district Kotaanyar). For precise locations, see the BAKOSURTANAL map series Peta Rupabumi Digital Indonesia (1: 25,000), Sheets 1608-224 (Kraksaan) and 1608-331 (Paiton).

265. The existence of a river named Mandala on the eastern side of Gading adds strength to this argument.

266. Noorduyn and Teeuw (2006), p. 259 (BM 832–834). Identifiable with present Kamalkuning in the district of Krejengan.

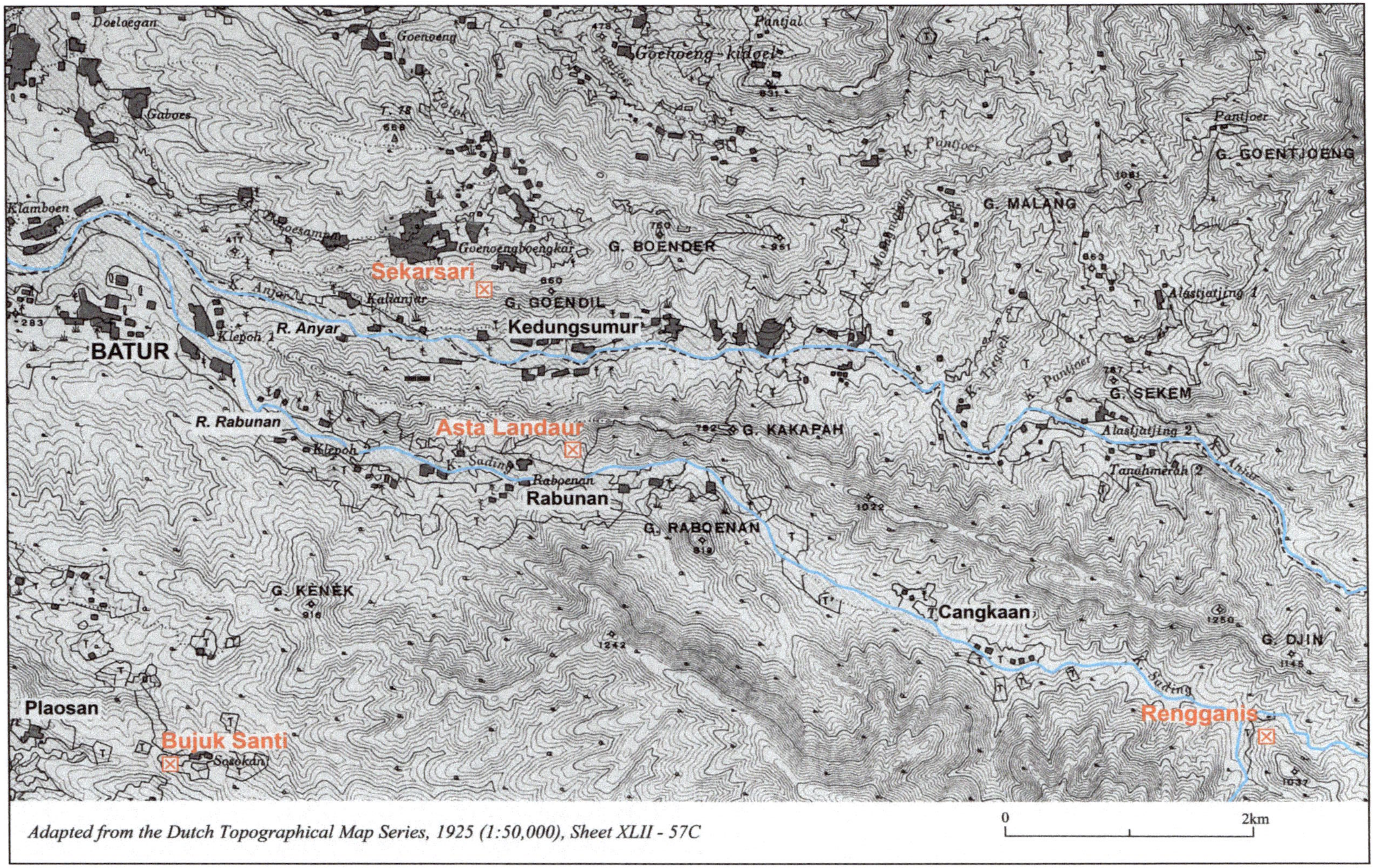

Figure 45 Map showing archaeological sites in the vicinity of Batur (2).
Adapted from: Name: 05120-420; Scale: 1: 50,000; Type: Topographic map; Year: 1925

the Rabunan, which follow a parallel course before converging on the north side of the village. Further substantial archaeological remains are to be found nearby, notably in the hamlets of Kedungsumur and Rabunan. The former is located on the banks of the river Anyar, ± 3 km east of Batur. Here, on the mountain ridge named Gundil, can be found the remains of an ancient hermitage, together with a series of natural caves (see Figure 46).

Known locally as Sekarsari, this place was first mentioned in the 1860s by Hageman, who observed a seated statuette identified as a "Recoguru" image.[267] Four decades later, Knebel described an *offerplaats*, where he encountered a four-armed male statue.[268] Although both images have long since disappeared, an impressive *makāra* spout was unearthed some years ago near a water source located below the caves, suggesting the presence of a sacred structure (see Figure 47).[269] Taken together, these discoveries would seem to provide sufficient reason to consider a connection with one of the *maṇḍala* referred to in the TP.[270]

Today the mountain sanctuary of Sekarsari continues to function as a hermitage under the management of a resident caretaker, whose forbears are said to have occupied the site for several generations.[271] These newcomers, however, can hardly claim to be the guardians of an unbroken tradition. Massive displacement of the native population in the seventeenth and eighteenth centuries, along with a steady influx of Madurese settlers to the region, have helped to sever all ties with the earlier period. The legacy of Ki Kabhayan-panglayar has, in turn, been replaced by myths of more recent origin, notably those surrounding the figure of Dewi Rengganis.[272]

267. Krom (1916), p. 427.
268. Knebel (1904), p. 108.
269. This item is now preserved at Sekarsari.
270. In support of this argument I draw attention to a Dutch topographical map of the Probolinggo area dating from 1885 (scale 1: 100,000), where the mountain above Kedungsumur is clearly labelled Petapan (= hermitage).
271. The graves of these former inhabitants can be found beside the path leading to the principal dwelling, which consists of a wooden structure perched on a ledge below the cliff face. Further down the hill, to the north, lies the site of Asta Jamar, dedicated to the memory of an eighteenth century Madurese pioneer.
272. According to local tradition, Rengganis was a female anchorite who subsisted on the nectar of flowers and had the ability to fly. To this day she is believed to reign over an invisible kingdom from a palace on the summit of Mt Argopura (3,088 m), highest peak in the Hyang Massif. The legend of Dewi Rengganis is generally regarded as belonging to a literary genre of the sixteenth century, which includes the Amir Hamzah cycle and the stories of Pañji. Variations are known in West Java, as well as on the island of Lombok. The Rengganis legend is further popular among the Madurese community, which might be a reason for its pervasive influence in the far eastern regions of Java (cf. Wirjo Asmoro 1926, p. 259; Sosrodanoekoesoemo 1927, p. 166).

Figure 46 Series of natural caves at the hermitage of Sekarsari (Batur), Probolinggo Regency. *Photo by Hadi Sidomulyo, 2018.*

Figure 47 *Makāra* spout at Sekarsari.
Photo by Hadi Sidomulyo, 2018.

Nonetheless, there still remains a curious piece of evidence at Sekarsari, which invites speculation. During an initial field investigation in 2006, my attention was directed to a mysterious stone, apparently connected with certain rituals once performed at the hermitage. Whether or not this object represented the *offerplaats* referred to by Knebel was, unfortunately, impossible to verify, as it had been intentionally concealed beneath a smooth layer of tiles and cement. Whatever the case, it is tempting to consider a connection with the stone named Ubhusan, described in the TP as a central feature of the *maṇḍala* at Waśaṇa.

Turning now to the southern valley, substantial remains exist on a hillside above the hamlet of Rabunan, 4 km east of Batur.[273] Here, at the site known as Asta Landaur,[274] can be found an extensive network of pathways, walled terraces and standing stones (menhirs) of varying size, some arranged in formation, giving the impression of a former religious settlement (see Figures 48 and 49). Although in archaeological parlance these remains might well be termed megalithic, the possibility that they represent one of the *maṇḍala* mentioned in the TP should not be ruled out. After all, the fact that Ki Kabhayan-panglayar needed to vanquish the demonic guardians (*rākṣasa*) at Talun and Waśaṇa with yoga and *samāḍi* suggests that he founded these *maṇḍala* communities on pre-existing settlements adhering to an animistic tradition.[275] The transformation of the site at Rabunan could thus be viewed as yet another permutation of the merging of Hindu-Buddhist and ancient Javanese beliefs, as observed earlier at the terraced sanctuary of Wadung Prabhu in the Tengger region.

Access through the valley to the east of Rabunan is limited to a footpath which ascends gradually, following the course of the river. During our brief survey of the region in November 2018, local inhabitants pointed out a second complex of terraces reinforced with walls of unworked stone, identified as a "resting place" of the legendary Dewi Rengganis. This site is located near the former hamlet of Cangkaan, from where the Batur copper plates and other assorted items were reportedly recovered in 1915.[276] It turns out, however, that the precise find spot of the inscription lies still further up

273. To my knowledge, this important site has not yet come to the attention of the scientific community.

274. The term *asta* is used by the Madurese to denote the site of a revered ancestor.

275. We are reminded here of the popular legends surrounding some of the early Muslim proselytizers in Java, who displayed their superior skills by engaging in mystical combat with the guardians of sacred sites. A good example is to be found in Budiman (1978), pp. 133–35.

276. The settlement of Cangkaan no longer exists, having been abandoned in the years before World War II. Early Dutch topographical maps place it on the north side of the river, ± 3 km to the east of Rabunan. For details of the archaeological discoveries, see note 257 above.

Figure 48 Entrance to the site of Asta Landaur at Rabunan (Batur), Probolinggo Regency.
Photo by Hadi Sidomulyo, 2018.

Figure 49 A group of menhirs at Asta Landaur.
Photo by Hadi Sidomulyo, 2018.

the river in an elevated tract of forest known today as Alas Persilan.[277] Unfortunately, both time and weather conditions have not yet permitted direct observation in the field, but according to villagers at Rabunan the place has yielded a number of antiquities in recent years, among them a stone image and at least one large earthenware jar (*guci*).

To recapitulate, the principal aim of the above discussion has been to determine the locations of the trio of *maṇḍala* established by Ki Kabhayan-panglayar on Mt Hyang, namely Talun, Waśaṇa and Sāgara. In order to achieve this purpose, we have consulted a number of textual sources, as well as examined the archaeological record for the region in question. These combined data direct our attention to two specific areas on the northern side of the Hyang Massif, each of which requires closer investigation. The first is the saddle of the mountains Hyang and Lemongan, to the south of Pajarakan, while the second is situated further east in the district of Gading.

Concerning the origin of the *maṇḍala* named Sāgara, the TP describes a renowned cemetery on a hilltop (*arga*) known as Kalyasěm, where people from the regions north and east of the mountain came to conduct funerary rites.[278] The place subsequently became the centre of a cult of Bhairawa, inhabited successively by the sages Mahāmpu Palyat and Mpu Barang. Their legacy, in turn, passed to the figure known as Ki Kabhayan-panglayar, who transformed the site into the Sāgara *maṇḍala*. It is noteworthy that the close relationship between Sāgara and the sacred ancestral seat at Kalyasěm is unequivocally confirmed in the fourteenth century charter of Batur.

From Prapañca's detailed account of the royal visit to Sāgara in 1359, we can be quite confident that the place described in the Deśawarṇana was located near present day Ranu Segaran at Tiris (Probolinggo). It is nonetheless curious that the poet consistently describes Sāgara as a forest hermitage (*wanāśrama*), rather than a *maṇḍala*, and even more so when in one instance a *maṇḍala* at Gěḍe is mentioned in the same stanza.[279] This makes it difficult to argue that the poet's choice of terminology was prompted solely by metrical considerations. In short, we have reason to doubt that the community visited by king Rājasanagara was the *maṇḍala* of Sāgara described in the TP.

277. This is presumably the modern rendering of the name "Gunung Perceel", mentioned in the 1915 report by Bosch (1915b, p. 105).

278. Part 1, p. 53.

279. DW 32: 2a–c. Robson translates as follows:

> When the King departed to go on, it was the forest hermitage [*wanāśrama*] of Sāgara that he headed for;
> His way southward was steep, passing through the riverbed of Buluh,
> As well as the religious community [*maṇḍala*] of Gěḍe, and soon after he betook himself to Sāgara …

As already noted, Prapañca refers to Sāgara on another occasion in the Deśawarṇana, listing it among the four *maṇḍala* known as *caturbhasma*. In the course of time these revered institutions doubtless found reason to establish additional centres in different parts of the country. This was certainly true for the Kasturi order, which appears to have had numerous affiliates. The *wanāśrama* visited by king Rājasanagara could thus have represented a regional branch of the Sāgara lineage,[280] while the ancestral seat at Kalyasĕm, site of the original *maṇḍala*, was located somewhere else on Mt Hyang. As to precisely where, an obvious choice would be the district of Gading, perhaps near the discovery site of the Batur inscription. Not only is this region especially rich in archaeological remains, but its strategic position and rugged topography agree more closely with the description in the TP.

The same argument holds good for the *maṇḍala* of Talun and Waśaṇa, each of which is quite possibly identifiable with one of the sites discussed above. Regrettably, we have been unable to make use of a valuable clue to the position of Talun. As will be recalled, Ki Kabhayan-panglayar established his first *maṇḍala* on land granted to him by the village elders of Bĕsar, a toponym which unfortunately remains elusive.

At this point the discussion must come to an end, as we have exhausted the available data. Despite the temptation to speculate further it is clearly wiser to be patient, while awaiting new discoveries in the fields of archaeology and epigraphy, as well as the publication of hitherto unstudied texts.

Further historical and topographical aspects

Throughout section III of the present commentary, the "historical" events of the TP have been viewed principally against the backdrop of the kingdom of Kaḍiri in the twelfth and early thirteenth centuries. This image becomes clearer when we observe the parallels existing between the TP and the text of the Pararaton, the early part of which is set in almost precisely the same period. Linguistic similarities aside, the narrative content of these two literary works can be seen to overlap, suggesting a shared body of tradition. Clear evidence of this is provided in the opening sections of the Pararaton, where the early life of the hero Ken Angrok is portrayed in the environment of ascetic communities and *maṇḍala* which are also described in the TP (see Figure 50).[281]

---

280. Another representative might have been the place named Sagara Dalĕm, located in the region of Malang and mentioned in the Bujangga Manik (line 1047). Cf. Noorduyn and Teeuw (2006), pp. 263, 452–53.

281. Brandes (1920), pp. 3–20.

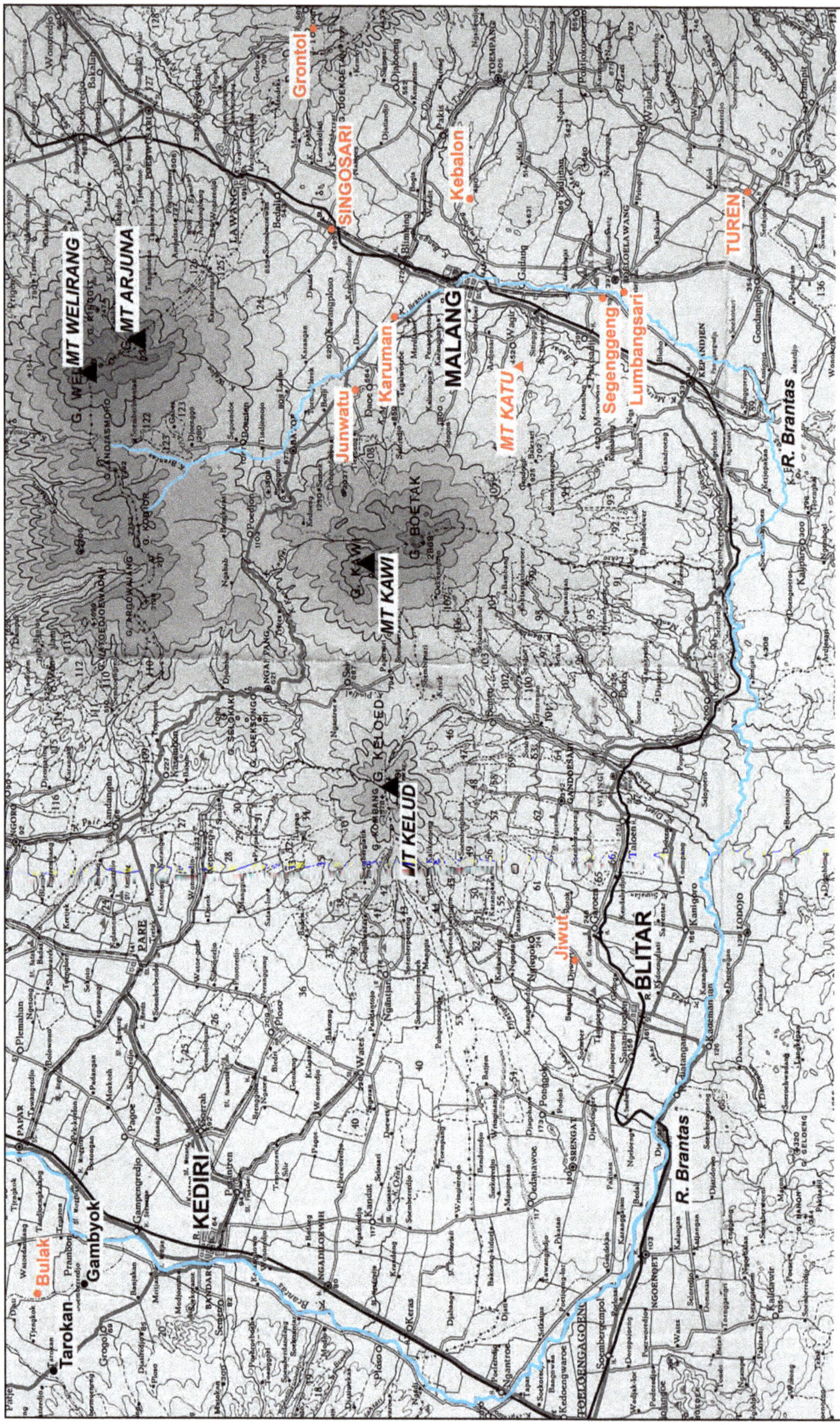

Adapted from the Dutch Topographical Map Series, 1929 (1: 250,000), Ja-a en Madoera, Sheet IX

0 20km

Figure 50 Map showing geographical locations referred to in the Pararaton.
Adapted from: Name: 05270-09; Scale: 1: 250,000; Type. Topographic map; Year: 1929

As will be recalled, the text of the Pararaton opens with the description of a wayward youth, son of a widow from Jiput,[282] who took refuge with the sage Mpu Tapa-wangkĕng at Bhulalak. Upon hearing that the holy man's hermitage could not be completed without a sacrifice to the guardian spirit of the gateway, the young visitor offered himself as victim in return for an elevated rebirth on the eastern side of Mt Kawi. Mpu Tapa-wangkĕng accepted the proposal and the youth was duly sacrificed, thereby securing his destiny as the future king of Java.

The figure of Mpu Tapa-wangkĕng features prominently in the TP. Together with his colleague Tapa-palet, he was a foremost disciple of Mpu Barang, founder of the first Kasturi *maṇḍala* at Tūryan. Mpu Tapa-wangkĕng had for many years served at the court of Daha, both before and after his ordination as a *wiku*. It is said that he eventually retired to open his own *maṇḍala* at Bhulalak.[283] Although the precise location of this establishment remains uncertain, it is noteworthy that the toponym Bulak is not uncommon in the present regency of Kediri. The fact that the TP describes the *maṇḍala* as lying "by the side of the road", where "people passed by", allows a tentative identification with the present hamlet of Bulak in the district of Tarokan, which lies 20 km north of Kediri and not far from the well known archaeological remains at Gambyok.[284]

Returning now to the Pararaton, through the intervention of the sage Tapa-wangkĕng, the youth from Jiput was reborn as Ken Angrok on the eastern side of Mt Kawi, a result of the union of the god Brahmā and a woman from Pangkur[285] named Ken Ĕndok. Abandoned in a graveyard shortly after his birth and subsequently adopted by a thief, the young Ken Angrok later spent some time with the family of a renowned gambler named Bango-samparan at Karuman,[286] before finally settling at Sagĕnggĕng,[287] where he studied literature and learned the rudiments of the Old Javanese calendar.

282. Quite possibly to be identified with the present village of Jiwut in the district of Nglegok (Blitar Regency), not far south of the famous temple complex named Candi Panataran.

283. Part 1, pp. 60–61.

284. This ancient site features a relief panel depicting the legendary hero Pañji, discussed by both Stutterheim (1935, pp. 139–43) and Poerbatjaraka (1968, pp. 406–8), and more recently by Kieven (2013, pp. 66–72). Further archaeological discoveries in the vicinity include a stone image of Parwatī at Tarokan, reported by Stutterheim (1936, p. 14).

285. Position uncertain, but probably not far from Kepanjen in the southern part of the regency of Malang.

286. A settlement named Karuman can still be found at Tlogomas (Lowokwaru), on the northwestern outskirts of the city of Malang, where archaeological remains are preserved at the village *punden* (sacred site).

287. Identifiable today with the hamlet of Segenggeng at Wonokerso (district Pakisaji), about 8 km south of the city of Malang on the western bank of the river Brantas.

Upon entering adulthood, Angrok's exceptional abilities and supernatural power became plainly manifest, coupled with increasingly antisocial behaviour. This came to the attention of the ruler at Daha, who sent orders to Tunggul Amĕtung, the local ruler at Tumapĕl, to get rid of the troublemaker. As a consequence, Ken Angrok was forced to flee from Sagĕnggĕng and seek refuge with one ascetic community after another.[288] He finally gained a respite at Lulumbang, where he befriended Mpu Palot, spiritual head of the *maṇḍala* at Tūryan. Mpu Palot was on his way home from Kabalon, and happened to be transporting a large amount of gold. Ken Angrok offered to protect him on his journey and in return was adopted as a son and pupil of the *dewaguru*, who imparted to him the secrets of the goldsmith's art. It was not long before Ken Angrok's skill matched that of his teacher.

Here, once again, we find a parallel in the TP, where the founder of the *maṇḍala* at Tūryan, Mpu Barang, is said to have overseen the creation of a golden image of Wiṣṇu, carved by his disciples Tapa-wangkĕng and Tapa-palet. Although admittedly no more than conjecture, the possibility that Mpu Tapa-palet succeeded Mpu Barang as *dewaguru* at Tūryan is quite plausible, since the TP informs us that the latter "left the *maṇḍala* of Bapa (Tūryan) and took himself to the west", where he subsequently founded a second *maṇḍala* at Ḍupaka (see Figure 51).[289] This allows us to connect Mpu Tapa-palet with the figure named Mpu Palot in the Pararaton.

As to the positions of Kabalon and Lulumbang, if it is accepted that the former is identifiable with the hamlet of Kebalon at Cemorokandang (Kedungkandang), on the eastern side of the city of Malang, it follows that Lulumbang was in all probability

---

288. Among the places which are still identifiable, we can mention the *maṇḍala* at Junwatu, described as a place of the "enlightened ones" (*wong sampūrṇa*). There is still a settlement named Junwatu in the district of Junrejo, a hill region to the northwest of the city of Malang. The profusion of archaeological remains in the vicinity supports an identification with the place described in the Pararaton. Another place, named *rabut* (sacred) Katu, clearly refers to present day Mt Katu at Wagir, 8 km southwest of Malang. Local tradition acknowledges this hill as the "grave site" of Ken Angrok. Legend aside, the location of the holy *dharma* at Kagĕnĕngan was in all probability located nearby (cf. Bosch 1923, pp. 85–86). Lastly, it seems quite possible that the place named *rabut* Gorontol is identifiable today with the hamlet of Grontol at Tlogosari (Tutur, Pasuruan), to the east of Singosari.

289. Possibly identifiable with the present settlement of Dupak at Ngadirejo (Kawedenan), Magetan, where a stone pillar dated Śaka 1379 (?) can still be found (Knebel 1905–6, p. 59; Nastiti and Suhadi 1996, p. 32). See Figure 38 above.

Figure 51 Dated stone pillar at Dupak (Kawedenan), Magetan Regency.
Photo by Hadi Sidomulyo, 2019.

located at present day Lumbangsari in the district of Bululawang, which lies on the road leading southward to Turen, across the river from Segenggeng.[290]

While perhaps not leading us much further towards solving the mystery of the identity of Ken Angrok himself, the data presented above at least help to bring the landscape, both historical and geographical, into clearer perspective. Taken together, the texts of the TP and Pararaton give the impression that the area comprising the present regency of Malang, in the past known simply as "the land to the east of Mt Kawi" (*bhūmi wetan ing Kawi*), was formerly a renowned spiritual centre. Since at least the age of Pu Siṇḍok, the sacred sites of Himad, Walaṇḍit and Pangawān had served as channels of communication with the holy mountain Brahmā in the Tengger

290. In this connection it is worth drawing attention to the stele of Muñcang, which dates from the reign of Pu Siṇḍok (Krom 1913a, OJO 51). The *sīma* territory marked out in the inscription is said to have shared a boundary with Lumbang-lumbang and Sa(*ng*)tingging (8–10 *recto*), which is perhaps a misreading of Sagĕnggĕng. If so, this not only establishes the location of the original site of Muñcang, but allows us to conclude that the Lulumbang of the Pararaton is an abbreviated form of Lumbang-lumbang.

highlands. Later, when the kings of Kaḍiri reigned supreme, the region of Malang was apparently dotted with numerous religious establishments, classed under various headings such as *patapan*, *maṇḍala*, *rabut* and *kabuyutan*. The famed *maṇḍala* of Kukub on the Mahāmeru, as well as that of Kasturi at Tūryan, probably exerted a strong influence on the local population.

Moving on to the early years of the thirteenth century, the text of the Pararaton portrays the rise to power of Ken Angrok against the backdrop of the ascetic communities in the countryside. These revered establishments doubtless helped to legitimize the founding of the Rājasa dynasty by drawing the sympathy of the religious leaders at Daha, who were becoming increasingly disenchanted with the decadence at the royal court.[291] At the same time they provided a firm doctrinal base for the future rulers at Singhasāri and Majapahit.

Afterword

By way of conclusion, it would seem pertinent to say a few words about the native Tenggerese, who have for centuries inhabited the highland region dominated by the mountains Bromo and Semeru.[292] Considering that the majority of the Tengger community still adhere to the old Hindu-Javanese religion, and further claim close ties with the former kingdom of Majapahit, one would expect them to be familiar with at least a few of the myths preserved in the TP. Such, however, does not appear to be the case. On the contrary, the evidence suggests that, at least since the eighteenth century, the Tenggerese have for the most part come to embrace the popular "historical tradition" of a later age. The influence of Islam, and more recently the move towards a closer affiliation with neighbouring Hindu Bali, have further helped to obscure any direct links with the distant past.

This is not to say, however, that the connection has been severed entirely. A glance at some of the ritual items employed by the Tengger *dukun*, namely shirt (*baju*), ritual sash (*sampĕt*), bell (*gĕnta*) and "zodiac beaker" (*prasen*), is sufficient to recall the official insignia of the *dewaguru*, i.e. headdress (*singhĕl*), jacket (*kalambi*), earrings (*kuṇḍala*), headband (*badḍa*) and parasol (*payung*). In short, the symbols remain, but their former significance is no longer understood. A closer study of these isolated threads of continuity, preserved for posterity in the Tengger highlands, might yet lead to a deeper understanding of the spiritual legacy concealed in the text of the Old Javanese Tantu Panggĕlaran (see Figures 52–56).

291. The Pararaton alludes to the arrogance of the Kaḍiri king Dandang-gĕndis (Kṛtajaya), who openly flaunted his spiritual powers in front of his court priests, demanding their obeisance.

292. For a useful introduction to Tengger tradition and culture, see Hefner (1985).

Figure 52 Ritual bell (*gĕnta*), possession of *dukun* Misari at Pakel (Gucialit), Lumajang Regency. *Photo by Hadi Sidomulyo, 2018.*

Figure 53 Ritual sash (*sampĕt*), bell (*gĕnta*) and a "zodiac beaker" (*prasen*) dated Śaka 1261 (AD 1339), possession of *dukun* Harjo Ta'i at Kandangan, Lumajang Regency. *Photo by Hadi Sidomulyo, 2018.*

Figure 54 Sūrya symbol on the base of a *prasen* dated Śaka 1250 (AD 1328), possession of *dukun* Misari at Pakel (Gucialit), Lumajang Regency. *Photo by Hadi Sidomulyo, 2018.*

Figure 55 *Unan-unan* procession at the Tengger village of Ledokombo (Sumber), Probolinggo Regency.
Photo by Hadi Sidomulyo, 2018.

Figure 56 Senior *dukun* at Ledokombo presiding over the *Unan-unan* ceremony, performed every five years.
Photo by Hadi Sidomulyo, 2018.

APPENDIX 1

Notes on names and titles occurring in the text

Aḍidarwa	Variant Aḍiparwa. The name of a book (*puṣṭaka*), left behind at the hermitage of Kalyasĕm by Mpu Barang, subsequently acknowledged as the sage's spiritual legacy.
Agaṣṭi, Bhagawān	Variant Anggaṣṭi. Lord of Mt Kawi and adopted father of the twins Tṛṇawindu and Anggira. Succeeded Bhagawān Mārkaṇḍeya as *dewaguru* of the *maṇḍala* Sukayajña.
Agni, Hyang	God of fire.
Amanguyu-guntung	A name of Bhaṭāra Guru (?) as a *manguyu* ascetic. See also Pamanguyon-agung.
Analaga, Bhaṭāra Hyang	A name of Bhaṭāra Guru.
Anaman	The name of a *maṇḍala* founded by the *wiku* Buyut Arĕng. See also Andrala, Jun-maṇik, Kĕpuh-rĕbah.
Anantabhoga, Sang Hyang	Divine serpent, foundation of the earth.
Aṇḍawar	The name of a *maṇḍala* founded by Ki Kabhayan-panglayar. Located on thc saddle of the mountains Mahāmeru and Brahmā.
Andrala	The name of a *maṇḍala* founded by the *wiku* Buyut Arĕng. See also Anaman, Jun-maṇik, Kĕpuh-rĕbah.
Anggang-anggang, *gunung*	The remnants of Mt Gaḍa-wĕsi.
Anggara	Tuesday, the seventh *wiku* ordained by Bhaṭāra Guru. See also Budḍa, Raditya, Saneścara, Soma, Śukra, Wṛhaspati (days of the week).
Anggaṣṭi, Hyang	Guardian of the southern "opening" of the Mahāmeru at Paḍang. See also Agaṣṭi.
Anggira, Bhagawān	One of the twins born to the princess Śrī Wīratanu of Daha, later adopted by Bhagawān Agaṣṭi. See also Tṛṇawindu.

Anggirah	Variant Anggarah. A hermitage established by the sages Mpu Barang and Mpu Waluh-bang. See also Girah.
Anungkāla	One of two demons (*rākṣasa*) who emerged from the ashes of a trinity of Kāla on Mt Wihanggamaya, becoming guardians of the western "opening" of the Mahāmeru at Pangawān. See also Kāla, Pañātūr-mukā.
Anungkurāt, Bhaṭāra	A name of Bhaṭāra Guru.
Arĕng, Buyut	Formerly a butcher named Dṛwyānak, Buyut Arĕng became a *wiku* through the mediation of a black dog from the *maṇḍala* of Ḍingḍing. He later founded the sect known as Kasturi Arĕng. See also Anaman, Andrala, Jun-maṇik, Kĕpuh-rĕbah.
Arga-kleṣa	Variant Arga Kelaśa. Name of the hermitage of Buyut Jala-Giri on Mt Wĕlahulu. See also Kajar, Tĕnggĕk.
Arga-maṇik	The name of a *maṇḍala* on Mt Kawi, founded by the *wiku* Buyut Gĕnting. See also Bhamana, Brajahning, Gumantar, Jangkanang.
Arga-tilas	A *maṇḍala* propagating the spiritual legacy of Ḍingḍing. Founded by a palm-wine tapper turned *wiku* named Buyut Lĕsung-burut. See also Jawa, Lulumpang-burut, Rĕbhālas.
Aribhāṇa	Variant Karibawana. A *maṇḍala* of the Sukayajña order, located at the foot of Mt Wilis (East Java). Founded by a butcher named Suka. See also Bhāṇa, Jiwaṇa, Talutug.
Arjuna, *gunung*	One of the mountains formed from the earth which fell from the Mahāmeru in the course of its journey from Jambuḍipa. Identifiable with present day Mt Arjuna in eastern Java.
Aśoṣṭi, Bhagawān	The name given to the brahmin Ḍang Hyang Kacuṇḍa, following ordination at the *maṇḍala* of Kukub. See also Labdawara.

Astitijāti	A manifestation of Bhaṭāra Guru.
Bakal, Ki	The name given to *wiku* awaiting ordination from Ki Kabhayan-panglayar. See also Aṇḍawar.
Bakar	Variant Byakar. A place passed by Ki Kabhayan-panglayar on his journey to Kukub. See also Cangcangan, Duk, Kuḍampilan, Pacelengan, Payaman, Ragḍang, Tambangan, Untehan.
Bañcak, *gunung*	A mountain connected with the story of the widow Rāga-runting and the merchant Parijñana. Identifiable with present day Mt Bancak in the East Javanese regency of Magetan. See also Mĕḍang-tañjung.
Bapa	First *maṇḍala* of the Kasturi order, founded by the sages Mpu Barang and Mpu Waluh-bang at Tūryan.
Barang, Mpu	The Śaiwa emanation of the *bhujangga* Mahāmpu Palyat and joint founder of the first *maṇḍala* of the Kasturi order at Bapa. See also Waluh-bang.
Baruṇa	One of the four World Guardians (*caturlokapāla*).
Bāyu, Hyang	God of the wind.
Bĕsar	A village near the *maṇḍala* of Talun, on the northern slope of the Hyang Massif in eastern Java.
Bhamana	The name of a *maṇḍala* on Mt Kawi, founded by the *wiku* Buyut Gĕnting. See also Arga-maṇik, Brajahning, Gumantar, Jangkanang.
Bhāṇa	A *maṇḍala* of the Sukayajña order, located at the foot of Mt Wilis in eastern Java. Founded by a butcher named Suka. See also Aribhāṇa, Jiwaṇa, Talutug.
Bhatati, Mahārāja	Variant Tati. King of Galuh.
Bhairawa	Variant Bherawa. A Śiwaite sect (*pakṣa*), promulgated by the sages Mahāmpu Palyat and Mpu Barang.
Bhujangga	A name given to Kumāra-siddḍi, a son of the goddess Umā.

Bhulalak	A *maṇḍala* of the Kasturi order, founded by Mpu Tapa-wangkĕng. See also Botahi, Samĕgĕt-bagañjing.
Boddḍa	The Buddhist sect (*pakṣa*), and a name of Mpu Kumāra-raray, youngest son of the goddess Umā and Kumāra-gohphala. See also Sogata.
Botahi, Kaki	A name of Mpu Tapa-wangkĕng, founder of the Kasturi *maṇḍala* at Bhulalak. See also Samĕgĕt-bagañjing.
Brahmā, Bhaṭāra	Second of the divine Trinity of Lords (*trisamaya*), along with Iśwara and Wiṣṇu.
Brahmā, *gunung*	Mt Bromo, one of eastern Java's active volcanos.
Brahmāloka	The realm of Brahmā, highest level of creation according to Hindu conception.
Brajahning	Variant Mrājahning. The name of a *maṇḍala* on Mt Kawi, founded by the *wiku* Buyut Gĕnting. See also Arga-maṇik, Bhamana, Gumantar, Jangkanang.
Bret, *gunung*	The place where the goddess Umā emerged from the underworld following a period of penance. Identifiable with the hill named Bret in the district of Singosari (Malang), East Java.
Bṛnggiriṣṭi	Demonic manifestation (*wil*) of the god Kumāra, son of the goddess Umā.
Bubukṣa, Sang	One of two sons born to Mpu Siddḍayoga and Dewi Kasingi. See also Gagang-aking, Siddḍayogi, Tĕkĕn-wuwung.
Budḍa	Wednesday, the third *wiku* ordained by Bhaṭāra Guru. See also Anggara, Raditya, Saneścara, Soma, Śukra, Wṛhaspati (days of the week).
Bugoleng	A *walyan* in the service of king Uṇḍal of Daha. See also Lĕsung-burut, Lulumpang-burut.
Bulon	The first *katyāgan* (hermitage) of the *caturāśrama*, established by Bhaṭāra Guru. See also Huluwanwa, Kupang, Pacira.

Burukah, *gunung*	Variant Bareka. A mountain associated with the sage Bhagawān Anggira.
Cakrawarti, Mahārāja	King of Jambuḍipa (The Indian subcontinent).
Calakuṇḍa	A discus (*cakra*) wielded by Bhaṭāra Wiṣṇu in his effort to defeat the sage Siddḍawangsitadewa. See also Rĕbhawinuk, Tarĕnggabāhu.
Cañcurāja, Tuhan	A prince of Galuh. See also Śrī-manggala.
Cangcangan	Variant Tarawang. A place passed by Ki Kabhayan-panglayar on his journey to Kukub. See also Bakar, Duk, Kuḍampilan, Pacelengan, Payaman, Ragḍang, Tambangan, Untehan.
Cĕmpa	The kingdom ruled over by the wife of king Taki, following her forced departure from the palace at Daha.
Cintamaṇi	Variant Cintamaṇik. One of the offspring of the goddess Umā and Kumāra-gohphala.
Ciptagupta, Bhagawān	The divine sage responsible for introducing the visual arts to Java. See also Ciptangkara.
Ciptangkara, Mpu	The name adopted by Bhagawān Ciptagupta during his earthly incarnation.
Daha	Capital of the kingdom of Kaḍiri in eastern Java.
Damalung	The name of a legendary wild boar, associated with Mt Merbabu in central Java. See also Mawulusan, Pamrihan.
Ḍarmarāja, Bhaṭāra	An emanation of Bhaṭāra Guru as the supreme ascetic, incarnated in the sages Siddḍawangsitadewa, Taruṇa-tapa-yowana and Ḍarmahūtpṭi.
Ḍarma-ūtpṭi, Sang Ṛṣi	See Ḍarmarāja.
Dewaputra	A manifestation of Bhaṭāra Guru in the form of a handsome prince.
Dewata-kaki	The name of a deity bound to earth. See also Swarga.

Ḍihyang	Variant Wihyang. The place where Bhaṭāra Guru first performed yoga, identifiable with the Dieng Plateau in central Java.
Ḍingḍing	The place where the goddess Umā washed her menstrual cloths, later a *maṇḍala* founded by Aji Uṇḍal of Daha. See also Ranupuhan, Ulu-kĕmbang-pakalpan.
Ḍingḍing-Manuñjang	A *maṇḍala* under the leadership of Ki Buyut Samaḍi. See also Manuñjang.
Dṛĕwyānak	The former name of Buyut Arĕng.
Duk	A place passed by Ki Kabhayan-panglayar on his journey to Kukub. Identifiable with the mountain Duk at Cepoko (Sumber), Probolinggo Regency. See also Bakar, Cangcangan, Kuḍampilan, Pacelengan, Payaman, Ragḍang, Tambangan, Untehan.
Ḍupaka	The first *maṇḍala* to represent the Tyāga branch of the Bhairawa sect, founded by the sage Mpu Barang.
Durgādewī, Bhaṭārī	The demonic form adopted by the goddess Umā during her period of penance.
Gaḍa	A weapon granted by Bhaṭārī Umā to a monkey (*lutung*), one of the goddess's children by Kumāra-gohphala.
Gaḍa-wĕsi, *gunung*	A mountain situated in the vicinity of Kampud (Kelud), to the west of Mt Mahāmeru. See also Anggang-anggang.
Gagang-aking, Sang	One of two sons born to Mpu Siddayoga and Dewi Kasingi. See also Bubukṣa, Siddayogi, Tĕkĕn-wuwung.
Galuh	The kingdom ruled over by Mahārāja Bhatati, identifiable with Kaḍiri. See also Daha.
Gaṇa, Sang Hyang	A son of Bhaṭāra Guru and the goddess Umā.
Ganḍamaḍana, *gunung*	A name of Mt Mahāmeru.

Gantĕn	A village guarding the northern access to the holy Mahāmeru, in the charge of Bhaṭārī Ghorī. One of the Pañātūr-mukā.
Garga	One of a group of five deities (*dewata*), along with Kuśika, Metri, Kuruṣya and Patañjala.
Gĕgĕr-katyāgan	The name of one of Bhaṭāra Guru's hermitages on the Mahāmeru.
Gĕnting, Buyut	The name given to an actor (*widu*), following ordination as a *wiku* of the Kasturi order. Founder of several *maṇḍala* on the slopes of Mt Kawi. See also Arga-maṇik, Bhamana, Brajahning, Gumantar, Jangkanang.
Gĕrĕsik	The second of three *maṇḍala* created by Bhaṭāra Guru on Mt Mahāmeru, located on the mountain's eastern slope. See also Hahāh, Śūnyasagiri.
Ghorī, Bhaṭārī	Guardian of the northern access to Mt Mahāmeru at Gantĕn. See also Pañātūr-mukā.
Gilingan	The name of a *maṇḍala* on the shore of the southern ocean, founded by Buyut Śrī-manggala. See also Panimbangan, Rājamaṇik, Wungkal-ibĕk.
Girah	Location of the hermitage named Anggirah, established by the sages Mpu Barang and Mpu Waluh-bang.
Giri, Buyut	Title chosen by the *pujut* Tĕnggĕk, a former retainer of Aji Uṇḍal of Daha and a self-appointed *wiku*. See also Jala, Jala-Giri.
Gora, Sang Hyang	A weapon granted by the goddess Umā to "*tabĕ-habĕt*", one of her offspring by Kumāra-gohphala.
Guḍuhā, Sang Hyang	Variant Guruha. A weapon granted by the goddess Umā to Mpu Kumāra-raray, her third son by Kumāra-gohphala. See also Mṛṣa, Trikurungan.
Gulingaṇḍara, *gunung*	A mountain connected in legend with the amorous union of the goddess Umā and Kumāra-gohphala. See also Cintamaṇi.

Gumantar	The name of a *maṇḍala* on Mt Kawi, founded by the *wiku* Buyut Gĕnting. See also Arga-maṇik, Bhamana, Brajahning, Jangkanang.
Guru, Bhaṭāra	The Supreme Lord. See also Analaga, Jagatnātha, Jagatpramāṇa, Jagatwiśeṣa, Mahāguru, Mahākāraṇa, Nandiguru, Nīlakaṇṭa, Parameśwara.
Gurudeśa	A name of the god Iśwara in his role of teacher of village headmen.
Guruh	A *maṇḍala* deriving its name from the thunderous sound (*gumuruh*) of the gods' praises. Probably located near Pekalongan in central Java.
Gutuk, *watu*	The name of a stone (*watu*), said to have been thrown by Ibu-tĕngahan (daughter of Mpu Barang) at her second husband, a religious teacher.
Hahāh	The first of three *maṇḍala* created by Bhaṭāra Guru on Mt Mahāmeru, located on the mountain's southeastern slope. See also Gĕrĕsik, Śūnyasagiri.
Hari, Bhaṭāra	A name of the god Wiṣṇu.
Haricaṇḍana, Bhaṭāra	Uncertain. Apparently a reference to either Śiwa or Wiṣṇu.
Huluwanwa	Variant Luwano. Third *katyāgan* (hermitage) of the *caturāśrama*, established by Bhaṭāra Guru. See also Bulon, Kupang, Pacira.
Hyang, *gunung*	An important ancestral seat. Identifiable with the present Hyang Massif at the far eastern end of Java.
Ibu-tĕngahan	A daughter of the sage Mpu Barang and an incarnation of the goddess Smarī.
Ijo, *gunung*	The name of a mountain of the goddess Umā. Probably identifiable with present day Mt Ijo, to the southwest of Mt Bromo.
Ileru	A place of Bhaṭāra Guru, probably somewhere in central Java.

Indra	One of the four World Guardians (*caturlokapāla*).
Iśwara, Bhaṭāra	The first of the divine Trinity of Lords (*trisamaya*), along with Brahmā and Wiṣṇu.
Itip-ing-lěmbu, *gunung*	A mountain, named after a bull cursed by the goddess Umā to fall to earth. See also Kědyangga.
Jagatnātha, Bhaṭāra	A name of Bhaṭāra Guru.
Jagatpramāṇa, Bhaṭāra	A name of Bhaṭāra Guru.
Jagatwiśeṣa, Bhaṭāra	A name of Bhaṭāra Guru.
Jala, Buyut	The title chosen by the *pujut* Kajar, a former retainer of Aji Uṇḍal of Daha and a self-appointed *wiku*. See also Giri, Jala-Giri.
Jala-Giri, Buyut	The combined title of the self-appointed *wiku*, Kajar and Těnggěk.
Jala-parwata	A mountain, site of a sanctuary (*kahyangan*) and *maṇḍala* established by Bhaṭāra Brahmā. See also Nangka-parwata, Tigāryan-parwata.
Jambuḍipa	The Indian subcontinent.
Janaḍipa, Mpu	The title adopted by Mpu Kalotan following ordination by Mahāmpu Palyat. See also Narajñāna.
Jangkanang	The name of a *maṇḍala* on Mt Kawi, founded by the *wiku* Buyut Gěnting. See also Arga-maṇik, Bhamana, Brajahning, Gumantar.
Jaṭa, *gunung*	A mountain to the east of the *maṇḍala* at Kukub, formed from the twisted hair (*jaṭa*) of Bhaṭāra Guru. Described as the "border" of Tanděs and Mt Maṇik. See also Kampil, Manuñjang.
Jawa, *nūsa*	The island of Java. See also Yawaḍipa.
Jawa	A *maṇḍala* founded by Buyut Lěsung-burut, a former palm wine tapper ordained by the *walyan* Bugoleng. See also Arga-tilas, Rěbhālas.
Jiwaṇa	A *maṇḍala* founded by the butcher named Suka, a follower of Bhagawān Mārkaṇḍeya. See also Aribhāṇa, Bhāṇa, Talutug.

Jun-maṇik	The name of a *maṇḍala* founded by the *wiku* Buyut Arĕng. See also Anaman, Andrala, Kĕpuh-rĕbah.
Kabhayan-panglayar, Ki	A disciple of Bhaṭāra Guru at Kukub. Founder of the *maṇḍala* named Aṇḍawar, as well as the *maṇḍala trisamaya* on Mt Hyang (Sāgara, Talun and Waśaṇa).
Kabyang	A hermitage of Bhaṭārī Umā on Mt Mahāmeru.
Kacuṇḍa, Ḍang Hyang	An Indian brahmin-sage who travelled to Java. Later ordained as Bhagawān Aśoṣṭi.
Kajar, Si	A *pujut* (slave) in the service of Aji Uṇḍal of Daha. Later entitled Buyut Jala following ordination as a *wiku*. See also Bugoleng, Tĕnggĕk.
Kaki-dewata	A name of Bhaṭārī Umā.
Kāla	One of two demons (*rākṣasa*) who emerged from the ashes of a trinity of Kāla on Mt Wihanggamaya, becoming a guardian of the western "opening" of the Mahāmeru at Pangawān. See also Anungkāla, Pañātūr-mukā.
Kālakūṭa	The poisonous water which emerged from Mt Mahāmeru in the course of its journey from Jambuḍipa.
Kālarūdra, Sang Hyang	A terrific form of Bhaṭāra Guru, adopted in anger after cursing his wife Umā to undergo penance as Dūrgādewī.
Kalotan, Mpu	One of two officials (*pangambehan*) in the service of king Bhatati of Galuh. Later known as Mpu Janaḍipa following ordination by Mahāmpu Palyat. See also Waju-kuning.
Kalpataru	The wish-granting tree, a manifestation of Bhaṭārī Umā.
Kalyasĕm	The name of a mountain and cemetery on the northern slope of the Hyang Massif, the hermitage of Mahāmpu Palyat and Mpu Barang. Original site of the *maṇḍala* of Sāgara.

Kāmadewa, Sang Hyang	A son of Bhaṭārī Umā and husband of Bhaṭārī Smarī.
Kamaṇḍalu, Sang Hyang	A jewelled pot containing the holy Śiwāmba, elixir of immortality.
Kambangan, *nūṣa*	Site of a *maṇḍala kabhujanggan* and residence of the sage Mahāmpu Palyat. Probably identifiable with the present day island of Nusa Kambangan, located off the south coast of central Java near Cilacap.
Kampil, *gunung*	A mountain to the east of the *maṇḍala* at Kukub, formed from the twisted hair (*jaṭa*) of Bhaṭāra Guru. See also Jaṭa, Manuñjang.
Kampud, *gunung*	One of the mountains formed from the earth which fell from the Mahāmeru in the course of its journey from Jambuḍipa. Identifiable with present day Mt Kelud in eastern Java.
Kaṇḍayun, Hyangta	A reference to Wṛtti-kaṇḍayun, the youngest son of Rahyang Kaṇḍyawan. See also Turuk-manis.
Kaṇḍyawan, Rahyang	An incarnation of Bhaṭāra Wiṣṇu in the land of Mĕḍang-gaṇa. See also Kanyawan.
Kanyawan, Sang	An incarnation of Bhaṭārī Śrī in the land of Mĕḍang-gaṇa. The wife of Rahyang Kaṇḍyawan.
Kapila	The name of a divine sage (*dewarṣi*). See also Ketu, Nārada, Sapaka, Tumburu, Wiśwakarma.
Karmaṇḍeya, Bhagawān	See Mārkaṇḍeya.
Karung-kalah, Sang	Variant Karukala. The fourth son of Rahyang Kaṇḍyawan at Mĕḍang-gaṇa. See also Katung-malaras, Mangukuhan, Saṇḍang-garbha, Wṛtti-kaṇḍayun.
Karurungan, *gunung*	Variant Karungrangan. A mountain featuring in the story of the widow (*raṇḍa*) Rāga-runting at Mĕḍang-tañjung. Identifiable with Mt Ungaran in central Java.

Kasingi, Dewi	A daughter of the king Wawu-langit of Mĕḍang-gaṇa and wife of Mpu Siddayoga. See also Madumali.
Kasturi	The name of a *maṇḍala* and religious order, founded by the sages Mpu Barang and Mpu Waluh-bang. See also Bapa, Tūryan.
Katiha	Identity uncertain. Apparently a member of the ruling family at Mĕḍang-gaṇa.
Katong, *gunung*	One of the mountains formed from the earth which fell from the Mahāmeru in the course of its journey from Jambuḍipa. Identifiable with the mountain Lawu on the provincial boundary of Central and East Java.
Katu-katu	A name of Sang Kumāra.
Katung-malaras, Sang	Variant Katung-mararas. Third son of Rahyang Kaṇḍyawan at Mĕḍang-gaṇa. See also Karung-kalah, Mangukuhan, Saṇḍang-garbha, Wṛtti-kaṇḍayun.
Kawi, *gunung*	One of the mountains formed from the earth which fell from the Mahāmeru in the course of its journey from Jambuḍipa. Later placed in the charge of Bhagawān Agaṣṭi by Bhaṭāra Guru. Identifiable with present day Mt Kawi in eastern Java.
Kayutaji	The first hermitage established by Bhaṭāra Guru on Mt Mahāmeru.
Kĕba-kĕba, Bhaṭārī	A name of Bhaṭārī Umā.
Kedman	A place to the east of Bhagawān Aśoṣṭi's *maṇḍala* at Labdawara.
Kĕdyangga, *gunung*	Variant Kĕnyāngga. A mountain where Bhaṭāra Guru's bull underwent a period of penance, having been cursed by Bhaṭārī Umā.
Kelāśa-parwata	Variant Kailāśa. The base of the holy Mt Mahāmeru, left behind at the western end of Java. Probably located near the Dieng Plateau.

Kelaśabhumisampūrṇawan	A name of Mt Mahāmeru, associated with the burial place of Bhaṭāra Ḍarmarāja.
Kĕṇḍĕng, *gunung*	A mountain associated with the widow Rāga-runting of Mĕḍang-tañjung. Probably located in the Boyolali region of central Java.
Kĕpuh-rĕbah	The name of a *maṇḍala* founded by the *wiku* Buyut Arĕng. See also Anaman, Andrala, Jun-maṇik.
Keśawa, Bhaṭāra	A name of the god Wiṣṇu.
Kĕtĕk-Mĕlĕng	The name given to the holy receptacle Kamaṇḍalu by the demons Rātmaja and Rātmaji.
Ketu	The name of a divine sage (*dewarṣi*). See also Kapila, Nārada, Sapaka, Tumburu, Wiśwakarma.
Kombala, *ranu*	Variant *ranu* Kbo-kuning. A lake created by Bhaṭāra Guru. Identifiable with Ranu Kumbolo in the Tengger highlands.
Kowera	One of the four World Guardians (*caturlokapāla*).
Kuḍampilan	A place passed by Ki Kabhayan-panglayar on his journey to Kukub. See also Bakar, Cangcangan, Duk, Pacelengan, Payaman, Ragḍang, Tambangan, Untehan.
Kukub	A *maṇḍala* founded by Bhaṭāra Guru on the southern slope of Mt Mahāmeru. See also Śūnyasagiri.
Kulikuli, Sang	Wife of the king Wawuh-langit of Mĕḍang-gaṇa.
Kumāra, Sang	A son of Bhaṭāra Guru and the goddess Umā, and a brother of Sang Hyang Gaṇa.
Kumāra-gimbal, Mpu	The eldest of three sons collectively known as Mpu Kuna, who emerged from Bhaṭārī Umā's big toe following her encounter with the herds-boy Kumāra-gohphala. See also Kumāra-raray, Kumāra-siddi.
Kumāra-gohphala, Sang	A manifestation of Bhaṭāra Guru as a handsome herds-boy, adopted for the purpose of testing the fidelity of Bhaṭārī Umā.

Kumāra-raray, Mpu	The youngest of three sons collectively known as Mpu Kuna, who emerged from Bhaṭārī Umā's big toe following her encounter with the herds-boy Kumāra-gohphala. See also Kumāra-gimbal, Kumāra-siddi.
Kumāra-siddi, Mpu	The second of three sons collectively known as Mpu Kuna, who emerged from Bhaṭārī Umā's big toe following her encounter with the herds-boy Kumāra-gohphala. See also Kumāra-gimbal, Kumāra-raray.
Kumukus, *gunung*	One of the mountains formed from the earth which fell from the Mahāmeru in the course of its journey from Jambuḍipa. Identifiable with the mountain Welirang in eastern Java.
Kuna, Mpu	The collective name for the three infants Kumāra-gimbal, Kumāra-siddi and Kumāra-raray, who emerged from Bhaṭārī Umā's big toe.
Kupang	The second *katyāgan* (hermitage) of the *caturāśrama*, established by Bhaṭāra Guru. Located near Pekalongan in central Java. See also Bulon, Huluwanwa, Pacira.
Kuruṣya	One of a group of five deities (*dewata*), along with Kuśika, Garga, Metri and Patañjala.
Kuśika	One of a group of five deities (*dewata*), along with Garga, Metri, Kuruṣya and Patañjala.
Kutritusan	The name of the religious establishment (*kabhu-janggan*) where the manuscript of the Tantu Pang-gĕlaran was copied in Śaka 1557. Located in the region of Gianyar on the island of Bali.
Labdawara	The name of a *maṇḍala* founded by Bhagawān Aśoṣṭi.
Lamunwiku	A temporary residence of Aji Uṇḍal of Daha, situated on the eastern slope of Mt Kawi.
Lawu, *gunung*	The former hermitage of Bhaṭāra Guru in the form of Kālarūdra, identifiable with present day Mt Lawu. See also Katong.

Layu-watang	Variant Malayu-watang. The name of a *maṇḍala* founded by the sage Anggira, located in central Java. See also Panatmaku.
Lĕbĕng, *gunung*	Variant Sbĕng. Formerly the summit of Mt Kampud (Kelud), hurled to the southwest by Bhaṭārī Umā in a fit of rage.
Lĕmah-bang, Ki	Variant Lmabāng. One of two demons (*rākṣasa*) who escorted Ki Kabhayan-panglayar from Waśaṇa to the peak of Kalyasĕm. See also Maraṇak.
Lĕsung-burut, Buyut	The title of a palm wine tapper named Lulumpang-burut, following ordination as a *wiku* of the Kasturi sect by the *walyan* Bugoleng.
Limohan, *gunung*	The place where Bhaṭāra Guru stood when he created Mt Hyang. Probably identifiable with Mt Lemongan in the regency of Lumajang, eastern Java.
Lodra	A form of the god Brahmā, one of a trinity of Kāla manifestations intended to destroy the sage Siddawangsitadewa. See also Samaya, Sambu.
Lulumpang-burut, Si	Variants Lulumpang-gurut, Lpung-burut, Lphung-burut. The name of a palm wine tapper, ordained as a *wiku* entitled Buyut Lĕsung-burut by the *walyan* Bugoleng.
Lumanglang	One of the five Yakṣa, an emanation of the demons Kāla and Anungkāla. See also Lumangling, Lumangut, Mangdulur, Manginte.
Lumangling	One of the five Yakṣa, an emanation of the demons Kāla and Anungkāla. See also Lumanglang, Lumangut, Mangdulur, Manginte.
Lumangut	One of the five Yakṣa, an emanation of the demons Kāla and Anungkāla. See also Lumanglang, Lumangling, Mangdulur, Manginte.
Madumali, Dewi	A daughter of the king Wawu-langit of Mĕḍang-gaṇa. See also Kasingi.

Mahādewa, Hyang	A manifestation of the god Śiwa, credited with introducing the art of the goldsmith to Java.
Mahāguru, Bhaṭāra	A name of Bhaṭāra Guru.
Mahākāraṇa, Bhaṭāra	A name of Bhaṭāra Guru.
Mahāmeru, Sang Hyang	The holy mountain Mahāmeru, transported from the Himalaya in order to stabilize the island of Java. Identifiable with Mt Semeru in eastern Java.
Makuṭa	A crown, attribute of Bhaṭārī Umā.
Maṇḍalagiri, Sang Hyang	A name of Mt Mahāmeru.
Mandaragiri, Sang Hyang	A name of Mt Mahāmeru.
Mandaraparwata, Sang Hyang	A name of Mt Mahāmeru.
Mandiki	A club wielded by Bhaṭāra Wiṣṇu in his effort to defeat the sage Siddawangsitadewa. See also Nandaka, Pañcajanya, Suḍarṣana.
Mangdulur	One of the five Yakṣa, an emanation of the demons Kāla and Anungkāla. See also Lumanglang, Lumangling, Lumangut, Manginte.
Manginte	One of the five Yakṣa, an emanation of the demons Kāla and Anungkāla. See also Lumanglang, Lumangling, Lumangut, Mangdulur.
Mangukuhan, Sang	Variant Mangakuhan. The eldest son of Rahyang Kaṇḍyawan at Mĕḍang-gaṇa. See also Karung-kalah, Katung-malaras, Saṇḍang-garbha, Wṛtti-kaṇḍayun.
Manguyu	The name of an ascetic order, founded by Bhaṭāra Guru.
Maṇik, *gunung*	A mountain in the vicinity of the Mahāmeru, hermitage of Bhaṭārī Umā.
Manuñjang, *gunung*	A mountain, site of a *maṇḍala* founded by Hyang Gaṇa and later inherited by the *wiku* Ki Buyut Samaḍi. Situated on the eastern side of Mt Mahāmeru. See also Ḍingḍing-Manuñjang.

Maraṇak, Ki	Variant Maraṇan. One of two demons (*rākṣasa*) who escorted Ki Kabhayan-panglayar from Waśaṇa to the peak of Kalyasĕm. See also Lĕmah-bang.
Marapi, *gunung*	Variants Marawi, Marapwi. A mountain, formed from the semen spilled by Kumāra-gohphala during his amorous encounter with Bhaṭārī Umā. Probably identifiable with Mt Merapi in central Java.
Mārkaṇḍeya, Bhagawān	Variant Karmaṇḍeya. A scholar (*paṇḍita*) from heaven (*swarga*), who replaced Bhaṭāra Iśwara as *dewaguru* at the *maṇḍala* of Sukayajña on Mt Kelāśa.
Maśin	A residence of Bhaṭāra Guru and Bhaṭārī Umā, origin of the *manguyu* ascetics. Probably identifiable with the village of Masin in the regency of Batang, Central Java.
Mawulusan, *gunung*	An alternative name for Mt Pamrihan (= Merbabu), created by Bhaṭāra Wiṣṇu. See also Damalung.
Māyana	The second *maṇḍala* created by Bhaṭāra Guru (after Sukayajña), probably located in central Java.
Mĕḍang	The name of an ancient settlement in central Java (cf. Mĕḍang-gaṇa, Mĕḍang-kamulan, Mĕḍang-tañjung).
Mĕḍang-gaṇa	An ancient settlement in central Java, founded by Rahyang Kaṇḍyawan, an incarnation of Bhaṭāra Wiṣṇu.
Mĕḍang-kamulan	Site of the earliest community in Java, following the introduction of carpentry by Sang Hyang Wiśwakarma. Located in the regency of Grobogan, Central Java.
Mĕḍang-tañjung	Residence of the goddess Śrī in the form of the widow (*raṇḍa*) Rāga-runting. Probably situated in the regency of Boyolali, Central Java.
Metri	One of a group of five deities (*dewata*), along with Kuśika, Garga, Kuruṣya and Patañjala.

Mṛṣa, Sang Hyang	Variant Mṛṣya. A weapon granted by the goddess Umā to Mpu Kumāra-siddi, her second son by Kumāra-gohphala. See also Guḍuhā, Trikurungan.
Nāmaśiwaya, Bhaṭāra	A name of Bhaṭāra Guru.
Nandaka	A dagger wielded by Bhaṭāra Wiṣṇu in his effort to defeat the sage Siddawangsitadewa. See also Mandiki, Pañcajanya, Suḍarṣana.
Nandiguru, Bhaṭāra	A name of Bhaṭāra Guru.
Nangga-parwatā	A mountain, site of a religious establishment (*kabuyutan*).
Nangka-parwata	A mountain, the sanctuary (*kahyangan*) of Bhaṭāra Wiṣṇu. Site of a *maṇḍala* named Panasagiri. See also Jala-parwata, Tigāryan-parwata.
Nārada	The name of a divine sage (*dewaṛṣi*). See also Kapila, Ketu, Sapaka, Tumburu, Wiśwakarma.
Narajñāna, Mpu	The title adopted by Mpu Waju-kuning following ordination by Mahāmpu Palyat. See also Janaḍipa.
Nīlakaṇṭa, Bhaṭāra	Literally "blue throat". The name by which Bhaṭāra Guru was known after drinking the Kālakūṭa poison from Mt Mahāmeru.
Nini, Aji	A form of the goddess Śrī in a future incarnation, prophesied by the queen of Daha following banishment by her husband king Taki.
Niṣada, *gunung*	A name of the Mahāmeru as a symbol of stability.
Pacelengan	A place passed by Ki Kabhayan-panglayar on his journey to Kukub. See also Bakar, Cangcangan, Duk, Kuḍampilan, Payaman, Ragḍang, Tambangan, Untehan.
Pacira	Variant Macira. The fourth *katyāgan* (hermitage) of the *caturāśrama*, established by Bhaṭāra Guru, probably identifiable with the district of Pasirian on the southeastern foot of Mt Semeru. See also Bulon, Huluwanwa, Kupang.

Paḍang	A village serving as the southern access to the holy Mahāmeru, guarded by the sage Anggaṣṭi. Identifiable with present day Kalipadang (district Amadanom) in the regency of Malang. See also Pañātūr-mukā.
Paguhan	Variant Pagulan. A village to the northwest of the hermitage of Mahāmpu Palyat at Kalyasĕm.
Palet, Kasturi	A name of Mpu Tapa-palet following his ordination as *dewaguru* at the *maṇḍala* of Śelagraha-rong.
Palyat, Bhaṭāra Mahāmpu	An incarnation of Bhaṭāra Guru as a *bhujangga* of the Bhairawa sect.
Pamanguyon-agung	A *manguyu* hermitage on Mt Mahāmeru, residence of Bhaṭāra Guru and the goddess Umā. See also Amanguyu-guntung.
Pamrihan, *gunung*	The name of a mountain created by Bhaṭāra Wiṣṇu, identifiable with Mt Merbabu in central Java. See also Damalung, Mawulusan.
Panasagiri	Variant Panagiri. The name of a *maṇḍala* established on the mountain Nangka-parwata, seat of Bhaṭāra Wiṣṇu.
Panatmaku	Variant Panatan. A name given to the *maṇḍala* of Layu-watang, founded by Bhagawān Anggira.
Pañātūr-mukā	The four "openings" of the holy Mt Mahāmeru, comprising the villages of Gantĕn, Paḍang, Pangawān and Pūrṇajiwa.
Pañcajanya	A conch wielded by Bhaṭāra Wiṣṇu in his effort to defeat the sage Siddawangsitadewa. See also Mandiki, Nandaka, Suḍarṣana.
Pangawān	A village serving as the western access to the holy Mahāmeru, guarded by the demons Kāla and Anungkāla. See also Pañātūr-mukā.
Pangeran, Bhaṭāra	A name of Bhaṭāra Guru.
Pangkeśwara	The first hermitage of Bhaṭāra Iśwara, probably located in central Java.

Panimbangan	The name of a *maṇḍala* on the shore of the southern ocean, founded by Buyut Śrī-manggala. See also Gilingan, Rājamaṇik, Wungkal-ibĕk.
Parameśwara, Bhaṭāra	A name of Bhaṭāra Guru.
Parameśwara-śiwapaḍa	A reference to the heavenly realm of Śiwa.
Parameśwarī, Bhaṭārī	A name of the goddess Umā, wife of Bhaṭāra Guru.
Parijñana	Variant Paringjñāna. The name of a greedy merchant (*walija*), admonished by the widow Rāga-runting at Mĕḍang-tañjung.
Pasanggaman, *gunung*	A mountain named after the intimate encounter of Bhaṭārī Umā with the herds-boy Kumāra-gohphala.
Pāwaka, Bhaṭāra	A name of the god Brahmā.
Pawinihan, *gunung*	The mountain where the gods Brahmā and Wiṣṇu created the first human beings. Identifiable with Mt Pawinian in the regency of Banjarnagara, Central Java.
Pawitra, *gunung*	The summit of Mt Mahāmeru, which became detached during the transport of the mountain from Jambuḍipa. Identifiable with present day Mt Penanggungan, to the south of Surabaya, East Java.
Payaman	A place passed by Ki Kabhayan-panglayar on his journey to Kukub. See also Bakar, Cangcangan, Duk, Kuḍampilan, Pacelengan, Ragḍang, Tambangan, Untehan.
Phala, *wukir*	A hill in the vicinity of the Mahāmeru, where Bhaṭāra Guru performed yoga.
Pilan, *gunung*	Variants Kampil, Wilān. A mountain named after an episode involving Bhaṭārī Umā and her son Kumāra.
Pinton, *arga*	A mountain peak in the vicinity of the Mahāmeru, site of a hermitage established by Bhaṭārī Umā.
Patañjala	One of a group of five deities (*dewata*), along with Kuśika, Garga, Metri and Kuruṣya.

Pṛthiwī, Bhaṭārī	The goddess Earth.
Puṇḍutan-śawa	Variant Punduta-sawa. A place to where the body of the sage Siddawangsitadewa was transported by the four World Guardians (*caturlokapāla*).
Pūrṇajiwa	A village serving as the eastern access to the holy Mahāmeru, guarded by Sang Hyang Gaṇa. Probably identifiable with present day Pronojiwo, Lumajang Regency. See also Pañātūr-mukā.
Raditya	Sunday, the fifth *wiku* ordained by Bhaṭāra Guru. See also Anggara, Budḍa, Saneścara, Soma, Śukra, Wṛhaspati (days of the week).
Raditya, Sang Hyang	The holy Sun.
Rāga-runting, *raṇḍa*	An incarnation of the goddess Śrī as a widow at Mĕḍang-tañjung.
Ragḍang	A place passed by Ki Kabhayan-panglayar on his journey to Kukub. See also Bakar, Cangcangan, Duk, Kuḍampilan, Pacelengan, Payaman, Tambangan, Untehan.
Rāhu	A demon (*rākṣasa*) who posed as a god and endeavoured to steal a draught of the Śiwāmba, elixir of immortality.
Rājamaṇik	The name of a *maṇḍala* on the shore of the southern ocean, founded by Buyut Śrī-manggala. See also Gilingan, Panimbangan, Wungkal-ibĕk.
Rājapati, Sang Hyang	Variant Mrājapati. A name of the god Brahmā.
Ranubhawa	A hermitage (*patapan*) of Bhaṭāra Guru on Mt Mahāmeru.
Ranupuhan, Sang Hyang	A holy stream on Mt Mahāmeru, where Bhaṭārī Umā washed her menstrual cloths. See also Ḍingḍing, Ulu-kĕmbang-pakalpan.
Ratih, Bhaṭārī	An emanation of Bhaṭārī Smarī, the wife of Kāmadewa.

Rātmaja	One of two demons (*rākṣasa*) who stole the jewelled pot Sang Hyang Kamaṇḍalu. See also Kĕtĕk-Mĕlĕng, Rātmaji, Śiwāmba.
Rātmaji	One of two demons (*rākṣasa*) who stole the jewelled pot Sang Hyang Kamaṇḍalu. See also Kĕtĕk-Mĕlĕng, Rātmaja, Śiwāmba.
Rĕban	Variant Rĕbyan. The religious sect (*pakṣa*) followed by Bhaṭāra Iśwara at Sukayajña. See also Rĕrĕban.
Rĕbhālas	Variant Rĕgālas. A *maṇḍala* situated at the foot of Mt Suṇḍawiṇi, founded by Buyut Lĕsung-burut. See also Arga-tilas, Jawa.
Rĕbhawinuk	A discus (*cakra*) wielded by Bhaṭāra Wiṣṇu in his effort to defeat the sage Siddawangsitadewa. See also Calakuṇḍa, Tarĕnggabāhu.
Rĕnĕb	The southern limit of a fissure on Mt Kampud (Kelud), created by the goddess Umā in a fit of rage.
Rĕrĕban, *gunung*	Variant Rĕban. A mountain, described as the "shelter of the gods", possibly associated with the village of Reban in the regency of Batang, Central Java. See also Rĕban.
Ṛṣi	The religious sect (*pakṣa*) adhered to by the sages Mpu Tapa-wangkĕng and Mpu Tapa-palet.
Rudra	The wrathful form of Bhaṭāra Iśwara.
Sāgara	One of the *maṇḍala trisamaya* on Mt Hyang, founded by Ki Kabhayan-panglayar. See also Kalyasĕm, Sanggara, Talun, Waśaṇa.
Śaiwa	A reference to the religious sect associated with the cult of Śiwa.
Samaḍi, Ki Buyut	The name of a *wiku* ordained at the *maṇḍala* of Ḍingḍing, later *dewaguru* at Manuñjang. See also Ḍingḍing-Manuñjang.
Samaya	A form of the god Iśwara, one of a trinity of Kāla manifestations intended to destroy the sage Siddawangsitadewa. See also Lodra, Sambu.

Sambadagni, *gunung*	Variant Sambudaghni. A name of the mountain Kampud, identifiable with Mt Kelud in eastern Java.
Sambu	A form of the god Wiṣṇu, one of a trinity of Kāla manifestations intended to destroy the sage Siddawangsitadewa. See also Lodra, Samaya.
Samĕgĕt-bagañjing, Ki	A name of Mpu Tapa-wangkĕng. See also Bhulalak, Botahi.
Saṇḍang-garbha, Sang	Second son of Rahyang Kaṇḍyawan at Mĕḍang-gaṇa. See also Karung-kalah, Katung-malaras, Mangukuhan, Wṛtti-kaṇḍayun.
Sandijñāna	Variant Sandiyajña. A "holy key" (*sang hyang kuñci*), bestowed upon Ki Kabhayan-panglayar by Bhaṭāra Guru.
Saneścara	Saturday, the sixth *wiku* ordained by Bhaṭāra Guru. See also Anggara, Budḍa, Raditya, Soma, Śukra, Wṛhaspati (days of the week).
Sanggara	Variant Sanggar. The name initially given to the *maṇḍala* of Sāgara.
Sañjaya, *gunung*	A mountain created by Bhaṭāra Iśwara, probably located in central Java.
Sapaka	The name of a divine sage (*dewarṣi*). See also Kapila, Ketu, Nārada, Tumburu, Wiśwakarma.
Sarayu	The name of a river (*loh*) in the vicinity of the Mahāmeru.
Sarjawa-Jambuḍipa	The name of the hermitage of the sage Sidḍawang-sitadewa on Mt Mahāmeru.
Sarwasidḍa	A *maṇḍala* near Mt Rĕrĕban in the region of central Java, initially presided over by Bhaṭāra Brahmā as *dewaguru*, later inherited by Bhagawān Anggira.
Śelagraha-rong	A *maṇḍala* of the Kasturi order, founded by the *wiku* Mpu Tapa-palet.

Siddawangsitadewa, Sang Ṛṣi	Variant Siddiwangsitadewa. A title borne by Bhaṭāra Ḍarmarāja following ordination as a *wiku.*
Siddayoga, Mpu	The title borne by the brahmin Těkěn-wuwung following ordination as a *wiku.*
Siddayogi, Sang	The title borne by Dewi Kasingi, wife of Mpu Siddayoga, following ordination as a *wiku.*
Śiṇḍo	A ravine (*jurang*) on Mt Mahāmeru, temporary residence of Aji Uṇḍal while awaiting ordination as a *wiku.*
Śiwa, Bhaṭāra	A name of Bhaṭāra Guru, the Supreme Lord.
Śiwāmba	The "water of life", distilled from the Kālakūṭa poison of Mt Mahāmeru by Bhaṭāra Guru.
Śiwa-raditya, Sang Hyang	The holy Sun. See also Raditya.
Smarī, Bhaṭārī	The wife of Bhaṭāra Kāmadewa.
Sogata	The Buddhist sect (*pakṣa*), and a name given to Mpu Kumāra-raray, youngest son of the goddess Umā and Kumāra-gohphala.
Soma	Monday, the second *wiku* ordained by Bhaṭāra Guru. See also Anggara, Budda, Raditya, Saneścara, Śukra, Wṛhaspati (days of the week).
Śrī, Bhaṭārī	The spouse of Bhaṭāra Wiṣṇu.
Śrī-manggala, Buyut	The title adopted by the prince Cañcurāja following ordination as a *wiku* of the Kasturi order by Buyut Jala-Giri.
Sudarṣana	A discus (*cakra*) wielded by Bhaṭāra Wiṣṇu in his effort to defeat the sage Siddawangsitadewa. See also Mandiki, Nandaka, Pañcajanya.
Sujiwana, Mpu	A name of the god Brahmā in his role as divine metal smith.
Suka, Si	The name of a butcher (*abhelawa*), follower of Bhagawān Mārkaṇḍeya. Founder of the *maṇḍala* of Jiwaṇa in the vicinity of Mt Mahāmeru, and the *maṇḍala* of Bhāṇa, Aribhāṇa and Talutug at the foot of Mt Wilis.

Sukawela	A *maṇḍala* whose name was derived from the "happiness of all the gods", located near Mt Rĕrĕban in central Java.
Sukayajña	The first *maṇḍala* to exist, established by Bhaṭāra Guru in the vicinity of the Dieng Plateau.
Śukra	Friday, the fourth *wiku* ordained by Bhaṭāra Guru. See also Anggara, Budḍa, Raditya, Saneścara, Soma, Wṛhaspati (days of the week).
Suṇḍawiṇi, *gunung*	Variant Śundawiṇi. A mountain, probably situated near the Mahāmeru. Original site of a golden image of Wiṣṇu created by Mpu Barang, later the location of the *maṇḍala* of Rĕbhālas, founded by Buyut Lĕsung-burut.
Śūnyasagiri	The third of three *maṇḍala* created by Bhaṭāra Guru on Mt Mahāmeru, located on the mountain's southern slope. Later named Kukub. See also Gĕrĕsik, Hahāh.
Swarga	The realm of heaven, hermitage of a certain Dewata-kaki.
Taki, Mahārāja	A king of Daha, son of king Bhatati of Galuh.
Talun	One of the *maṇḍala trisamaya* on Mt Hyang, founded by Ki Kabhayan-panglayar. See also Sāgara, Waśaṇa.
Talutug	A *maṇḍala* of the Sukayajña order, located at the foot of Mt Wilis. Founded by a former butcher named Suka. See also Aribhāṇa, Bhāṇa, Jiwaṇa.
Tambangan	A place passed by Ki Kabhayan-panglayar on his journey to Kukub. See also Bakar, Cangcangan, Duk, Kuḍampilan, Pacelengan, Payaman, Ragḍang, Untehan.
Taṇḍĕs	The name of a hermitage (*patapan*) of Bhaṭāra Guru on Mt Mahāmeru.
Tantu Panggĕlaran, Sang Hyang	Variant Tantu Paglaranya. The text translated here as "Threads of the unfolding web".

Tapa-palet, Mpu	One of two brothers in the service of king Taki of Daha. See also Palet, Tapa-wangkĕng.
Tapa-wangkĕng, Mpu	One of two brothers in the service of king Taki of Daha. See also Botahi, Samĕgĕt-bagañjing, Tapa-palet.
Tapi	A mountain ridge (*gĕgĕr*), site of the hermitage of Ibu-tĕngahan, daughter of Mpu Barang.
Tarĕnggabāhu	A discus (*cakra*) wielded by Bhaṭāra Wiṣṇu in his effort to defeat the sage Siddawangsitadewa. See also Calakuṇḍa, Rĕbhawinuk.
Taruṇa-tapa-yowana, Sang Ṛṣi	The title borne by Bhaṭāra Ḍarmarāja following ordination as *dewaguru* of the *maṇḍala* at Kukub.
Tasik-lĕbu	A "sea of dust", created by Bhaṭāra Guru in the vicinity of the holy Mahāmeru. Probably identifiable with the sand sea of Mt Bromo.
Tawungan, *gunung*	A mountain, former hermitage (*patapan*) of Sang Kumāra. Identifiable with present day Mt Penawungan in the regency of Probolinggo, East Java.
Tĕkĕn-wuwung, Sang Hyang	A brahmin from Jambuḍipa (India), ordained with the title Mpu Siddayoga by Bhaṭāra Iśwara.
Tĕnggĕk, Si	A *pujut* (slave) in the service of Aji Uṇḍal of Daha. Later entitled Buyut Giri following ordination as a *wiku*. See also Bugoleng, Kajar.
Tigalana	Variant Tigarahana, Tigāyana. A religious text recited by Mpu Tapa-wangkĕng when residing on Mt Brahmā. See also Tigarahaṣya, Tigatĕpĕt.
Tigapatra	The name of the *maṇḍala* established at the mountain sanctuary (*kahyangan*) Tigāryan-parwata by Bhaṭāra Iśwara.
Tigarahaṣya	Variant Tigaraṣya. A religious text recited by Mpu Barang when residing on Mt Brahmā. See also Tigalana, Tigatĕpĕt.

Tigāryan-parwata	A mountain, site of a *maṇḍala* established by Bhaṭāra Iśwara. Later inherited by the sage Mpu Waluh-bang. See also Jala-parwata, Nangka-parwata.
Tigatĕpĕt	A religious text recited by Mpu Tapa-palet when residing on Mt Brahmā. See also Tigalana, Tigarahaṣya.
Trikurungan, Sang Hyang	Variant Trikumara, Trikurungarantā. A weapon granted by the goddess Umā to Mpu Kumāra-gimbal, her eldest son by Kumāra-gohphala. See also Guḍuhā, Mṛṣa.
Triśṛngga, *gunung*	Variant Tisnangga. A name of the holy Mt Mahāmeru.
Tṛṇawindu, Bhagawān	One of two sons born to the princess of Daha (Tuhan Galuh Śrī Wīratanu) and Bhagawān Aśoṣṭi. See also Anggira.
Tuhan, Bhaṭāra	A name of Bhaṭāra Guru.
Tumburu	The name of a divine sage (*dewarṣi*). See also Kapila, Ketu, Nārada, Sapaka, Wiśwakarma.
Tunggĕng, *gunung*	A mountain associated with the sage Siddawang-sitadewa, probably located in the vicinity of Mt Mahāmeru.
Turuk-manis, Sang	The wife of Sang Wĕngan in the land of Mĕḍang-gaṇa. An incarnation of Bhaṭārī Ratih. See also Kāmadewa, Smarī.
Tūryan	The location of the first *maṇḍala* of the Kasturi order, founded by the sages Mpu Barang and Mpu Waluh-bang. See also Bapa.
Tyāga	A branch of the Bhairawa sect (*pakṣa*). Mentioned specifically in connection with the sage Mpu Barang as *dewaguru* of the Kasturi *maṇḍala* of Ḍupaka.
Ubhusan	Variant Hubuṣā, Ucusan, Hususan. The name of a stone (*watu*) serving as "an offering to the teacher" at the *maṇḍala* of Waśaṇa.

Ulu-kĕmbang-pakalpan, Ki	An official in the service of Bhaṭāra Ḍarmarāja at the *maṇḍala* of Kukub. Later the name given to a rock where the goddess Umā washed her menstrual cloths. See also Ranupuhan.
Umā, Bhaṭārī	The spouse of Bhaṭāra Guru. See also Parameśwarī.
Uṇḍal, Aji	A king at Daha, enemy of Mahārāja Taki, later founder of the *maṇḍala* at Ḍingḍing.
Uṇḍal	The name of a well created by Aji Uṇḍal of Daha, located on Mt Kawi.
Untehan	A place passed by Ki Kabhayan-panglayar on his journey to Kukub. See also Bakar, Cangcangan, Duk, Kuḍampilan, Pacelengan, Payaman, Ragḍang, Tambangan.
Waju-kuning, Mpu	One of two officials (*pangambehan*) in the service of king Bhatati of Galuh. Later known as Mpu Narajñāna following ordination by Mahāmpu Palyat. See also Kalotan.
Walaṇḍita, *gunung*	The name of a mountain where the goddess Umā buried the blood, body-hair and marrow of her son Kumāra. Located to the east of Singosari in the regency of Malang, East Java.
Walangbangan, *gunung*	A mountain created by Bhaṭāra Brahmā, probably located in central Java.
Waluh-bang, Mpu	The Sogata (Buddhist) emanation of the *bhujangga* Mahāmpu Palyat. Joint founder of the Kasturi order. See also Barang.
Wanisari	Variant Pangning-sari. A holy site associated with the goddesses Umā and Smarī. Probably located in north central Java.
Warag	Variant Warug. The location of a settlement founded by the sage Mpu Waluh-bang.
Wariguh	A *maṇḍala* of the Kasturi order on the northern slope of Mt Wilis. Founded by the sage Mpu Barang.

Warunggama	A place associated with the rituals observed by Bhatāra Guru on Mt Pawitra.
Waśaṇa	One of the *maṇḍala trisamaya* on Mt Hyang, founded by Ki Kabhayan-panglayar. See also Sāgara, Talun.
Wawu-langit, Sang	A ruler in the land of Mĕḍang-gaṇa, husband of Sang Kulikuli and father of Dewi Kasingi and Dewi Madumali.
Wĕlahulu, *gunung*	Variant Walawulu. A mountain, site of the hermitage of Buyut Jala-Giri. Identifiable with present day Mt Muria in northern central Java.
Wĕngan, Sang	The husband of Sang Turuk-manis at Mĕḍang-gaṇa. An incarnation of Sang Hyang Kāmadewa. See also Ratih, Smarī.
Wihanggamaya, *gunung*	Variants Wiyanggāmaya, Wiranggāmaya, Wahang-gāmaya. A mountain formed from the ashes of the Kāla *trisamaya*. See also Anungkāla, Kāla, Pangawān.
Wija, *gunung*	The name of a mountain, formerly a hermitage of the god Gaṇa.
Wilis, *gunung*	One of the mountains formed from the earth which fell from the Mahāmeru in the course of its journey from Jambuḍipa. Identifiable with present day Mt Wilis in eastern Java.
Winduprakāśa	A place preserving the memory of Bhaṭāra Brahmā in his role as the smith Mpu Sujiwana.
Winihatya, *gunung*	Variant Winih-satya. The name of a mountain, symbolizing the loyalty of Bhaṭārī Umā to her husband Bhaṭāra Guru.
Wīratanu, Tuhan Galuh Śrī	Variant Rakryān Galuh Śrī Wīratanu. A princess from Daha, daughter of the king Taki.
Wiṣṇu, Bhaṭāra	Third of the divine Trinity of Lords (*trisamaya*), along with Brahmā and Iśwara.

Wiṣṇu, *arcā*	A golden image in the land of Jambuḍipa, reproduced by the sage Mpu Barang and presented to king Taki of Daha. See also Suṇḍawiṇi.
Wiśwakarma, Sang Hyang	The deity responsible for introducing the art of carpentry to Java. Also the name of a divine sage (*dewaṛṣi*), along with Kapila, Ketu, Nārada, Sapaka, Tumburu.
Wṛhaspati	Thursday, the first *wiku* ordained by Bhaṭāra Guru. See also Anggara, Budḍa, Raditya, Saneścara, Soma, Śukra (days of the week).
Wṛtti-kaṇḍayun, Sang	Variants Kṛti-kaṇḍayun, Kṛtthi-kaṇḍayun. The fifth and youngest son of Rahyang Kaṇḍyawan at Mĕḍang-gaṇa. See also Karung-kalah, Katung-malaras, Mangukuhan, Saṇḍang-garbha.
Wungkal-ibĕk	The name of a *maṇḍala* on the shore of the southern ocean, founded by Buyut Śrī-manggala. See also Gilingan, Panimbangan, Rājamaṇik.
Wurung, *ranu*	The name of a dry lake bed in the region of Mt Mahāmeru.
Yama	One of the four World Guardians (*caturlokapāla*).
Yawaḍipa	Variant Yawaḍipāntara. The island of Java.

APPENDIX 2

Archaeological record for the Tengger Highlands and Hyang Plateau

TENGGER HIGHLANDS

Adapted from: Name: 05271-10; Scale: 1: 250,000; Type: Topographic map; Year: 1943

MALANG REGENCY

Item	Origin	Present Location	Reference
Copper plates of *pabañolan*, Ś1303	Ds. Gubugklakah (Poncokusumo)	Nat. Museum, Jakarta	NBG 47 (1909): 190–91. Boechari 1985–86: 110–11, no. E.48
1 dish and 2 pots	Ds. Pamotan (Dampit)	Nat. Museum, Jakarta	Groeneveldt 1887: 341, Cat. nos. 1928, 1929
Site of "Patih Ngurawan"	Ds. Pamotan (Dampit)	*Loc cit*	Rangkuti 2000: 16
Brick structure at Sumberayu	Ds. Pamotan (Dampit)	*Loc cit*	Rangkuti 2000: 16
Lumpang "Mbah Tugu"	Ds. Pamotan (Dampit)	*Loc cit*	Sidomulyo, field observation 10/9/2018
Gaṇeśa image (bronze)	Ds. Dampit (Dampit)	Nat. Museum, Jakarta	JBG X (AV 1948–1951): 73–74, no. 7953
Gold coin and items of jewellery	Ds. Jambangan (Dampit)	Nat. Museum, Jakarta	JBG I (AV 1930–1932): 218, no. 6026
Bronze incense burner	Ds. Baturetno (Dampit)	Nat. Museum, Jakarta	TBG LXV (AV 1924): 658, no. 5828
Candi Jawar (terraced structure). 2 *dwārapāla*	Ds. Mulyosari (Ampelgading)	*Loc cit*	Rangkuti 2000: 16–17
3 inscribed stones from Gerbo	Ds. Tamansari (Ampelgading)	*Loc cit?*	NBG 27 (1889): 73–74. Knebel 1902: 342–43
Stone *lingga* from Gerbo	Ds. Tamansari (Ampelgading)	Volk. Mus. Leiden	Juynboll 1909: 40, Cat. no. 3190
Collection of statues from "Soengipetoeng" (Lemahduwur?)	Ds. Simojayan (Ampelgading)	Banyubiru (Grati) Pasuruan	Krom 1916: 450–51
Standing Gaṇeśa (stone)	Ds. Simojayan (Ampelgading)	Volk. Mus. Leiden	Juynboll 1909: 21, Cat. no. 1759
Stone inscription. 2 *dwārapāla* statues. Stones dated Ś1360, 1362	Ds. Simojayan (Ampelgading)	?	Knebel 1902: 340–41
Earthenware pot. Stone image of Hanuman (?)	Ds. Simojayan (Ampelgading)	Nat. Museum, Jakarta	Groeneveldt 1887: 338, Cat. no. 1894. NBG 27 (1889): 86, no. 3398. ROC 1912: plate 8

MALANG REGENCY *(continued)*

Item	Origin	Present Location	Reference
Miniature temple from Petungombo	Ds. Tamansatriyan (Tirtoyudo)	Trowulan Museum	Wibowo 1975: 48–61
Gold and silver items. Decorated bronze container	Ds. Ampelgading (Tirtoyudo)	Nat. Museum, Jakarta	JBG VII (AV 1939): 91, nos. 6918–6939
4 stone *lumpang*. Damaged stone image	Desa Gadungsari (Tirtoyudo)	*Loc cit*	Sidomulyo, field observation 10/9/2018

PASURUAN REGENCY

Item	Origin	Present Location	Reference
Various bronze items. Earthenware pot	Ds. Watulumbung (Lumbang)	Nat. Museum, Jakarta	NBG 36 (1898): 2f, nos. 3860–3864
Bronze nāga	Ds. Panditan (Lumbang)	Nat. Museum, Jakarta	JBG VII (AV 1939): 85, no. 6847
Bronze musical instruments, 3 *ketuk*, 4 *kencreng*	Ds. Pancur (Lumbang)	Nat. Museum, Jakarta	TBG LXV (AV 1923): 597, nos. 5824 (a–c), 5825 (a–d)
6 copper trays. 2 pots. 2 chisels. 3 unidentified objects	Ds. Galih (Pasrepan)	Nat. Museum, Jakarta	NBG 3 (1865): 145c. NBG 4 (1866): 2ff. nos. ?
2 zodiac beakers	Ds. Tosari (Tosari)	?	NBG 4 (1866): 263 (IVa). Scholte 1920: 69, 82
Bronze lime container. Copper plates of Walaṇḍit, Ś1327	Desa Wonokitri (Tosari)	Nat. Museum, Jakarta	NBG 37 (1899): 62, nos. 3938, E.28 Boechari 1985–86: 87–89
Pot and ladle (bronze)	Ds. Podokoyo (Tosari)	Nat. Museum, Jakarta	NBG 37 (1899): 62, nos. 3939, 3940
Zodiac beaker, Ś1253	Ds. Ngadiwono (Tosari)	?	Scholte 1920: 69, 82
Zodiac beaker, Ś1274	Ds. Sedaeng (Tosari)	?	Scholte 1920: 69, 82
Candi Sanggar Ś1267, Ś1431	Ds. Pusungmalang (Puspo)	*Loc cit*	Istari 2015: 59–72

PASURUAN REGENCY *(continued)*

Item	Origin	Present Location	Reference
3 bronze items	Ds. Pusungmalang (Puspo)	Nat. Museum, Jakarta	JBG VII (AV 1939): 97, nos. 7043–7045
Components of a musical instrument (*gĕnding*)	Ds. Puspo (Puspo)	Nat. Museum, Jakarta	TBG LXV (AV 1924): 659, nos. 5830 (a–j)
Zodiac beaker	Ds. Ngadirejo (Tutur)	?	Scholte 1920: 69, 82

PROBOLINGGO REGENCY

Item	Origin	Present Location	Reference
Bima statue (stone)	Ds. Sapih (Lumbang)	?	Knebel 1904: 102–3
Gold ear ornament	Ds. Tandonsentul (Lumbang)	Nat. Museum, Jakarta	JBG VI (AV 1938): 103, no. 6481
Copper plates of Rameśwarapura Ś1197	Ds. Sapikerep (Sukapura)	Mpu Tantular Museum	Suhadi 2003: 2
Zodiac beaker Ś1266	Ds. Ngadisari (Sukapura)	?	Scholte 1920: 69, 81 (note 8)
Zodiac beaker Ś1251	Ds. Wonotoro (Sukapura)	?	Scholte 1920: 69, 81 (note 8)
Zodiac beaker Ś1246	Ds. Ngadas (Sukapura)	?	Scholte 1920: 69, 81 (note 8)
Zodiac beaker Ś1284	Ds. Ngadirejo (Sukapura)	?	Scholte 1920: 69, 81 (note 8)
Zodiac beaker Ś1269	Ds. Pakel (Sukapura)	?	Scholte 1920: 69, 81 (note 8)
2 porcelain dishes. Bronze lamp. Various gold and metal objects	Ds. Gunungtugel (Bantaran)	?	Knebel 1904: 101–2
Zodiac beaker Ś1252	Ds. Ledokombo (Sumber)	?	Scholte 1920: 69, 81 (note 8)
Unidentifiable bronze object	Ds. Gemito (Sumber)	Nat. Museum, Jakarta	NBG 58 (1920): 337, no. 5784
Zodiac beaker undated	Ds. Pandansari (Sumber)	?	Scholte 1920: 69, 81 (note 8)

PROBOLINGGO REGENCY *(continued)*

Item	Origin	Present Location	Reference
Collection of ceramic items	Ds. Cepoko (Sumber)	*Loc cit*	Sidomulyo, field observation 5/9/2018
Collection of silver earrings. Gold necklace	Ds. Wonoasri (Kuripan)	Nat. Museum, Jakarta	Groeneveldt 1887: 297, 305. Cat. nos. 1438, 1439, 1443, 1445–1447, 1517

LUMAJANG REGENCY

Item	Origin	Present Location	Reference
Stone images of Brahmā (*caturmukha*) and Wiṣṇu. *Yoni* pedestal	Ds. Burno (Senduro)	Mpu Tantular Museum. *Yoni* still *in situ*?	Nawawi 1990: 8
Rock inscription in the river at Mlambing	Ds. Burno (Senduro)	*Loc cit*	Sidomulyo, field observation 8/9/2018
Menhir "Watu Tugu"	Ds. Burno (Senduro)	*Loc cit*	Sidomulyo, field observation 8/9/2018
Dancer's headdress (gold)	Ds. Senduro (Senduro)	Nat. Museum, Jakarta	JBG X (AV 1948–1951): 75, no. 7966
Earthenware dish. Zodiac beaker. *Yoni* pedestal	Ds. Kandangan (Senduro)	*Loc cit*?	Knebel 1904: 122. Scholte 1920: 69, 70, 81 (note 8)
Menhir "Wadungprabhu"	Ds. Kandangan (Senduro)	*Loc cit*	Nitihaminoto 1990: 25
Stone grave "Mbah Dariah"	Ds. Kandangan (Senduro)	*Loc cit*	Sidomulyo, field observation 21/10/2018
Menhir "Ki Dadap Putih"	Ds. Kandangan (Senduro)		Sidomulyo, field observation 21/10/2018
Lumpang "Ki Demang Apus"	Ds. Kandangan (Senduro)	*Loc cit*	Sidomulyo, field observation 21/10/2018
Copper tray and bell. 2 plates. *Guci*	Ds. Kandangan (Senduro)	*Loc cit*?	Nawawi 1990: 9
Bronze bell. Zodiac beaker Ś1261	Ds. Kandangan (Senduro)	*dukun* Harjo T'ai	Sidomulyo, field observation 6/9/2018

LUMAJANG REGENCY *(continued)*

Item	Origin	Present Location	Reference
Zodiac beaker 2 prehistoric axes	Ds. Bedayutalang (Senduro)	?	Scholte 1920: 69, 81 (note 8). Nawawi 1990: 9
Zodiac beaker	Ds. Argosari (Senduro)	?	Scholte 1920: 69, 81 (note 8)
Zodiac beaker Ś12?1	Ds. Kandangtepus (Senduro)	?	Scholte 1920: 69, 81 (note 8)
2 bronze lamps	Ds. Wonocepokoayu (Senduro)	Nat. Museum, Jakarta	TBG LXV (AV 1924): 659, nos. 5831, 5832
Pair of silver armbands	Ds. Bedayu (Senduro)	Nat. Museum, Jakarta	TBG LXV (AV 1930–1932): 134, nos. 7360, 7361
Collection of bronze items	Ds. Jambekumbu (Pasrujambe)	Nat. Museum, Jakarta	JBG VI (AV 1938): 100, nos. 6432–6435
Inscribed stone of Tesirejo Ś1113. Stone *lumpang*	Ds. Kertosari (Pasrujambe)	Mpu Tantular Museum *Lumpang in situ*	Sukarto Kartoatmodjo 1990: 13–14. Sidomulyo, field observation 7/9/2018
Headless Nandi statue at Dadapan	Ds. Kertosari (Pasrujambe)	*Loc cit*	Sidomulyo, field observation 7/9/2018
Inscribed sheet of copper. Spout figure. Bronze lime container	Ds. Pasrujambe (Pasrujambe)	?	Knebel 1904: 123
± 25 inscribed stones, 3 dated Ś1381. Collection of bronze and ceramic items	Ds. Pasrujambe (Pasrujambe)	Mpu Tantular Museum. Lumajang Museum	Sukarto Kartoatmodjo 1990: 16–19. Nastiti et al. 1994–95: 6–11
2 bronze mirrors. Bronze lamp	Ds. Sukorejo (Pasrujambe)	Nat. Museum, Jakarta	JBG VII (AV 1939): 94, nos. 6976–6978
4-armed stone image of Umā/ Parwatī	Hill of Giring-sapi (Pasrujambe)	Nat. Museum, Jakarta	TBG LXV (AV 1925): 747, no. 5870
Menhir "Demang Alap-alap"	Ds. Padang (Sukodono)	*Loc cit*	Nawawi 1990: 6
Bronze, silver and copper items. Zodiac beaker	Ds. Tunjung (Gucialit)	Nat. Museum, Jakarta	JBG IX (AV 1942): 103, nos. 7660–7666

LUMAJANG REGENCY *(continued)*

Item	Origin	Present Location	Reference
Zodiac beaker	Ds. Gucialit (Gucialit)	?	Scholte 1920: 69, 81 (note 8)
Collection of iron implements	Ds. Wonokerto (Gucialit)	Nat. Museum, Jakarta	NBG 47 (1904): 10, Bijl. XX, nos. 1575d, 1627e–g, 1652a
Beads and Chinese ceramic fragments at Jenggolo	Ds. Wonokerto (Gucialit)	?	Nawawi 1990: 9
Menhir “Mbah Karyo Leksono”. Hill of Jenggolo-manik	Ds. Wonokerto (Gucialit)	*Loc cit*	Sidomulyo, field observation 20/10/2018
Bronze lamp	Ds. Kertowono (Gucialit)	Nat. Museum, Jakarta	JBG VII (AV 1939): 97, no. 7041
Stone pillar support dated Ś1330. 5 stone *lumpang*. Chinese ceramics	Ds. Kertowono (Gucialit)	*Loc cit*	Nitihaminito 1990: 15. Nastiti et al. 1994–95: 13–14
Holy water ladle (copper)	Ds. Sombo (Gucialit)	Nat. Museum, Jakarta	TBG LXV (AV 1924): 659, no. 5833
Bronze ritual bell. Beads, earthenware	Ds. Dadapan (Gucialit)	Lumajang Museum	Sidomulyo, field observation 14/9/2018
Bronze ritual bell. Zodiac beaker, Ś1250	Ds. Pakel (Gucialit)	*dukun* Misari	Sidomulyo, field observation 6/9/2018
Bronze ritual bell. Zodiac beaker	Ds. Kenongo (Gucialit)	*dukun* Jumat	Sidomulyo, field observation 20/10/2018
Candi Gedung Putri. *Yoni* pedestal	Ds. Candipuro (Candipuro)	*Loc cit*	Verbeek 1891: 309–10. Knebel 1904: 120–22
Collection of bronze items	Ds. Penanggal (Candipuro)	Nat. Museum, Jakarta	JBG III (AV 1934): 191, no. 6078. JBG VIII (AV 1940): 134, nos. 7354–7359
Collection of stone *lumpang*	Ds. Sumberrowo (Pronojiwo)	*Loc cit*	Sidomulyo, field observation 14/9/2018
Collection of archaeological items	Ds. Sidomulyo (Pronojiwo)	*Loc cit*	To be investigated
Stone Gaṇeśa image. Gold items and beads	Ds. Bulurejo (Tempursari)	?	Nastiti et al. 1994–95: 18
Late Ming ceramics (16th–17th centuries)	Ds. Kaliuling (Tempursari)	Property of Bp. Sukir	Nastiti et al. 1994–95: 18

BROMO/SEMERU

Item	Origin	Present Location	Reference
Bronze image representing the Trimūrti	Sand sea (Mt Bromo)	?	OV 1914: 209. Photo O.D. Serie A, nos. 281, 314, 329
Sĕrat Damarwulan (*lontar* manuscript)	Tengger highlands	?	NBG 42 (1904): 30 (c, 4)
Zodiac beaker	Tengger highlands	?	NBG 47 (1909): 158 (c)
Statues of Śiwa and Umā	Arcapodo (Mt Semeru)	*Loc cit*	Krom 1916: 421–22
Rock inscription Ś1232	Ranu Kumbolo (Mt Semeru)	*Loc cit*	Bosch 1920: 100–101. Bosch 1926a: 33
2 stone images, male and female	Tengger highlands (Probolinggo)	Nat. Museum, Jakarta	Groeneveldt 1887: 91, Cat. nos. 253, 254
Zodiac beaker Ś1253	Tengger highlands	Leiden Museum	Juynboll 1909: 139, Cat. no. 876/9
Earthenware *tempayan*	Tengger highlands, south of Mt Semeru	Nat. Museum, Jakarta	NBG 41 (1903): 54, no. 4522

HYANG PLATEAU

Adapted from: Name: 05271-10; Scale: 1: 250,000; Type: Topographic map; Year: 1943

PROBOLINGGO REGENCY

Item	Origin	Present Location	Reference
Candi Kedaton	Ds. Andungbiru (Tiris)	*Loc cit*	Knebel 1904: 113–18
Stone altar. Gaṇeśa image. 2 *dwārapāla.* 4-armed female statue	Ds. Krucil (Krucil)	?	Krom 1916: 428–29
Kramat Watu Lancang	Ds. Watupanjang (Krucil)	*Loc cit*	Krom 1916: 429–30
Stone platform and pillar supports at Telogo Indro	Ds. Plaosan (Krucil)	*Loc cit*	Krom 1916: 430–31
Site of Bujuk Santi (Telogosari?)	Ds. Plaosan (Krucil)	*Loc cit*	Krom 1916: 431
Inscribed rock displaying a chronogram, Ś1324	Ds. Wangkal (Gading)	*Loc cit*	Knebel 1904: 111–12 Krom 1916: 431 Brandes 1920: 246
2 Śiwa statues. Gaṇeśa image. *Dwārapāla*	Ds. Wangkal (Gading)	?	Knebel 1904: 111–12 Krom 1916: 431
2-armed female statue	Ds. Gadingwetan (Gading)	?	Knebel 1904: 112–13
2 Śiwa statues. Gaṇeśa image. Statue pedestal. Stone pillar support	Ds. Batur (Gading)	?	Knebel 1904: 111 Krom 1916: 426–27
2-armed female statue	Ds. Sentul (Gading)	?	Knebel 1904: 111
2 copper plate inscriptions. 2 bronze bells. 2 sets of scales	Dsn. Cangkaan Ds. Batur (Gading)	Nat. Museum Jakarta	NBG 53 (1915): 105–6, 130–32, nos. 5629–5632, E.50 (a–d), E.51. Boechari 1985–86: 112–14
Terraced sanctuary at "Somergo"	Ds. Keben (Gading)	*Loc cit*	Krom 1916: 427
Site of "Asta Landaur" at Rabunan	Ds. Batur (Gading)	*Loc cit*	Sidomulyo, field observation 20/11/2018

PROBOLINGGO REGENCY *(continued)*

Item	Origin	Present Location	Reference
4-armed male statue. "*Reco guru*" at Sekarsari (G. Gundil)	Ds. Kedungsumur (Pakuniran)	?	Knebel 1904: 108–9. Krom 1916: 427
Makāra spout at Sekarsari (G. Gundil)	Ds. Kedungsumur (Pakuniran)	*Loc cit*	Sidomulyo, field observation 19/11/2018

LUMAJANG REGENCY

Item	Origin	Present Location	Reference
2 bronze statuettes. Iron spearhead. Bronze *kudi*	Ds. Bence (Kedungjajang)	Nat. Museum, Jakarta	TBG LXV (AV 1923, 1926): 597–98, 713, nos. 5827–5829, 5872. Bosch 1926a, b: 32, 77–80
Items of gold jewellery. Chinese porcelain	Ds. Pandansari (Kedungjajang)	Nat. Museum, Jakarta	JBG IV (AV 1936): 163, nos. 6206–6210[293]
2 bronze items. Gold finger ring	Ds. Jenggrong (Ranuyoso)	Nat. Museum, Jakarta	TBG LXV (AV 1924): 659–60, nos. 5837a–b, 5838

293. The discovery site is listed simply as Pandansari, Lumajang, allowing for the possibility that these items originate from the village of Pandansari at Senduro.

APPENDIX 3

The Old Javanese text of the Tantu Panggĕlaran (Pigeaud 1924, pp. 57–128)

TEKST.

Eerste Hoofdstuk.

Awighnam āstu.

Nihan sang hyang Tantu paglaranya [1]), kayatnakna de mpū [2]) sanghulun, sa [3]) māharĕpā [4]) wruherikā; [5]) ndah ndah pahenak tangdenta [6]) mangrĕngĕ ring kacaritanikā nuṣa Jawa ring açitkala. Iki [7]) manuṣa tanana, nguniweh [8]) sang hyang Mahāmeru tan hana ring nuṣa Jawa; kunang kahananira sang hyang Maṇḍalagiri [9]), sira ta gunung magöng aluhur [10]) pinakalinggāning bhuwana, [mungguh ring bhūmi Jambuḍipa] [11]). Yata matangnyān henggang henggung [12]) hikang nuṣa Jawa, sadakāla molah marayĕgan [13]), hapan tanana sang hyang Mandaraparwwata [14]), nguniweh janma manuṣa [15]). Yata matangnyan mangadĕg [16]) bhaṭārā Jagatpramaṇā, rĕp mayugha ta sira ring nuṣa Yawaḍipa [17]) lawan [18]) bhaṭārī Parameçwarī; yata matangnyan hana ri Ḍihyang [19]) ngaranya mangke, tantu bhaṭāra mayughā nguni kacaritanya [20]).

Malawas ta bhaṭāra manganakĕn [21]) yugha, motus [22]) ta sira ri sang hyang Brahma Wiṣṇu magawe [23]) manuṣā. Ndah tan wihang [24]) hyang Brahmā Wiṣṇu, magawe ta [25]) sira manuṣā; lmah kinĕmpĕlkĕmpĕlnira [26]) ginawenira manuṣā lituhayu pāripūrṇṇā [27]) kadi rūpaning dewatā. Mānūṣā jalu hulih sang hyang Brahmāgawe, mānūṣā histri hulih sang hyang Wiṣṇu gawe,

---

[1]) C. D. E.: Tantu panggĕlaran. [2]) D. E.: ḍerasang hĕmpu. [3]) B. C. D. E: sang. [4]) C: sang maharĕp. [5]) D. E: sang mahyun wruha ring tātwa bhūwaṇa. [6]) B: pahenak angdenta. C: tadenta. D: nda mahenak denta. E: pahenak denta. [7]) B. C: Ikang. D. E: uniweh ikang. [8]) D. E: mwang. [9]) D. E: kahanan s. h. Mahāmeru ring Jambudipa (D: ring Jamudipa). C: Mandaragiri. [10]) D. E: hagungmaluhur. [11]) D, E: ontbreekt. [12]) B: hegang hegung. D, E: matang yan hegung. [13]) D. E: marajĕgan. [14]) B: Maṇḍalaparwwata. [15]) D. E: hirikang nūṣa Jawwa, uniweh tananā hikang nūṣa (B: manuṣā). Mangkanā nimitanya ngūni duk sang hyang Mahameru hangadĕg. [16]) D. E: Ndah kacaritaha. [17]) D. E: Yāwwadīpantara. [18]) D. E: hakaliyan ring. [19]) B: ring Wihyang. [20]) D. E: yata hana radītya ngaranya (D: ring Ḍihyangan aranya) mangke, tantuning yuganing bhaṭāra kācaritanya ngūni. [21]) D. E: manganakna. [22]) D. E: tumon. [23]) D. E: magāweya. [24]) D. E: Tarwihang. [25]) D: magawe yata. E: magawe hāta. [26]) B: kinpĕlnira. E: kĕpĕlnira. D: kinĕpĕlkĕpĕlnira. [27]) B. D. E: listuhayu.

paḍa lituhayu paripūrṇṇa [1]). Yata matangnyan hana gunung Pawinihan ngaranya mangke [2]), tantu hyang Brahmā Wiṣṇu magawe manūṣa kacaritanya [3]).

Pinatmokĕn pwa hulih [4]) hyang Brahmā Wiṣṇu magawe manuṣa, sama hatūt madulur mapasihpasihan. Mānak taya, maputu, mabuyut, mahitung, munihanggas [5]); wṛddhi karmma [6]) ning janma manuṣa. Ndah tanpa humah taya [7]) lanang wadwan mawuḍawuḍa haneng alas [8]), manikĕsnikĕs [9]) hanggas, apan tan ana pagawe ulahnya [10]), tanana tinirūtirūnya [11]); tanpa kupina [12]), tanpa ken, tanpa sāmpursāmpur, tanpa baṣahan, tanpa kĕṇḍit, tanpa jambul [13]), tanpa gunting. Mangucap tan wruh ring ujaranya, tan wruh ri raṣahanya [14]); sing ronḍon mwang wohan pinanganya [15]); mangkana hulah ning janma mānūṣa ring usana.

Yata matangnyan mapupul mapulungrahi sang watĕk dewatā [16]) kabeh, manangkil ri bhaṭāra Guru [17]). Tuwan [18]) bhaṭāra Jagatnātha manuduh watĕk dewata [19]) gumawayakna katatwapratiṣṭa [20]) ri Yawaḍipāntara. Nā ling bhaṭāra Mahākaraṇa [21]):

«Anaku kamu hyang Brahmā, turuna pwa [22]) ring Yawaḍipa; panglandĕpi pĕrang pĕrang [23]) ning mānūṣa, lwirnya: āstra, luke, tatah, usu, pĕrkul, patuk, salwirning pagawayaning mānūṣa [24]). Kita mangaran [25]) pande wsi; kunang denta manglaṇḍĕpanāstra, ana [26]) Windu prakāça ngaranya. Mpune sukunta kalih mangapita nabuka [27]); paradakĕn [28]) tang ayah çarasantana. Malaṇḍĕp tang astra [29])

---

[1]) D. E: manūṣa histrī kakung wulih sanghyang Brāhma Wiṣṇū magawe manūṣā, paḍa listubayu paripūrṇṇa, ulih sanghyang Brāhma Wiṣṇū magāwe manūṣā. [2]) D. E: katkaning mangke. [3]) D. E: kacaritanya ngūni. [4]) D. E: Yata pinatĕmwakĕnholih. [5]) B: maïtung mani hanggāsya. D: mattbapihenggal. E: matamapihenggal. [6]) D. E: krama. [7]) D. E: Anghing tayāndatan pomahomah taya. [8]) D. E: lanang wadon paḍa mawuwuḍa tayaneng halas. [9]) D, E: paḍa manikĕlnikĕl. [10]) B: pagawayulahnya D, E: yapwan tan bhiṣā magawe humah. [11]) D. E: tinirun tirun. [12]) B: tanpa kuping. [13]) D. E: tanpa jambuljambul. [14]) B: ring bhaṣāhanahā. D. E: ring bhaṣānya. [15]) D: goḍong mwang wwahwwahan pinanganya. E: ontbreekt. [16]) D, E: mapupulpulangrah hikang watĕk dewata. [17]) D. E: bhaṭāra Guru Parameçwara. [18]) D. E: tumurun. [19]) B: duh watĕh dewata, D. E: matuduh pwa bhaṭāra ring para watĕk dewata kabeh. [20]) B. C: tatwapratiṣṭa. D. E: gumawe taya tantu praçiṣṭā. [21]) D. E: mojar (E: mwajar) pwa bhaṭāra Parameçwara, lingnira. [22]) D: tumuruna maring. E: tumurun maring. [23]) D: manglaṇḍĕpin kita hastra. E: panglaṇḍĕpi kita hastra. D. E: magawaya (D: magaweya) kita pĕrang pĕrang. [24]) D. E: lwirnya: luke, tatah, waḍung (E: wadung), patjul, bingkung, usu (E: wusu), linggis, sakalwiraning pagaweyaning manūṣā. B: pagawening manuṣā. [25]) D. E.: makangaran. [26]) D. E: anatā. [27]) E: pangāpitānābuka. D: paṇapitanāmuka. [28]) D: parudakĕn. [29]) D. E: manglaṇḍĕp ikang astra.

59

dene mpune sukunta kalih; matangnyan mpu Sujiwana [1]) ngarantāpaṇḍe [2]), [apan mpune sukunta manglandĕpi hayah. Matangnyan mpu ngaranta paṇḍe wsi] [3]), apan mpune sukunta çaraṇa [4]). Samangkana pawkasangku [5]) ri tanayangku.

Muwah tanayangku [6]) sang hyang Wiçwakarmma, turun pwa ring [7]) Yawaḍipa, magawe umah [8]) tirunĕn ring manuṣa [9]); tinhĕr ngarananta huṇḍahagi [10]) [Kita tirunĕn ing manuṣa magaweyumah, kitangaran huṇḍahagi] [11]).

Kunang kamu [12]) hyang Içwara, turun pwa [13]) ri Yawaḍipa, pawarahwarah [14]) tikang manuṣa warah ring sabda wruhanya ring bhāṣā, nguniweh warah ring daçaçilā, pañcaçikṣā [15]). Kita guruwa [16]) ning rāma deça, matangnyan Gurudeça ngaranta [17]) ring Yawaḍipa.

Kunang kamu [18]) hyang Wiṣṇu, turun pwa ring [19]) Yawaḍipa; kunang pituhun sawuwusta [20]) dening mānuṣa, sapolahta tirunĕn dening manuṣa [21]). Kita guru ning janma manuṣa [22]), amawā rāt kitānaku [23]).

Kunang kita [24]) hyang Mahādewa, turun pwa ring [25]) Yawaḍipa, papaṇḍe mās [26]), pagawe hanggonanggoning [27]) manuṣa. Bhagawān Ciptagupta manglukisa [28]), hamarṇṇamarṇṇaha lĕngkara, sakarūpaka ri cipta [29]), maçaraṇa [30]) mpune tanganta; matangnyan mpu Ciptangkāra [31]) ngarananta nglukis [32]).

Samangkana pawkas [33]) bhaṭara Guru ring dewatā kabeh;

---

[1]) B: Sutiwana. D. E: hèmpu Tajīwarṇṇa. [2]) D. E: ngaranya pande wsi. [3]) D. E: ontbreekt. [4]) D. E: makasarananta. [5]) D: pawkaṣkwiri kita. E: pawkas kwing kita. [6]) D. E: tanayangku kamu. [7]) D. E: tumurun tā kita maring. [8]) D. E: magawe ta humah. [9]) D. E: hana tinirutiru dening manuṣa. [10]) D. E: thĕr pwa hananta mahuṇḍagi (E: mahuṇḍagihā). B: huṇḍagi. [11]) D. E: ontbreekt; D. E: kita marahā ring maṇūṣa krama ning hukur magawe(E: wwe)yumah. [12]) E: kita. [13]) D. E: tumurun pwa kita hamarahmarah ring manūṣā ring çabda sakalwiring sakalwiranya, mwang wruhanya ring baṣabhasiki. [14]) B: warahwarah. [15]) D.E: uniweh wruha ring ḍaçaçilā pāñcāçilā. [16]) D. E: makaguru. [17]) D. E: harananta. [18]) D. E: tanayangku kamu. [19]) D. E: tumuruna kita maring. [20]) D: mwah den pintuhu. E: mwah denta pintuhu. D. E.: sawuwusta. [21]) D. E: saparipolahta tirutirunĕn ing rat kabeh. [22]) D. E: kita wruha ring manūṣa. [23]). D. E: kita hamawaha rat ngarananta, mangkana pawkaskwiri kita. [24]) D. E: muwah kita. [25]) D. E: tumuruna sira maring. [26]) B: hapande mās. D. E: makahapande mās. [27]) D. E: magaweha sahanggonanggoning manūṣā. [28]) B: Bhagawan Cittagupta. D. E: Muwah kamu bhagawān Ciptagupta, tumurun maring Yawadipā hanglukis. [29]) D. E: sakarakara ning cipta. [30]) D. E: makasarana. [31]) B: Cittangkāra. [32]) D. E: matang yan mpu Ciptakara (E: Ciptaka) ngaranya manglukis. [33]) D. E: Mangkana pawkasnira.

yata sama tumurun maring Yawaḍipa. Hyang Bhahmā paṇḍe wsi, inarṣayanira [1]) tang pañcamahābhuta [2]), lwirnya: pṛthiwī, āpah, teja, bāyu, ākāça. Ikang pṛthiwī pinakaparwan [3]), āpah pinakacapit [4]), teja pinakahapuy [5]), bayu pinakahububan, ākāça pinakapalu; yata matangnyan hana gunung Brahmā ngaranya mangke, tantu hyang Brahmā paṇḍe wsi ngūni kacaritanya yata tkaning mangke [6]). Palu parwan [7]) sawit ning tal göngnya, susupitnya sapucang [8]), hyang Bāyu mtu saking guhā, hyang Agni hana rahina wngi, apan tantu hyang Brahmā kapaṇḍe [9]) wsi kacaritanya.

Tumurun ta bhagawan Wiçwakarmma huṇḍahagi [10]) magaweyumah, [maniruniru tang manuṣa magaweyumah] [11]), paḍa taya momahomah [12]). Yata hana deça ring Mḍang Kamulan ngaranya mangke, mulaning mānuṣāpomahomah ngūni kacaritanya [13]).

Tumurun bhaṭāreçwara mawarahmarah ring çabda rahayu [14]), nguniweh ring daçaçila pañcaçikṣa [15]). Sira ta Gurudeça panĕnggah ringkana [16]).

Jĕg [17]) tumurun ta bhaṭāra Wiṣṇu kalih bhaṭārī Çrī jĕg ratu sakeng awangawang. A ngaraning tanana, wa ngaraning maruhur, hyang ngaraning bhaṭāra; matangnyan ta rahyang Kaṇḍyawan ngaran bhaṭāra Wiṣṇu. Sang Kanyawan ngaran bhaṭārī Çrī ri nagara ring Mḍang Gaṇa, [18]), apan mulamulaning nagara kacaritanya ngūni, [19]) apan sira [20]) amarahmarah ring manuṣa; yata wruh [21]) mangantih manĕnun [22]) makupina madodot matapih masampursampur.

Bhaṭāra Mahādewa sira tumurun mapaṇḍemās [23]); bhagawān Ciptagupta sira tumurun anglukis.

---

[1]) B: inayanira. [2]) D. E: yata tumurun sang hyang Brāhma pande wsi, nhĕr çayanira pañcamahābhuta. [3]) D. E: paron. [4]) D: spit. E: supit. [5]) D. E: hapwinira pande. [6]) D. E: dyapi tkaning mangke. [7]) D. E: Hana ring gunung Brahma palu paron. B: Ana gunung Brahma paluparon. [8]) D. E: supit sawitning pucang. B: capit sawitning pucang. [9]) B. D. E: pande. [10]) D: mauṇḍagi paḍa. E: huṇḍagi paḍa. [11]) D. E: ontbreekt. [12]) D. E: yata paḍa momah ikang manūṣā. [13]) D. E: mulaning janma momahumah kacaritanya ngūni. [14]) D. E: amarahmarah içabda ring manūṣā. B: marahmarah. [15]) D. E: pañcaçīlā. [16]) D. E: sira ta pinakaguruhaning ramadeçā, matangnyan kaki Gurudeṣā panĕnggahanira, apan pinakaguru ning ramadeṣā sirā [17]) D. E: Rĕp. [18]) B: ring nagara ring Mḍangkilnyang gaṇā. [19]) E [5]: invoegsel begint. D. E: hawang pwa haraning haluhur, matangnyan hingaranan (E: hinarahta) hyangta Kaṇḍyawan bhaṭāri Çrī, nāgharā ring Mḍang ghaṇna. D: ingevoegd: nimitanya hana nagara ring Mḍang ghaṇna hapan mulaning hana nagara kacaritanya ngūni. [20]) D: sang Kanyawan sira. [21]) D. E: matangnyan tikang manūṣa wruh anggantih. [22]) B. E. E[5]. manunun. [23]) D. E: Muwah bhaṭāra Mahadewa, sira tumnrunnapaṇḍemās.

61

Kahucapa ta sira hyang[1]) Kaṇḍyawan, manak ta sira limang siki; sang Mangukuhan[2]) anak panuha[3]), sang Saṇḍang garbha panggulu, sang Katung malaras[4]) panngah[5]), sang Karung kalah[6]) kakang ring pamungsu, sang Wṛtti kaṇḍayun[7]) pamungsu. Rĕp tka ta wahana bhaṭārī Çrī, manuk patang[8]) siki kwehnya, lwirnya: kitiran, putĕr,[9]) wuruwuru spang, ḍara wulung[10]). Binuru denikang pañcaputra, katututan, tumap ring warwang, diniwal ta[11]) de sang Wṛtti kaṇḍayun. Ruru tlih tikang manuk: ikang kitiran mesi wija putih, ḍara wulung mesi wija hirĕng, ikang wuruwuru spang mesi wija mirah, ikang putĕr mesi wija kuning, mṛbuk awangi gandhanika. Harṣa tāmbĕk sang pañcaputra, ginugut[12]) nira tlas; yata matangnyan orana wija kuning tamapi tkaning mangke, apan hĕnti ginugut sang pañcaputra. Sang Mangukuhan sira mangipuk[13]) ikang wija putih [bang] irĕng, yata dadi pari tamapi tkaning mangke. Kunang kang wija kuning kulitnya pinĕṇḍĕmnira, matmahan kunir; yata gnĕp ikang wija caturwarṇṇa tamapi tkaning mangke.

Kunang kahucapa ta çri bhaṭāra Mahākāraṇa magawe tantu pratiṣṭa ri[14]) Yawaḍipa, tuminggalaknatantu hyang[15]), yata gumlar ing āṇḍa bhuwana, kumĕṇḍĕng tan pgat, rumeka[16]) tan lbur; mangkana kramanya[17]). Kunang ikang nuṣa Jawa ring āçītkāla enggangenggung[18]) sadākāla molah marayĕgan, apan tanana tiṇḍihnya; matangnyan bhaṭāra Mahākāraṇa mamet pagĕhan ikang nuṣa Jawa sira ring atita nātgata[19]) warttamāna. Rĕp mayuga bhaṭāra Guru, madĕg[20]) sang hyang umarĕp wetan; taya pinutĕrnira, mangdadi wĕrĕhwĕrĕh, mangdadi gunung. Yata matangnyan hana gunung Hyang tamapi katkaning mangke, yuganira bhaṭāra guru kacaritanya nguni; lmah ri suku bhaṭāra matmahan gunung Limohan.

Nhĕr tikang nuṣa Jawa tan[21]) apagĕh, sadākāla molah marayĕgan. Ndah irika ta bhaṭāra Parameçwara kumon i sang dewata mawusana magawe jagat pratiṣṭa[22]), mantuka ring swargga-

[1]) B: bhaṭāra hyangta. D. E: bhaṭāra. [2]) D. E[3] Mangakuhan. [3]) D. E[3] atuha. E: matuha. [4]) B. E: Katungmararas. [5]) E: manngah. [6]) B. E. E[3] Karung kala. D: Karukala. [7]) D: Kṛti kaṇḍayun. E. E[3]: Kṛtthikaṇḍayun. [8]) D: begin gaping. [9]) E[3] titiran, putĕh. [10]) E. E[3]: dara hulung. [11]) E: begin gaping; dus: diniwal ta de wwang tani. [12]) A: ginutut. [13]) E[3]. mangipun. [14]) A: mratiṣṭa. E[3]: einde invoegsel. B: praçiṣṭā. [15]) B: tantu lmah hyang. [16] C: rumake. [17]) B: yitigni, mangkana kramanya. [18]) B: egangegung. [19]) B: natkata. [20]) B: mandĕg hyang. [21]) B: tan ontbreekt. [22]) B: praçiṣṭā.

62

nira sowang sowang [1]). Mantuk sira kabeh, paḍa sirātinggal anak yuga gumantya ri [2]) sakramaning manuṣa.

Rĕp kahucapa ta sira hyangta [3]) Kaṇḍyawan; nhĕr sira manilar ing anakira [4]) kalima gumantyanana ratu ring [5]) sira. Ndah tanana ta sira angga [6]) salahtunggal. Wkasan ta sira magawe huṇḍi halangalang [7]); sing mandudut [8]) ikang winuntĕlan, sira gumantyanana ratu. Mandudut ta [9]) sira kapat, ndatan kadudut ikang winuntĕlan; wkasanta katuju sang Wṛtti kaṇḍayun adudut ikang [10]) winuntĕlan. Yata rinatwakĕn sang Wṛtti kaṇḍayun. Kunang sang Mangukuhan makakrama wwang tani [11]), sangkaning pinanganira [12]) sang ratu. Sang Saṇḍang garbha makakrama adagang [13]), sangkaning pirakira sang ratu. Sang Katung malaras [14]) makakrama [15]) amahat, sangkaning [16]) twaknira sang ratu. Sang Karung kalah [17]) makakrama [18]) ajagal, sangkaning iwaknira [19]) sang ratu. Ratu sang Wṛti kaṇḍayun [20]) gumantyani bapanira [21]). Mantuk ta bhaṭāra Wiṣṇu saking kahananya muwah kalawan bhaṭārī Çrī. [22]) Kunang ikang manuṣa sayākweh matambĕh [23]).

Tweede Hoofdstuk.

Rĕp kahucapa ta [24]) sang watĕk dewata sama sumambah ri bhaṭāra Guru [25]), sakweh ning dewata kabeh, ṛṣigaṇa, [26]) çuranggaṇa wiḍyādara, gandarwwa, paḍa ngimpunakĕn [27]) lĕbuni pāḍadwaya bhaṭāra Mahākāraṇa [28]). Uwusnira mawwat sĕmbah, paḍamaçilā [29]) mataraptap [30]) manangkil ri bhaṭāra guru [31]):

[1]) B: swawang swawang. [2]) B: gumantyani. [3]) B: bhaṭāra hyangta. [4]) B: sira manālar ingānaknira. [5]) A: ring outbreekt. [6]) B: tan hana manggā. [7]) B: saṇḍi halanghalang. [8]) A: mandunut. [9]) A. C.: mandududuta. [10]) B.: handudut ikang sang. [11]) Eind gaping D. en E. [12]) D.: pinangkanya. [13]) D.: kramanya madagang. E.: kramanyādagang. [14]) D: sang Ratung malaras. [15]) D. E: kramanya. [16]) D. E: panangkaning. [17]) B. E. D: Sang Karung kala. [18]) D: kermma kramanya mangjagal. E: kramanya jagal [19]) D. E.: hulamnira. [20]) E: Sang Kṛti kandayun ratu. [21]) D. E: gumantening sang bāpa. [22]) D. E: Kunang sira hyang Kandyawan mantuk. (E: mantuk bhaṭara Wiṣṇu) muwah sang Kanyawan, mantuk bhaṭārī Çrī sira. [23]) D. E: mawuwuh makweh hikang wwang. [24]) D: Ucapa. E: Kucapa. [25]) D. E: masomahan sumambah (D: sumbah) ring bhaṭara Prameçwara. E: hierna invoegsel: „hikang kitiran meçi wijā putih" tot „yata matang nyan nora wija kuning mapi katkaning mangke". [26]) D. E: mwang dewa ṛṣigaṇa. [27]) B: rimpunakĕn. [28]) D. E: paḍa mitanakning (E: mintakning) paḍa bhaṭāra Makaraṇa. B: lbūni paḍa mangwija. [29]) D. E: Ri wuwusnira mawot ṣkar paḍa masilih atut. [30]) B: maharaptap. [31]) D. E: bhaṭāra Jagatnatha, lingnira.

«Uḍuh kamu kita hyang dewata kabeh [1]), ṛṣigaṇa, çūrānggaṇa, widyādara, ganḍarwwa, laku, pareng [2]) Jambuḍipa, tanayangku kita kabeh, alihakna sang hyang Mahāmeru [3]), parakna ring [4]) nuṣa Jawa, [makatitinḍih paknanya] [5]) marapwan apagĕh mari enggangenggung ikang nuṣa Jawa, [6]) lamun tka ngke [7]) sang hyang Mandaragiri [8]). Laku, tanayangku kabeh!» [9])

Mangkana wuwus bhaṭāra ring dewata kabeh [10]), mwang ṛṣigaṇa, widyāḍara, ganḍarwwa, çurānggaṇā. Tan wihang sira kabeh, paḍa sirāmit lumampaha [11]) ḍatĕnga ring Jambuḍipa, kumĕmbulana [12]) sang hyang Mandaragiri. Prāpti ring gunung Jambuḍipa [13]), magĕng aruhur, tutug tka ring ākāça, satusewu yojana ruhurnya [14]). Matangnyan satusewu yojana dwahning ākāça [15]) lawan pṛthiwi, apan satusewu yojana ruhur sang hyang mahāmeru ngūni [16]). Inalih pwa maring nuṣa Jawa [17]), satngah karing Jambuḍipa; matangnyan satngah [18]) ring ākāça ruhur sang hyang Mahāmeru mangke [19]), sira ta bungkah [20]) sang hyang Mahāmeru; pucaknira inalih [21]) maring Jawa.

Yata kinambulan [22]) de sang watĕk dewata kabeh. Bhaṭara Wiṣṇu matmahan nāga [23]), tanpahingan dawa-gĕngira [24]), makatali [25]) ning amutĕr sang hyang Mahāmeru. [26]). Sang hyang Brahmā matmahan kūrmmarāja [27]), tanpahingan göngnira, pinakadasaring amutĕr [28]) sang hyang Mahāmeru. Rĕp ambĕbĕd ikang nāga ri [29]) sang hyang Mahāmeru, parĕng mayat sira kabeh mamupaka ri sang hyang Mahāmeru [30]). Mijil tang [31]) teja prabhāwa

[1]) D. E: Uduh tanyangku kita kabeh, mwang dewa. [2]) B: mareng D. E: lakwa mareng. [3]) D. E: alihĕn ikang gunung Sampora. [4]) D. E: parakneng. [5]) B: paknahnya. D. E: ontbreekt. [6]) D. E: marapwan mapagĕh hikang bumi Jawa, mari heguheguh. B: heganghegung. [7]) D. E: lamun uwus tka ring Jawa. [8]) B: Maṇḍalagiri. [9]) D. E: matangnyan ta lakū kita kabeh tanayanku. B: tūnaku kabeh. [10]) D. E: Samangka ta huwus bhaṭāra Guru ikang watĕk dewata kabeh. [11]) D. E: Tan wihang sira kabeh, sang ṛṣighaṇa, widyadara, gandarwwa sama (D: samanyan) lumampah sira kabeh. [12]) D. E: humaliha. [13]) D. E: gunungnyawa Jamudipa. [14]) D. E: hagĕng aluhur, tutug (D: tutugnya) tkeng hakaça, satusyu (E: satusi) yojjāṇna luhurnira. [15]) E: matangnyan satusi (D: satusiyu) yojjāṇna hdohing akaça. [16]) D. E: apan satuçyu (E: satusi) yojjāṇa luhurnika duk ing Jamudipa. B: ruhur ring sang hyang Mahāmeru ngūni. [17]) D. E: Yata hinalih (D: pinalih) mareng Jawa. [18]) E: pitngah. [19]) D. E: sang hyang Mahāmeru ring Jamudipa kang mangke. [20]) D. E: bungkahira. [21]) D: pinalih. [22]) B: kinĕmbulan. [23]) D. E: Yatthā bhaṭāra Wiṣṇu matmahanaghā. [24]) D. E: gĕngira lawan dawanya. [25]) D. E: yata pinakatali. [26]) B: mangke. [27]) D. E: kurma rajā bhaḍawang. [28]) D. E: pinakaddasar hamutĕr. [29]) D. E: ikang naghā hambĕbĕd ta. [30]) D: yata sira kabeh sarĕng habungkah gunung. E: yata parĕng mayat āmukah gunung sira kabeh. [31]) D. E: Hamijilakĕn ta sira.

saha ktug mwang prahāra. Jag lĕs [1]) parĕng amuṇḍut [2]) sang dewatā kabeh; umung [3]) mangastungkārajayajaya [4]) sang watĕk ṛṣigaṇa, dewānggaṇā [5]). Bhaṭāra Bāyu sira dewatā kāskaya, rĕp tumumpakni tunggir sang hyang kūrmmarāja [6]), sang hyang Mandaragiri pinutĕr [7]) dening watĕk dewata kabeh, umung majayajaya [8]) mangusung [9]) ri sang hyang Mahāmeru.

Kunang wong Jambuḍipa [10]) tumon ing sang hyang Mahāmeru malakulaku [11]), ndah tan katwan kang dewata denya [12]). Yata matangnyan umung gumuruh çabdanya [13]), paḍa mangastuti sira sang brāhmāṇa kabeh ri sang hyang Mandaragiri [14]); jag perat lĕs [15]), mangkana pangastuti sang brāhmāṇa [16]) kabeh.

Kahucapa [17]) ta sang watĕk dewata kabeh, paḍa kangelan sira mamutĕr i [18]) sang hyang Mandaragiri, yata sira paḍa malapa way [19]). Ana ta way mijil saking [20]) sang hyang Mahāmeru, wai wiṣya Kālakūṭa ngaranya; yata pinakamedane hikang gunung [21]); sangka ring helning [22]) dewata kabeh tinahapnira tang wai [23]) wiṣya Kālakūṭa. Nhĕr pjah ta sang [24]) dewata kabeh dening çakti nikang wai wiṣya Kālakūṭa ngaranya. Mulat sira bhaṭāra Parameçwara [25]):

«I, pjah kita sang [26]) dewata kabeh; ah mapa nimitanya pjah kabeh arih [27])? Ih, umisnikang gunung [28]), pilih ininumnya [29]), matangnyan [30]) pjah kabeh. Ah, uh, dak tahapnya.» [31])

Tinahapnira tang wai [32]) Kālakūṭa; mahirĕng gulu bhaṭāra kadi twah [33]) rūpanya. Matangnyan bhaṭāra Guru mangaran [34])

[1]) D: sag rĕp. E: sagṛh. [2]) D. E: parĕng ta mundut sang hyang Mahāmeru. [3]) D. E: ontbreekt. [4]) D: ajayajaya. E: mañjayajaya. [5]) D. E: suranggaṇa. [6]) D. E: tapṛngsĕṛg, yata tumumpang sira gigirira bhadawang. [7]) D. E: pinundut kinambulan. [8]) B. D. E: mañjayajaya. [9]) D. E: mangĕmbuli mangusung. [10]) D. E: Wwang Jambuḍipa humwang (E: humung) gumĕntĕr. [11]) B: maring Jawa. D. E: tumon ing gunung malakulaku mareng Jawa. [12]) D. E: tuhun katon gunung malakulaku juga. [13]) D. E: yata humung gumĕntĕr çwaranya. [14]) D. E: paḍa mangastungkara hikang dewata kabeh i sang hyang Mahameru Mandaragiri. [15]) B: peraklĕs. D. E: saglĕs. [16]) D. E: pangastuti ning dewata. [17]) E: kucapa. D: kunang. [18]) A: mīnutĕri. D. E: hamutĕr. [19]) D. E: sama ta malapa wwe (D: wweh). [20]) D. E: saking ṛngatira. [21]) D. E: pinaka medanikang guṇung. [22]) D: sangarangelning sang. E: sangaranghelnika sang. [23]) D. E: yata tinahappikang we. [24]) D. E: Pjah tekang. [25]) D. E: mulata bhaṭāra Guru. [26]) D. E: kita para watĕk. [27]) B: hari. D. E: paranimitanya pjah harih (D: ngarih). [28]) D. E: inumā (E: ihuma) medanikang gunung. [29]) D. E: pilih iki gane hinūmnya. [30]) D. E: nimitanira. [31]) D. E: lah hiko (E: siko) dak tahap. [32]) D. E: Yata tinahap hikang we. [33]) B: kadi wwah. D. E: kadi toh. [34]) D. E: Yata nimitanya bhaṭāra Guru hinaranan.

bhaṭāra Nīlākaṇṭa, apan ahirĕng kadi twah [1]). Mojar ta bhaṭāra Guru [2]):

«Ih, mahāçakti dahat ngko arih [3]); kasakitan aku denya [4]).»

Rĕp dinĕlĕngnira tang wai wiṣya Kālakūṭa, yata matmahan tatwāmṛtha çiwāmba [5]). Yata pinakaïsi sang hyang Kamaṇḍalu, pinakapaniramnira ri sang [6]) dewata kabeh. Jag lĕs pwa sumiram [7]) sang hyang tatwāmṛta çiwāmbha ri sang dewata kabeh; yata mahurip sira kabeh mwang [8]) caturlokaphala, widyaḍara, ganḍarwwa, paḍa sumambah ri bhaṭāra Guru sang dewata kabeh. Jag lĕs [9]) mojar ta bhaṭāra Parameçwara:

»Ndah putĕr ta manih [10]) sang hyang Mandaragiri, den tkeng nuṣa Jawa. Arah, anaku [11])!»

Mangkana ling bhaṭāra ring dewata kabeh; tan wihang sira kabeh. Yata inaweṣya [12]) ta detya danawa rakṣasa kabeh apulihana [13]) sang watĕk dewata kabeh [14]). Pinutĕr ta sang hyang Mandaragiri; jag lĕs [15]), ḍatang ta sireng nuṣa Jawa tungtungan kulwan. Rĕp mangadĕg ta sang hyang Mahāmeru, makiris [16]) makelahkelah tampak sang dewata; matangnyan Kelāça-parwwata ngaran sang hyang Mahāmeru, apan makelahkelah tampak sang dewata.

Col aṇḍap kulwan, maluhur wetan ikang nuṣa Jawa; yata pinupak sang hyang Mahāmeru, pinalih [17]) mangetan. Tunggaknira hana kari kulwan; matangnyan hana argga Kelāça ngaranya mangke, tunggak sang hyang Mahāmeru ngūni kacaritanya. Pucaknira pinalih [18]) mangetan, pinutĕr kinĕmbulan dening dewata kabeh; runtuh teka [19]) sang hyang Mahāmeru. Kunang tambe [20]) ning lĕmah runtuh matmahan gunung Katong; kaping rwaning lmah runtuh matmahan gunung Wilis; kaping tiganing lmah runtuh matmahan gunung Kampud; kaping pat ing lmah runtuh matmahan gunung Kawi; kaping limaning lmah runtuh matmahan gunung Arjjuna; kaping nĕm ing lmah runtuh matmahan gunung Kumukus.

---

[1]) D. E: hapan ahirĕng gulu kadi toh rupanika. [2]) D. E: mwajar ta bhaṭāra Mahakaraṇa. [3]) B: ko hari. D. E: Ih, mahaçakti ko medanya yarih. [4]) B: denyu. D. E: kasaktinya mangkana denya. [5]) D: tirtthamṛttha çiwamba. E: tirttha çiwamba. [6]) B: pinakapaniramniramnira ring sang. D. E: pinakahurip ning watĕk. [7]) B: Jhag perat çwar carĕm, sumirat. D. E: Rĕp peret reg cap sumirat ta. [8]) D. E: manglilir kang para watĕk dewata. [9]) B: jhag lĕs. D. E: sag rĕp lĕs. [10]) D. E: Nimitanya mahurip tanayanku dening tatwamṛtthā çiwāmba, mangko ta putĕrĕn manih hanaku. [11]) B: denya tka ring nuṣā Jawa. Halah hanaku! D. E: den tĕka riṇg Jawa tanayanku. [12]) D. E: hinaçaya. [13]) D: hamangĕmbuli hiring. E: hamuliha ring. [14]) D. E: begin gaping. [15]) B: jhag lĕs. [16]) B; pakiris. [17]) B: hinalih. [18]) B: inulih. [19]) B: runtuh ta. [20]) B: tĕmbe.

66

Goweng sisih ring iswar dening runtuh sang hyang Mahāmeru, yata coṇḍong [1]) mangalwar pangadĕgnira, [molah pukah pucaknira] [2]). Yata inadĕgakĕn dening watĕk dewata pucak sang hyang Mahāmeru. «Ih pawitra» [3]) ling ning dewata kabeh; yata ring Pawitra ngaranya mangke pucak sang hyang Mahāmeru kacaritanya ngūni. Kunang pwa tan apagĕh sang hyang Mahāmeru, sumaṇḍa ring gunung Brahmā sira wkasan, apan [4]) wyakti rubuh sang hyang Mahāmeru, yan tan sumaṇḍaha ring gunung Brahmā, apan sira goweng sisih iswar. Nimitanira apagĕhana ring gunung Brahmā, rĕp mapagĕh pangadĕg [5]) sang hyang Mandaragiri; yata matangnyan apagĕh tikang nuṣa Jawa mari molah marayĕgan, nisaḍapagĕh [6]). Yata matangnyan sang hyang Mahāmeru inaranan gunung Niṣaḍa.

Ndan irika ta bhaṭāra Parameçwara kumwan [7]) ing sang dewata kabeh mamūjāha ri sang hyang Mandaragiri, kumnakna hiṣi [8]) sang hyang Mahāmeru. Tĕhĕr tikang dewa trisamaya sinung nugraha wāhana: wṛṣabha putih pinakawāhana [9]) bhaṭāra Içwara; hangsa putih pinakawāhana [10]) bhaṭāra Brahmā; garuḍadwaja [11]) pinakawāhana bhaṭāra Wiṣṇu. Tlasnira dewata trisamaya sinung nugraha wāhana, asamūha tang dewata kabeh amujāha ri [12]) sang hyang Mahāmeru girirāja. Jag [13]) lĕs yeki mangke bhawanira.

Ana kuṇḍi maṇik, sang hyang Kamaṇḍalu ngaranya, mesi sang hyang tatwāmṛta çiwāmbha, makahiji [14]) sang hyang Mandaragiri. Yatika pinūjā dening sang watĕk dewata kabeh. Ri huwusnira pinūjā, pinupu ijinira [15]) sang hyang Mahāmeru, lwirnya: mirah [16]), komala, intĕn [17]); inaturakĕn ri [18]) bhaṭāra Parameçwara; tan kahuninga sang hyang Kamaṇḍalu. Jag lĕs [19]) lungha sang dewata kabeh, kari sang hyang kuṇḍi maṇik.

Ana ta rākṣasa roro [20]) kwehnya, sang Rātmaja sang Rātmajī ngaranya [21]). Amĕngamĕng maring sang hyang Mandaragiri, harĕp amupuha mas mirah komala intĕn ri iḍĕpnya [22]). Ndah tan pantuka [23]) mas mirah komala intĕn, kapanggih ta sang hyang

[1]) B sondo. [2]) B: ontbreekt. [3]) B: pawitra pawitra. [4]) B: apanya. [5]) B: mangadĕg. [6]) B: niçaḍḍa mapagĕh. [7]) B: tumwan. [8]) B: haji. [9]) B: pinakawahananira. [10]) A: pinakahawahana. [11]) B: garuḍa putih. [12]) B: amūjāhering. [13]) B: Jhag lĕs. [14]) B: makahaji. [15]) B: hinira. [16]) B: mas, mirah. [17]) B: wintĕn. [18]) B. inaturakna ring. [19]) B: Jhag lĕs. [20]) D. E: einde van de gaping; kalih siki. [21]) D. E: makangaran sang R. R. [22]) D. E: harĕpwa hamupu mās mirah idĕpnya. [23]) B: tan pantukya. D. E: tan manmu taya.

67

Kamaṇḍalu[1]) denya. Pinupuwiring[2]) anggonya, pinakamengameng-anya ri iḍĕpnya[3]); tan wruh taya ri paknanya[4]). [Tuhu mlĕng-mlĕng rūpanya][5]), yata inaranan sang hyang Ktĕk-mĕlĕng[6]) sang hyang Kamaṇḍalu denya. Jag lĕs[7]) lungha ta sang Rātmaja Rātmajī.

Ucapĕn[8]) ta sang watĕk dewata kabeh ḍatang paḍā nĕmbah ri[9]) bhaṭāra Guru. Mwajar ta bhaṭāra[10]):

«Um anaku[11]) dewata kabeh, ndi ta iji[12]) sang hyang Mahāmeru [dentānaku][13])? Inaturakĕn ta ikang mas mirah komala intĕn, tanana ikang[14]) kuṇḍi maṇik sang hyang Kamaṇḍalu, mesi sang hyang tatwāmṛtha[15]) çiwāmbha, pinakahurip[16]) ring dewata kabeh ika».

Mangkana ling bhaṭāra Mahākārana[17]). Ndah tanana wruh sang dewata kang umalap sang hyang Kamaṇḍalu; nguniweh ṛṣi[18]) Nāraḍa, Kapila, Ketu, Tumburu, [Sapaka, Wiçwakarmmā][19]), ndah tanana wruh tikang jumumput[20]) sang hyang Kamaṇḍalu[21]). Ikang caturlokapala[22]), Indra, Yama, Baruṇa, Kowera, ṛṣigaṇa, dewānggana, çūrānggaṇā[23]), widyāḍara, ganḍarwwa, sami tan wruh ika[24]). Kemngan ikang para watĕk[25]) dewata kabeh; wkasan ta sang hyang rāditya wulan tinakonan de sang watĕk dewata[26]). Mojar ta sang hyang rāditya wulan[27]):

«Ana ta rakṣasa roro kwehnya[28]), sang Rātmaja sang Rātmajī ngaranya; ika mangalap[29]) sang hyang Kamaṇḍalu»

Mangkana ling sang hyang rāditya wulan[30]). Kunang bhaṭāra Brahmā Wiṣṇu sira mara ri kahanan[31]) sang Rātmaja Rātmajī. Jag lĕs[32]) prāpta irikang rākṣasa[33]). Mwajar ta sang Rātmaja Rātmajī:

«Uḍuh, dingaryyan sang watĕk dewata yan parangke[34]). Punapi dwaning ḍatang pwangkulun[35])?»

[1]) D. E: maṇi Kamanḍalu. [2]) B: pinupu jiring. D. E: pinupu winawanya. [3]) D. E: hamngamngan hiḍĕpnya. [4]) D. E: ndah tan wruh paknohnya. [5]) D. E: ontbreekt. [6]) D: sang ktikyangmlĕng. [7]) D. E: Lĕslĕs. [8]) D. E: Tucapa. [9]) D. E: paḍa sumĕmbah ring. [10]) D. E: bhatāra Mahakarana. [11]) D: Yata hanaku. E: Iya hanaku. [12]) B: haji. D. E: hi hĕndi ta hisinira. [13]) D' E: ontbreekt. [14]) D. E: ta hasi tan iku wijinira sang hyang Mahāmeru. [15]) D. E: tirtthāmṛttha. [16]) E: pinakaning hurip. [17]) D. E: Parameçwara. [18]) D. E: uniweh ika dewaṛṣi. [19]) D. E: ontbreekt. [20]) B: jumput. [21]) D. E: hapan tanana wruh (E: tanawruh) hikang dewata ikang dumpilya (E: dumpil) sang hyang kuṇḍi maṇik. [22]) A. B. D. E: lokaphala. [23]) D. E: makaḍḍi çuranggaṇna. [24]) D. E: tanana wruh ika kabeh. [25]) D. E: Iya ta kerangan ikang. [26]) D. E: awkasan (E: awkas) sang hyang haditya tinañan. [27]) D. E: hādītya. [28]) D. E: detya kalih aki kwehnya. [29]) D. E: hikā hana wwangalap. B: inalap. [30]) D. E: hādītya. [31]) D. E: sira ta marok (E: mangrok). [32]) B. D. E: Jhag lĕs. [33]) D. E: prapti ri kahanan ikang detya bhaṭara Brahmā mwang bhaṭara Wiṣṇu. [34]) D. E: dingaren pukulun sang dewata. [35]) B: Punapa dwaning ḍatĕng pwakulun?

68

Mwajar ta sang hyang Brahmā Wiṣṇu: [1])

«Dwaning hulun datang: paran hulihta sakeng Mandaragiri?»

Sumawur tikang rākṣasa:

«Tan panĕmu mās [2]) mirah komala wintĕn [3]) nghulun bhaṭāra [4]). Ana si Ktĕk-mlĕng ulihning hulun».

Sumawur sang dewata:

«Apa Ktĕk-mlĕng ngaranya? [5]) [Apa rūpanya?] [6])»

Pinintonakĕn ta kuṇḍi maṇik. Nhĕr pinalaku de sang watĕk dewata; ndatan [7]) paweh tikang rākṣasa. Pinalaku tinukwing mās maṇik [8]); tan paweh tikang rākṣasa [9]). Wkasan matakwan tikang rākṣasa [10]):

«Apa gatinikang [11]) kuṇḍi maṇik?»

Mwajar ta sang dewata [12]):

«Ikang kuṇḍi maṇik sang hyang Kamaṇḍalu ngaranya, mesi tatwāmṛtha [13]). çiwāmbha, pinakahurip ing dewata».

Rĕp sinambutnya [14]) tang kuṇḍi maṇik dening rākṣasa [15]), nhĕr kinmitnya kalihan [16]). Ndah kerangan [17]) sang hyang Brahmā Wiṣṇu. Saka ri prajñā [18]) sang hyang Brahmā Wiṣṇu molaha [19]), marūpa ta sirestri lituhayu [20]); rĕp yeki mangke bhāwanira. Ḍatang ri kahanan ikang Rātmaja Rātmajī [21]), pinalakunira tang kuṇḍi maṇik, tĕhĕr minanismanisanira [22]). Hāmhām buddhinikang rākṣasa [23]) tumon ing istri lituhayu [24]); yata winehaknira tang [25]) kuṇḍi maṇik. Kāgĕm ta [26]) de bhaṭāra Wiṣṇu. Jag lĕs pinalaywaknira de hyang Brahmā Wiṣṇu. Tinūt de sang Rātmaja Rātmajī [27]), ndatan katututan [ta sang hyang Brahmā Wiṣṇu] [28]) denya, apan tanpahingan [29]) drĕsnira. Kerangan [30]) ta sang Rātmaja Rātmajī.

Kahucapa [31]) ta sang dewata kabeh samānangkil ri bhaṭāra

---

[1]) D. E: gaping tot „hinurupan mirah komalā hintĕn". [2]) B: hmās. [3]) B: hintĕn. [4]) B: hulun bhaṭāra. [5]) B: haranya. [6]) B: ontbreekt. [7]) B: ndah tan. [8]) B: pinalakwi hmās manik. D. E: pinalaku hinurupan mirah komalā hintĕn. [9]) D. E: ikang detya. [10]) D. E: sang Rātmaja Rātmajī. [11]) D: paran gaḍeyanikang. E: paranke gawene hikang. [12]) D. E: sang hyang Brahmā. [13]) D: tirtthāmṛttha. [14]) B. D. E: sinambut. [15]) D. E: sang hyang Brahmā. [16]) D. E: hinètĕtakĕnira (E: denira). [17]) D. E: kari kerangan. [18]) B: prājanira. [19]) D. E: bhiṣanira bhaṭāra Wiṣṇu, yata hamet upaya. [20]) D. E: stri mantyanta listuhayunya. [21]) D. E: sang detya. [22]) D. E: minanismanisan. [23]) D. E: yata kneng (E: tan kneng) rĕs manah ikang detya. [24]) D. E: tuminghāl ing histrī hayu. [25]) D. E: winehakĕnníkang. [26]) E: tinanggapan. [27]) D. E: ri sāmpun kagĕgĕm tang kuṇḍi maṇik, yata sirā marūpajati muwah. Lĕs lunghā bhaṭāra Wiṣṇu, binuru de (D: den) sang Rātmajā Rātmajī. [28]) D. E: ontbreekt. [29]) D. E: tan sipi. [30]) D. E: kari kerangan. [31]) D. E: Kucapa.

69

Parameçwara[1]). Tĕhĕr manāhap[2]) tatwāmṛtha çiwāmbha, phalanira tan kneri tuwa pati; rwaning wandira[3]) pinakatahapanira ngkana[4]). Ana ta rākṣasa Rahu[5]) ngaranya, [mĕnggĕp kadi dewata swabhāwanya][6]), umor ing dewatā nahap[7]) tatwāmṛtha çiwāmbha; rwaning awarawar tahapanya[8]). Tuminghal[9]) ta sang hyang rāditya[10]) wulan, inaruharuhan tang kāla nahap[11]) tatwāmṛtha çiwāmbha; yata dinagĕl[12]) ring cakra[13]) [kang kālā][14]) de bhaṭāra Wiṣṇu. [Pgat tĕnggĕknya][15]) pjah laweyanya; ikang amṛta wahu kahmū durung tka ring awaknya[16]). Matangnyan mahurip tĕṇḍasnikang Rahu; sang hyang rāditya[17]) wulan kinawuyunganya, yata sang Rahu[18]) pinakawikalpanya[19]) sang hyang rāditya[17]) wulan yadyapi tkaning[20]) mangke.

Ri huwusnikang[21]) dewatā nahap tatwāmṛtha[22]) çiwāmbha, rĕp mayuga ta[23]) bhaṭāra Çiwa; mijil tang gunung Wlahulu[24]). Rĕp mayuga ta bhaṭāra Içwara; mijil tang gunung Sañjaya. Rĕp mayuga ta bhaṭāra Brahmā; mijil tang gunung Walangbangan. Rĕp mayuga ta bhaṭāra Wiṣṇu; mijil tang gunung Pamrihan; twĕk ning wĕk[25]) Damalung pjah, yata inaranan gunung Mawulusan[26]), mangkana kacaritanya.

Derde Hoofdstuk.

Kahucapa ta[27]) bhaṭāra Jagatpramāṇa, tyāga[28]) tāmbĕknira; matangnyan hana kategan ing Bulon ngaranya mangke, tambayan ing bhaṭāra magawe katyagan[29]) kacaritanya ngūni. Kaping kalih ring Kupang[30]), kaping tiga ring Huluwanwa[31]), kaping pat ring Pacira[32]). Ana ta nāga magalak arĕp angalahakna ri[33])

---

[1]) D. E: ring pasamwanirā (E: pasamohanirā) nangkil ring bhaṭāra Guru. [2]) D. E: Nhĕr ikang. [3]) D. E: mandira. [4]) D. E: gwanira nahapnirengkana. [5]) D: Rawu. C: Rāhu ontbreekt. [6]) D. E: ontbreekt. [7]) D. E: hamor ing dewata milu manahap. [8]) D. E: panahapanya. [9]) D. E: Wruh ta. [10]) D. E: aditya. [11]) D. E: ta yan anahap. [12]) B: dinasĕl. [13]) D: dinaglis cinakra de. [14]) D. E: ontbreekt. B: hikang kāla. [15]) D. E: ontbreekt. [16]) B: ikang nahap mṛtta wahu katmu wurung tka ring awaknya. D. E: ikang tatwāmṛtthā durung tkeng lawehanya. [17]) D. E: aditya. [18]) B: si Rahu. [19]) D. E: matangnyan sang Rahu (D: Rawu) pinakawikāra (E: sangpūrṇnā). [20]) B: yadyan katkaning. D: dyapi katkaning. E: dyapin tkaning. [21]) D. E: ri sampunikang. [22]) D. E: tirṭthāmṛtthā. [23]) D. E: malĕkasira yugā. [24]) D. E: Walawulu. [25]) D. E: tawĕk (E: tangwĕk) ri wka (D: wkas). [26]) E: Damalusan, Damalungan? D: ontbreekt. [27]) D. E: Kucapa. [28]) D. E: twega. [29]) D. E: tĕmbeyenira gawe kategan ringuni. [30]) D. E: Kapiṇḍonya gawe kategan (D: katwegan) ing Kupang. [31]) D. E: kaping tiganya ring Luwano. [32]) B: Macira. D. E: kaping patnya ring Pacira, madya ngĕmbung hamrang gĕsing. [33]) D. E: mangalahaning.

bhaṭāra; pinrangnira ring kuḍi [1]); pjah tang nāga, dadi tumuwuh marwan akĕmbang [2]). Nhĕr ingaranan nagasari, matangnyan ing Pacira tambehan ing hana kĕmbang nagasari [3]). Hana ta tuñci [4]) tininggalakning kayu, matmahan satwa lutung nga-ranya [5]) mangkana kacaritanya.

Tindak bhaṭāra saking Pacira mangulwan maring Maçin. Atapa [6]) ta sira kalih bhaṭārī Humā, amangunmangun ayu sira; matang-nyan hana manguyu, sira tinūt hana bhāwa hamanguyu, magawe phalapalupi ring jagat. Maharĕp ta bhaṭāra Guru manaka litu-hayu; mijil ta anak bhaṭārī. Inaranan ta sang hyang Kāmadewa, lituhayu [7]) lwih sakeng dewata kabeh; ikang istrī inaranan bhaṭārī Smarī. Mogha ta sira waliwitan amangan; kamasḍihĕn [8]) ta bhaṭārī, hinguntitakĕnira [9]) tang sga pinĕṇḍĕmnira, dadi tumuwuh malung kumĕṇḍung; matangnyan hana gaḍung ngara-nya, sga ngūni kacaritanya.

Ing Ileru hunggon [10]) bhaṭāra Guru; bhaṭārī Humā kalih bhaṭārī Smarī lungha sira anger ing kubonkubon ing Wanisari; [11]) tĕhĕr ta hunggon bhaṭārī Umā ring Wanisari [12]), katamapi tkaning mangke tantu bhaṭārī Umā.

Sah bhaṭāra Guru saking Masin; kari ta sang hyang Kāma-dewa [13]) lawan bhaṭārī Smarī ring argga Kelāça. Kunang bhaṭāra Guru ḍatang sireng Mahāmeru kalawan bhaṭārī Parameçwarī, paḍa sirā mangunakĕn tapa. Bhaṭārī Humā umintonakĕn bhawanira, tinhĕr ing argga Pinton patapan bhaṭārī Umā, hlĕtañ jurang [14]) saking patapan bhaṭāra Guru. Prāpta bhaṭārī Umā ring patapan bhaṭāra Guru, kasaṇḍung ta sira ring kayu malaṇḍĕp kadi taji wsi, tinhĕr ta ring Kayutaji [15]) ngaraning patapan bhaṭāra Guru. Rahĕn ta suku bhaṭārī, manangis ta sira; tangisnira matmahan pañcaçilah, luhnira matmahan ktakning ptung, sisinira matmahañ jamūrning paḍali [16]).

Sah ta bhaṭāra Guru saking Kayutaji, atma ring ranu bhāwa-nira; tinhĕr i Ranubhawa ngaraning patapan bhaṭāra Guru. Tumūt ta bhaṭārī Parameçwarī, lagi mabyangbyangan rahning [17]) suku bhaṭārī; tinhĕr ing Kabyang araning patapan bhaṭārī Umā. Masiga tāmbĕk bhaṭārī, mahyas ta sira. Tumwan ta bhaṭāra Guru

[1]) B: kuṇḍi. E: kuṇṭi. D: yata pinrang ta kundi. [2]) D. E: dadi tapwa tu-muwuh makĕmbang marondon. [3]) D: begin gaping. [4]) B. E: tudḍi. [5]) B. E: haranya. E: begin gaping. [6]) B: antapa. [7]) B: listuhayu [8]) B: kamasḍĕhĕn. [9]) B: nguntĕtakĕn. [10]) B: Iñilerahungo. [11]) B: kubonkubon i Pangning sāri. [12]) B: Pangning sāri. [13]) B: Lakṣmining dewa. [14]) B: hlĕtantura. [15]) B: hikang Kayutaji. [16]) B: jamūrning paduli. [17]) B: ngaraçrangning.

71

bhaṭārī hayunira; mara ta bhaṭāra Parameçwara ring bhaṭārī Humā; masangyoga ta sira, kaworan ta bhaṭārī Umā ring jĕro wtangnira. Sah ta sira ring patapanira, amanguyu ta sira wkasan; ring Pamanguyon-agung unggonira. Uwi talĕs ḍinaharnira; matangnyan anglĕmbu-guntung bhaṭāra, tinhĕr ngaranira Amanguyu-guntung.

Mijil ta anak bhaṭārī, jalujalu kalih sira. Mwajar ta bhaṭāra Guru: «Ingūni [1]) gaṇaku mara iri kita [2]), bhaṭārī, matangnyan Gaṇa Kumāra arananyānakning hulun». Bhaṭārī Umā ta sirā masĕhmasĕh iṇḍing baruñjing [3]) ri tusan sang hyang Ranupuhan; matangnyan ring Ḍingḍing [4]) aranya mangke. Iṇḍingira amoh, yata rineknira [5]); rinubung ring lalĕr umung mabyungan. Matmahan arwan aḍaḍung, tinhĕr ingaranan turuk-umung.

Kahucapa ta sang hyang Kāmadewa lawan bhaṭārī Smarī, sira maring argga Kelāça. Maharĕp ta sang hyang Kāmadewā sanggamaha [6]) lawan bhaṭārī Smarī, awdi ta kaglĕngana de bhaṭāra Guru. Pinalih tāwaknira bhaṭārī Smarī; matangnyan bhaṭārī Ratih manakbi ri sang hyang Kāmadewa. Mangjanma ta bhaṭārī Ratih sira ri hyangta [7]) Kaṇḍayun, matmahan sang Turuk-manis; [sang Kāmadewa mangjanma matmahan sang Wngan, sira pinakalaki sang Turuk-manis] [8]). Matangnyan pinaleçawi, makestri sang Katiha; mangkana [9]) sang Kulikuli, nagara ring Mḍang-gaṇa, makestri sang Wawuh-langit ring nagara [10]) ring Mḍang-gaṇa.

Kahucapa ta bhaṭāra Guru mwang bhaṭārī Humā, sira ta haneng [11]) Pamanguywan-agung, makānak sang Gaṇa mwang sang Kumāra. Wkasan ta bhaṭāri Umā amet raka sang Gaṇa Kumāra; tumurun maring ratharatha [12]) sira, phalawa kĕmbang binaktanira. Bhaṭāra Guru kari among [13]) sang Gaṇa mwang sang Kumāra, sukāmbĕk mamĕng sira. Kacaritā bhaṭārī Humā manangsinangsi ta sira; ndatan wruh tikang wwang ri manangsinangsi. Kerangan ta bhaṭārī Humā, wkasan ta sinamburatakĕn tang phalawa kambang. Jag, lĕs, mantuk ta bhaṭārī Umā, sinungsung [14]) de sang Gaṇa Kumāra. Mogha ta sira doyan amangan, apoyah [15]) ta bhaṭārī Humā, winwaran ta spĕt sganira.

Kahucapa ta bhaṭāra Parameçwara, tuminggalakning bhaṭārī Humā mwang sang Gaṇa Kumāra. Tyāga tāmbĕknira, mungguh ri gĕgĕrgĕgĕr; yata ri Gĕgĕr-katyagan ngaraning patapan bhaṭāra

---

[1]) B: Ih, ngūni. [2]) A. C: irika ta. [3]) B: baruñci. [4]) ri Ḍiḍing. [5]) B: hinenira. [6]) B: masanggamahā. [7]) B: ring hye. [8]) B: ontbreekt. [9]) B: makānak. [10]) B: rinatara. [11]) B: maring. [12]) B: raṣāraṣā. [13]) A: hanmong. [14]) A: sinungsang. [15]) kamohay.

72

Guru. Kunang bhaṭārī Umā momahomah mwang sang Gaṇa sang Kumāra; iniḍĕp ta laki kalih sira, matangnyan Gaṇa Kumāra hyang ning ambulungan ing kili; yata agöng papa pinangguhnya [1]) sang mabhāwa kili, yan katurun alaki [2]), apan ngūni bhaṭārī Umā kacaritanya. Tumutur sang Gaṇa ri bhaṭāra Guru; lunghā ta bhaṭāra Guru, kari ta sang Gaṇa ring Gĕgĕr-katyagan. Bhaṭāra Guru tumaṇḍĕs hiḍĕpnira, tinhĕr ing Taṇḍĕs ngaraning patapan bhaṭāra Guru.

Kunang ucapa ta [3]) bhaṭārī Humā, sah ta saking Pamanguywan-agung, magawe ta sira patapan. ‹Aku maṇik haneng wukir› hiḍĕpnira; tinhĕr ing gunung Maṇik ngaraning patapan bhaṭārī Humā. Makuṭa ta bhāwanira, Makuṭa ngaranya. Kadi tingkah ning dewata mabasahan, tinhĕr Kaki-dewata nāmanira [4]) bhaṭārī [5]), katamapi tkaning mangke.

Kunang sang Kumāra tumutur i [6]) bhaṭāra Guru sira, kaputangpati ta [7]) sira. ‹Ih, katuhon ring [8]) tumut ring bhaṭāra› lingnira; tinhĕr Katukatu [9]) ngaranira. Yata [10]) matangnyan sang Kumāra hyang ning katukatu [11]), yata magöng pāpa kapangguh de sang bhāwa katukatu [12]), yan sira katurun arabi [13]), apan bhaṭāra [14]) Guru kacaritanya. Sang Kumāra [pwa sira malapa susu, mantuk ta sira manuswing bhaṭārī Humā [16]); warĕg sira manusu, mantuk maring bhaṭāra Guru. Malapa ta [17]) sira sumusu muwah, [18]) pakṣanira maraha ring bhaṭārī [19]); wruh ta bhaṭārī Humā [20]) yan ḍatang sang Kumāra, mahĕthĕtan [21]) ta sira bhaṭārī. Wruh sira sang Kumāra, tinūt nira bhaṭārī [22])] [15]) matmahan ta sira Kalpataru [23]). Pinĕhnira ta [24]) susu bhaṭārī, katwan ta umis [25]) tang Kalpataru [26]) de sang Kumāra, yata linanggangnira [27]). Arasa ta kadi susu bhaṭārī [28]), wruh

[1]) A: pinanggunya. B: ,pangguhnya. [2]) B: yan turun halaki. [3]) B: kahucapa ta. [4]) B: kadi dewatayanira. [5]) C: bhaṭāra. [6]) D. E: einde gaping. [7]) B: kapuntangpanting. D. E: kabuntangbanting. [8]) D. E: katuhon dening. [9]) A: Katutatuta. [10]) D. E: ontbreekt. [11]) D. E: katu. [12]) D. E: yata matangnyan hagung pataka kūpanggih de (D: den) sang hārawwa katukatu. B: sang mabhâwa katukatu. [13]) B: katurunanārabi. [14]) D. E: apan ramanira bhaṭara. B: bhāwa bhatara. [15]) E: ontbreekt. [16]) D: maring bhaṭārī. [17]) B. malapāsṭi. [18]) B: susu muwah. D: susu malih. [19]) D: mareng bhaṭārī. [20]) D: ontbreekt tot tinūtnira bhaṭārī: nhĕr linunggan sira, tinutā bhaṭārī den sang Kumāra, awlas pwa bhaṭārī Umā, rĕp matmahan pwa sira kalpataru. [21]) B: matĕhĕr tan [22]) B: tinūt nira bhaṭārī ontbreekt. [23]) E: awlas pwa bhaṭārī Uma, rep matmahan pwa sira taru kalpa. [24]) D: yata pinĕntang. E: yata pinĕh. [25]) D. E: umisulurikang. [26]) E: tarukaghā. [27]) D: linanggahika. E: linangguhika. B: sinanggahnira. [28]) D. E: mwang karaṣa kadi duh ning susu ning bhaṭārī.

ta sang Kumāra wkasan yan tmahan bhaṭārī Umā tikang kayu. [1]) Sinantwanira tang kalpataru [2]) wkasan.

«Non duh duk amangguh susu ning indung karing dangu [3])». Matangnyan hano [4]) ngaranya mangke; duk ngaraning [5]) wulunya [6]), dangu ngaraning [5]) sulurnya [7]).

Mangkana ling sang Kumāra. Jag lĕs [8]), lunghā ta bhaṭārī Humā, mangulwan larinira; tinūt ta de sang Kumāra, katututan ta sira, pinipilan ing [9]) sang Kumāra; matangnyan hana gunung Pilan [10]) ngaranya. Malara ambĕk sang Kumāra, matapa ta sira ring gunung Tawungan [11]) ngaranya mangke, patapanira sang Kumāra ngūni kacaritanya [12]).

Ḍatang ta sang hyang Gaṇa ri bhaṭārī Humā, mogha ta paḍapaḍa rūpanira lawan sang Kumāra; matangnyan ahijo sang hyang Gaṇa, tinhĕr gunung Hijo ngaraning gunung bhaṭārī Humā. Malara tambĕk sang hyang Gaṇa, matapa ta sira; matangnyan hana gunung Wija ngaranya mangke, patapan sang hyang Gaṇa ngūni kacaritanya [13]).

Inanugrahan ta sang hyang Gaṇa de bhaṭāra Guru mandi çwara [14]), sawuwusnira tuhu [15]). Wikalpa ta manah sang hyang Brahmā Wiṣṇu tumon kasiddhan [16]) sang hyang Gaṇa; yata hetunirāgaweya cangkriman [17]). Ḍatang ta sang hyang Wiṣṇu ri harĕp [18]) sang hyang Gaṇa, [mwajar ta sang hyang Gaṇa] [19]):

«Apa [20]) gawenta, sang hyang Wiṣṇu?»

[Mwajar ta sang hyang Wiṣṇu lingnira:] [19])

«Cpani cangkriman ing hulun, hyang Gaṇa» [21]).

«Apa ta [22]) cangkrimanta [23]), sang hyang Wiṣṇu?»

«Apa pinakawadangku [24])?».

---

[1]) D. E: yan bhaṭārī matmahan taru. [2]) D. E: sinatyanira kayu wkasan. [3]) D. E: Yata kapanggih (E: Dadi kapanggih) sapa ring dangū. B: koṇḍuh duk amanggih pungih susu ning indung kang ring dangū. [4]) B: Hako. [5]) D. E: harane. [6]) B: araninghulun. [7]) B: araning susurnya. [8]) D. E: Lĕs. [9]) D. E: bhaṭārī Uma tinututan pinipilnira ta de. B: kapipitan. [10]) B: Wilān. D. E: Kampil. [11]) D. E: Tuwu ngaranya. [12]) D. E: patapan sang Gaṇa kacaritanya ngūni. D. E: volgende alinea ontbreekt. [13]) B: ngūni kunangnya. [14]) D. E: inugrahan ta sira mandi çwara de bhaṭāra Guru. [15]) B: wuwusira tuhu. D. E: yata sa wuwusira mogghā tutuha (D: mogaha). [16]) D. E: wruh ta sang hyang Brāhma Wiṣṇu, tuminghāl kaṣidenira. [17]) A: sangkriman. B: hetunirācangkrimān. D. E: yata magawe cacangkriman. [18]) B: harĕp. D. E: tka bhaṭara Wiṣṇu ri kahanannira hyang Gaṇa. [19]) D. E: ontbreekt. [20]) D. E: paran. [21]) D. E: Cĕpaniñ (E: Cĕmpaniñ) cacangkriman ing hulun, sang Gaṇa. [22]) D. E: Mapa. [23]) A: sangkrimanta. [24]) B: pinakapaḍangku. D. E: Ndah, paran medaning hulun, sang Gaṇa?

74

«Ah, brahmātya pinakawadanta [1])»

«Apa brahmahatya ngaranya [2])?»

«Amatimati paḍanta dewata kita»

«Taha, durung tāku amatimati paḍangku dewata [3])»

«Ah, mamatimati kita paḍanta dewata [4]); apa ta yan [5]) kumĕlĕm polah mangkana [6])?»

Jag lĕs [7]), lunghā ta bhaṭāra Keçawa, ḍatang [8]) ta sang hyang Brahmāgawe sangkriman [9]). Lima ngūni tĕṇḍas [10]) sang hyang Brahmā; intĕtakĕn çirahnira kang [11]) ring tngah, papat katwan çirahnira [12]), yeki mangke [13]) bhāwanira. Jag lĕs, ḍatang ri kahanan sang hyang Gaṇa [14]).

«Apa [15]) gawenta, sang hyang Brahmā?»

Sumahur bhaṭāra Pāwaka [16]):

«Cpani kwehe tĕṇḍasku denta [17]), hyang Gaṇa»

«Apa ta yan kacpan kwehe tĕṇḍasta [18])?»

«Dak sambah kita, hyang Gaṇa; tan kacpan [19]), ḍak pangan kita, hyang Gaṇa. [Lah, pira kwehe tĕṇḍasku denta, hyang Gaṇa?] [20])»

»Papat kwehe tĕṇḍasta, hyang Brahmā [21])».

«Ah [22]), pjah si kita denku, hyang Gaṇa, apan lilima kweh ning tĕṇḍasku, hyang Gaṇa. [23])»

Tuminghal ta bhaṭāra Parameswara; «Uḍuh, pjah syanak ning hulun de bhaṭara Brahmā mne [24])». Matangnyan pinĕgat çirah sang hyang Brahmā kang ring tngah de bhaṭāra Guru ri tangan kiwa [25]). Kunang pinakatangan tngĕn sang hyang Brahmā, sang hyang Wiṣṇu tangan kiwa [26]); matangnyan sang hyang Wiṣṇu

---

[1]) B: pinakawwanganta D. E: Ah, brāhmantā pinakamedanta. [2]) D. E: Paran ta brāhma ninghulun. [3]) D. E: Ah, durung hulun amateni paḍanta dewata. [4]) D. E: Hah iya kita mateni dewata. [5]) B: mapa tanayan. [6]) D. E: hapan tan mangkanā polah ning dewa hlĕmhlĕm. [7]) D. E: Lĕs. [8]) B: anḍatang. [9]) D. E: ḍatang bhaṭara Brāhma, hamalahu (D: halaku) cinta. [10]) D. E: lilima pwa tĕṇḍasnira. [11]) D. E: sawiji ta. [12]) D. E: katon papat tĕṇḍasnya. [13]) D. E: mangko. [14]) D. E: Lĕs mareng sang hyang Gaṇa. Mojar hyang Gaṇa. [15]) D. E: Paran. [16]) D: Mojar bhaṭāra Brahma. E: ontbreekt. [17]) D. E: Pira kehe tĕṇḍas ning hulun. [18]) B: yen kacĕpanya. D. E: mapā lamun (D: laku) kacpan? A: tĕṇḍastu. [19]) B: denta. D. E: lamun tan kacpan. [20]) D. E: ontbreekt; mangkana wuwusnira bhaṭara Brāhma. Mojar hyang Gana. [21]) D. E: Yi, papat kehe tĕṇḍasta bhaṭara Brahmā. [22]) D: Ah lah. E: Alah. [23]) D. E: apan lilima tĕṇḍas ning hulun. [24]) D. E: dene si Brahmā. [25]) D. E: Matangnyan pinĕgat sang hyang Rājapati ri tngah denira bhaṭara Guru, yata katon papat hulunya. Pĕk tĕk, yata pintĕkakning tangan kiwa tĕṇḍasnireng tĕngah. [26]) D. E: Kunang pinakatangan kiwa tngĕn de bhatara Guru (E: bhaṭara Bratuwan), sang hyang Brāhma tanganira kiwa, sang hyang Wiṣṇu tanganira tngĕn.

kinonira umalapana[1]) tĕṇḍas sang hyang Brahmā. Katuju kapacupi[2]) sang hyang Gaṇa ri sang hyang Wiṣṇu yan sira brahmahatya[3]).

Kahucapa ta wuwus sang hyang Brahmā lawan sang hyang Gaṇa[4]):

«Papat kwehning[5]) tĕṇḍasta, sang hyang Brahmā.»

«Ah tahā, lilima kwehning tĕṇḍasku, hyang[6]) Gaṇa.»

[Mangkana ling sang hyang Brahmā.][7])

«Ah, mati ngko denku, hyang[8]) Gaṇa.»

Mangkana ling hyang Brahmā; pakṣanira umijilakna tĕṇḍasnira[9]), mogha wus pinĕgat[10]) de bhaṭāra, [muñcar ta rudiranira][11]). Kroḍa ta bhaṭāra Brahmā; yata matangnyan yinuganira tang ruḍira[12]) maṭmahan mahakāla rākṣasa[13]) satus ḍolapan kwehnya, kinwan umjahana[14]) ri hyang Gaṇa. [Jag lĕs, malayu sang hyang Gaṇa][15]), sumambah ri bhaṭāra Guru[16]), sinambut ta lunghayanira de bhaṭāra Parameçwara[17]).

«Uḍuh, kami umalapi[18]) tĕṇḍase si Rājapati[19]); uwus pjah kita yen tan aku mangalapana çirah[20]) sang hyang Brahmā, apan den tĕtakĕn[21]) çirahnya kang ring tngah[22]), hetunya katwan[23]) papat denta[24]».

«Kroḍa mangke pun[25]) Rājapati, pwangkulun[26]); matangnyan manganakĕn surakāla[27]) rākṣasa ṣatus ḍolapan kwehnya, ahyun umjahana ri[28]) tanayan bhaṭāra mangke, pwangkulun, dwan[29]) ing tanayan bhaṭāra sumambah ri pāduka Parameçwara[30])».

«Uḍuh, tan sangçayaha kitānaku sang hyang Gaṇa; yan ṣang hyang Brahmāyuga rākṣasa, kami mayuga dewa».

---

1) D. E: umalapa. 2) B: kapaḍāpi. D. E: Kunang katuju kacĕmpan. 3) D. E: brāhmamaptyā. 4) D. E: Tucapa ta sang hyang Gaṇa lingira. 5) D. E: Ah, papat kehe. 6) D. E: lilima tĕṇḍasku. 7) D. E: ontbreekt. 8) D. E: Ah, dak panganko. B: mati ko denku. 9) D. E: humintokna tĕṇḍasnya. 10) D. E: pinupak ta. 11) D. E: ontbreekt. 12) D. E: yata yinugaḍira. 13) D. E: matmahan kāla mwang rākṣasa. 14) D. E: hamjahana. 15) D. E: ontbreekt. 16) D. E: Prameçwara. 17) D. E: Guru. 18) D. E: „Uḍuh, padūka bhaṭara manghalapi tĕṇḍase pun Brahmā, pukulun?" „Ya, kami humalapi. 19) B: Mrājapati. 20) B: dentanaku mangalapana. D. E: yen tan hulun humalapā tĕṇḍase. 21) A: den tatakĕn. 22) D. E: dene si Rājapati. 23) D. E: sangkane katon. 24) D. E: yata dak alapi sawiji tĕṇḍase hyang Brahmā". 25) D. E: punang. 26) D. E: pukulun. 27) D. E: yata mangnakĕn mahaçūra mwang kalā. 28) D. E: maharĕpwa matespana (D: mangetana) tanayan. 29) D. E: ya don. 30) D. E: ring pada bhaṭara, pukulun.

76

Çeg rĕp[1]), yinuga ta kukunira[2]) kalima[3]); tĕp, bĕt, yata yinuganira[4]), matmahan dewata limang siki kwehnya, inaranan Kuçika[5]), Gargga, Metri, Kuruṣya, Pratañjala [samangkana kweh nya][6]). Kinwanira manglawana ikang mahāsurakāla; ndah tan wihang sang pañcadewata. Tan ucapĕn prangnira[7]) pañcadewata lawan rākṣasa[8]).

Kahucapa ta taṇḍas sang[9]) hyang Brahmā, linabuhnira ring sāgara[10]) [asat kang sāgara][11]); sinalahakĕn ing ākāça, [gsĕng kang ākāça kadi sinanga][12]); sinalahakĕn ing pṛthiwī[13]), tĕrus tkeng jro pātāla. Katiban çirah[14]) sang hyang Anantabhoga[15]), nāga pinakadasar ing pṛthiwī; sira ta kaholaholah[16]) çarīranira, matangnya liṇḍu bhaṭārī pṛthiwī, ogah[17]) sang hyang Mahāmeru. Sawet ning drĕs nikang liṇḍu matakut ta bhaṭāra Guru rubuha[18]) sang hyang Mahāmeru; yata inalapanira çirah sang hyang Brahmā sangkeng jro pātāla.

Kahucapa[19]) ta mahasurakāla sampun alah matakut denikang pañcadewata; matangnyan paḍa marĕk sang[20]) pañcadewata ring sira bhaṭāra Guru [aminta upadeça][21]). Tan wineh ta bhaṭārī Humā rumĕngwakna[22]) upadeça de bhaṭāra; yata dinohaknira[23]), kinwan ta sirāmeta pĕhan ing lĕmbu kanya hirĕng. Tan wihang ta bhaṭārī Humā, jag lĕs[24]) lunghā ta bhaṭārī Humā. Enak ta pangupadeçanikang pañcamahādewata ri sira bhaṭāra Guru[25]).

. Kunang çirah sang hyang Brahmā dinĕlĕng de bhaṭāra[26]) pinĕṇḍĕm ta ring gunung Kampud wkasan; matangnyan gunung Sambadagni[27]) ngaraning gunung Kampud wkasan. Tumuwuh çirah sang hyang Brahmā wkasan, matangnyan haṇa nyu ngaranya mangke[28]), tmahaning çirah [sang hyang Brahmā][29]) kacaritanya ngūni.

---

[1]) D. E: Sag rĕp. B: Jhag lĕs. [2]) D. E: mayugghā ta sira kukunira tiaugĕlan. [3]) B: lima. [4]) D. E: tap pĕk, yata yinuga hikang kuku. [5]) B: Kurçika. [6]) D. E: ontbreekt. [7]) D. E: paprangira. [8]) D. E: lawan sang mahāçūrakalā. [9]) D. E: kucapa tĕṇḍase. [10]) D. E: linabuhakning. [11]) D. E: ontbreekt. [12]) D. E: ontbreekt; kadi singhā. [13]) D. E: ingevoegd: bubul ikang pṛthiwī. [14]) D: katinghalan. E: kaciyyan. B: sira. [15]) B. D. E: Nantabhoga. [16]) B: sira ta kang holahholah D. E: kolaholahta. [17]) D. E: lwirug. [18]) D. E: marmma rubuha. [19]) D. E: Kucapa. [20]) E: maçewāka. D: masewa. [21]) D. E: ontbreekt. [22]) D. E: kunang bhaṭāri Uma tan wineha humarĕkna. [23]) matangnyan dinohakĕn pwa sira. [24]) D. E: sag lĕs. B: sagya lĕs. [25]) D. E: pañcadewata ring bhaṭāra Guru. [26]) D: ingevoegd: yata mahularĕpanasnira, wkasan. E: ingevoegd: yata mari hulap panasnira, wkasan. [27]) D. E: Sambudaghni. [28]) D. E: Wkasan tumbuh (E: tumut) ikang çirah, matangnyan hamangke (E: tka ning mangke). [29]) D. E: ontbreekt.

77

Kahucapa ta [1]) bhaṭārī Humā, mahas ta [2]) sira ring swargga loka, amet ta sira pĕhan ing lĕmbu kanya hirĕng; tka ring saptapātāla, ndah tan panmu sira pĕhan ing lĕmbu kanya irĕng. Mahas ta sira ring [3]) maḍyapada, mogha ta sira kasaṇḍung ring watu karang; blah ta mpu ning [4]) sukunira kiwa, matangnyan lumampah matkĕn sira [5]). Binañcana ta de bhaṭāra Guru, pinarikṣa [6]) kasatyan bhaṭārī Umā; matangnyan bhaṭāra Guru matmahan sang kumāra gohphala [7]), raray angon, tanpahingan lituhayunya [8]). [Ikang andaka putih wahananira] [9]) wineh atmahana [10]) lĕmbu kanya irĕng, yata ingonira [11]); rĕp yeki bhāwanira. Sḍang mamöh [12]) pĕhan ing lĕmbu kanya irĕng sang kumāra gohphala [mogha ta] [13]) kapanggih de bhaṭārī Humā. Mwajar ta bhaṭārī Humā:

«Ih, sang raryyangon, ndak aminta pĕhan iri kita, arih [14])».

[15]) «Tan paweh pinun, arih [16])».

«Ah, tan aweh; [17]) ih, ḍak tukuneng [18]) mās maṇik, arih».

«Ah, tan paweh; makaparan [19]) ta gawehaning hmās maṇik dening pinun [20])?»

Mangkana lingnira. Wkasan ta sang kumāra gohphala amalaku linawanan; wirangrwang buddi bhaṭārī Umā, yeka ta warṇna kasatyanira [21]); yata hana gunung Winihatya [22]) ngaranya. Matngĕ ta bhaṭārī Humā ri pĕhan [23]) ing lĕmbu kanya irĕng; matangnyan linawananira sang kumāra gohphāla. Satya matapi sira ri [24]) bhaṭāra Guru; masanggama tan linawananira ta ring rahasya, linawananira pupu [25]), dinĕngkulaknira [26]) kadi rahasya rūpanya. [27]) Rĕp asanggama ta sira, matangnyan hana gunung Pasanggaman [28]) aranya mangke. Kunang pasangyoga [29]) bhaṭāra lan bhaṭārī

---

[1]) D. E: Kucapa. [2]) D: umastana. E: umahas ta. [3]) D. E: mara ta sirong. [4]) D. E: blak pwa hĕmpune. [5]) D. E: matkĕntăkĕn. B: matkyan. [6]) D. E: pinarikṣanira ring. [7]) D. E: guphala. [8]) D. E: raryyangon tan sipi listuhayunya. [9]) D. E: ontbreekt. [10]) D. E: winehira matmahana. [11]) D. E: pinakahingonira. [12]) D. E: sḍĕng ring angonira. B: sḍĕng mamĕspĕs. [13]) D. E: ontbreekt. [14]) D. E: dak jaluke pehan ing lembu kanya hireng. A: pehaning ri kita. B: Ih, sang raryyāngwāng haminta pĕhan irikita, hari. [15]) D. E: ingevoegd: Mojar sang rāryyangon. [16]) D. E: momaharih. [17]) D. E: tan paweh, pinun. [18]) A: dak tuneng. D. E: dak tukone. [19]) A: pakaparan. [20]) D. E: paran gawene mas maṇik deninghulun? [21]) A: ta satyanira. D. E: yeki ta kasatyanira. B: yekā taghna ring kasatyanira. [22]) D. E: Winasatya. B: Winih satya. [23]) D. E: ikang pĕhan. [24]) Satyanira ring. [25]) B: tan linawan ikang mupu. D. E: masanggama ta sira linawanan tang pupu. [26]) B: winĕngkulakĕnnira. D. E: dinkungakĕnira (D: dinĕngkungakĕn) tang pupunira. [27]) D. E: kadi raṣya paraparanya. (D: parapanya). [28]) D. E: Sanggama. [29]) D: masangyogya.

matmahan tang komara Cintamaṇik [1]) [masanggama pwa sira lawan pupu] [2]) tinhĕr kasamputa ngaraning sang Cintamaṇi [3]). Kinarangulonira ta sĕmbung [4]), kinalaçanira ta papa [5]); kari ta sira sang Cintamaṇi kagulinggulingan [6]); yata matangnyan hana [7]) gunung Gulingaṇḍara [8]) ngaranya mangke [9]). Kāmanira wutah haneng [10]) lmah, inurugan [11]) ta de bhaṭārī Humā, matmahan ta gunung Marapi [12]). Blaḳ ni mpumpu ning [13]) suku bhaṭārī mesi ta kāma katitisan de bhaṭāra; yata matangnyan abĕh [14]) mpumpu ning suku bhaṭārī [15]).

Winehnira [16]) ta bhaṭāri Umā pĕhan [17]) ing lĕmbu kanya irĕng. Jag, lĕs, msat ta sang kumāra gohphala, waluya ta bhaṭāra Guru; [18]) muwah tikang [19])andaka paḍa manglayang [20]), sinapa ta de bhaṭārī Humā, tibaheng [21]) pṛthiwī, tan wĕnang mūra [22]); yata matangnyan hana gunung Itip-ing-lĕmbu [23]) ngaranya mangke. Manaḍah ta sapatanira [24]) bhaṭārī Humā, kinwanirā mangunakna tapa [25]). Atapa tikang andaka; yata matangnyan hana gunung Kĕdyangga [26]) ngaranya mangke [27]).

Ikang pĕhan kang sinwaknira [28]) matmahan silodaka.

Kahucapa ta [29]) bhaṭārī Humā, maböh mpumpu ning sukunira kiwa [30]); marepota [31]) sira, pinijĕtira, mtu rahnya, mtu pilapilunya, mtu kawahkawahnya [32]); pinijĕtnira muwah, mtu tang raray [33]) tigang siki kwehnya, mtu ariarinya. Yata matangnyan kroḍa bhaṭārī Humā; rĕp rinĕgĕp tang [34]) sañjata ning para watĕk [35]) dewata, yeki [36]) mangke bhāwanira; sumyuhkna [37])

[1]) B: komara sang Ciṇṭamaṇi. D. E: sang kumara Ciṇṭāmaṇik. [2]) D. E: ontbreekt. [3]) D. E: nher ta sāmpun ta haranira sang Ciṇṭāmaṇik. [4]) B: tang sĕmbu. [5]) B: kinaraçānira tang papa. D. E: kalasanira hapahapā. [6]) B: kagulingguling ngaranya. D. E: magiling gilingan. [7]) A: tana. [8]) A. B: Guling haṇḍara. D. E: Gilingan. [9]) A: mangkā. [10]) D: hutamaneng. [11]) D. E: inurutan. [12]) A: Marawi. D. E: Marapwi. [13]) A: pupuning. B: blahning. D. E: blakning hĕmpune. [14]) B: habah. [15]) D. E: matangnyan kasiṣyan kama katimpal de bhaṭārī, hiya ta (E: ikata ta) pagĕh ning (D: ring) hĕmpune suku bhaṭārī. [16]) D. E: Wus mangkana wineh. [17]) B: halapĕhān. [18]) D. E: maluya reh bhaṭara muwah. [19]) A: kitang. [20]) D. E: muwah tando msat anglayang. [21]) D. E: tiba tayeng. [22]) B: takna wnang murah. D. E: tan awrĕng (E: tan mrĕng) tan maraṇa. [23]) D. E: Hiṣyalĕmbu. [24]) D. E: Manaḍah ta pĕhan pwa sapaning. [25]) D. E: kinon ta mamanguna (E: mamangana) sapa. [26]) B: Kĕnyāngga. [27]) D. E: Matuwa tang andakā; matangnyan bhaṭārī matmahan gunung Marapwi (E: Marapuy), datĕng ring (E: dati ring) pasaba bhaṭārī ikā; matang yan ta siṣyanta makatisan de bhaṭāra (D: mwang katisan); matangnyan nanggĕh (D: nagĕh) ning (D: ring) suku bhaṭārī. [28]) D. E: Ikang pĕhan pinoknira. [29]) D. E: Tucapa ta. [30]) D. E: manggĕlĕt puḍata kawa, ya. [31]) B: mara ring pot ta. [32]) D. E: yata pinijĕtira turanya, ya mtu kawah kā. [33]) B. D. E: ingevoegd: jalujalu. [34]) manggĕlĕpwa. [35]) D. E: nawa. [36]) D. E: rĕp, yeki. [37]) B: sumyuḳna.

ikang raray paryyanira [1]). Rĕp tikang raray katrini sumambah ri [2]) bhaṭārī Parameçwarī; mwajar tang raray:

‹Apa deya ranak bhaṭārī yan pjahana de Parameçwarī [3]); prasidanĕn [4]) tanayan bhaṭārī, pwangkulun [5])›.

Mangkana ling ning raray katrini; rĕp, mari kroda bhaṭārī Humā, yata matangnyan pinratiṣṭhanira tang raray [6]) wkasan:

‹Uḍuh tanayanku kita raray katrini, kita pwa mijil sakeng [7]) mpumpune sukungku [8]) kiwa, matangnyan mpu kuna [9]) ngaranta katrini. Kunang kita sang matuhā, dak sangaskara [10]) kita, dak rarapusane romanta [11]); tinhĕr mpu Kumāra-gimbal ngaranta [12]), wiku ṛṣyangarĕmban [13]) ta ngaranta mangke. Mangkana ta panugrahangkwiri kita [14]): sañjāta sang hyang Trikurungan ta [15]); [kayatnakĕn ta panganugrahangku] [16])›.

‹Kunang kita raray panngah, dak sangaskara [17]) kita, ndah ta suhun wulune [18]) rahāṣyangku [19]), tinhĕr mpu Kumāra-siddi ngarananta [20]). Pasewa ta [21]) kita ri hyang Gaṇa, matangnyan wiku çewa ta ngaranta ring rāt. Warahwarah tang mānusa ring akṣara wijjāna [22]), kita haṣṭapaḍasāri [23]) ning bhuwana. Bhūjā [24]) ngaraning tangan, angga ngaraning çarīra, tinhĕr ta mpu Bhūjangga ngarananta. Mah panugrahangku ri ko [25]): sañjāta sanghyang Mṛṣa [26]) ngaranya. Kayatnākĕn panganugrahangku [27])›.

[28]) ‹Kunang kita raray pamungçu, dak sangaskara [29]) kita mangke, mpu Kumara-raray ta ngaranta; tiñjo ta rahaṣyangku yan samahita [30]); wiku boḍḍa ta nga[ra]nta ring rāt, pamiṇḍa [31]) kita ring bhaṭāra Buḍḍa dlahā. Ço ngaraning hyang, gata ngaraning rĕm; tinhĕr ta çogata ngaranta ring rāt. Mah panganu-

---

1) B: marāryyanira. D. E: sumrahakna ta rare wiprayanira mareng bhaṭārī Umā. 2) Rĕp ḍatĕng hikang rare katrini sumambaha. 3) D. E: Masa deya pjah ranak bhatari pukulun. 4) B: prasiddākĕn. 5) D. E: kunang riḍĕpni ranak paḍuka Prameçwari, prasiddakna tanayan bhatari. 6) D. E: ya pinrathiṣṭā (D: pinrastita) ikang rare. B: minanrānṣṭita sira tang rarāy. 7) B: sangke. D. E: mijile sakeng. 8) D. E: sukune hulun. 9) B: mpungku. D. E: mpu. 10) D. E: dak sangaskarani. 11) B: ko rarāy puṣāne romanta. D. E: dak rampase remonta. 12) D. E: nhĕr wu Komara-gimbal āranira. 13) B: ṛṣyāngarĕptan. D. E: ṛṣyabarĕban aranira mangke. 14) D. E: mangkanā nugrahangkwa ri kita. 15) D E: sambata bhatāra hyang Trikumara ngaranya mangke. B: Trikuru ngarantā. 16) B: panugrahangku. D. E: ontbreekt. 17) B. D. E: dak sangaskarani. 18) B: ndah mahta suhun hulune. 19) D. E: ndah suhun ulu de raṣyangku. 20) D. E: nhĕr wu Komara-siddi. 21) D. E: waçewa. 22) B: akṣarawijāna. D. E: hākṣara wyañjāna. 23) D. E: haṣṭasarira. 24) B: bhūjāngga. D. E: bhujanggāraning. 25) D. E: nihanugrahanku ringko. 26) D. E: Mṛṣya. 27) D. E: Ndah kayatnakna panugrahanku. 28) D. E: volgende alinea ontbreekt. 29) B: dak sangaskarani. 30) A: tan samāhitā. 31) B: mapiṇḍata.

grahangku: sañjāta sang hyang Guḍuhā [1]) ngaranya. Kayatnakĕn ta panganugrahāngku».

«Ih muwah raray, paran kita manglabtiryyāku [2]), ndi sangkanta?»

«Sājjā [3]) bhaṭārī, pratiṣṭanĕn [4]) tanayan bhaṭārī, pwangkulun; ranak bhaṭārī tmahaning [5]) kawahkawah nikang raray pwangkulun [6])».

«Lah, ḍak pratiṣṭa [7]) kita; patapa [8]) kita pinggir ing a[wa]n. Ki[ta] ngūni manglabt [9]) iryyāku [10]); tinhĕr ta tabĕhabĕt ngaranta [11]). Nihan panganugrahangkwa riko [12]): sañjāta sang hyang Gora [13]) ngaranya. Kayatnakĕn ta [14]) panganugrahangku».

«Muwah raray, paran kitānambah [15]) iryyāku, lanang wadwan kita?»

«Sajjā bhaṭārī, [16]) praçiṣṭanĕn [17]) tanayan bhaṭārī pwangkulun; ranak bhaṭārī tmahan ing harihari ning raray [18]) pwangkulun».

«Lah, ḍak pratiṣṭa [19]) kita [20]); pamidĕr kita ring rāt, pamaṇḍagiṇa kita [21]), [den kadi bhawangku lawan bapanta ngūni] [22]) mangkana bhawahanta raray wadwan kita [23])».

«[Muwah kita raray lanang] [24]) den kadi bhawane bapanta [25]) duk anggoḍa hiryyāku [26]); pasawit kita ḍaḍung, paglangglang hada pinulir [27]); tinhĕr ta hambaṇḍagiṇānggoḍa ngarananta ring rāt [28]). Mangkana pawkasangku ring ko [29])».

«Ih, satwa [30]), paran ta kita sumambah [31]) iryyāku»?

«Sajjā bhaṭārī [32]), satwa lutung haran pinakanghulun [33]). Mraçiṣṭanĕn [34]) tanayan bhaṭārī pwangkulun [35])».

---

1) B: Guruha. 2) B: paran kita malabwiryyaku. D. E: Ih, paranta, rare humalang ireku. 3) B: Sajñā. 4) B. D. E: praçiṣṭanĕn. 5) D. E: dadening. 6) D. E: hikang raryyalā. 7) B. D. E: praçiṣṭā. 8) D. E: pwatapa. 9) B: malābt. 10) D. E: ngūniweh halangĕn karyyangku. 11) D. E: nhĕr angambĕtabĕt (D: angabĕtabĕt) aranta. 12) D. E: Nihanūgrahangku ringko. B: Tinhĕr ta tanghabĕt haranā panugrahanku ringko. 13) B: Ghora. 14) B: Yatnakĕn ta. D. E: Ndah kayatnakna. 15) B: kitang nĕmbah. 16) D. E: Sajñā bhaṭāri pukulun, B: Sajñā bhaṭārī. 17) D. E: pratiṣṭānĕn. 18) D. E: raryyalā. 19) B: ḍak praçiṣṭā. 20) B: kanyu. 21) D. E: pamañca bhūwaṇa. 22) D. E: ontbreekt. 23) D. E: mangkana bhawanta rare lanang (D: rare) wadon. 24) D. E: ontbreekt. 25) D: den kadi bhawane bapanta nguni den kadi bhawanta nguni. E: den kadi bhawantengūni. 26) D. E: apantā duk anggowa hiryyaku ringūni. 27) D. E: pagĕglang kita hardḍa pinūlir. 28) D. E: nhĕr anggoḍa ngarantā. B: hambaṇḍaginā goḍa. 29) D. E: pamkasku ri kita. 30) D. E: sato. 31) D. E: wani hanĕmbah. 32) D. E: Sajña bhatarí pukulun. B: Sajña. 33) D. E: Sato minakaraning hulun. 34) B. D. E: praçiṣṭānĕn. 35) D. E: ingevoegd: den paḍa lawan bhaṭari.

81

«Lah, ḍak praçiṣṭa kanyu [1]. [Mah, sañjāta Gaḍa [2] ngaranya;] [3] padodwata kita wiḍak [4], pacaritakĕn tang bhūwaṇa, rākṣaka pūjān sang prabhū [5]; tinhĕr ta widu ngarananta ring rāt [6]. Mangkana pawkasangku ri ko [7].

Kahucapa [8] ta sang Cintamaṇi [9], inĕmban kinudang [10] de sang watĕk dewatā. Bapa-hibunya tinakonakĕn [11], winarah ta sira dening watĕk dewata yan sira hanak de bhaṭāra Guru makebu [12] bhaṭārī Umā. Yata matangnyan [lumampah] [13] sang Cintamaṇi, ḍatang ri [14] bhaṭāra Parameçwara; tan hinaku hanak sira [15] de bhaṭāra Guru, pambeda [bhaṭāra ri] [16] bhaṭārī Huma; kamerangĕn ta bhaṭārī mangakuha ring anaknira [17]. Yata matangnyan manangisang Cintamaṇi, rĕp tumĕdun ta sira ring mahitāla. Liṇḍu tang pṛthiwī saha ktug mwang prahara [18]; manganakĕn ta sira tejā prabhawa [19] sawetning laranira [20] tan inaku hanak de bhaṭāra mwang bhaṭārī. [Kasiharĕp bhaṭāra] [21] wkasan, yata matangnyan sinambut [22] sang Cintamaṇi wkasan, inaku hanak de bhaṭāra mwang bhaṭārī.

Vierde Hoofdstuk.

Kahucapa tatwa sih [23] bhaṭāra Parameçwara tumulusakna [24] magawe tantu [praçiṣṭa] [25] ri Yawaḍipa. Makāryya ta [26] sira maṇḍala, makulambi [27] maguṇḍala sira, tumitihi su[ra]ngga [28] pataraṇa. Tinhĕr manganaknadewaguru sira, umiṣyani sira patapan [29] kabeh, kadyana: katyagan [30], pangajaran, pangubwanan, pa[ma]nguywan, pangabtan, gurudeça [31], hanguṇḍahagi [32], angarĕmban [33]; sirāgawe hika [34] kabeh. Masamoha ta sira [35] sang watĕk dewata kabeh [36], mangambuli [37] ta sira makāryyā [38] humah sing kayu tan wurung [39], sarwwasiddā

[1]) D. E: kita. [2]) B: gaḍdā. [3]) D. E: ontbreekt. [4]) B: padodwata kita ring wana kanya. D. E: padodot pwa kita wikwa. [5]) D. E: rikṣakeng pujān pawkas sang prabhu ring ko. [6]) D. E: nhĕr wanda pwa ngarantā. [7]) D. E: pāwkasku ri kita. [8]) D. E: kucapa. [9]) B: Ciṇṭamaṇī. [10]) D. E: kinudangkuḍang. [11]) B: tinakonakĕnya. D. E: tinakonanira. [12]) D. E: makaïbū. [13]) D. E: ontbreekt. [14]) D. E: ḍatĕngeng. [15]) D. E: hinaku wka. [16]) C: ontbreekt. [17]) D. E: pambeda hikā umerang ta bhaṭara mangakwanaknira. [18]) D. E: ingevoegd: hudan miris. [19]) D. E: mangnakĕn prabhawa pwa sira mwang tejā. [20]) D. E: larane hatinira dumehira. [21]) D. E: ontbreekt. [22]) D. E: wkasan rĕp sinambut. [23]) D. E: Tucapa ta. [24]) D. E: ingevoegd: denira. [25]) D. E: ontbreekt. [26]) D. E: makāryyaha [27]) D. E: hakalambi. [28]) D. E: manitihi çūragā. [29]) D. E: humisenana pataman. [30]) D. E: ngūniwehikang katwegan. [31]) D. E: gradeça. [32]) D. E: uṇḍahagi. [33]) B: angarĕmbak. [34]) D. E: sira hikā magawe kabeh. [35]) D. E: pasamohan pwa. [36]) D. E: sang dewa kabeh. [37]) D. E: makĕmbulan. [38]) D. E: magawe. [39]) D. E: ginawenira huwus. B: tan hurung.

[mun huwusa][1]), matangnyan ring Sarwwasiddḍā ngaraning maṇḍala mangke. Çighra sirāgawe humah, maluwaran sang dewata sira kabeh[2]), arĕp ta sira magaweha rĕrĕban[3]); tinhĕr ing gunung Rĕrĕban[4]) ngaranya mangke, pangrĕban[5]) sang dewata[6]) ngūni kacaritanya Mawelawela sukaning[7]) dewata kabeh, tinhör maṇḍala ri Sukawela[8]) ngaranya mangke. Bhaṭāra[9]) sira mayajñā suka[10]), matangnyan ring Sukayajña ngaranya wkasan. Bhaṭāra Guru sira mapūrwwa taruka[11]), Sukayajñā tambeyaning[12]) hana maṇḍala.

Akweh manūṣa[13]) harĕp wikuwa[14]), yata sinangāskaran de bhaṭāra Guru. Tambehaning mangaskarani[15]) bhagawan Wṛhaspati, kaping kalih bhagawan Soma, kaping tiga bhagawan Budḍa, kaping pat bhagawān Çūkra, kaping lima bhagawan Raditya[16]), kaping ĕnĕm bhagawan Saneçcara, kaping pitu bhagawan Hanggara. Samangkana kwehning çikṣa[17]) bhaṭāra Guru duk ing Sukāyajñā[18]).

Tan hucapĕn lawasnira, arĕp[19]) ta sirāmangetana[20]), ḍatnga ri sang hyang Mahāmeru [prayanira][21]). Yata winkas bhaṭāra Wiṣṇu gumantyanana[22]) dewaguru sira; ndah tanangga[23]) bhaṭara Wiṣṇu. Pinarikḍĕh de bhaṭara Parameçwara, tininggalan ta [payung][24]) kuṇḍala kalambi[25]), panugraha sang hyang; wkasan manglalu bhaṭāra Wiṣṇu. Jag lĕs[26]) lunghā ta bhaṭāra Guru sira, mapakṣa wukir[27]) ta sira; uminte polah[28]) hyang Wiṣṇu sira. Mayamaya paḍanira hyang Guru[29]); tinhör hing Mayana hunggwanira hyang[30]) Guru; matangnyan ring Sukayajña muwah pakṣa ring[31]) Mayana, kaping kalih ing[32]) maṇḍala hika.

Kahucapa[33]) ta bhaṭāra Wiṣṇu gumantyani lungguh ring

---

[1]) D. E: ontbreekt. [2]) D. E: maluwanta sira dewa kabeh. [3]) B: parĕrĕban. D. E: pangarĕmban. [4]) B: Rĕban. D: Mĕngĕrĕmban. E: Marĕmban. [5]) B: pangrĕrĕmban. [6]) D. E: parĕrĕmbaning nawa dewata. [7]) D. E: sahaning. B: çubhāning. [8]) D. E: ring dya Çukayajñā. [9]) B: bhaṭāra bhaṭārī. [10]) D. E: sukasukanya. [11]) B: mamūrwwatarukā. D. E: mapūrwwa matarukā. [12]) D. E: tĕmbening. [13]) D. E: datang pwa tang manūṣā. [14]) D. E: hingaskaran. B: harĕp awikuha. [15]) D. E: ring tĕmbening hangaskarani sira. [16]) D. E: Radite. [17]) B: siçyan. D. E: çiṣya. [18]) D. E: da Sukayajñā. [19]) D. E: hayun. [20]) B: mangetan ḍatnga maring. [21]) D. E: ontbreekt. [22]) D. E: manggantenana. [23]) D. E: ndah tan mangkanā pwa. [24]) B: tininggal tang payung. D. E: ontbreekt. [25]) D. E: kulambi guṇḍala. [26]) D. E: sag lĕs. [27]) D. E: pakṣa wukiran. [28]) D. E: polahnira. [29]) D. E: mapadiwwa sang hyang. [30]) D. E: hunggon i bhaṭara. [31]) D. E: ing Sukayajñā pakṣa mawa ring. [32]) D. E: kaping kalih bhaṭara Guru magawe. [33]) D. E: tucapa.

bhaṭāra Guru [1]) tumitihi surangga [2]) pataraṇa; ndah tanpamitra sira [3]). Ana wwang arĕp lumakuha [4]) wiku, almĕh ta sira mangaskāranana [5]). Tuminghāl [6]) ta bhaṭāra Guru, yata ḍatang ri kahanan sang hyang Wiṣṇu, mwajar ta sira hyang Guru, lingnira:

«Ih, tanayanku hyang Wiṣṇu, apa dwāning tanpaçiṣya [7])? Akweh manuṣa [8]) harĕp wikuhā, ndan tonton [9]) kita tanpamiçwa [10]); mangaskarani [11]) kitānaku!»

Sumahur sang hyang [12]) Wiṣṇu:

«Almĕh tanayan bhaṭāra hangaskāranana; hasukĕr hakwehana mantara [13]). Sukaning hatapa prihawak [14]).»

Mojar ta [15]) bhaṭāra Guru:

«Kapan ta kang manuṣa limpada sakeng pañcagati sangsara? Dwaning makāryya [16]) maṇḍala panglpasana [17]) pitarapāpa. Antukaning manuṣa mangaskara hayun wikuha: matapa sumambaha dewata [18]), dewata sumĕngkaha [19]) watĕk hyang [20]), watĕk hyang [20]) sumĕngkāha [19]) siddārṣi, siddārṣi sumĕngkāha [19]) watĕk bhaṭāra [21]). Lena sakerikā [22]) hana pwa wiku [23]) sasar tapabratanya; tmahanya tumitis ing rāt, mandadi [24]) ratu cakrawarthi wiçe[ṣa] ring bhuwaṇa [25]), wurungnya [26]) mandadi dewata. Matangnyan wuwurungan dewatā prabhū cakrawarthi [27]), apan tmahan ing [28]) wiku sasar tapabratanya hika. Matangnyan ta kita, hyang Wiṣṇu, pangaskārani kanyu [29])!»

Sumahur bhaṭāra Wiṣṇu tinhĕr maçugal [30]):

«Tambe tanayan bhaṭāra mangaskārani wwang, lamun ana wwang sasiwak; samangkana tambe pangaskārani [31])».

«Uḍuh, tanpangaskārani si kita [ta]nayan mangkana [32]), apan tanana wwang [33]) sasiwak ngaranya».

---

[1]) D. E: mangganteni palinggihira bhaṭāra Prameçwara. [2]) D. E: manitihi çuraga. [3]) D. E: ndah tanpamikoni ta sira. [4]) D. E: Yan anā wwang hamalaku. [5]) D. E: ngaskarani. [6]) D. E: tumon. [7]) D. E: paran gawenta tanpamikuni. [8]) D. E: wwang manūṣā. [9]) B: ndak tonton. [10]) D. E: tanpamimitra. [11]) B. D. E: pangaskarani. [12]) D. E: sumawur bhaṭāra. [13]) B: mangtara. D. E: sukĕran makwehana pantara, pukulun. [14]) D. E: sukā rame ring amrih dawak. [15]) D. E: Sumawur. [16]) D. E: dening magawe. [17]) B: panglpasaning. [18]) B: sumambah hadewata. D. E: hesihaning manūṣā ngaskara manūṣā yan awikū" Sumawur bhaṭara Wiṣṇu: „Almĕh tanayan bhaṭara pukulun". „Matasa hawiku matapa, dewata sumkaha dewata. [19]) D. E: sumkaha. [20]) D. E: watĕk ahyang. [21]) D. E: watĕk dewata. [22]) B: sakwerika. D. E: den ana lwih sakirikā. [23]) D. E: tanantāwikū. [24]) D. E: tumitisa yata dadi [25]) D. E: ring bhūmi. [26]) D. E: wurung ikā. [27]) D. E: matangnyan hurungan ngaraning sang prabhū. [28]) D. E: katmuning. [29]) D. E: kitā. [30]) D. E: masugal çahur bhaṭara Wiṣṇu. [31]) C. B: mangaskarani. D. E: samana tĕmbe tanayan bhaṭara ngaskarani. [32]) D. E: kitenaku hyang Wiṣṇu. [33]) D. E: tanāwang.

84

Jag lĕs, lunghā [1]) ta bhaṭāra Guru; yata matangnyan sirārūpa [2]) wwang çasiwak, [matangan masuku tunggal, acangkĕm [m]atha sisih][3]). Rĕp ḍatang ri kahanan sang ẖyang Wiṣṇu [yeki mangke bhawanira][4]). Tuminghal ta bhaṭāra Wiṣṇu [5]), yata gumuyu sira:

«[Ci hāhāhāh] [6]), iḍĕp ning hulun [7]) tanana wwang çasiwak; [ih, dadi hana wwang çasiwak] [8]). Ih, paran ta donta marangke [9])? Ndak ton kita sarosa, apa gawenta marangke [10])»?

«Uḍuh pukulun hyang kaki, dwaning ḍatang hayun awikuha, mahyun [11]) manaṇḍanga bhawa lakṣa[ṇa] bhaṭāra pwangkulun».

«Uḍuh, gung ri ḍaṇḍa [12]) bhaṭāra mangrehakĕn [13]), tan wnang hulun mundura çabda ya [14])».

Rĕp, sāmpun akāryya [15]) puṣpa sira, mamiçwaguru [16]) bhaṭāra Wiṣṇu; tanangga [17]) ta sira kapapasa. Masinghĕl makuṇḍala badḍa [18]) ḍawak; sāmpun sangaskāra [19]), sūkṣma muwah sira manglayang. Umung gumuruh [20]) pangastuti ning watĕk dewata sira kabeh, matangnyan hana maṇḍala ring Guruh [21]) ngaranya mangke.

Kahucapa ta [22]) bhaṭāra Parameçwara, sah ta sira saking Manis [23]), mangetan sira; tumut [t]a sira [24]) bhaṭārī Parameçwarī. Marāryyan ta sira ring gunung Wilis; mwajar tta bhaṭāra:

«Sājñā bhaṭārī, pakari ngkene, pakbakbata kita [25])».

Tinhĕr ngaran bhaṭārī Kbakba.

«Kami ḍatĕngeng Mahāmeru; [yan wuwus abcik tĕmbe caracara sang hyang Mandaragiri [27]) kami hundang kita tĕmbe. Haywa ta kita tka yan tan hinundang!»

Mangkana pawkas bhaṭāra ring bhaṭārī. Jag lĕs lunghā [28]) bhaṭāra Guru mare sang hyang Mahāmeru; [29]) magawe ta sira maṇḍala ring Hahāh, ri lambung sang hyang Mahāmeru] [26])

[1]) D. E: Lĕs, lunghā. [2]) D. E: yata sira matmahan. [3]) D. E: ontbreekt. [4]) D. E: ontbreekt: iku hingaskaran, masuku tunggal, matangan tunggal, marakĕt saçiwak, sagama pratama kang sarwwa saçiwak, ring hayunira bhaṭara Wiṣṇu. [5]) D. E: ingevoegd: ri wwang saçiwak. [6]) D. E: ontbreekt. [7]) D. E: Citta idping hulun. [8]) D. E: ontbreekt. [9]) D. E: Ih para watĕk dewata merene. [10]) D. E: dak tonton kitā kadi pamadani tan sarese magamā, gawento wang saçiwak. [11]) D. E: hayun. [12]) B: durung ring ḍĕṇḍa. [13]) D. E: munggah hinĕṇḍak de bhaṭāra maratakĕn. [14]) B: sabḍāyu. D. E: tan wnang ta masañjarya (magama sañjayyu). [15]) D. E: Sag lĕs rĕp, sampun hagawe. [16]) D. E: yata hingaskaran de. [17]) B: tan maga. [18]) B: masingĕl mabadḍa. D. E: Yata maçīla mawiku. [19]) D. E: rĕp sampun sira ngaskara. [20]) B: Umung gumuh. D. E: matangnyan humungguh Merū. [21]) B. ring Guru. D. E: maṇḍalagiri Gumuruh. [22]) D. E: Kucapa. [23]) B. D. E: Masin. [24]) D. E: manut buri. [25]) D. E: pakari kapwa kitī pakbakbat!" [26]) B: ontbreekt. [27]) D. E: lamun uwusan bcik pwa tĕmbe caraca sang hyang Mahameru. [28]) D. E: Lĕs, msat. [29]) D. E: ingevoegd: sapraptinireng Mahameru.

kidulwetan [1]). Sāmpun sira taruka [maṇḍala ring Hahāh] [2]) magawe ta sira maṇḍala ring Gĕrĕsik [3]), iringan sang hyang Mahāmeru wetan. Sāmpun magawe [4]) maṇḍala ring Gĕrĕsik, magawe ta sira maṇḍala hiringan [sang hyang Mahāmeru] [5]) kidul. Çūnya sagiri [6]) tan hanā tapa; tinhör hing Çūnyasagiri [7]) ngaraning maṇḍala.

Kahucapa [8]) ta bhaṭāra Wiṣṇu haneng Sukāyajñā; ndah sāmpun sira maçiṣyākweh, ḍatang ta sira ring patapan [9]) bhaṭāra Içwara ring Pangkeçwara [10]) ngaranya. [Mwajar ta sira bhaṭāra Wiṣṇu :] [11]) «Taganti manandang kuruwa [12]), hyang Içwara [13]), sira dewaguruwa [14]) mangke».

Sinrahakĕn tang payung guṇḍala kalambi [15]) ring bhaṭāreçwara, sira gumanti dewaguru ring Sukāyajñā. Bhaṭāra Wiṣṇu mangher hing Mayan[a], mapakṣa wukir ta sira; bhaṭāreçwara sira Sukāyajñā pakṣa Rĕban [16]).

Hana ta brahmaṇa sakeng [17]) Jambuddipa, sang hyang [18]) Tkĕn-wuwung aranya; anggagaṇacara [19]) anūt[t]a lari sang hyang Mahāmeru. Manwan [20]) ta tejā putih: «Ika pawitra nggoning sang hyang [21])» lingnira. Anger ta sira luhurning thirtha mili [22]) maring Sukāyajñā; tuminggal [23]) ta sang hyang Içwara [24]):

«Jah [25]) sang brahmāṇa» [ling sang hyang Içwara] [26]) «haywa sira hangher hing ruhuring kene [27]). Tunggal hikang bañu hiki [28]), sugyan kita rinangkuṣa [29]), acĕpĕl tikang bañu [30]). Pamet hunggon maneh, hangruhuri dahat kita [31])».

Ndah pakṣa tinanggĕhan [32]) sang brahmāṇa [33]); kewalya

---

[1]) B: kidulya wetanya. D. E: magawe ta sira maṇḍala hiring kidul. [2]) B: ontbreekt. D. E: Ri sāmpunira mataruka maṇḍaling Ahah. [3]) B: ingevoegd: maṇḍala ring Hahāh, ring lambung sang hyang Mahāmeru kidul wetan. Sāmpunira taruka maṇḍala ring Hāhāh, magawe ta sira maṇḍala ring Gĕrĕçik. [4]) D. E: Sampunira mataruka. [5]) D. E: ontbreekt. [6]) D. E: Buĕr, sunya giri. [7]) D. E: nhĕr ring Sunya. [8]) D. E: kocapa. [9]) D. E: ḍatanga sireng. [10]) D. E: Paseçwara. [11]) D. E: ontbreekt. [12]) B: guruwa. [13]) D. E: Ih, bhaṭāra Hiçwara, taganti hamañcaguru. [14]) D. E: dewaguru. [15]) D. E: Rĕp sinrahakĕn ika kālambi guṇḍala. [16]) D. E: mapakṣa Rĕbyan. [17]) B: sakweng. D. E: ḍatĕng sakeng. [18]) D. E: ḍang hyang. [19]) D. E: gaghāṇacara sira mangajāwa. [20]) B: māwan. D. E: hanon. [21]) D. E: „Sakeng (E: ingevoegd: Pawitra) gonira sang hyang". [22]) D. E: luhuring tirttha, ikang tirttha milwi. [23]) B: tuminghāl ta. [24]) D. E: tumon ta hyang Hiçwara, mwajar ta sira. [25]) B: ndah, D. E: Ih. [26]) D. E: ontbreekt. [27]) D. E: aywa kita ngeri luhuring kono. B: hiring luhur hing kene. [28]) D. E hikā. [29]) D. E: sanggonta ring akaçā. [30]) B: acĕcĕl hikang bañu. D. E: malĕtuh ikang bañu. [31]) B: angruhur dahat kita. D. E: kita mahrūhuri tmĕn. [32]) B: Kḍāh pākṣa tikanggĕha. [33]) D. E: Kḍĕh ta sang brāhmaṇa ngering luhur ikang bañu mili mareng Sukayajñā.

86

juga tanangga [1]), ḍaraḍah sama rinangkuṣa [2]), mtu [3]) cirinya tan yogya [4]). Awamana ri sang paṇḍita [5]): maḍahar manglarut hajang maring swah [6]), angising taya ring bañu [7]):

«Kadi wruhanira [8]) sang paṇḍita» [lingnira] [9]) «yan mamyāngising ring lwah [10])»,

Mulih ta sang brahmāṇa hapuyapuy [11]); tuminghāl ta bhatāreçwara [12]):

«Uḍuh, riṇangkuṣa hikang brahmāṇa [13]), keli tahine sne [14]). Ih, walu[ya] ta ko, bañu [15]), [pareng natare ḍang hyang Tkĕn-wuwung] [16])!»

[Lĕs mawlar [17]) bañu mili minḍuhūr. Mwajar ḍang hyang Tkĕn-wuwung:] [18])

«Ih, bañu mili maring natar, ising mangan tajang [19]) mami, huni wus lĕpas keli, mangke ta mungswing [20]) natar. Ih, mantyanta [21]) bañu mili minḍuhur amamanek; apūrwwa bañu hiki, apan sing lĕbak paraning banyu. Ih, çakti tmĕn sang pāṇḍita [22])!»

Rĕp ḍatang [23]) ḍang hyang Tĕkĕn-wuwung ri kahanan sang hyang Içwara [24]):

«Uḍuh sangtabya [25]) ranak sang pāṇḍita; apa dwaning [26]) bañu mili miṇḍuhur, pwangkulun? Tan ya don sing lbak [27]) paraning bañu [28]); kapuhan [29]) kami dening [30]) bañu mili miṇḍuhur [31]). Mapa kalinganya [32])?»

Sumahur bhaṭāra Içwara:

«Ah, nirangkuṣa tan sipi dahat, harih, mangileknājang mangising ring lwah [33]). Ika tan kaharĕp [34]) ingwang.»

[1]) D. E: kewala jugā tan anggĕtan (D: tinanggĕtan). [2]) B: caraḍah saparinangkuṣā. D. E: taranda yatā rinangkusa. [3]) B: ptung. [4]) D. E: mtu tiki cirinya takrog. [5]) D. E: awwapana ri rasang paṇḍita. [6]) B: manglaruta hajā maring lwah. [7]) D. E: habañu tajang ring bañu. Mwajar sang brāhmaṇa: [8]) D. E: kadi wruha. [9]) D. E: ontbreekt. [10]) D. E: yan kami mangising i lwah. [11]) D. E: maminḍapuy. [12]) D. E: sawulatira. [13]) D. E: nirakusa tikang ta brāhmaṇa hika. [14]) B. C. D. E: mne. [15]) D. E: Ih, dak walikakĕn ikang bañu. [16]) D. E: ontbreekt. [17]) D. E: Lĕr wla tā. [18]) D. E: ontbreekt; Sawulatnira sang brāhmaṇa. [19]) B: isingan tājang. [20]) B: munggwing. [21]) C: mantya. [22]) D. E: „Ih, paran gāwenikang bañu malwi, kapuhan ikang bañu hamamanek. Tandon si lĕbak paraning bañu; abañu tajang keli lpas maling natar. Ih, paranane sang paṇḍita." [23]) D. E: Jhag, lĕs, prapti. [24]) D. E: ingevoegd: mwajar taya: „Paran gāweyanta sang brāhmaṇa?" [25]) D. E: sangtabe. [26]) D. E: paranimitane hikang. [27]) D. E: Tan don si lbak. [28]) D. E: ingevoegd: Uḍuh, çakti dahat sang paṇḍita. [29]) Begin invoegsels E³. [30]) B: denta. [31]) D. E: kapuhannikang bañu hamamanek. [32]) D. E: Paran kalinganya, pukulun? [33]) D. E: rinakuça tan çiddi dahat, areh kitajangising i loh. [34]) D. E: hapan tan karĕp.

87

«Duh, ndi ta nggonta wruh [1]) [yan angising ring lwah] [2])?»

[«Haneng umah kamyālungguh, katon kita ngising [4]) ring lwah [5]); matangnyan dakwalekĕn ikĕna kang [6]) bañu.»

«Duh, mahāçakti dahat sang paṇḍita. Ih, paran rika kaçaktinira [7])? Mahyun warahĕn sirānaknira [8]); hana hmās akweh ring [9])) Jambuḍipa] [3]) mangĕmbanganiran [10]) sang pāṇḍita, pwangkulun [11]).»

«Lah, sang brahmāṇa yan ahyun warahĕn [12]), [lamun si kita] [13]) haywa salah rūpa [14]); den tunggal kang warṇṇa; pawiku kita hiri kami [15]), manaṇḍanga hupakāra bhaṭāra [16]), [matangnyan tunggal kang warṇna] [17]).»

«Uḍuh, bhahagya [18]) yan mangkana, pwangkulun.»

Wilaça [19]) lakṣaṇa ning wiku; rĕp sḍang sinangaskāra [20]) sang brahmāṇa, kinĕn [21]) çiwopakārana [22]); inaranan mpu Siddayogi [23]). Winarah ring upadeça de bhaṭāreçwara.

Ucapĕn ta [24]) lawasnirāmpu [25]) Siddayogā mangunakĕn [26]) tapa, kāṇḍĕhan ta sira ragiwaça [27]), ikang parakrama inuntitakĕn [28]) dening ṣadwargga [29]). Matangnyan matur i sang gurunira [30]):

«Sājñā bhaṭāra, mahyun manambuta karmma tanayan bhaṭāra, pwangkulun [31]). [Kdĕh mahyun marabiha] [32]) tan kawaça tutunggala [33]).»

«Lah, daraṇakna, mpu [34]) Siddayoga; satya masilunglung brata [35]), den hana sidda tkeng çwarggakāraṇa [36]), kadungkapa [37]) ikang Parameçwara çiwapaḍa sing sakārṣa [38]); nora

---

[1]) B: ndi ta nggonang sang wruh. E^3: ndi ta nggonang çawruh. D. E: ndi tanggonira wruh. [2]) D. E: ontbreekt. [3]) E^3: ontbreekt. [4]) D. E: yata katon kami mangising. [5]) D. E: ingevoegd: mabañu tajang ring bañu kita. [6]) B: dak walekĕn ikang. [7]) D. E: punapa çaktinira? [8]) D. E: ḍuh, warahĕn pukulun ranak sang paṇḍita. [9]) D. E: hmāsakeng. [10]) C: pangĕmbanganira. B. E^3: apāpangĕmbanganira. [11]) D. E: pinaketambangan ing ranak sang paṇḍita". [12]) D. E: yan kita harĕp wruha. [13]) D. E^3: lamun sih kita. D. E: ontbreekt. [14]) D. E: aywa si kita kakehan warṇna. [15]) D. E: pawiku kita den tunggalawan kami. [16]) D. E: manandang kita dalupakara". [17]) D. E: ontbreekt. [18]) D. E: bhageyan si. [19]) D. E: mawilaçaheng. [20]) D. E: sḍĕng ingaskarān. [21]) B E^3: kinĕnan. [22]) D. E: tinwan çiwahpataraṇna. [23]) B. D. E. E^3: Siddayoga. [24]) D. E: Tan ūcapĕn. [25]) B. E^3: Hucapĕn ta lāmpahnira. [26]) D. E: mangnakĕn sira. [27]) B. E^3: lagiwaça. [28]) B. E^3: hinguṇḍitakĕn. [29]) D. E: hinutitakĕn harĕp makarmmāha sira. [30]) D. E: humatūr ing hyang Guru nikā. [31]) D. E: hayun makramaha ranak pukulun. [32]) D. E: ontbreekt. Eind invoegsel E^3. [33]) D. E: tan kawaça nunggal ranak bhaṭāra pukulun". Sumahur bhaṭāra Hiçwara. [34]) D. E: Daranakĕn hĕmpu. [35]) D. E: satya masilunglunge tapa brata. [36]) D. E: den hana çiddanta mareng swarggā. [37]) D. E: madungkap. [38]) B: çiwahpaḍa ring sakarmmā. D. E: çiwapadḍa sah sakeng manūṣa.

dewata sidḍa yan tan lumkasa tapa brata¹). Apranga kiteng
çamara²), sing wani gañjarĕn ika³); angusir⁴) satya puruṣa⁵),
lot daraṇakna ring spaspi⁶), kadyāprang tngah ning raṇa⁷),
tan kangneng⁸) hanak rabi. Tĕmpuh ing si ḍaraṇakĕn⁹); pira¹⁰)
wkas doh ning tgal¹¹), n̊on lo tanpabiṣa mamrih¹²). [Aywa
mundur ing raṇa]¹³), ḍaṇḍa patita hawakta¹⁴). Mne pwa yan
huwusiddātapa, padum pamilih sakārṣa¹⁵).»

Mangkana wuwus sang hyang Içwara.¹⁶) Kḍĕh sirārĕp mara-
biha¹⁷), tanpangur¹⁸) atutunggal¹⁹).

«Ih, yan ahyun kita harabiha²⁰), ana ta rājaputrī ring Mḍang-
gaṇa, mangaran dewi Kasingi lawan dewi Madumali²¹), anak de
mahārāja Wawu-langit²²). Alap ta denta kang atuha ngaran
dewi Kasingi.»

Mangkanā²³) mpu Siddayoga henggal, hapan hambaramarg-
ga²⁴). Prāpta ring nāgara²⁵), pinintanira ta sang rākryan rāja-
putri²⁶); tan tinĕngĕt de mahārāja Wawulangit²⁷). [Kinon ta
sira mpu Siddayogāmilihana; pinilihnira kang atuhā. Mojar tta
sira çrī mahārāja Wawu-langit:

«Masyārĕpa sang pāṇḍita ryyānak ning hulun kang atuha,
hapan wuta, nirwwang gumulak tang²⁸) swaca, tanpanwan hanggagap ika.»

Mangkana ling çri mahārāja Wawu-langit. Jag lĕs]²⁹), mantuk

¹), D. E: yen pangnĕknĕkan atapa. ²) D. E: haprang kiteng habyantara.
³) D. E: sang wani ginañjar ikā. ⁴) B: angungsi. ⁵) D. E: mangungsiha kaçatyan
puruṣā. ⁶) D. E: daraṇakĕn ikang spaspi. ⁷) D. E: den kadi haprang ring
raṇa. ⁸) D. E: tan kangéna ring. ⁹) B: tĕmpuh i siddaraṣān. D. E: manĕmpuh
ajana katolih. ¹⁰) B: para. ¹¹) D. E: tikang tgal. ¹²) D. E: linonlon biṣa mrih.
¹³) D. E: ontbreekt. ¹⁴) B: ḍĕṇḍa pati tahadanta. D. E: ḍĕṇḍa pwa kita hawak.
¹⁵) D. E: tĕmbe pwa dummapilih yan uwus atapa. ¹⁶) D. E: ingevoegd: matangnyan dinaraṇakĕn de sang Siddayoga; tan kocapa lawaçira, sang hĕmpu
Siddayoga. ¹⁷) D. E: kḍĕh arĕp akramaha sira. ¹⁸) B: tanpahur. ¹⁹) D. E: bayah
Siddayoga tan kawasa nununggal. Ingevoegd: Matangyan amarĕk ing hyang
Guru nikā, mojar taya sang ĕmpu Siddayoga. Sumahur bhaṭāra Hiçwara.
²⁰) B: ma yan hayun harabihā. D. E: Lah, angapa si yan sira tan kawaçanak
mami. ²¹) Begin invoegsel E³. ²²) D. E: rājā Wuwulangit. ²³) D. E: ingevoegd:
wuhusnira hyang Hiçwara. Yata mangkat. B. E³: Mangkat[t]a. ²⁴) D. E: apan
abramaga pwa sira. ²⁵) D. E: Prapteng Mḍanggaṇa; ingevoegd: sinapa taya:
„Lah, bahageya pukulun sang paṇḍita". Sumahur sang Çiddayoghā: „Sangka-
ningsun marangke, sang Wuwulangit, hanĕngguh sira hanak rajāputrī kalih
siki; lamun sirā weh suñ jaluke kang atuwa." Sumahur sang Wuwulangit:
„Pukulun, maça si harĕpa sang paṇḍita ring hanakingsun kang atuwa, hapan
wuta dling, hanggagap tanpanon". ²⁶) D. E: yata pinintokĕn sang rajāputrī.
²⁷) B: ingevoegd: halap ta denta kang atuha ngaran. ²⁸) B: nirwwang humulatti
çwaca. ²⁹) D. E: ontbreekt.

ta sira mpu Siddayoga, prapta sumambah ri gurunira [1]), umajar sira yan wuta sang rājaputrī kang atuhā.

«Lah, wali halap ika, dumling mari wuta; kunang kita yan apanggih [2]), aywa kitārāryyan ing nāgara; bwat amanguyu lkasanta.»

Mangkana ling bhaṭāreçwara. Lumāmpah tāmpu Siddayogi [3]). Prāpta ring nāgara, kapanggih [4]) lawan dewi Kasingi. Sampuning mangkana amit [t]a sira manguyuha. Mantuk dinularakĕn [5]), prāpta sumambah ri gurunira:

«Sajjā [6]) bhaṭāra, sāmpun apanggih [7]) tanayan bhaṭāra lāwan dewi Kasingi. Lah, den paḍa bhawalakṣaṇa».

Rĕp sinangaskāra dewi Kasingi, hingaranan wiku Siddayogi. [8]) «Atapitapi tāpadadwan [9]) humah, aywa kita gulawĕṇṭah. Tatkala kaṇḍĕhan ragiwaça, pamareng tapinta».

Mangkana pawkas bhatareçwara. Sang Siddayogi hoyeng gĕgĕr lwar ing Māyana [10]), hlĕtan lwah lāwan mpu Siddayoga. Tan ucapĕn lawasnya, mānak ta sira kalih siki çami jalu, sang Gagang-aking [11]) panuhā, sang Bubukṣah kang anom; paḍa nwam awiku paḍa lumakwātapa [12]) sira.

Kahucapa ta sang hyang Brahmā, sira ta dewaguru ring Sarwwasidda, mapakṣa wukir ta sira. Ana ta sira paṇḍita saking swargga, bhagawan Karmmaṇḍeya ngaranya; marūpa ta sira kbo bule, ḍatang ta sireng ārgga Kelaça. Arĕp ta bhaṭāra hamupuha, matakut ta sira kapupuhā; yata matangnya maluy pāṇḍitārūpa. Rĕp sumambah sira ring bhaṭāreçwara. Kunang bhaṭāra Içwara harĕp ta ḍatngeng sang hyang Mahāmeru tumutura ri bhaṭāra Guru. Rĕp sinrahaknira tang payung guṇḍala kalambi ring bhagawān Karmmaṇḍeya [13]), sira gumantyani dewaguru umungguh ring harggā Kelaça. Matangnyan sang wiku ring Sukāyajñā tanpa[ma]ngan kbo bule, apan bhagawān Karmmaṇḍeya marūpa kbo bule ngūni kacaritanya.

Kahucapa ta bhaṭāra trisamaya, Içwara, Brahmā, Wiṣṇu, datang ri sang hyang Mahāmeru tumutur ing bhaṭāra Guru. Jag lĕs, prāpta bhaṭāra trisamaya ri sang hyang Mahāmeru; kunang bhaṭara Guru sḍang haneng Çūnyagiri-maṇḍala, umawasakĕn sang hyang hastitijāti. Ḍatang hyang Içwara Brahmā

[1]) D. E: mawaraha ring hyang Guru nikā: saḍatangnya ring hyang Guru nikā. Hierna gaping. Eind invoegsel E^3. [2]) B: amanggih. [3]) B: Siddayoga. [4]) B: amanggih. [5]) B: dinuluraknya. [6]) B: Sajñā. [7]) B: amanggih. [8]) Begin invoegsel E^3. [9]) B. E^3: madūdwan. [10]) B. E^3: Sang Siddiyogi woyeng gĕgĕr ing lwah ring Mayana. [11]) B. E^3: sang Gagak-haking. [12]) B. E^3: lumaku tapā [13]) Eind invoegsel E^3.

Brahmā Wiṣṇu, sumambah ri bhaṭāra Guru, mwajar tta bhaṭāra Parameçwara:

«Uḍuh, bhahagya tanayanku sang trisamaya, rowanganangku [1]) gawe tantu praçiṣṭa ri sang hyang Mahāmeru. Tanpasrĕhan tang bhuwana; kita katrini humilangkna lkalkaning bhuwana; glar tawur sĕrĕhanyu. Kunang sang hyang Içwara Brahmā Wiṣṇu, masĕhana, wruha [2]) ri sisikusung kita dewata. Den paḍāgawe kahyangan tanayanku katiga. Nihan panganugrabāngku: payung, guṇḍala, kalambi guru, muwah pustaka samuṣṭi pañjangnya, binbĕd hing nāga sinuntagi; kunang hisinya kami hiki. Ndah kayatnākĕn panugrahangku muwah sang hyang Brahmā Wiṣṇwīçwara».

Samangkana panugraha bhaṭāra Guru ri dewata trisamaya. Paḍa ta mawot sĕmbah katiga; jag, lĕs, lunghā bhaṭāra trisamaya, paḍa hagawe maṇḍala sowangsowang. Kunang pustaka panugraha bhaṭāra kari tan kahuninga de bhaṭāra trisamaya; anghing payung guṇḍala kalambi kasambut. Tuminghal ta bhaṭāra Guru:

«Duh, kari si kang [3]) pustaka de bhaṭāra trisamaya; pilih lali katriṇinya [4]).»

Sināmbut hikang pustaka de bhaṭāra Guru, winawanira mareng jro pahoman; rĕp kinukubanira tan wineh katona; matangnyan ring Kukub ngaraning maṇḍala wkasan, Kukub kahyangan bhaṭāra Guru.

Kahucapa ta sira bhaṭāra trisamaya magawe maṇḍala; bhaṭāra Içwara pupus ing sang hyang tiga, matangnyan Tigaryyanparwwata kahyangan . . . . . ; . . . . . bhaṭāra Brahmā; ring Nangka-parwwata kahyanganira bhaṭāra Wiṣṇu. Mapanaçapaça sira [5]), matangnyan ring Panasagiri [6]) ngaraning maṇḍala. Paḍa mengĕt ri [7]) sĕrĕhanira sowangsowang.

Kahucapa ta bhaṭāra Guru sĕḍangnira haneng Kukub, linolyākĕñ jaṭanira mangetan, matmahan gunung Jaṭa; yata pinakawatĕs ning Tandĕs lāwan ing gunung Maṇik. Matangnyan lmah larangan tan wnang hinambah ikang gunung Kampil, apañ jaṭa bhaṭāra [8]) kacaritanya ngūni. Mwajar ta bhaṭāra Guru:

«Tanayangku kamu hyang Gaṇa, tuñjang jaṭangku!»

Ndah tan wihang hyang Gaṇa, tinuñjang jaṭa bhaṭāra; yata

[1]) B: rowanganku. [2]) B: masrĕhana, wruhana. [3]) B: hikang. [4]) B: katriṇi. [5]) B: Mapanāçapanasa sirā. [6]) B: Panagiri. [7]) B: mengĕtning. [8]) B: apan jaṭan bhaṭāra.

matangnyan hana maṇḍala ring gunung Manuñjang ngaranya mangke. Hyang Gaṇa sira pratiṣṭangkāna [1]).

Vijfde Hoofdstuk.

Hana ta sira brahmāṇā mangajawa, hanūta ta larinira sang hyang Mahāmeru, ḍang hyang Kacuṇḍa ngaranya, brahmāṇa siddi çakti. Ḍatang ri sang hyang Mandaragiri, kahāmpir ta sireng Kukub, sumambah ri bhaṭāra Mahākāraṇa, amintā [2]) nugraha upakāra bhaṭāra. Yata sinangaskāran de [3]) bhatāra ring Kukub, inaranan bhagawān Açoṣṭi, sira brahmāṇa hanusun brata. Tlas kṛtta sangaskāra, sah sira saking Kukub-maṇḍala, naḍahamba [4]) haminta bhumi prayanira. Jag lĕs lunghā ta sira bhagawān Açoṣṭi, kahampir ta ring maṇḍala Panaçagiri. Mojar ta bhaṭāra Wiṣṇu:

«Bhahagya yan ḍatang sang dwijārṣi, apa dwaning ḍatang, lawandi parana sang dwijawara»?

Sumahur sang dwijārṣi:

«Ahyun ḍatĕngeng Mḍang hameta hunggona çwacaranira.»

Sumahur tta bhaṭāra Keçawā:

«Yan ahyun hunggwān si hangera [5]) kulwan ing Kedman, rāmyāparĕk lwah jurang».

Sumahur bhagawan Açoṣṭi:

«Yogyā dahat sih pwangkulun [6]), yan mangkana gocaranira lakṣaṇa milu tarukaha [7])».

Rĕp sāmpun sira matarukā, matur bhagawan Açoṣṭi ri bhaṭāra Guru ring Kukub, nhĕr hamintānugraha payung kuṇḍala kalambi, mapajar yan sinung hunggon de sang hyang Wiṣṇu. Mwajar tta bhaṭāra Guru:

«Duh, labdawara dahat tanayangku, wineh unggon de bhaṭāra Hari».

Mangkana ling bhaṭāra; tinhĕr hing Labdawara ngaraning maṇḍala. Mangkana kacaritanya ngūni.

Ana ta taruṇi hatuhā tanpalaki, sumambah ri bhaṭāra Guru, amintānugraha bhaṭāra [8]). Sinangaskāra ta de bhaṭāra, wineh mabadahāroma hinangit [9]), madodota wiḍak, midĕra ring bhuwana; kamawaçyahara [10]) katunggalanya, tinhör mangawasi ngaranya. Mangkana mulaning anāngawasi.

---

[1]) B: sirā praçiṣṭāngkāna. [2]) B: ānminta. [3]) B: hingaskara. [4]) B: nādḍahamba. [5]) B: sira hangher ing dmakya. [6]) B: bhāgya dahat sih pukulun. [7]) B: milu taruka. [8]) B: ring bhaṭāra. [9]) B: wineh manasaha roma hinabit. [10]) B: katamawaçyahara.

92

Anā ta strī pjah swaminya, sumambah ri bhaṭāra hamintānugraha bhaṭāra. Sinangaskāra de bhaṭāra, tĕhĕr ta wineh makĕṇḍita walatung, cihnanya yan [1]) ṣatya malaki, kahiḍĕpnya wkasan ing lakinya; tĕhĕr ta māmbulungana kalihkalih, matangnyan hakili ngaranya. Mangkana mulaning ana bhāwa kili.

Ana ta wwang lanang wadwan sumambah ri bhaṭāra Guru amintānugraha bhaṭāra. Sinangaskāra ta de bhaṭāra Jagatnātha, tan wineh tayāmagĕhana [2]) brata, mabaḍaha [3]) ri kālaning pūrṇnama tilĕm; «uwus kapwa tĕmbe suruhaṭa [4]), wnanga magĕhakna [5]) brata»; tinhĕr ta bharubharu ngaranya.

Hana taruna hanwam ring wayah, sumambah ri bhaṭāra Guru amintānugraha kawikun. Yata hingāskara de bhaṭāra Guru, tan sininglan taya daluwang, sininglan taya rwan ing halalang; tinhĕr wiku hijo ngaranya. Mangkana mulaning wiku hijo.

Ucapĕn ta lakṣaṇa bhaṭāra Jagatwiçeṣa, anggaṣṭa yinuganira hinaṣṭi, siniramnira ring Tatwāmṛtha çiwamba, yinuganira matmahana dewata puruṣangkāra. Inaranan bhagawān Agaṣṭi, inanugrahan kawikun de bhaṭāra, kinwan matapaha ring gunung Kawi. Tinhĕr makadṛwya kang gunung Kawi, pinakapacihnā pawkas bhaṭāra Guru.

Muwah bhaṭāra Nandiguru [6]) manghanakĕn ta sirā yuga, pinalih ta hajñānanira, mijil ta bhaṭāra Ḍarmmarāja. Kinahanan sangaskāra, siniramning Tatwāmṛtha çiwamba, inaranan sang ṛṣi Siddawangsitadewa [7]). Inanugrahan kawikun, sumusuk sang hyang sima brata [8]), kinwan tā mangunakna tapa de bhaṭāra. Tan wihang ta sang ṛṣi Siddawangsitadewa [7]), malĕnggita [9]) sirā mangunkna tapa, malāghna monaçrī [10]), tan kalangkahan dening rahina wngi, tan pa[nu]wukning pangan turu. Kalinganya: tan hana hiniṣṭinira, tan bhuwana, tan swargga, tan bhaṭāra, tan kamokṣan, tan kalĕpasĕn, tan suka, tan ḍuhka; tan hana hinalĕmnira [11]), tan hana keliknira; yata sinangguh tapa ngaranya. Tĕpĕt sḍĕng sarjjawa juga sira, yata hinaranan Sarjjawa Jambuḍipa, patapan sang ṛṣi Siddawangsitadewa [7]). Sira mūrttining atapa ngūning ārdḍi, sira ta bhaṭāra Ḍarmmarāja.

Sḍĕng rumgĕp samaddi nirmmala sang ṛṣi Siddawangsitadewa, tuminghal ta bhaṭāra Içwara Brahmā Wiṣṇu ri polahira sang ṛṣi Siddawangsitadewa [7]), ri sḍĕng rumgĕp samaddi nirmmala. «Sumadya syuhan ing bhūwana» mangkana iḍĕp bhaṭāra

[1]) B: cinanya yanyan. [2]) B: pagĕhana. [3]) B: mabanḍaha. [4]) B: suruhanta. [5]) B: amagĕhana. [6]) B: bhaṭāra Guru. [7]) B: Siddiwangsitadewa. [8]) B: siman ruta. [9]) B: malĕnggitta. [10]) mala monaghnāçrī. [11]) B: tan hana hinalĕm monanira.

93

trisamaya, ndah tan wruh ta sira yan bhaṭāra Ḍarmmarāja sang matapa; «kewala [1]) samanya paṇḍita», ri hiḍĕpnya, «sumadya syūhan ing bhuwana», ri hiḍĕpnya sang hyang trisamaya. Wikalpa ta manahnira; yata matangnyan mijil tang kāla trisamaya. Kāla Lodra mtu saking bhaṭāra Brahmā, kāla Sambu mijil saking bhaṭāra Wiṣṇu, kāla Samaya mijil saking bhaṭāra Içwara; rĕp yeki mangke bhawanira. Yata kinonira humjahana sang ṛṣi Siddiwangsitadewa; ndah tan wihang ta sang kāla trisamaya.

Jag, lĕs, lumāmpah tang kāla, prāpta ri kahanan sang ṛṣi Siḍdawangsitadewa [2]) sḍang mangrĕgĕp samaḍi nirmmala. Tka tang kāla sahaça hamigrahā, paḍa taya mamṛp mangdĕdĕl mapupuh [3]) manahut maṇḍĕkung; nirwikara sang ṛṣi sira. Mamrĕp tang kāla kaprĕp rowangnya ḍawak, mandĕdĕl kadĕdĕl rowangnya ḍawak, mamupuh kapupuh rowangnya ḍawak, manahut kasahut rowangnya ḍawak, manujah katujah rowangnya ḍawak; ndatan kawnang sang paṇḍita winigrahan. Kerangan buddi sang kāla dening tan pjah sang ṛṣi Siddiwangsitadewa; jag lĕs lunghā tang kāla, mungsir i sang hyang Brahmā Wiṣṇu Içwara; mawarah taya dugaduga yan tan kawnang winigrahan sang ṛṣi.

Matangnyan paḍa lumampah bhaṭāra trisamaya humjahana [4]) sang ṛṣi prayanya. Jag rĕp mawak Āgni sang hyang Brahmā, gumsĕnghana sang ṛṣi prayanya [5]); ndātan wikara sang ṛṣi. Mapa nimitaning tan pjah de sang hyang Brahmā? Apan sang hyang Ḍarmma tan gsĕng dening apuy; yata matangnyan kawĕs matakut sang hyang Brahmā. Tumandang ta bhaṭāra Wiṣṇu, māwak ta Wiṣṇu kroḍa sira, atĕṇḍas [s]ewu [6]), atangan rongiwu. Sarwwasañjāta rinĕgĕpnira, sang ṛṣi pinarajayanya, dinagĕlnira ring cakra Suḍarṣana, pinupuh ring gada Mandiki, tinujah ri twĕk Nandaka, pinngĕnganira sangka Pañcajanya; ndātan wikāra sang ṛṣi Siddiwangsitadewa. Muwah bhaṭāra Hari [7]) hamutĕr cakra Calakuṇḍa, cakra Tarĕnggabāhu, cakra Rĕbhawinuk [8]), yata dinagĕlaknira ri sang tapa. Ndatan kawnang dening āmbĕ[k] kroḍa hyang Darmmarāja sira; alah matakut kawĕs ta bhaṭāra Wiṣṇu. Rĕp māwak Rudra ta bhaṭāra Içwara, sang ṛṣyātapa sinahasanira [9]); ndah sang ṛṣi Siddiwangsitadewa, sḍang rumgĕp samaddi nirmmala, langgĕng tunggĕng sira. Tan kagyat [t]an wikalpa sira, nirawaraṇa sira, inurugan lmah tankorugan sira,

---

[1]) B: kewalya. [2]) B: Siddiwangsitadewa [3]) B: mamupuh. [4]) B: ndah mjahana. [5]) B: paryyanira. [6]) B: ingevoegd: amata rongewu. [7]) B: bhaṭāra Wiṣṇu. [8]) B: cakra Rĕgarahu, cakra Rĕgawinuk. [9]) B: sinaharṣānira.

langgĕng tunggĕng sira; matangnyan hana gunung Tunggĕng aranya. Ingilen [1]) bañu tan kahilen, tintĕl sira [2]). Apa hetunira yan mangkana? Kalinganya: sang hyang Ḍarmma pinĕṇḍĕm sira tan awuk, tinunu sira tan gsĕng, linabuh sira tan keli. Mangkana kasiddan sang ṛṣi Siddiwangsitadewa.

Matangnyan matakut sang hyang Brahmā Wiṣṇu Içwara tumon kasiddanira sang ṛṣi tapa [3]). Jag lĕs malayu ta bhaṭāra trisamaya ḍatngeng Kukub-maṇḍala. Tuhun bhaṭāra sḍĕng tinangkil dening dewata catūrlokaphala, ḍatang ta bhaṭāra trisamaya, sumambah ri bhaṭāra Jagatnātha. Jag rĕp [4]):

«Sājñā bhaṭāra, dwan ing tanayan bhaṭāra sumambah ri paḍadoja bhaṭāra pwangkulun: ana paṇḍita malĕkasakĕn [5]) tapa, masadya syuhan ing bhūwana, mangkana hiḍĕp tanayan bhaṭāra. Mantyanta [6]) siddi çaktinya, tamapi tanayan bhaṭāra katrini [7]) kaswaran prabhawa denya. Dwan ing tanayan bhaṭāra sumambah: aminta çaraṇa tanayan bhaṭāra [8])».

Mangkana ling bhaṭāra trisamaya. Sumahur bhaṭāra Guru:

«Uḍuh, tanayanku kita hyang Brahmā Wiṣṇu Içwara, [9]) sang ṛṣi Siddiwangsitadewa [10]) hika kanyu sĕngguh [11]) masadya syuhan ing bhuwana? Taha, tan mangkana hika; apan bhaṭāra Ḍarmmarāja sang ṛṣyātapa. Nimitanya tan alah denyu [12]), apan sākṣat [13]) kami sang ṛṣyātapa, apan pamalihan mami hajñana hika [14]), matangnyan tan alah denyu [12]). Kita pwa manganakĕn rakṣasa [15]), byaktawas kita kāla [16]); matangnyan haroharaning bhuwana, apan sākṣat kanyu [17]) rākṣasa hika. Matangnyan pjah ikang kāla denyu [18])!»

Mangkana ling bhaṭāra Guru. Mwajar ta bhaṭāra trisamaya:

«Sājña bhaṭāra, tan pjah ikang kāla, yan tan pjah [19]) sang ṛṣi Siddiwangsitadewa.»

Mangkana ling bhaṭāra trisamaya [20]); yata matangnyan bhaṭāra Guru humangsil hing urip [21]) sang ṛṣi Siddawangsitadewa,

---

[1]) B: Inilen. [2]) B: tan tĕlĕs [s]ira. [3]) B: sang ṛṣyātapā. [4]) B: seg rĕp. [5]) B: mangnakĕn. [6]) B: matangnyan ta. [7]) Eind gaping D. E. [8]) D. E: mangkanā don i ranak bhaṭara, haminta pwa ranak bhaṭāra. [9]) D. E: kamu hyang Hiçwara Brahmā Wiṣṇu. [10]) D.E. Siddiwasçitadewa. [11]) D. E: kana sanggu. [12]) D. E : denta. [13]) D. E: sasat. [14]) D. E: hapan pamalihane hajñāṇan kami hikā. B: samāsihan mami. [15]) D. E: mapa sangkanya mangnakĕn rakṣasa? [16]) D. E: byakta malah kawus ika. B: byaktāwas kita kāla. [17]) D. E: sakṣasat kana. [18]) D. E: matangnyan ikā tan pjah ing kalā". [19]) D. E: tan pjahha rakwa tang kalā, yan tan pjahha. [20]) D. E: hyang Hiçwara Brahma Wiṣṇu. [21]) D. E: umangsal huripnira.

apan bhaṭāra wiçeṣanira [1]). Kinwanira kang dewata caturlokaphala mananggaha çawanira sang ṛṣi, apan byakta matmahan hekanarwwa [2]) tang bhuwana, yan tumibāha ring pṛthiwi çawanira sang ṛṣi Siddiwangsitadewa. Yata lumampah tang dewata catūrlokaphala, ḍatang ri kahanan sang ṛṣyātapa. Binañcut tang huripnira de bhaṭāra Guru, pjah [3]) sang ṛṣyātapa; sinangga ta çawanira de bhaṭāra catūrlokaphala. Pinundut [t]a sira mangetan, yata sinangguh [4]) Punḍutan-çawa [5]) ngaranya. Pinĕṇḍĕm ta ring pucaknira sang hyang Mahāmeru [çawanira sang ṛṣi Siddiwangsitadewa wkasan] [6]); matangnyan tan hana wnang mangruhurana [7]) pucaknira sang hyang Mahāmeru, apan pinĕṇḍĕmnira [8]) bhaṭāra Ḍarmmarāja kacaritanya. Mogha [9]) bayu tan ana wani [10]) mangruhurana [11]) [pucaknira sang hyang Mahāmeru] [12]), yadyan sang hyang Raditya Wulan tuwi tanpangruhuri [13]), [ngūniweh tang janma manūṣa tan wnang mangruhurana pucaknira sang hyang Mahāmeru] [14]).

Kelaça bhumi sāmpurnṇāwan pinĕṇḍĕm bhaṭāra Ḍarmmarāja [15]). [Kelaça ngaraning gunung; bhumi ngaraning lĕmah] [16]); sāmpūrṇnawangan ngaraning awa ruhur [17]); tinhĕr tta Kelaça bhumi sāmpūrṇnāwan [ngaran sang hyang Mahāmeru] [18]). Yata sinangguh [19]) susuk ṣima brata ngaranira, lmah larangan ikang prasadḍa lingga [20]), tan wnang rinug [21]); tinhĕr pinakapraçiṣṭa susuk ṣima [brata] [22]) sang hyang kawikun.

Kahucapa [23]) ta sang hyang Brahmā Wiṣṇu Içwara [24]) umjahi tang kāla trisamaya; dinĕlĕngnira hikang dṛṣṭiwiṣya, [25]) bhaçmibhūta matmah[an] awu [26]). Awunikang kāla trisamaya matmahan gunung Wihanggamaya [27]); [gunung Wihanggamaya] [28]) ring

[1]) D. E: bhaṭara Guru wiçeṣā. [2]) D. E: hekārṇnawa. B: hekarnāwwa. [3]) B: rĕp pjah ta. [4]) B: yata siranangguh. [5]) D. E: Punduta-sawa. [6]) D. E: ontbreekt. [7]) D. E: sangkanya tananā wani mangungkuli. [8]) B: apāna pĕṇḍĕmnira. D. E: apan unggonya pinĕṇḍĕm. [9]) B. D. E: Megha. [10]) B: wani ontbreekt. [11]) D. E: tananāngungkuli. [12]) D. E: ontbreekt. [13]) D. E: dyapin sang hyang Adītya Wulan tuwi tan wani mangluhuri harghgā sang hyang Mahameru. [14]) D. E: ontbreekt. [15]) B: Kelaçā bhūmi sāmpūrṇnāwwanya, pĕṇḍĕm bhaṭāra Ḍarmmarāja. D. E: Wuhus paripūrṇnā hagĕng aluhur, pinĕṇḍĕm sawanira bhaṭāra Ḍarmmā. [16]) D. E: ontbreekt. [17]) B: sāmpūrṇnāwan ngaraning hawan aruhur. D. E: sampūrṇnāwananing agĕng aluhur. [18]) D. E: ontbreekt; pinĕṇḍĕm sang ṛṣi Çidḍiwaçitadewa; mangkanā kacaritanya. [19]) B: yata mā sinangguh. [20]) B: prasaḍi linggā. D. E: lmah larangan ngaranya, praçidḍa linggih. [21]) B: tan wnang rug. [22]) D. E: ontbreekt. [23]) D. E: Tucapa. [24]) D. E: Içwara Brahma Wiṣṇu. [25]) B: wiṣya ontbreekt. D. E: dṛṣṭiwiṣa. [26]) B: bhūta matmahan awu. D. E: syūh bhaṣmi tanpatmahan awu. [27]) B: Wiyanggāmaya. D. E: Wiranggāmaya. [28]) B: ontbreekt.

Pangawan awunikang kāla trisamaya, ya [1]) kacaritanya ngūni. Ri wuwusnikang kāla trisamaya pjah mantuk ta bhaṭāra trisamaya; bhaṭāra Içwara mantuk maring Tigapatra-maṇḍala; bhaṭāra Brahma mantuk maring Jalaparwwata-maṇḍala; bhaṭāra Wiṣṇu mantuk maring Nangkāparwwata-maṇḍala.

Kahucapa ta hatmajiwanikang [2]) kāla trisamaya matmahan taya rākṣasa rwang çiki kwehnya, mijil saking [3]) gunung Wiyanggamaya; sang Kālānungkāla ngaranya. Sumambah ri bhaṭāra Parameçwara aminta kumawaçakna [4]) bhūwana lāwan janma mānūṣa; mwajar ta bhaṭāra Guru:

«Anaku Kālānungkāla, astu kita kumawaçakna [5]) bhuwana kalāwan janma mānūṣa. Yan tĕngĕta yughanta [6]) [ma]hapralaya, irika ta yan pamūktya ya [7]); mangunakna [8]) tapa kamung rumuhun. Patunggu [9]) ta kita babahan sang hyang Mahāmeru [kulwan] [10]), irika ta kamung mangunakna [11]) tapa. Kunang pawkasanangkwiri ko: yan ana bharibhari mangrāmpa dṛwyaçwa, [12]) umalap [13]) lmah larangan, lumbur susuk ṣima [brata] [14]) sang ṛṣi, rumugakĕn [15]) sang hyang praçiṣṭa kawikun, kamung makadṛwya [16]) hika, nguniweh salwirning sisikusung sarampadan, kamung makadṛwya hika kabeh [17]). Kunang yan rumugakĕn [18]) sang hyang [praçiṣṭa] [19]) kawikun, astu tibāha ring mahārorawa, [20]) tan [21]) tkaha ring swargga. Ndah kayatnākĕnta sapawkasning hulun [22])».

Mangkana ta ling bhaṭāra Guru. Yata sang Kālanungkāla matungku [23]) babahan sang hyang Mahāmeru kulwan, [24]) ring Pangawan ngaraning babahan [25]), [matangnyan hana deṣa ring Pangawan babahan sang hyang Mahāmeru hika] [26]). Sang Kālānungkāla praçiṣṭa kinabhaktyan [27]) ing Pangawan; manganakĕn ta

---

[1]) D. E: Wahanggāmaya ngaranya gunung Pangawan, hawan sang kāla triṣamaya. [2]) D. E: Kucapā hatmanikang. [3]) D. E: mijil maṇḍĕlĕng. [4]) D. E: kumawaçakĕn ikang. [5]) D. E: kumawaçaha. ring B: kumawaçakning. [6]) B. C: ya tngĕta yuganta. D. E: yan ḍatngeng yuggātan. [7]) D. E: irikā ta kamu yan pwa muktyaṣā. [8]) D. E: mangnakna. [9]) B: matunggu. D. E: palunggu. [10]) D. E: ontbreekt. [11]) D. E: kamu padekĕn. [12]) D. E: yan anāngbharingbhara paranparan pwa dewaçwa. B: mangramparampa. [13]) B: umayap. D. E: umalapa. [14]) B. D. E: ontbreekt. [15]) B: rumurugakĕn. D. E: murugākĕn. [16]) D. E: kamu mangkwadṛwya. [17]) D. E: ngūniweh sakalwir ing sisikusung salanya paḍana kamu sakadṛwya hikā kabeh. [18]) B: kunang hanaku murugakĕn. D. E: kunang yan kamu rumugakĕn. [19]) B: ontbreekt. [20]) B: mahābhairāwa. D. E: astu ko tiba ring mahaberawi. [21]) D. E: ingevoegd: kamu. [22]) D. E: Ndah kayatnakna pawkasku! [23]) B. C: matunggu. D. E: mungguh ring. [24]) B: kilyan. D. E: ontbreekt. [25]) D. E: ingevoegd: babahanira marĕp kulon; sang Kalanungkalā çira tunggu. [26]) D. E: ontbreekt. [27]) B: praçaṣṭi kinabhaktyan. D. E: sira ta kinabakten.

97

yuga sang Kālānukāla, çabdanira mangdadi gĕrĕh, kḍapira [1]) mangdadi kilat, sihung-huntunira mangdadi glap. Ikang naka matmahan pañcayakṣa [2]), aranya sang Lumanglang, sang Lumangling, sang Lumangut, sang Mangdulur, sang Manginte [3]). Ika mangingĕtakĕn yan hana salah ulah salah çabda [4]); mangkana kacaritanya.

Kunang hyang Gaṇa kinon kumĕmita [5]) lmah larangan, matungguha babahan sang hyang Mahāmeru marĕp wetan [6]); matangnyan hana deça ring Pūrṇnajiwa [7]) ngaranya mangke, babahan sang hyang Mahāmeru marĕp wetan. Sang hyang Gaṇa sira praçiṣṭa [8]) kinabhakten sira ring Pūrṇnajiwa [9]).

Kunang sang ṛsy Anggaṣṭi [10]) kinon kumĕmita [11]) lmah larangan, atungguha babahan sang hyang Mahāmeru marĕp kidul; matangnyan hana deça ring Paḍang aranya mangke, babahan sang hyang Mahāmeru hika. Sang ṛsy Anggaṣṭi [10]) kinabakten ing Paḍang.

Kunang bhaṭārī Ghorī kinon kumĕmita [12]) lmah larangan, matungguha babahan sang hyang Mahāmeru marĕp lwar. Matangnyan hana deça ring Gantĕn [13]) ngaranya mangke, babahan sang hyang Mahāmeru marĕp lwar; bhaṭārī Ghorī praçiṣṭa [14]) kinabhakten ing Gantĕn [15]).

Papat babahan sang hyang Mahāmeru; yata sinangguh [16]) Pañātūr-mukā ngaranya.

Ucapĕn [17]) ta bhaṭāra Ḍarmmarāja, mijil ta saking ārgghānira sang hyang Mahāmeru. Blah [18]) pucaknira sang hyang Mahāmeru [apatiga; yata matangnyan tiga pucaknira sang hyang Mahāmeru] [19]) katamapi katkaning mangke [20]). Tinhör gunung Triçṛngga [21]) ngaran sang hyang Mahāmeru, apan tiga hārghanira [22]). Mṛbuk hawangi pwa ganḍanira [23]) [bhaṭāra Darmmarāja duk mijil saking hārghanira sang hyang Mahāmeru] [24]); yata

[1]) D. E: kdepnira. [2]) D. E: ingevoegd: rakṣasa limang siki kwehnya. [3]) D. E: sang Lumanglang, sang Lumabut, sang Mangmit, sang Mandulu, sang Manginte. [4]) D. E: wwang salah polah sabḍanya. [5]) D. E: makmit. [6]) D. E: babahan marĕp mangetthan. [7]) B: Pūrṇnaçīwa. D: Purwwadiwa. E: Purwwadḍipa. [8]) B: praçaṣṭi. D. E: pratiṣṭā. [9]) D. E: sira ta kinabakten. B: ring Pūrṇnasīwa. [10]) D. E: hyang Anggaṣṭi. [11]) D. E: mangmit. [12]) D. E: makmit. [13]) B: Bantĕn. D. E: Lantĕn. [14]) B: praçaṣṭi. D. E: pratiṣṭā kang. [15]) D. E: Lantĕn. [16]) B: Mañaturmuka. [17]) D. E: Kucapa. [18]) D. E: Mlèdos ta hamatiga. [19]) D. E: ontbreekt. [20]) D. E: hatamapi tkaning mangke. [21]) D. E: Tisnangga. [22]) D. E: hargagranira. Ingevoegd: Sanghyang Ḍarmmarājā mtu sakeng pucakira sang hyang Mahāmeru. [23]) D. E: yata mrik awangi ganḍanira. [24]) D. E: ontbreekt.

98

matangnyan [1]) sang hyang Mahāmeru inaranan gunung Gaṇḍamaḍana wkasan. Liṇḍu pwa bhaṭārī Pṛthiwī, kadi ruga [2]) sang hyang Mahāmeru, mĕṇḍĕk bhumiwaçaṇa [3]), kumucak wai nikang hudadi [4]), atgata [5]) bhaṭāra Parameçwara [ruga sang hyang Mahāmeru] [6]).

Yata matangnyan mara bhaṭāra Guru maring ārghā [ambara margga sira lawan handakadewa] [7]). Jag lĕs prāpta ring ārgghanira sang hyang Mandaragiri, katingalan [8]) ta bhaṭāra Ḍarmmarāja mijil saking blahnira [9]) sang hyang Mahāmeru. Atrinayanā catūrbhuja sira, samasama lāwan rūpa [10]) bhaṭāra Guru. Rĕp, mangadĕg ta bhaṭāra Ḍarmmarāja ri punuknikang wṛṣabhadewa [11]); matangnyan tuṣṭāmbĕk nikang wṛṣabhadewa. Muwah bhaṭāra Ḍarmmarāja kinanān sira sangaskāra [12]), inaranan sang ṛṣi Taruṇā-tapa-yowana, inugrahan sira kawikun de bhaṭāra Guru, susuk [ṣima] [13]) sang hyang çima brata. Winkas ta sira sang ṛṣi Taruṇā-tapa-yowana sambegaha ring rāt kabeh; sinrahakĕn tang dṛwyāçwa [14]). Ço ngaraning dewa; matangnyan dṛwyāçwa sang hyang Mahāmeru, sira ta lmah larangan bhaṭāra ngaranira, pinakasusuk-ṣima sang ṛṣi; sira pinakatambrapuraṇa [15]), yeka sinangguh mantra tanpasurāt ngaranya.

Muwah bhaṭāra Guru winehaknira tang wṛṣabhadewa ri sira sang ṛṣi Tapa-taruṇa-yowana, pinakaçaraṇanira ngrākṣa [16]) bhuwana. Muwah sinrahakĕnira tang payung kuṇḍala kalambi; sira gumantyani dewaguru ring Kukub-maṇḍala [17]). Matangnyan yen ana

---

[1]) D. E: sangkan. [2]) D. E: Rĕp mangnakĕn ta liṇḍu sira, lwirug. [3]) D. E: sabhūmi Yawa sira. [4]) D. E: wenikang wahudadi. [5]) D. E: kaget pwa. [6]) D. E: ontbreekt. [7]) D. E: ontbreekt; manitihi tang andakadewa. [8]) D. E: katon. [9]) D. E: mtu saking rĕngatira. [10]) D. E: paḍa lawan. [11]) B. C: ingevoegd: yata dinĕhanira, yaya pjahha ikang hanḍaka dinĕhanira. Yata pinangku bhaṭara Ḍarmmarāja de bhaṭara Guru, winawanireng Kukub-maṇḍala. Linunggahakĕn ta sira ring rātnapakajā, tĕhĕr siniram ring Tatwāmṛtta çiwambā. Kalukū makādyusnira ring wṛṣābhādewa. D. E: yata dinuhanira, pjah tikang handaka denira. Matakut pwa bhaṭara Guru pjah wahanānira, yata pinakaratha sang hyang Ḍarmmaraja. Winawa ta mareng Kukub, inunggahakĕn ta ring ratha, nhĕr siniram ring Tatwāmṛtthā çiwambhā. Kinaluku sira, dinyus tang wṛçabadewa; matangnyan harituṣṭambĕk ikang handakā. [12]) D. E: kinon ta ngaskaraha. [13]) B. D. E: ontbreekt. [14]) B: dṛwyaçwang. [15]) B: sira hinaranan tambrapūraṇā. [16]) D. E: pinakaçarananta rākṣakā. [17]) D. E: ingevoegd: manitihi çūraga pataraṇa, inidĕpira tang dewata kabeh, mangastwani ring sang ṛṣi Taruṇa-tapa. Rĕp kinon ta sira byasana, inastwakĕn dening para watĕk dewata kabeh, wastu bhaṭāra Mahaguru ngaranira kaping roning dewaguru ring Kukub, sira ta sang ṛṣi Taruṇa-tapa. Sangkanya hinaranan sang ṛṣi Taruṇa-tapa-yowaṇā.

ṛṣi taruṇa tapa yowana, mijil saking rĕngatnira [1]) sang hyang Mahāmeru, tanpabapa tanpababu [2]), tanpakaḍang [tanpawwang-sanak] [3]), sira tālapĕn pinakalingga [4]) sang hyang Mahāmeru, mungguha ring Kukub-maṇḍala; sira ta sang ṛṣi Ḍarmmahūtpṭi [5]) ngaranira.

Muwah ana ta dewata kalmahan tan wnang mura [6]), kna sapa de sang ṛṣi Sidḍiwangsitadewa nguni kacaritanya. Sumambah ri bhaṭāra Parameçwara, aminta [7]) winaluyākning swargga. Sumahur bhaṭāra Guru:

«Uḍūh hanaku dewata kna sapa, astu kamung mantuka ring swargga [8]); yan mantuk maring swargga sang ṛṣi Tapa-yowana [9]), tan kantuna kamung [10]). Kunang pawkasangkwiri ko: panganakĕn [11]) tapa kamung rumuhun. Nihan ta panganugrahangkwiri ko: payung kuṇḍala mwang kulambi. Ndah tanpangaskāraha, tinhör ta Dewata-kaki panĕnggahan ing rāt hiri kita, idĕp ta ring Swargga patapanta [12]).»

Mangkana pawkas bhaṭāra Guru; matangnyan hana ring Swargga ngaranya mangke, mangkana kacaritanya. Muwah sang Kālānungkāla winkas ta de bhaṭāra Guru, rumakṣaha ri sang ṛṣi Taruṇā-tapayowana: «Yan mantuk maring swargga, tan kantuna kamung». Mangkana ling bhaṭāra Guru.

Zesde hoofdstuk.

Kahucapa ta lakṣaṇa bhaṭāra Guru [13]) tumulusakna magawe praçiṣṭa [14]). Mayoga ta ring ārgghanira sang hyang Mahāmeru [15]), apatitis [16]) anggraṇaçika humarĕp kulon; matangnyan harĕpning kahyangan kulon, apan kulwan arĕpan ing bhaṭāra mayoga [17]). Tumungkul mulat mingsor [18]) sira, sahulatnira mingsor matmahan Tasik-lĕbu; mangkana kacaritanya. Mayoga ta sira muwah [19]), maphala swastahaning rāt kabeh; matangnyan hana wukir Phala ngaranya. «Tan hana pwa way paçucanya» iḍĕpnira [20]); magawe ta sira ranu paçucyananira [21]).

1) D. E: pucakira. 2) D. E: tanpahibū. 3) D. E: ontbreekt. 4) D. E: sira yogya gawenĕn linggā. 5) D. E: sang hyang Ḍarmmahupti. B: sang ṛṣi Ḍarmmahupti. 6) D. E: tan wĕnaug mangamĕr. 7) D. E: hamalaku. 8) D. E: antukanmu mulihheng çwarggā. 9) D. E: Taruṇa-tapa. 10) D. E: tan hana ta kami. 11) D. E: mangnakĕn. 12) D. E; idĕpĕnta ring Çwarggā tapanta. 13) D. E: Kucapa bhaṭara Prameçwara. 14) D. E: lakṣaṇ a sira magawe tantu. 15) B. D. E: Mandaragiri. 16) B: amatitis. 17) D. E: hapan mangulon harĕpnira bhaṭara Guru duk ayoggā. 18) D. E: mulat ing çwargga. 19) D. E: Muwah kucapa bhaṭāra, denira mangnakĕn yoggā ring sang hyang Mandaragiri. 20) B: wway paçucyana iniḍĕpnira. D. E: „Tan anā pwa wah panaçūnya" iḍĕpnira. 21) D. E: magawe ta siranu maçūnya.

100

Kahucapa ta [1]) bhaṭārī Huma, alawas [s]ira haneng gunung Wilis, [alal ta sira bhaṭāra [2]) mangundangeng sira] [3]). Tan daraṇa pwa bhaṭārī [4]), yata sira lumampah ḍatĕngeng Mahāmeru [5]). Sḍangnira bhaṭāra magawe raṇu, datang ta bhaṭārī Huma; mwajar ta bhaṭāra Guru:

«Ah bhaṭārī, paran [n]imitaning [6]) ḍatang? Tan hana hulih mami sangketa lawan kita [7])? «Kami hundang kitā dlahā, yan huwus rāmya caracaranira [8]) sang hyang Mahāmeru», mangkana hujarku ngūni».

Rĕp kroḍa ta bhaṭārī Huma; wurung ta de bhaṭārāgawe raṇu[9]), matangnyan hana raṇu Wurung [10]) aranya mangke. Jag lĕs, lunghā bhaṭārī Huma, mara ta maring [11]) gunung Hārjjuna. Kunang bhaṭāra Guru tumulusaknāgawe [12]) raṇu; amasĕhmasĕh ta sira kombala [13]); matangnyan hinaran raṇu Kombala [14]) tkaning mangke talaganira sang hyang Mahāmeru.

Tindakning bhaṭāra [15]) saking Mahāmeru maring gunung Pawitra. Atrisadyabrata bhaṭāra [16]), madyus ta sira ping tiga sarahina ping tiga sawngi. Tustusnira manring Warunggama [17]); matangnyan hana [18]) bañu ring gunung Pawitra [19]), apan ĕnti makādyus bhaṭāra ngūnī kacaritanya. Tindaknira [20])saking Pawitra; mayoga sira ri hargghaning gunung Kumukus. Atihangĕyĕh [21]) bhaṭāra Guru, kumukus mangdadi warirang [22]), katamapi tkaning mangke.

Kahucapa ta [23]) bhaṭārī Huma, sah saking gunung Harjjuna ḍatĕngeng gunung [Kawi, tumuluy maring][24]) Kampud. [Patampuh ning kroḍa bhaṭārī] [24]) pinupaknira ta pucakning gunung Kampud [25]), inuntalaknira mangidul mangulwan [26]); matangnyan hana gunung Lĕbĕng [27]) aranya mangke [28]), pucaknira gunung

---

[1]) D. E: Kucapa. [2]) B: alawas ta sira bhaṭāra tan. [3]) D. E: ontbreekt; ḍatĕnga ri kahananirā bhaṭāra Guru. [4]) D. E: Tan kawasa hamgĕng bhaṭārī Umā-B: tan ḍaraṇā pwāmbĕk bhaṭārī. [5]) D. E: ingevoegd: Jhag lĕs, kapanggih bhaṭāra Guru. [6]) D. E: paran ta sangkānta. [7]) D. E: tan anā hulih ring amkas ring kita. B: mami masangketa lawan kita. [8]) D. E: tĕmbe, lamun uwus mamyacaracaraning. [9]) D. E: wurung ta bhaṭāra denirā magawe raṇū. [10]). D. E: Urung. [11]) D. E: prapti sireng. [12]) B. D. E: tumulusakna magawe. [13]) B: ya tbahtbah ta sira kombalā. D. E: masĕh ta sira kbo kuning. [14]) D. E: raṇu Kbo-kuning. [15]) D. E: Sah. [16]) D. E: Trisaddyā ta butmangke bhaṭāra. [17]) B. C: tustusnira maring Warugama (C: Warunggama). D. E: tusanya mareng Parunggarmmā. [18]) B: tan hana. [19]) D. E: sangkanya norana bañu pawitra. [20]) D. E: Sah. [21]) B: Atihabĕsĕh. D. E: Tangĕyĕh. [22]) B. D. E: walirang. [23]) D. E: Kucapa. [24]) D. E: ontbreekt. [25]) D. E: pinukah pucaknira. [26]) B: ingevoegd: lĕs bĕng. [27]) B: gunung Sbĕng. [28]) D. E: matmahan gunung Sĕmbĕng, hatamapi tkaning mangke.

101

Kampud ngūni kacaritanya. Dindĕlnira saçeṣaning [1]) gunung Kāmpud, bubul trus tkeng sagara kidul [tkeng Rĕnĕb, saka ri wuyung bhaṭārī Huma] [2]); matangnyan mili wwayning gunung Kāmpud amjahi janma mānūṣa. «Tuhan, Rahadyan [3]), Pangeran» sāmbatning rāt kabeh. Bhaṭāra Guru sḍang mayoga ring [4]) gunung Kumukus, mangrĕngĕ ta panangis [5]) ning rāt kabeh. Sawulatnira kidul katon ta pukah pucaknikang gunung Kāmpud; wruh ta sira yan bhaṭārī makāmbĕknika [6]). Mwajar ta sira:

«Uḍūh, paran ta mne lwiraning rāt kabeh [7]), yan tan aku hasiha [8])? Aku hamahayu [9]) rāt kabeh».

Marūpa ta sira dewaputra lituhayu [10]), tinhĕr Dewaputra [11]) ngaranira, sira mahayu rāt kabeh. Tinambaknira [12]) kroḍa bhaṭārī, mangĕmbŏng manalaga [13]), mangdadi raṇu ring gunung Kāmpud [14]); tinhĕr bhaṭāra hyang Hanalaga [15]) ngaranirā. Sira humandĕl iring [16]) gunung Kāmpud, umadĕgakĕn [17]) ta gadānira wsi, agŏng aruhur tumutug [18]) tkeng akaça. Jag lĕs, lunghā ta bhaṭārī Huma [19]), nhĕr mari kroḍanira [20]). Mwajar ta bhaṭāra Guru:

«Uni haku [21]) duk pinaka-[gurunikang rāt kabeh, duk] [22]) guruning dewata kabeh, bhaṭāra Guru haranku. Mangke [23]) pwāku hamahayu [24]) rāt kabeh; «Tuhan, Rahadyan [25]), Pangeran [26]),» hujar ning wwang kalaran masambat iryyaku. Matangnyan bhaṭāra Tuhan ngaranku, aku bhaṭāra Pangeran, aku kinabhaktyan ikang mānūṣa, aku sumungku ring rāt [27]) kabeh; matangnyan bhaṭāra Hanungkurāt [28]) ngaranku waneh. Aku byapaka [29]) ning rāt kabeh [30]), aku pasajen ing rāt kabeh [31]); wastu tuliha kang wwang marĕk [32]) ing gunung Kāmpud yan tanpadṛwe sasajen [33]).»

---

1) D. E: Dindĕl tunggaknya. 2) D. E: ontbreekt. 3) D. E: Radyan. 4) D. E: Kucapa ta bhaṭāra Guru sḍangnya mayogghā ring hagraning. 5) D. E: tangis. 6) D. E: wruh tambĕkanira bhaṭāri. 7) D. E: paran ta beikane tang rāt kabeh. 8) D. E: yen tan kami wilasāha. 9) D. E: hamahayuha. 10) B. D. E: listu hayu. 11) D. E: bhaṭāra Putra. 12) D. E: hinambĕkan. 13) D. E: mangŏmbĕng managga. 14) D. E: ya mandadi raṇū hikang gunung Kampud. 15) B: hyang Hatalagā. D. E: sang hyang Ngatalaga. 16) D. E: umandĕl ikang. 17) D. E: umandĕgakĕn. 18) D. E: agĕng adawa kumutug. 19) D. E: Kunang bhaṭāri Uma lunghā sira. 20) B: mari kroḍa sira. 21) D. E: Ngūni kami. 22) D. E: ontbreekt. 23) D. E: Mangko. 24) D. E: hāmayu. 25) D. E: Radyan. 26) B: Pangeranku. 27) D. E: sumungkuning rat. 28) D. E: bhaṭara Nungkurat. 29) B: wyapaka. 30) D. E: Aku hampĕki rat kabeh. 31) D. E: aku sinadyan ing manūṣā kabeh. 32) B: wastu tulika wwang marĕk. D. E: aku wwang tulikatangka marĕk. 33) B: pasajenya. D. E: sangkanya dṛwya pasajyan.

Mangkana ling bhaṭāra Tuhan; yata paḍādṛwe pasajen [1]) kang wong marĕk [2]) ing gunung Kāmpud; pasajen ing rāt kabeh ring gunung Kāmpud mārĕp kulon [3]). Kunang bhaṭāra Tuhan ring Kumara pajanma-māṇuṣanira ngūni [4]).

Kunang hikang gaḍā wsi matmahan silādri, gunung watu kumutug tka ring akaça [5]). Tatkāla pwa [6]) lumingsir sang hyang Çiwa-raditya [7]) kulwan, tan kasuluhan [8]) sang hyang Mahāmeru de sang hyang Raditya [9]), apan katingkĕran denikang gunung Gaḍā-wsi [10]). Yata hinalapanira tang gunung Gaḍā-wsi, linabuhakning sāgara mangdadi karang. Çeṣanya sinalahning pṛthiwi, [hanggang-hanggang] [11]); matangnyan hana gunung Hanggang-hanggang ngaranya mangke [12]).

Kahucapa ta [13]) bhaṭārī Huma, umgil sira maring [14]) gunung Ganḍamaḍana [15]). Ḍatang ta sang Kumara, sumambah ri bhaṭārīçwarī [16]), tumakwanakning bhaṭāra Guru. Sumahur bhaṭārī Huma [17]):

«Apa denta takwanakĕn bhaṭāra, apan tan wruh kahananira [18]).»

Sumawur ta sang Kumāra:

«Mahyun sumambaha ri pāḍa bhaṭāra ranak bhaṭārī [19]), apan bhaṭāra sangkaning ranak bhaṭārī, apan paḍa [20]) bhaṭārī panlangañ juga, [awan de rānak bhaṭārī] [21]).»

Mangkanā ling sang Kumara. Kroḍa [tāmbĕk] [22]) bhaṭārī Huma rehira [23]) sinangguh panlangan de sang Kumara. Yata matangnyan sinambut sang Kumara, inalapan ikang rah-wulu-sumsumnira. Nhĕr sinapa de bhaṭārī Huma matmahana wil rūpa sang Kumara; atmahan Bṛnggiriṣṭi ta sira. Sḍĕng minangkana [24]) sang Kumara de bhaṭārī Huma, datang ta bhaṭāra Guru; katwan minangkana sang Kumara [25]) de bhaṭārī Huma. Kroḍa ta bhaṭāra Guru, sinapa ta bhaṭārī Huma:

---

[1]) D. E: matangnyan paḍadṛwya pasadyan. [2]) B: wong parĕk. [3]) D. E: pinakasadya sira dening rat ring gunung Kampud tang humarĕp kulon. Ingevoegd: matangnyan hanarāning pasadyan kang mangke. [4]) D. E: mañjanma ta sireng manuṣā, ring Kumara pagwanirāñjanma. [5]) B: gunung watu tumūlya tka ring akaçā. [6]) D. E: Wawu. [7]) B: sang hyang Çiwahaditya. D. E: hyang Aditya. [8]) D. E: kaslĕhan. [9]) D. E: dening dilah ning Haditya. [10]) D. E: apan katawngan dening gunung wsi. [11]) D. E: ontbreekt. [12]) D. E: nimitanya hana gunung Hagangagang aranya. [13]) D. E: Kucapa. [14]) D. E: umungguh ta sireng. [15]) B: Gadḍāpawanā. [16]) D. E: ri paduka Prameçwarī. [17]) D. E: bhaṭari Guru. [18]) D. E: tan wruh paranya. [19]) D. E: „Hayun sumĕmbahana bhatari. [20]) B: paḍa ontbreekt. D. E: kunang paḍa. [21]) D. E: ontbreekt. B: lāwan de ranak bhaṭārī. [22]) D. E: ontbreekt. [23]) D. E: karehanya. [24]) D. E: sḍĕngnya mangkana. [25]) D. E: katon sang Kumara sinangkala.

103

«Jhah, bhaṭārī Huma, apa doṣanyānaku demu [1]), matangnyan demu wehi matmahan wil [2]), tĕhĕr demu halapi rāhnya sumsum-wulunya? Dūrgga dahat kamung, bhaṭārī Huma [3]), agila haku tumon ing rūpamu [4]).

Mangkana ling bhaṭāra Guru ri bhaṭārī Huma. Tanpendah duduk wuluh mangnani lagḍu [5]), [kang paribhaṣa] [6]), tan wyartha [7]) tumañcĕb çabda bhaṭāra ri bhaṭārī Huma. [Yata matangnyan rĕp tang rūpajuti] [8]), matmahan rakṣasi rūpa bhaṭārī Huma, mabho mangi ta sira [9]), tinhĕr bhaṭārī Dūrggadewī [10]) ngaranira. Jag, lĕs, lunghā ta bhaṭāṛī Dūrgga saking Mandaragiri, ininditnira sang Kumara nhĕr lunghā, pinĕṇḍĕmnira wulu-sumsumnirāh [11]) ning Kumara. Wala pwa ngaraning rare, tinhĕr ta ring Walaṇḍita ngaraning gunung, pamĕṇḍĕman ing rāh [12]) wulu sumsum sang Kumara kacaritanya ngūni. Jag lĕs, lunghā maring sma kisidul palayaçara [13]).

Kunang bhaṭāra Guru tapwan kahanan kroḍa sira ngūni, [mangke sira kapwa tan kanan [14]) kroḍa] [15]); yata sumapa [16]) hawaknira matmahan rākṣasa. [Rĕp rūpa bhaṭāra Guru marūpa ta rākṣasa] [17]) matrinayanā catūrbhuja; tinhĕr ta ngaranira sang hyang Kālarūdra. Girigirin [18]) tang watĕk dewata kabeh, ngūniweh tāng rāt kabeh tumon rūpa bhaṭāra Kālarūdrā [19]); mahyun sira manaḍaha sahisining bhūwana [20]).

Rĕp sakṣaṇa bhaṭāra Içwara Brahmā Wiṣṇu umawara panaḍah [21]) bhaṭāra Kālarūdrā; [tumurun maring maḍyapaḍa hawayang sira] [22]), umucapakĕn tatwa bhaṭāra mwang bhaṭārī ring bhuwana [23]). Mapanggung maklir [24]) sira, walulang hinukir makawayangnira [25]), kinudangan [26]) pañjang langonlangon. Bhaṭāra Hiçwara sira hudipan [27]), rinakṣa sira de hyang Brahmā Wiṣṇu [28]).

---

[1]) D. E: „Mapa ta donyanaku demu ḍaṇḍa, bhāṭari. [2]) D. E: sangkanya matmahan wil. [3]) D. E: ingevoegd: demu napa. [4]) D. E: tuton ing rūpanta. [5]) D. E: Tanpendah dukduk wuluh mangnāni lgĕḍu. [6]) D. E: ontbreekt. [7]) D. E: wyakti. [8]) D. E: ontbreekt. [9]) D. E: habo hamis habunya. [10]) D. E: Durggadewati. [11]) B: rah. [12]) D. E: pamdĕn rah. [13]) B: maring sma si Dūrggā sayāṣāṇa. D. E: Lĕs lunga bhaṭārī Dūrggā, yeki mangke bhawanira. [14]) B: kapwa (tan ontbreekt) kahanan. [15]) D. E: ontbreekt. [16]) D. E: sumapu. [17]) D. E: ontbreekt. [18]) D: E: Kagirigiri ruhurira lawan gĕngira, tuminghāl. [19]) D. E: mūlat ring bhaṭara Kala. [20]) D. E: mahyun ya manaḍaha rāsinikang bhūwaṇā. [21]) D. E: mangawarah tadahira. [22]) D. E: ontbreekt. B: hangwayang. [23]) D. E: mangucapakĕn kacaritthanikang bhūwaṇa. [24]) D. E: mapanggung māglar. [25]) D. E: minakawayang, ingevoegd: tinabĕhtabĕhan. [26]) D. E: kiniḍungan. [27]) B: hucapan. [28]) D. E: Bhaṭara Hiçwarā sirengiḍĕp, pratyakṣa mwang bhaṭara Brāhma Wiṣṇu.

Midĕr sira ring bhuwana masang giṇa hawayang [1]), [tinhĕr habaṇḍagiṇa hawayang [3]); mangkana mula kacaritanya ngūni.

Muwah pangawara bhaṭāra Hiçwara Brahmā Wiṣṇu ri bhaṭāra Kāla, midĕra ring bhuwana, bhaṭāra Kāla tiniñjonira, ijohijo molah ta sireng bale, lumawulawu hawaknira] [2]). Sang hyang Içwara dadi çwari, sang hyang Brahmā dadi pederāt [4]), sang hyang Wiṣṇu dadi tkĕs [5]); midĕr mangidung hamenamen, [tinhĕr baṇḍagina menmen] [6]) ngaranya [7]). Mangkana mulaning hanābaṇḍagiṇa menmen [8]).

Kunang bhaṭāra Guru lumawulawu ring çarīranira [9]); matangnyan hana gunung Lawu ngaranya mangke, patapanirā bhaṭāra Kālarūdrā ngūni kacaritanya. Malawas ta bhaṭāra Kāla hamangunakĕn [10]) tapa, waluya marūpajati muwah [11]) sira bhaṭāra Guru. Kunang bhaṭārī Dūrgga anaḍah antasapa ri bhaṭāra Parameçwara [12]); kinon ta sirāmangunakna tapa [13]). Matapa ta sira ri jro patala; alawas ta sirāmangun tapa [14]), waluya jati marūpa [15]) bhaṭārī Humadewi. Umijil ta sira saking [16]) jro patala, matangnyan hana gunung Bret ngaranya mangke, awan bhaṭārī Huma saking jro patala kacaritanya. Kunang sang Kumāra-Bhṛnggiriṣṭi manaḍah antasapa ring bhaṭārī Huma [17]); kinon tā mangunakna tapa [18]); waluya marūpajati Kumara [19]).

Zevende Hoofdstuk.

Kahucapa [20]) bhaṭāra Guru, tumulusaknamagawe tantu ri Yawaḍipa; matilĕl atantu [21]) satampakning kuntul anglayang, kumĕṇḍĕng tan pgat, rumeka tan lbur, satampak bhaṭāra Guru. Marūpa ta sira wiku, bhujangga [22]) çewapakṣa ta sira, sira bhaṭāra mahāmpu Palyat ngaranira. Dumunung ta sira ring sma Kalyasĕm, sma ginawe patapan, wetan kidul sakeng Paguhan [23]). Kunang denirā mangun tapa bherawapakṣa lkasnira, amangan

[1]) B: makagiṇā hangwayang. D. E: makaguṇānira wayang. [2]) D. E: ontbreekt. [3]) B: tinhăr hana giṇā hangwayang. [4]) B. D. E: peret. [5]) D. E: tkas. [6]) D. E: ontbreekt. [7]) D. E: ta ngaranira. [8]) D. E: hana mañcagiṇā. [9]) D. E: Kunang bhaṭāra Kāla lumawulawu ta hawakira. [10]). D. E: mangunakĕn. [11]) D. E: walūya rupajatī. [12]) D. E: manaḍah sapa bhaṭāra Guru. [13]) D. E: kinon ta matapā. [14]) D. E: sirā mangnakna tapā. [15]) D. E: walūya rupajatī. [16]) D. E: mijil sireng. [17]) D. E: manaḍah sapa bhaṭārī Dūrggā. [18]) D. E: kinwan ta sirā mangnakna tapā. Ingevoegd: Malawasirātapā. [19]) D. E: malūya rupajātī sang Kumara. [20]) D. E: Tucapa. [21]) B: matinggal atantu. D. E: matinggala; tantu ontbreekt. [22]) D. E: wiku mwang bhūjanggā. [23]) D. E: Pagulan.

çawa [ning wwang][1]), inayĕmnira tang çawa, tatkala tngah wngi sira npanaḍah [2]).

Gnĕp ta [dwidaça] [3]) rwawlas tawun lawasnira [4]), mangrĕngö ta sang prabhū ring Galuh, çrī mahārāja Bhatati [5]) ngaranira, yan Brahmāloka [6]) sang wiku; mangundanga ta [7]) sira para wiku, manganakna [8]) yajñā sira. Pininangan ta sang para gowantĕn kabeh [9]), pininangan ta sirāmpu Mahāpalyat. Sadanantara [10]) tka tanggungning rājasokāryya [11]), ring pañcādaçi çuklapakṣa ning kasanga [12]); ḍatang kang wong sakidulning Galuh, sakulon ing Galuh. Mangkat sira mahāmpu Palyat lawan kang atunggu sma [13]), yata hamawa mahāmangsa [14]). Kaphalaning wwang pinakatahapanira [15]), lawan kaṇṭora [16]) lima kwehnya, yata makawaḍahnirā [ngayĕm çawaning wwang] [17]). Ḍatang sira mahāmpu Palyat [ring taratag] [18]); matakwan tā haj i Bhathati [19]) ring pangambehan [20]), lingnira:

«Mpu Waju-kuning, mpu Kalotan, ndi ta sang wiku Palyat hunggonya? Apa rūpanira [21])?»

«Unya, pwangkulun, sang malinggih kilyan sira [22]).»

«Ih, mapa dening hulun tuminghal[eng sira] [23]); purungul-purungul yaya dayaka ta rūpanira [24]). Iḍĕpning hulun habhrangga [25]) mabadḍa makalambi-guru [26]) [mapayung makuṇḍala] [27]), iringĕn dening anak-ṣiṣyanira [28]) satus rongatus kwehnya.»

Mangkana ling çrī mahārāja; sumahur mpu Kalotan:

«Tahā si pwangkulun, apan sira bhūjangga wiku [29]) çewapakṣa sira, yata nimitaning tanpabadḍa [30]).»

[«Ah, mangkana kupwa] [31]). Apa pwa [32]) mungguh ring arĕpnira?»

---

[1]) D. E: ontbreekt. [2]) D. E: ywatara tngah wngi yan sirāuaḍah. [3]) D. E: ontbreekt. [4]) D. E: lawasnyātapā. [5]) D. E: Bataki. [6]) D. E: brāhmaṇaloka. [7]) B: mangundang ta. D. E: maṇḍala tu. [8]) D. E: mangnakĕn. [9]) D. E: para dewata kabeh. [10]) B: Tadānantara. D. E: Sanghaneng hantara. [11]) B: tkā gungning rājasokāryya. D. E: tkahata kāryya. [12]) D. E: pūrṇnammā ning kasanga. [13]) D. E: walana ta wwang kungga çma. [14]) D. E: ya mawa basangku. [15]) D. E: makatapanira. [16]) D. E: lawan kajorā ya wanawanya. [17]) D. E: ontbreekt. [18]) D. E: ontbreekt. [19]) D. E: Bhataki. [20]) D. E: pangabehan. [21]) D. E: „Waju-kuning, mpu Kalotan, daṣṭa sang ĕmpu Palyat ngaranya, mpu rupanira?" [22]) D. E: „Dan sang malinggih, pukulun, lambung kilyan sira". B: lambang kilyan sira. [23]) D. E: ontbreekt. [24]) B: yaya dayaka rūpā sira. D. E: kaya yeka rupanya. [25]) B. D. E: habhṛngga. [26]) D. E: kalambikuru. [27]) D. E: ontbreekt. [28]) D. E: kiniring dening mitra. [29]) D. E: sing bujangga tanpawiku. [30]) D. E: yan kanimitanya tan ahabādḍa, hapan mangkanā pwa". [31]) D. E: ontbreekt. [32]) D. E: „Paran haranya. B: Paran pwa.

«Kaphalaning wwang lāwan kaṇṭora [1]) ngaranya, pwangkulun.»

«Kang kaphala pinakaparan [2])?»

«Pinakatapahan [3]), pwangkulun.»

«Kang kaṇṭora pinakaparan [4])?»

«Waḍahnirāngayĕm [5]) [çawaning wwang] [6]), pwangkulun.»

U e golol kelĕ [7]), mutah çrī mahārāja: «Ye ñjuru pawohañ, [ñ]jaluk [k]inang [8]).»

«Ih, yāmangan wwang kapwa sira mahāmpu Palyat? Sākṣāt brahmālokasanghāra ngaraning wiku mangkana. Dohakna sangkeng nūṣa Jawa [9]), labuhakna ring sāgara [10]), marapwan tanana kārmma [11]) mangkana.»

Ḍuhka sirāji Bhatathi; mantuk sira mahāmpu Palyat, wruh yan ḍuhka sang prabhū. Gumuyu sira [12]): «ci hāh hāh hāh», mantuk sira mahāmpu Palyat maring patapanira ring Kalyasĕm.

Eñjang mara yatā mpu Kalotan lawan mpu Waju-kuning kinon tumilangakna [13]) sang paṇḍita. [Jag lĕs lunghā sang inutus, ḍatĕnga ring Kalyāsĕm; umaṇḍĕm anambah sirāmpu Kalotan lawan mpu Waju-kuning, umarahakĕn yan hinutus de sang prabhū lumabuhakna ring sāgara rakwa sang pāṇḍita.

«Um, hanglampu juga kami, bapa; wruh kami yan sang prabhū ḍuhka.»] [14])

Wusungan amanikĕp mangambuli mpu Kalotan lawan mpu Waju-kuning [15]), mambĕbĕd ring walatung [16]), linabuhakning [17]) sāgara sirāmpu Mahāpalyat. Jag lĕs mulih sang malabuh, mawarah ring çrī mahārāja [Bhatathi yen sāmpun linabuh sirāmpu Mahāpalyat] [18]). Ring eñjing mara yata [sirāmpu Kalotan lawan mpu Waju-kuning inutus de sang prabhū tumilikanāmpu Mahāpalyat. Jag lĕs lunghā sang inutus] [19]), kapanggih ta haring-haring [20])sirāmpu Mahāpalyat [21]). [Umaṇḍĕm anambah mpu Kalotan lawan mpu Waju-kuning, mwajar ta sirāmpu Mahāpalyat lingnira:] [22])

[1]) D. E: kajoran. [2]) D. E: „Paran tang kaphala?" [3]) D. E: pinakatapani. [4]) D. E: „Tang kajoran pinakapwa?" [5]) D. E: „Taḍahnirayĕm. [6]) D. E: ontbreekt. [7]) B: „Ah, mangkana kwa kupwa" u golol kelö. D. E: Lah matukupwa ubrah. [8]) D: jalukinang rare. E: jalu rare. [9]) D. E: dobakĕn sakeng Jawa. [10]) D. E: labuh ring sagara. [11]) D. E: hapan tananā kramma. [12]) D. E: Tumuli sira. [13]) B: humilangakna ring. D. E: mangilangakĕn. [14]) D. E: ontbreekt; satkanya ring Kalyasĕm, kapanggih sirampu Palyat. [15]) D. E: sinikĕp kinambulan. [16]) D. E: yata binĕbĕd winalatung. [17]) D. E: ya linabuh ring. [18]) D. E: ontbreekt. [19]) D. E: ontbreekt; daṣṭa ta sang prabhū: „Laku, Kalotan Waju-kuning, tumiliki sang ĕmpu Palyat". [20]) B: kapanggih aringhari. [21]) D. E: kapanggih sira papanas. [22]) D. E: ontbreekt; sinikĕpwa sira rinimpus sukunya tanganya. „Paran gawenta nora pjah?" Majar taya.

107

«[Tan mati kami] [1]); pamet watu sadĕdĕg dawahanya [2]), sawitning tal gönganya [3])».

Nhĕr binbĕd ta sira lawan watu [4]); ring eñjing mara yata linabuh malih sang inutus [5]), kapanggih sirāmpu Mahāpalyat. Bhinaṣmi ta sira wkasan, awunya [6]) linabuh ring sāgara. Ring eñjing mara yata malih [7]) sang inutus, kapanggih ta sira maçilā mpu Mahāpalyat [8]). Mpu Kalotan lawan mpu Waju-kuning [umnang kawongan] [9]) tumon ri kaçaktin sang paṇḍitā; samangkanā mpu Kalotan lawan mpu Waju-kuning mamĕkuli jöng sang yatiwara [10]), atĕhĕr dumilati jöngnira [11]) sang paṇḍita:

«Tan olih humjahi sang paṇḍita, pwangkulun [12])».

Sumahur tāmpu Mahāpalyat, lingnira:

«Mpu Kalotan [lawan mpu Waju-kuning] [13]), kami saha [14]) saking kene, apan hangiccā hamĕngamĕng [15]) kami maring nūṣa Jawa, apan bhūmi mami ring nūṣa Kāmbangan ngaranya; [irika maṇḍala kabhujanggan mami] [16]). Mangke pwa ḍuhka sang prabhū ring Galuh, ndah mulih kami [17]) mangke maring maṇḍala mami [18]) ring nuṣa Kāmbangan [19])».

«Pukulun, tumūt raputu sang paṇḍita [20]), tansaha ri jöng sang yatiwara, pwangkulun».

«Um, hapa [21]) lingan mami yan mangkana; kami hameta watu [22]) sapuluh ḍpa dawanya, pinakaparahu mamyālayar [23])».

Amintonakĕn kawakyan sira [24]); tumūt [t]āmpu [25]) Kalotan lawan mpu Waju-kuning. Amanggih ta sira tuñjung bang ri tĕlĕngning sāgara, sakala[nga]n ronya [26]) akĕmbang mās [27]). Prāpta sira ri [28]) nūṣa Kambangan, sinungsung dening çiṣyanira [29]),

---

[1]) D. E: ontbreekt. [2]) B: sawĕdĕg dawahanya. D. E: „Hameta kwa watu sadpa dawanya. [3]) D. E: ingevoegd: bĕbĕdi lawan hawak mami, labuh ring sagara!" [4]) D. E: Yata hinubalan watu linabuh ring sagara; mulih sang malabuh. [5]) B: mali sābinutus. D. E: mara sang malabuh. [6]) D. E: kinukup. [7]) D. E: ring eñjing malwi. [8]) B. D. E: kapanggih malungguh sang ĕmpu Palyat. Ingevoegd: Mbĕr sang. [9]) D. E: ontbreekt. B: umnĕng kawngan. [10]) D. E: tĕhĕr mĕṇḍĕk manĕmbah. [11]) D. E: mandilati talampakanira. [12]) D. E: „Tan ulih mandilah tthalampakan sang paṇḍita". Ingevoegd: Mangkana sambatnya mpu Kalotan Waju-kuning. [13]) D. E: ontbreekt. [14]) B: kami syuha. D. E: kami sah. [15]) D. E: hayun mangica B: apan tangis hamĕngamĕng. [16]) D. E: ontbreekt. [17]) B: muliha mami. D. E: mulihkami. [18]) D. E: maṇḍala kami. [19]) D. E: ingevoegd: Mangkanā lingira sang ĕmpu Palyat. Sumawur sira mpu Kalotan lawan Waju-kuning: [20]) „Ḍuh, sun milu, pukulun. [21]) D. E: Ḍuh, paran. [22]) D. E: hameta sela. [23]) D. E: ya pinakaparawu mami malayarāknā. [24]) D. E: Amĕtwakĕn çaktinira. [25]) D. E: milu sira mpu. [26]) B: lonya. [27]) D. E: makĕmbang māsnikang tuñjung. [28]) D. E: Datang sireng. [29]) D. E: sikṣanira.

wwang ayuhayu saha bhūṣaṇa [1]), satus wwalung puluh kwehnya. Umarĕk paḍānĕmbah [2]); matakwan tāmpu Kalotan [lawan mpu Wajukuning] [3]):

«Wong āpeki [4]), pwangkulun, ayuhayu saha bhūṣaṇa [5])?»

«Ah, dedening wwang pinangan mami [6]) duk ing nūṣa Jawa.»

«Mangkana kapwa, [pwa]ngkulun [7])».

Tinamitami ta [8]) sirāmpu Mahāpalyat dening çiṣyanira [9]) kabeh. Ri sāmpuning mangkana sinangaskāra ta sirāmpu Kalotan lawan mpu Waju-kuning; mpu Janaḍipa puspatanirāmpu [10]) Kalotan, mpu Narajñāna puspatanirāmpu Waju-kuning, apan mahning buddi kṛta sira [11]). Sāmpuning mangkana mangĕmbang [12]) tāmpu Janaḍipa lāwan mpu Narajñāna amwita mantuka [13]) maring nūṣa Jawa. Sāmpun ta sira mintar [saking nūṣa Kambangan, prāpta sira ring nūṣā Jawa muwah] [14]), dumunung ta sira ri haji ring Galuh. Mamarah sasokramanira ring [15]) çrī mahārāja; samangkanā [16]) mpu Janāḍipa pinakaguru [17]) de haji Batathi, sirāmpu Narajñāna pinakapurohita sira.

Kahucapa ta [18]) bhaṭārī Çrī mangraṇḍaraṇḍa ta sira [19]), tinhör sang raṇḍa Rāga-runting aranira. Hangantih ning tañjung humahnira [20]), matangnyan hana deça ring Mḍang-tañjung [21]) ngaranya mangke. Hana ta sang walija Parijñana [22]) ngaranira, sira ta wwang dibyalba [23]); [tan aharĕp ta sira sang raṇḍa Rāga-runting wanoha lawan wong dibyaloba] [24]). Dinūk ta ring sapu manglaru wetan [25]) tkeng gunung Bañcak [26]); [yata hana gunung Karurungan ngaranya mangke] [27]). Makĕṇḍangkaṇḍang [28]) ta sira lawan sang walija Parijana [29]); matangnyan hana gunung Kĕṇḍĕng aranya mangke.

---

[1]) D. E: paḍa bhūṣaṇa. [2]) D. E: paḍa mĕṇḍĕk manĕmbah ring sira. [3]) D. E: ontbreekt. [4]) B: wong hapweki. D. E: wwang apweki. [5]) D. E: hayu hapkik lwir ing tulis rupanya?" [6]) B. C: „A dadening wwang (C: Ah, dadening) pinangan mami. D. E: „Hajining wang tapangan. [7]) B: kapwakulun. [8]) D. E: Tanami ta. [9]) D. E: sikṣinira. [10]) D. E: ngaranya sangĕmpu. [11]) D. E: apan anâhning bhūmi kṛttha sira. [12]) D. E: Sāmpunira mangkana mangumbang. [13]) B: amit mantuka. D. E: amita mantuk. [14]) D. E: ontbreekt. [15]) D. E: Mawarah sakeng kramanya mareng. [16]) D. E: sāmpun mangkana. [17]) D. E: minakaguru. [18]) D. E: Kucapa. [19]) D. E: marangḍaradatang sira. [20]) B: Angantih ĕbning tañjung humahnira. D. E: hangantih ĕlĕtañjulumanira. [21]) D. E: Mḍang-tajung. [22]) B: walita Paringjñāna. D. E: sang walija Parañjaṇā. [23]) E: dibyaloba. D: dibyaloka. [24]) D. E: ontbreekt. B: dibyamoha. [25]) D. E: malurung mangetan. B: dinuk ta. sapu malaru wetan. [26]) D. E: tkeng gunung Karungrangan aranya. [27]) D. E: ontbreekt. [28]) D. E: Makḍukḍu. B: Makĕṇḍungkĕṇḍung. [29]) B: sang walita Paringjñāṇa. D. E: sang walijā Parañjaṇa.

109

Kahucapa [1]) tāmpu Mahāpalyat, mantuk ta sira maring [2]) nūṣa Jawa. Pinalihnirā ta çariranira matmahan ta çaiwa sogata, mangaran sirāmpu Barang, sirāmpu Waluh(-bang. Sirāmpu) Bārang çewapakṣa, (sirāmpu Waluh-bang [sogatapakṣa). Jag lĕs, prāpti sireng nūṣa Jawa] [3]); dumunung ta sira ring Girah [4]), manganakĕn ta sira patapan ring Hanggirah [5]), [sirāmpu (Barang lan sirāmpu) Waluh-bang] [6]).

Kahucapa ta [7]) sira hyang buyut ring Kukub, sang ṛṣi Taruṇatapa-yowana [8]), [bhaṭāra Mahāguru ngaranira] [9]). Akweh ta hanak-çiṣyanira, yata tiningkah ta çiṣyanira [10]) masĕrĕhan, lwirnyā: pangadyan, ulu-kĕmbang-pakalpan, pwamah, pajanan, atanĕk, abrih, akarapa, juru-hamañjang-hamañjing [11]), kabhayan-panglayar, [kabhayan-maṇḍala, mahawanĕtha [12]), bahudĕṇḍa, but-wiçeṣa [13]), asaṇḍing-among, kabhayan-pamkas. Mangkana lwirning masĕrĕhan.

Kunang bhaṭāra Mahāguru mangnakna kāryya bhojana; gungni wulan [14]) Haçujimaça dadyaning kāryyā. Yata kinwan manangsinangsiha ki kabhayan-panglayar] [15]); manangsinangsi mangetan larinira [16]). Çighra prāpta wulan Haçujimaça [17]), ḍatang kabeh çiṣya bhaṭāra, ngūniweh bhaṭāra trisamaya sami ḍatang [18]); sumambah [19]) ri bhaṭāra Guru sakwehning çiṣyanira kabeh; anghing kaki kabhayan-panglayar durung tkā [20]). Tlas kāryya bhaṭāra [21]), mantuk tikang para çiṣya kabeh, nguniweh tikang maṇḍala trisamaya [22]) sami mantuk maring maṇḍalanira [23]) sowang-sowang.

Kañcit ḍatang ki kabhayan-panglayar. Kahucapa [24]) ta larinira saka wetan, kablat [25]) hewĕh [26]) ariwĕd. Akweh ta hantukantukira [27]): guci, kṛci, matha lĕmbu [28]) nguniweh [tang gĕrang] [29]) kbo, sapi [30]), [asu] [29]) celeng, [bebek] [29]), hayam, pisaningū [31]) wwang

---

[1]) D. E: Kucapa. [2]) D. E: mantuka sireng. [3]) D. E: ontbreekt. [4]) D. E: sireng wukir Hyang. [5]) D. E: maugnakĕn sirā tapā ning Anggarah. [6]) D. E: ontbreekt. [7]) D. E: Kucapa ta. [8]) D. E: sang ṛṣi Taruṇā-tapā. [9]) D. E: ontbreekt. [10]) B: yata matangnyan tiningkah tang çiṣyanira. D. E: ya tiningka sirā [11]) B: juru-hamaji. D. E: pangajyan, ulu-kambang-pakalpa mwah pajagan. patanĕk, akarapa, habri, juru hamañjang. [12]) B: mahawanātha. [13]) B: twiçeṣa. [14]) B: gungbiwulan. [15]) D. E: ontbreekt. [16]) D. E: Lĕs lunga kaki kabayan-panglayar mangetan lakunirā. [17]) D. E: prapti tang karyya, ulan Asuji masanya. [18]) D. E: uniweh hikang mandalā trīsamaya, katwegan, [19]) D. E: prasama sirā mawa sĕmbah. [20]) D. E: juga tananā. [21]) D. E: Sāmpun siddha karyyaning bhaṭāra. [22]) D. E: maṇḍalā samadaya. [23]) D. E: marengnga simanira. [24]) D. E: Kucapa. [25]) B. D. E: kablĕt. [26]) B: hewĕr. [27]) D. E: hulihulinira. [28]) D. E: kuca, kṛci, pata lbu (D: matal bu). [29]) D. E: ontbreekt. [30]) B. D: sampi. [31]) D. E: sisaninghutang.

lanang wadwan ārĕp awikuha [1]) aminta sinambahakning bhaṭāra Mahāguru. Kablĕt lampahira ki kabhayan-panglayar; kunang tampaknira saka wetan [2]): ring Ragḍang unggonirātinggal gĕrang asu [3]), ri Tambangan hunggonirātinggal gĕrang kbo [4]), ring Pacelengan hunggonirāmakan celeng [5]), ring Untehan unggonirā nguntehunte, ring Kuḍampilan [6]) hunggonirā ṇḍampil sapi [7]), ring Cangcangan [8]) unggonirā nangcang pagor [9]), ring Bakar [10]) hunggonirā hababakar, ring Duk hunggonirā hamet hḍuk, ring Payaman hunggonirātinggal ayam [11]).

Kunang duk sira tkeng Kukub, amintāsih ring ki kabhayan-wiçeṣa umaturakna [12]) ring bhaṭāra Mahāguru. Wruh [13]) sira yan kacalana de hyang Mahāguru. Çighra mātur kabhayan-wiçeṣa [14]) ri bhaṭāra Mahāguru, mawarah [dugaduga] [15]) yan tka [16]) kabhayan-panglayar. Mwajar ta hyang Mahāguru lingnira:

«Aywa wineh marĕka si panglayar; doṣane tka sep ing kāryya [17]). Kon mangsula!»

Mangkana ling hyang Mahāguru [18]). Mangsul mantuk ta sang wiçeṣa [19]), mawarah [20]) ring kabhayan-panglayar, yan sira tan kasatmatha [21]) de hyang Mahāguru; doṣanira ḍatang [22]) sep ing kāryya. Wkasan ki kabhayan-panglayar makwan ing but-wiçeṣa [23]) amalenana hantukantuknira karing curahcurah kidul, kātureng [24]) bhaṭāra Mahāguru. Kunang kabhayan-panglayar mangetan larinira, makatali talingisnira [25]), makaswāng sāmpĕtnira [26]); jag lĕs lumampah bhagawan panglayar.

[Ucapĕn ta kang masĕrĕhan, ḍatang ring cucurah kidul, amaleni hantukantuknira ki panglayar, ikang guci, kṛci, tamapi gĕrang kbo, sami [27]), hasu, celeng. Ḍatang ring Kukub sang masĕrĕhan; ikang gĕrang karing Payaman, tan liwat ring loh Sarayu; ring kana makahangan] [28]).

Hucapĕn ta [29]) kabhayan-panglayar, matharuka ta sira maṇḍala

---

[1]) D. E: ingevoegd: yata milu. [2]) D. E: tampakira wetan. [3]) D. E: tinggal gĕdang. Ingevoegd: i Rayyūdan unggwanira megarayyū. [4]) D. E: nangcang kbo. [5]) D. E: nangcang bawi. [6]) D. E: i Kudampil. [7]) D. E: kbo sapi. [8]) D. E: i Tarawang. [9]) B. D. E: bagor. [10]) D. E: i Byakar. [11]) D. E: tinggal satha. [12]) D. E: Kukub wiçeṣa, haminta sirā hingaturakĕn. [13]) D. E: Prah. [14]) D. E: buktiçeṣa. [15]) D. E: ontbreekt. [16]) D. E: yan ḍatang ki. [17]) D. E: dumeh tka wus ing kāryya. [18]) D. E: sang hyang Ḍarmmarajā. [19]) D. E: Mangsula but-wiçeṣa. B: Lĕs mantuk ta buyut-wiçeṣa. [20]) D. E: mawarahha ring. [21]) D. E: polahnya tan kasapa. [22]) D. E: karehanya rawuh. [23]) D. E: kinon ta mbuktiseṣa. [24]) D. E: haturakneng. [25]) B. C: makataling (C: makatali) tangisnira. D. E: makahalihali tangisnirā. [26]) B: makagwa sampĕtnira. D. E: mkase sambatirā. [27]) B: guci, kṛci, matambrā wsi, gĕrang kbo, sampi. [28]) B: makahingan. D. E: ontbreekt. [29]) D. E: Kucapa kaki.

ri patĕnggĕk [1]) sang hyang Mahāmeru lawan sang hyang Brahmā, umgil ta sira ngaṇḍawar-haṇḍawar [2]); tinhĕr ta ngaraning maṇḍala ring Aṇḍawar. Ana ta panugraha bhaṭāra Mahāguru, sang hyang kuñci Sandijñāna [3]) ngaranya; yata pinanahaknireng [4]) jagat, matangnyan kerut kang rāt kabeh sumambaheng sira. Lanang wadon kang wong paḍārĕp wikuhā, ndatan ingaskāran denira, apan durung kṛtānugrahā saking bhaṭāra Mahāguru [5]). Matangnyan sira wineh masingĕla babakan ing kayu [6]), tinhĕr ta ngaran ki bakal [7]).

«Tĕmbe kita ḍak sangaskārani [8]), lamun huwus kṛtānugrahanira [9]) Nāmaçiwaya.»

[Mangkana lingnira] [10]); wruh ta sira yan hanandang wiḍi saking [11]) buyut ring Kukub. Sah sakeng Aṇḍawar sira, ḍatang sira mareng wukir Hyang, aminta sira bhumi ri mpu rāmarāma ring Bĕsar [12]). Pinintanira taluntalun katinggal, tan tinĕngĕt [dening rāma ring Bĕsar] [13]), winehnira hikang [14]) talun [tan ingĕtĕnira [15]); yata hinaranan maṇḍala ring Talun] [16]).

Ana ta rākṣasa ring kana, tanpaweh gawenĕn maṇḍala [17]). Linawananira ring yogha samaḍi, kalah [18]) tang rākṣasa [mawijaya] [19]), wkasan kesisan ta [20]) denira; pinanahaknira tang kuñci Sandijñana [21]), kerut [t]ang rāt kabeh denira.

Tindaknira [22]) sakeng Talun, mataruka maṇḍala ring Waçaṇa [23]). Ana ta rākṣasa ring kana, tanpaweh gawenĕn maṇḍala humahnya [24]); linawanira ring yoga, alah tang kāla denirā. [25]) Ana ta watu Hubhusan [26]) ngaranya, yata pinakaguruyaganya, ana [27]) mangke. Muwah ta pinanahaknira tang kuñci Saṇḍijjāna [28]), kerut [t]a kang rāt kabeh denira; akweh wwang lanang wadwān arĕp wikuha, ndatan sinangaskāranira.

[1]) B: tgĕkira. D. E: patgĕsan. [2]) B. D. E: umgil ta sireng ngandawar. [3]) B: sang hyang kañcing Saṇḍijñāṇa. D: Sandiyajña. [4]) D. E: yata minenak sireng. [5]) D. E: hapan sira durung hinugrahā de sang guru. [6]) D. E: Winehira maçingĕleng babaneng kanegara. [7]) D. E: tĕhĕr hingaran ki kbakal. [8]) D. E „Tĕmbe kwanuḍakṣiṇā mangaskarani. [9]) D. E: lawun uwus kami hinugrahan de bhaṭāra (D: bhaṭāra Nāwaya). [10]) D. E: ontbreekt. [11]) B: hanaṇḍang widḍi gsang ki hyang. D. E: manaṇḍing widḍi sangkeng hyang. [12]) B: maring mpu. D. E: himpu ra ring Bĕsar dami. [13]) D. E: ontbreekt. [14]) D. E: wineh ing kwi. [15]) B: tĕhĕr tinarukanira. [16]) D. E: ontbreekt. [17]) D. E: Talun hana rakṣasanya tan aweh tarukanĕn patapan, yata hingkana hunggonira. [18]) D. E: malah. [19]) B: mawijahya. D. E: ontbreekt. [20]) D. E.: wkasan malih kaṣiṣya. [21]) D. E: yapwan pinanah ri sang kuñci jñāna. [22]) D. E: Tumindak. [23]) B: ring Pathanā. [24]) B: maṇḍala humānya. D. E: patapan. [25]) D. E: ingevoegd: wkasan tang rakṣasa kaṣiṣyan denira. [26]) B: Hubuṣā. D: Ucusan. E: Hususan. [27]) B. D. E: ingevoegd: tkaning. [28]) D. E: sang hyang Sandijñana.

112

Kocapa [1]) sirāmpu Barang lawan sirāmpu Waluh-bāng, amet [t]a sira pakṣa [2]). Sirāmpu Waluh-bāng mangulwan, mataruka ring Warag [3]), sirāmpu Barang [mangetan] [4]), manganakĕn ta sira [5]) çetragamana. Ana ta sma ring gunung Hyang, ring ārggha Kalyasĕm [6]) ngaranya, sma bandung pasamohan ing wong [7]) hatitiwa; wong wetan ing gunung Hyang, lor [8]) ing gunung Hyang, paḍa titiwa ring Kalyāsĕm. Ring kana pasamuhan ing [9]) kunapākweh, yata pinakapatapanirā mpu [10]) Bharang; bhairawapakṣa sira, çawaning wwang tinaḍahnira.

Ana ta sira ratu siniwining Ḍaha, anak atuhā de haji Bhathati [11]), çrī mahārāja Taki [12]) ngaranira [13]). Sira ta siniwi ring Ḍaha [14]), mangrĕngĕ ta yan hana bhūjangga mambherawa matapa rikang sma ring ārggha Kalyāsĕm, kunapaning wwang pinanganya [15]). Agila [ta manah] [16]) çrī mahārāja mangrĕngö, yata motus ri [17]) sang çogata kalih sanak, mangaran sirā mpu Tapa-wangkĕng [18]) mwang mpu Tapa-palet. Kalih paḍa kinon de sang prabhū hamjahana [19]) sirāmpu Bharang.

Tan wihang sira sang inutus; lumāmpah hāmbaramārgga [20]), paḍa çaktinya, apan utpti bhaṭāra [21]) Brahmā Wiṣṇu; hyang Brahmā dadi Tapa-wangkĕng [22]), hyang Wiṣṇu dadi Tapa-palet [23]). Jag lĕs lungha lumampah sang çogata kalih [24]) {umjahane sang bhūjangga camah; [yeki bhawanira] [25]). Çīghra ḍatang ring gunung Hyang, dumunung ring [26]) sma Kalyasĕm; kapanggih ta sirāmpu Bharang malungguh [27]) mangarĕpakĕn kaṇṭora [28]) lawan mahāmangsa [29]), kaphalaning wwang tahapanya [30]), [çawaning wwang makataḍahanya. Ḍatang tāmpu Tapa-wangkĕng} [31]) lawan mpu Tapa-palet] [32]), mawarah ta sira [33]) yan ingutus de sang prabhū; manglampu juga [34]) sirāmpu Bharang. Sinikĕp kinĕmbulan, nhĕr

---

[1]) D. E: Kucapa ta. [2]) B: amalih sira pakṣa. [3]) B: Warug. [4]) D. E: ontbreekt. [5]) B: mangĕnakĕn ta sira. D E: hamangūn tapa ring. [6]) D. E.: aghra Kalesĕm. [7]) D. E: sma hagĕng pasamayan, hapan pasamuhan ing. [8]) D. E: kulwan. [9]) D. E: Inakā samuhan ing. [10]) D. E: nggonira tapa sirampu. [11]) D. E: maharaja Tati. [12]) D. E: maharaja Bhataki. [13]) Begin invoegsel E^3. [14]) D. E: Sira ta ratu ring Ḍaha samanā. [15]) D. E· kunapa pinanganira. Eind invoegsel E^3. Begin invoegsel E^3. [16]) D. E: ontbreekt. [17]) D. E: makoni. [18]) D. E: tampa Wangkĕng. [19]) B. D. E. E^3: umjahana. [20]) D. E: mangkātar hambramaga sirā kalih. [21]) B. E^3: hupti sang hyang. D. E: apan sirā sang hyang. [22]) D. E: tampa Wangkĕng. [23]) D. E: ingevoegd: matangnyan pada çakṭinirā. [24]) E^3: sang çewa sogata kalih. B: ingevoegd: tapa Wangkĕng. D. E.: sirā sang kalih sanak. [25]) D. E ontbreekt. [26]) D. E: jumujug sirā [27]) D. E: malinggih. [28]) D. E: kajoran. [29]) D. E: lawan mahamangsa ontbreekt. [30]) D. E: tapanya. [31]) E^3: ontbreekt. [32]) D. E: ontbreekt. [33]) D. E: Mawarah ta sang Tapa-wangkĕng. [34]) D. E.: matangnyan hala.

sira binbĕd ri walatung [1]), linabuh sireng sāgara [mangke] [2]) sirāmpu Bharang. Mulih [3]) sang manglabuh, mawarah ri çrī mahārāja ring Ḍahā yan sāmpun linabuh [4]) sirāmpu Bharang.

Ring eñjing [sang prabhū motus ri sang bhujangga kalih sānak tumilikana bhujangga camah. Tan wihang sang inutus, çighra prapta ring Kalyāsĕm] [5]), kapanggih sirāmpu Bharang. Sinikĕp ta sira muwah [6]), binbĕd ri walatung, inukalukalan wsi kaṭe [7]), linabuh ring [8]) sāgara. Lĕs mantuk sang inutus [9]).

Ring eñjing mara yata malih sang inutus; kapanggih muwah sirāmpu Bharang. Binaṣmi ta sira wkasan [10]); sāmpun dadi haṣṭi [11]) sirāmpu Barang, mantuk sang çwagata kalih [12]), mawarah ri sang prabhū yan sāmpun dadi haṣṭi [13]) sirāmpu Bharang.

Eñjing motus [s]ang prahbū tumilikana [14]) bhujangga camah; [tan wihang sang inutus. Lumāmpah enggal hapan sira hambaramargga] [15]); prāpting Kalyasĕm, kapanggih muwah sirāmpu Bharang. Binaṣmi muwah sirāmpu Bharang, haṣṭinira [16]) linabuh ring sāgara [17]); mantuk sang swagata [18]) kalih sanak, mawarah ring çrī mahārāja yan sāmpun pinañcadeça hawunirā mpu Barang.

Ring eñjing muwah motus sang prabhū tumilikana [19]) sang bhujangga camah. Tan wihang sira kalih, wawang prāpta ring ārggha ring Kalyāsĕm [20]), kapanggih muwah sirāmpu Barang. Samangkana [21]) sirāmpu Tapa-wangkĕng lawan sirampu Tapa-palet sumambah ri sirāmpu Bharang; wruh ta sira yan bhaṭāra Parameçwara. Samangkana sirāmpu Bharang mahyun saha saking gunung Hyang ḍatngeng bhumi Jambuḍipa paryyanira. Agawe ta sira puṣṭaka Haḍidarwwa ngaranya, lawan kalambi; yata tininggalakning sanggar puṣṭaka lawan kulambi. Jag lĕs, lumampah sira ḍatngeng Jambuḍipa, milu ta sirāmpu Tapa-wangkĕng muwah sirāmpu Tapa-palet; lumampah ta sira paḍa hambaramārgga.

Kunang ucapĕn ta kabhayan-panglayar, tindaknira sakeng maṇḍaleng Waçaṇa, ḍatang sira maring harggha Kalyāsĕm, same-

---

1) E^3: winalatung. 2) B. D. E. E^3: ontbreekt. 3) D. E: Malih. 4) D. E: pinjahan 5) Begin invoegsels E^2, D. E: ontbreekt; mara sang inutus madutani sang bhūjanggā camah. 6) D. E: Malih sinikĕp sirā kinambulan. 7) D. E: hinuntaluntalan wĕsi kati. 8) D. E: maring. 9) D. E: sang malabuh. 10) D. E: sinikĕp sirā binaçmi. 11) D. E: dadyawu. 12) D. E: sang kalih sanak. 13) D. E: hawu. 14) D. E: Ringeñjing mara sang inutus de sang prabhū maniliki sang. 15) D. E: ontbreekt. 16) B. E^2, E^3: ingevoegd: pinañcadeça. D. E: Sinikĕp binaçmi pinañcadeça hawunya. 17) D. E: linabuh pinañcadeça hana mungguh ring mâdya. 18) D. E: sewa çogata. 19) D. E: Muwah ring eñjing tumiliki. Hierna gaping. 20) B. E^2. E^3: ring argghā Kalyasĕm. 21) B. E^2. E^3: Mangkana.

114

ring lawan ikang rākṣasa, mapengaran [1]) ki Maraṇak [2]) lawan ki Lĕmah-bāng [3]). Ḍatngeng sirāmpu Bharang prayanira, mogha ta wus lunghā; wkasan ta sira hamanggih puṣtaka lawan kalambi ring sanggar. Inungkabanira tang puṣtaka, meṣi Hadidrawa [4]), palupuynirā mpu Bharang; kahiḍĕpnira panugrahanira bhaṭāra Guru hika. Wkasan tang sma tinaruka maṇḍala, nhör hanurud kalambi ring sanggar, yata ring Sanggara [5]) ngaraning maṇḍalanira.

Muwah tang rākṣasa kalih çiki aminta panugraha sira; wnang ta sirā ngaskārani [6]) hakalambi ring sanggar, yata sinangguh wiku sanggara [7]) ngaranya. Muwah pinanahaknira tang Sandijñāna [8]), kerut [t]ang rāt kabeh; ḍatang wwang lawan wadwan sumambah ri sira, mangaturakĕn sadṛwenya [9]). Embuh çiṣya sira makweh, aprameya ler sāgara [10]) kwehning çiṣya lawan drawya; matangnyan hinaranan maṇḍala ring Sāgara [11]) wkasan. Mari ta haran ki kabhayan-panglayar, bhaṭāra Guru panĕnggah ing sarāt wkasan ring sira [12]). Sira sang āpūrwwa [13])-taruka ring Sāgara-maṇḍala, mangasihasih ta sireng anak-ṣiṣyanira:

«Tanpabhaṣaha tanaya, putu bhuyut bhaṣahanteryyaku.»

Mangkana pangasihasihnira ring anak-ṣiṣyanira; matangnyan pangasih-bhaṣanira [14]): bhuyut ring Sāgara. Muwah sang dewaguru ring Sāgara tanpakalami hamanya [15]), makahingan adodot sinalusur [16]), apan durung kṛtānugraha saking hyang [Guru] [17]) bhuyut ring Kukub.

«Tambe pwa, yan uwus [18]) kṛtānugraha de hyang buyut ring Kukub, wnang akalambiha de Sāgara [19]). Aywa tan mengĕt yan Kukub kamulanya nguni, ndah kayātnakĕn ta wkasku. Kunang kanyu [20]) yan tan mengĕt ri pawkasku, astu [21]) ko tampuhan ing upadarwwa [22]).»

Mangkana lingira ki kabhayan-panglayar, sira ta pūrwwa-

---

1) E^{3}: mapangaran. 2) B. E^{2}. E^{3}: ki Maraṇan. 3) B: Lmabāng. 4) B. C. E^{3}: Hadidarwwā. E^{2}: Hadḍiparwa. 5) B. E^{2}. E^{3}: ring Sanggar. 6) B. E^{2}. E^{3}: ingevoegd: apan uwus nugraha. 7) B. E^{2}. E^{3}: wiku sanggar. 8) E^{3}: Saṇḍijjāṇna. 9) B. E^{2}. E^{3}: ingevoegd: uniweh tang wwang lumaku wiku. 10) B. E^{2}. E^{3}: ler sanggāra. C: lor sāgara. 11) B. E^{2}. E^{3}: ring Sagāra. 12) B. wkasnya ring ṣāṇa sirā. E^{2}: wĕkasasnya ring. E^{3}: wkasana ring sira. 13) B. E^{2}. E^{3}: amūrwwa. 14) B. E^{2}. E^{3}: bapanira. 15) B. E^{2}. E^{3}: tanpa kalambi hadomḍoman. 16) B. E^{2}. E^{3}: kalingane (E^{2}. E^{3}: kalingana) dodot sinulusur. 17) B. E^{2}. E^{3}: ontbreekt. 18) B. E^{2}. E^{3}: yan uwusā. 19) B. E^{2}. E^{3}: wnang bakalambi domdoman, wnang habhāṣā tanaya matangnyan kanyun mitra Sagāra. 20) B. E^{2}. E^{3}: kanyun. 21) E^{2}: pāstu. E^{3}: wastu. 22) B. E^{2}. E^{3}: hupadrawa.

taruka ring Sāgara, sira magawe maṇḍala trisamaya ring gunung Hyang.

Kahucapa ta bhaṭārāmpu Bharang, ḍatang sireng bhūmi Jambuḍipa; kapanggih ta sang brahmāṇa sḍang mamūjā sira ri sang hyang Haricaṇḍana, awyatara sewu kwehnya sira para brahmāṇa. Ḍatang ta sirāmpu Bharang mangadĕgadĕg [1]); mojar ta sang brahmāṇa:

«Jhah, paran kita [2]) mangadĕgadĕg, tanpanambah ri bhaṭāra Haricaṇḍana? Kami brahmāṇa pawitrajanma, mayan panambah ri bhaṭāra [3]), apan siran hagawe jagatraya.»

Sumahur sirāmpu Bharang:

«Almĕh kami manambahā [4]), apan nghulun brahmāṇa jawa.»

«Brahmāṇa kapwa kita [5]); lah, panambah [6]), brahmāṇa jawa!»

«Almĕh kami manambaha.»

Sinikĕp [ta rumuhun, hinagĕmakĕn lungayanira] [7]), sinĕmbahakĕn ring [8]) bhaṭāra Haricaṇḍana [9]). Wahu ta sira kasidĕkung [10]), linḍu bhaṭārī Pṛthiwī, bĕntar harccānira [11]) bhaṭāra Haricaṇḍani [12]), tamapi tkaning mangke [13]). Samangkana ta [14]) sang brahmāṇa paḍa kapuhan tumon ing kasidḍanirā mpu Bharang; samangkana ta sang brahmāṇa paḍa mamūjā [15]) ri sira bhaṭārāmpu Bharang, sakwehning sang brahmāṇa. Wkasan ta sang brahmāṇa haweh [16]) hmās mirah komala hintĕn; tan aharĕp ta sirāmpu Bharang. Hamalaku ta sirāhurupa bhaṣma, bhaṣmānirāmpu Barang [ganḍa, bhaṣmanira sang brahmāṇa] [17]) rātnadwada [18]). [Mahurup ta sira bhaṣma; rātnadwada [19]) bhaṣmanirāmpu Bharang wkasan, bhaṣmānirā [20]) mpu Bharang ganḍa] [21]), yata pinakabhaṣmanira sang brahmāṇa [22]).

Ri sāmpunirāhurup bhaṣma [23]), ḍatang sang prabhū ring Jambuḍipa, çrī mahārāja Cakrawartti [24]) ngaranira. [Umĕnḍĕk

1) Eind gaping D. E: Tka ngadeg sirāmpu Barang. 2) E^3: paran ta sira. 3) B. E^2. E^3: ing sira. D. E: Kami pawitraning janma, padene hanambah ring bhaṭāra Caṇḍani. 4) D. E: hanĕmbah. 5) D. E: Kalinganya brahmāṇa jawa kita. 6) B. E^2. E^3: lah, manĕmbah. 7) B. D. E. E^2. E^3: ontbreekt; kinudupung. 8) B. E^2. E^3: sinambutākning. 9) D. E: sang hyang ngarccā caṇḍani. 10) D. E: Mawu masidĕkung. 11) B. E^3: hañcarnira. E^3: bĕntar linĕga harñcanira. 12) B. E^2. E^3: Haricandanā. 13) D. E: ingevoegd: rĕngat harccānira. 14) D. E: Samanā. 15) B. E^2: mapūjā. D. E: muji hastuti. 16) D. E: paḍa sira hatūr. 17) B. E^2. E^3: bhinaṣmānira sang brahmāṇa. D. E: ontbreekt. 18) B. E^2. E^3: ratnaḍwajā. D. E: tratnanoja. 19) B. E^2. E^3: ratnaḍwajā. 20) B. E^2. E^3: ingevoegd: sang brahmāṇa. 21) D. E: ontbreekt. 22) D. E: mpu brāhmaṇa. 23) B. E^2. E^3: ahurupā bhaṣmā. 24) B. E^2. E^3: Cakrawatu.

manambah ri sirāmpu Bharang] [1]), mangaturakĕn dodot malit, mās mirah hintĕn rājayogya [2]). Ndatan tinanggap denirāmpu Bharang [3]), pinintanira kang kinabhakten [4]) de sang prabhu. Tan tinngĕt, winehaknira tang pratima mās bhaṭāra Wiṣṇu hinimba [5]), sira kinabhakten ing Jambuḍipa [6]). Yata winehakning [7]) sirāmpu Bharang, ndatan inalap sireka, tuhun tiniru [8]) rūpanya; yata pinakahantukantuknira maring Jawa.

Lumampah sirāmpu Bharang samering lawan sirāmpu [9]) Tapa-wangkĕng mwang Tapa-palet, paḍāhāmbaramārgga sira [10]). Prāpta ring Yawaḍipa [11]), dumunung ta sireng gunung Brahmā, ri tantunira hyang Brahmā paṇḍe wsi ngūni [12]). Irika ta sirāmpu Bharang mangaji Tigarahaṣya [13]), sirāmpu Tapa-wangkĕng [14]) mangaji Tigalana [15]), sirāmpu Tapa-palet mangaji Tigatpĕt. Kunang sirāmpu Bharang magawe ta sirā kañcana, dinadekĕn pratimma hmās winimba rūpa [16]) bhaṭāra Wiṣṇu; inukirnira dempu Tapa-palet Tapa-wangkĕng. Tahatahaning [17]) mangukir sumamburat lwir huddaka [18]), matmahan kṛṣṇā, katamapi katkaning mangke.

Sāmpun paripūrnna [19]) sang hyang pratima hmās, pinucakanira ta ring [20]) gunung Suṇḍawiṇi. [21]) Mangrĕngö ta sang prabhū ring Dahā, çri mahārāja Taki, yan ana sang hyang pratima hmās ring gunung Suṇḍawiṇi; yata hutusan sang prabhū mangundanga sirāmpu Bharang nguniweh sirāmpu Tapa-wangkĕng Tapa-palet. Tan wihang sang inutus, lumampah sīghra prāpta sumambah ri sirāmpu Bharang; [22]) [mojar taya:] [23])

«Ranak sang pāṇḍita hinutus de sang aji ring Ḍaha, hangun-

1) B. E^2. E^3: ontbreekt; ingevoegd: bhaṭāra Wiṣṇu ring [ma]nuṣā. 2) D. E: mangaturakna mās mirah komala hintĕn. B. E^2. E^3: mās mirah komalā hintĕn dodot halit rājayogya. 3) D. E: Tan tinanggāpan hikang rajāyogya. 4) D. E: pinintanira kinabaktyan. 5) D. E: Tan tinngĕt [t]ang winehakĕn, hana ta sang hyang pratima mās ngaranya, rinekā bhaṭāra Wiṣṇu. 6) D. E: de sang prabhū ring Jambudipa. 7) D. E: pinetakĕn ring. 8) D. E: ndah tan pinet ikā, yata tinirun tā. 9) D. E: padḍomiring sira. 10) D. E: paḍa braga sirā katrini. 11) D. E: Çighrā prapteng nūṣā Jawa. 12) D. E: duk hapande wsi. 13) D. E: Tiggaraṣya. 14) D. E: tampa Wangkĕng. 15) B: Tigarahana. E^2: Tigāyana. E^3: Tigarahana. 16) D. E: rupanya hinimba. 17) B: tahitahining. D. E: sirāmpu Tapa-wangkĕng tananing. E^2: tahitāhina. E^3: tahitahida. 18) D. E: sumamburat lwir uḍan ika. E^2. E^3: sumburat lwir huṇḍaka. 19) B. E^2. E^3: Sāmpun sapūrṇna. D. E: Sirampunya pinujā. 20) D. E: pinucakakning. 21) D. E: Çudḍawangi. B E^2. E^3: Sudḍawiṇī. 22) D. E: prapting kahananirāmpu Barang, sumĕmbah taya. 23) D. E: ontbreekt; ingevoegd: mwajar sirāmpu Barang: „Lah, paran gawenta?" „Pukulun, matur ranak sang pandita.

danga ri sang [1]) yatiwara ḍatngeng nāgara ta, pwangkulun» [2]).

[«Um» lingnirāmpu Bharang] [3]) «tan wihang kami [4])».

Lumampah [5]) sirāmpu Bharang samering lawan sirāmpu Tapa-wangkĕng Tapa-phalet, [çīghra prāpting Ḍaha sira katriṇi] [6]), dumunung ring aji Taki. [7]) Pinintanira tang pratima hmās de sang prabhū; tan tinngĕt [t]aya, winehaknira denirāmpu Bharang. Yata matangnyan sang hyang pratima hmās kinabhaktenira [8]) de sang prabhū ring Ḍahā, katamapi katkaning mangke [9]).

Kahucapa ta [10]) bhaṭārī Smarī marupa ta sira manūṣa, taruṇi tan pramaṇa [11]) ring ayu; sira Hibhu-tngahan [12]) aranira. Tumūt [t]aya sireng bapanira ring sira [13]) bhaṭārāmpu Bharang, matapa hlĕtañ jurang lawan sira bapanira; [14]) tapitapi bhawanira. [15]) Matangnyan gĕgĕr ing Tapi ngaranya mangke.

Kahucapa ta bhaṭāra [16]) Waluh-bāng, mapakṣa ṛṣi mabadḍa sira, tuminggalakĕn bhodḍapakṣa [17]). Sah ta sira saking [18]) Warag, ḍatang ta sire [19]) Tigāryyan. [20]) Mangadĕgadĕg ta sira tanpanambah ri bhaṭāra Içwara; mojar ta bhaṭara Içwara ring çiṣyanira: [21])

«Apa ganya [22]) sang wiku Waluh-bāng mangadĕgadĕg tanpanambah iryyaku?»

Sumahur çiṣyanira:

«Hakas turipun, pwangkulun» [23])

Tinhĕr ta wiku kasture [24]) ngaranya. Samangkana [25]) ta bhaṭāra Içwara supranāthaknira [26]) tā payung kuṇḍala mwang kalambi ri bhaṭāra Waluh-bāng; sira gumanti dewaguru ring Tigaryyan, [27]) tinhĕr makapakṣa kasturi. [28]) Bhaṭāra Içwara mantuk maring [29]) swargganira. [30])

---

[1]) B. E^2. E^3: angundang i rasang. [2]) D. E: ḍatnga ring rajā rĕke. B. E^2. E^3: nāgara rakwa. [3]) D. E: ontbreekt. [4]) D. E: „Tan wihanga kami". [5]) D. E: Mangkat ta. [6]) D. E: ontbreekt. [7]) D. E: jumug sireng marajā Taki. [8]) Einde invoegsels E^2. [9]) D. E: sang prabhū ring Jawa, dyapin tkaning mangke. Ingevoegd: Kunang bhaṭāra mpu Barang, mabada pakṣa ṛṣi ta sira, tuminggālakna sewapakṣa. Sirāmpu Tapa-wangkĕng Tapa-palet kari sireng Daha, sirāmpu Barang mangetan mangnakĕn tapa ring Mahameru. Haṛupa ta sira kakikaki, matangnyan hana gĕgĕr ing Kumaki ngaranya. [10]) D. E: Kucapa ta. [11]) B. E^3: tanpapramaṇa. D. E: tanpamṛmaṇā. [12]) D. E. E^3: Hibu-tngah. [13]) D. E: Tumuta ring ramanira i. [14]) D. E: matapa māhlĕt jūrang kalawan ramanirājalu. [15]) D. E: matapitapi bhawa lawan ramanira. [16]) D. E: Kucapa sirampu. [17]) D. E: tuminggālakna bodḍapaksa. B. E^3: tumingalakĕn (B: tuminggalakĕn) yan bodḍapakṣa. [18]) D. E: Sah pwa sireng. [19]) D. E: ḍatngeng. [20]) B. E^3: Tigayyan. [21]) D. E: sikṣanira. [22]) D. E: Mapa gane. [23]) B. E^3: „Hakas āturipun, pwangkulun". D. E: „Mangastuti ring pukulun". [24]) D. E: wiku hastuti. [25]) D. E: Mangkana. [26]) B. E^3: sumrahaknira. D. E: yata sinrahakĕn ta. [27]) B. E^3: Tigayyan. [28]) D. E: nhĕr kasturi Tigayyan haranya. [29]) D. E: mulih mareng. [30]) Einde van E^1.

118

Kahucapa ta sira bhaṭārāmpu Bharang, ḍatang ta sireng Tigāryyan maring sira bhaṭāra Waluh-bāng. Mojar ta bhaṭāra Waluh-bāng:

«Lah, den paḍānaṇḍang kurug, [1]) mpu Bharang, phalaningwang tunggal kalawan sira».

Rĕp sinrahakĕn tang payung kuṇḍala mwang kalambi:

«Dewaguru kita, bapa, pūrwwa-ḍarmma-kasturi mandalahanta, bapa.»

Mangkana ling bhaṭāra Waluh-bāng; tan wihang sirāmpu Bharang, mataruka ta [2]) sirā maṇḍala, tinhĕr ta ngaran ing maṇḍala pūrwwa-ḍarmma-kasturi Hantabapa. [3]) Ambhairawa ta sira, [4]) sing pangan tan ana liniwatan denira. [5]) Ḍatang ta rāmarāmāngaturakĕn ūryyanira; siniddikāranira tang hūryyan, matmahana skul aputih [6]) hapulĕn. Mantuk tang rāma hatūryyan, [7]) tinhör ta ngaraning deça ring Tūryyan, [8]) yata makamaṇḍala-kasturi pūrwwa-ḍarmma ring Bapa.

Kahucapa ta sirāmpu Tapa-wangkĕng Tapa-palet, sḍangnira hana ring Ḍaha sira kalih, sirāmpu Tapa-wangkĕng samgĕt-bagañjing [9]) haranira. Mahutang ta sirā lakṣa, asamayā nawura huwus [10]) tngah ngwe. Norāna ta panawuranira; pinĕgĕng ta sang hyang Çiwahaditya, langgöng ta sira tngah ngwe tan lumingsir. Sang prabhū sirābratāngajaya, [11]) tanpalabuhan yan durung lumingsir; luhya ta sira [12]) tanpalabuhan, apan durung lumingsir; mangucap ta sira sang prabhū:

«Apa ganyāsuwe tan lumingsir sang hyang Çiwahaditya? Luhya ngwang mangke.»

Mangutus ta sira pangalasan maring samgĕt [13])-bhāgañjing tumakwanakna ri kalinganira sang hyang Çiwahadityāsuwe tan lumingsir. Tan wihang sang hīnutus, mareng samgĕt [14])-bhagañjing:

«Raputu sang paṇḍita, pwangkulun, hinutus de sang prabhū: paran pwa nimitanira [15]) sang hyang Çiwahadityāsuwe tan lumingsir, pwangkulun?»

Sumawur samgĕt [16])-bhagañjing:

«Hawirang kami mawaraha, bapa; tan warahna [17]) manawa

[1]) D: gurug. Hierna gaping. [2]) B. E^3: matarukan ta. [3]) B. E^3: haran ta Bapa. [4]) B. E^3: kita. [5]) B. E^3: sing pinangan tan hana liniwatanira. [6]) B. E^3: sikulā-puputih. [7]) B. E^3: rāma huryyan. [8]) B. E^3: Tūyyana. [9]) B: sangmgĕt-bĕgañjing. [10]) B. E^3: nahura hutang wus. [11]) B. E^3: mabratāngajiya. [12]). B. E^3: sirā suwe. [13]) B. E^3: maraha ring sangmgat. (E^3: mgĕtya). [14]) B: sangmgat. E^3: sangpgat. [15]) B: paran pwaranira. E^3; paran pwanira. [16]) B. E^3: sangmgat. [17]) B. E^3: tan warah.

duhka [1]) sang prabhū. Mahutang lakṣa kami, bapa, samaya wus tngah ngwe, nora panahura mami. Matangnyan kami pgĕng [2]) sang hyang Çiwahaditya».

«Ah, mangkana ka[pwa], pwangkulun. Putunira mātura ring çrī mahārāja».

Jag lĕs, mawarah ring sang prabhū yan mangkana ki samgĕt [3])-bhagañjing. Wineh ta pirak de sang prabhū, yata panawur sira [4]) hutang; rĕp surup [5]) ta sang hyang Çiwahaditya.

Kahucapa ta mpu Tapa-palet manglawani rakryan bhinihaji. [6]) Uwdita [7]) çrī parameçwarī; wruh ta sira sang prabhū yan tan ulihira, [tan satya hisining wtangnira [8]) bhiṇihaji] [9]). Mwajar çrī mahārāja Taki ri pramiçwarī: [10])

«Tan satya kita ri kami, [dudu hulih mami hiṣine wtangta hiku.]» [11])

Sumahur rakryan bhiṇihaji:

«Sājñā haji, nghulun tan satyaheng sang prabhū?» [12])

«Lah, yan kita satya hiri kami, mtuha rare paripūrṇna lituhayu, [13]) han ulih [14]) ning hulun iṣine wtangta hiku. Kunang yan tan ulihning [hulun, kita tan] satya, [15]) astu mtuha salah rūpa».

Mangkana lingira haji Taki; [16]) yata mtu sapi [17]) wadwan bulalak rūpanya. Samangkana ta rakryan parameçwarī tinundung de sang prabhū. Jag lĕs lunghā ta sira, waluya bhaṭārī Çrī muwah. Mojar ta sira nhĕr lunghā: [18])

«Yen ana tambe ratu wadon wiçeṣa hangadĕg ing nūṣa Jawa ring Ḍaha, [19]) hingaranan aji Nini, kami hikā.» Lunghā ta sira, rika tāngadĕg ratu ring Cĕmpa. [20])

Kunang sapi bulalak iningu ta denira samgĕt [21])-bhagañjing. Sang Tapa-palet wruh sira yan ilangakna, yata lunghā sira sakeng Ḍahā. Jag lĕs, mangetan ta larinira [22]). Muwah lumrāh balanira haji Taki amet sirāmpu Tapa-palet [23]); ana mangetan, ana ma-

---

1) B. E^3: duka. 2) B. E^3: kami mgöng. 3) B. E^3: sāngmgat. 4) B. E^3: manahur sira. 5) B. E^3: sumurup. 6) D: einde gaping: rakwan binihaji. 7) B: udita. E^3: udḍita. 8) E^3: hiṣṭini wtĕngnira. 9) D: ontbreekt. 10) B. E^3: „Jhah, rakryan parameçwarī. 11) D: ontbreekt. 12) D: Taha ta nghulun tan satya". 13) B. E^3: listuhayu. 14) B. E^3: yan ulih. 15) D: yenya hulih tan satya. E^3: yan ulih kitan satya. 16) D: ingevoegd: tan satya rakwan binihaji. 17) B. E^3: sampi. 18) D: sambi lunga. 19) B. E^3: wiçeṣā ring nuṣā Jawa hangadĕg ing Dahā. D: wiçeṣā ring Jawa, mangadĕg ratu ring Dahā. 20) D: irika ta sira mangadèg ratu ring Cĕ... 21) B. E^3: sangmgĕt. 22) B. E^3: lakunira. 23) D: manututi sirampu Tapa-palet. Hierna gaping.

ngulwan, ana mangidul, ana mangalor. Kapanggih ta malayu mangungsi ring jro rong; mojar ta sirāmpu Tapa-palet:

[«Aja kami denta pateni; ana ta guṇa mami sumalah iri kita, guṇaning magawe praçada, sang hyang pratima mungguh heng jro, inukir ttaja hingĕṇḍĕkĕṇḍĕk. Muwah guṇaning magawe lumpang pamipisan, guṇaning magawe rong.»

Mwajar ta sira:

«Kunang ikang guhā hunggon mami hiki, mangkana hurip ajalagrahā.»

Jala ngaraning wwe, graha ngaraning rong, tinhĕr ta jalagrahā ngaranya. Wurung taya mamatyani sira, apan winehnira guṇa-n-mangkana; pūrwwaning jalagraga.

Kunang sira Tapa-palet] [1] mabadḍa masāmpĕt mapakṣa ṛṣi ta sira, tuminggalakna boddapakṣa sira. Aminta ta sirānugraha kalambi ri sang hyang maṇḍala pūrwwa-ḍarmma ring Bapa; tinhör ta sira dewaguru ri sang hyang maṇḍala-kasturi Çelagraha-rong [2]. Sira ta sang apūrbhwā-taruka [3], matangnyan kasturi Palet ngaranya; mangkana kacaritanya kasturi Palet.

Kahucapa tānaknirāmpu Bharang, sira Hibu-tngahan ngaranya [4], amalaku sirālakya tyaga; winehnirālakya tyaga. Warĕg sirālakya, rineknira hikang tyaga. Ndāh almĕh ikang tyaga pgata lawan sira, ginutuk [5] ta ring upih; yata matangnyan sang tyaga tan sah ring kajang kaṇḍi [6].

Muwah amalaku ta sirālakya cāryya; warĕg sirālakya, rineknira hikang cāryya. Almĕh ikang cāryya pgata lawan sira, ginutuknira ta ring watu; matangnyan hana watu Gutuk [7] ngaranya mangke, kidul sakeng Tūryyan.

Amalaku ta sirālakya widu [8], wineh sirālakya widu [8]. Warĕg ta sira halaki, rineknira tang widu. Apurik tang widu ri sira, tinhĕr tinigas tĕnggĕknira, lĕs lungha tikang widu. Kari mahurip tang çirah, çirahnya mangucap:

«Jhah, sang rāryyāngon, tpungakna nggone laweyangku [9])!»

«Hih, halumuh pinun [10].»

«Ḍah, poma harih.»

«Ah, halumuh; sapining pinun [11] tan kawruhan paranya [12].»

«Lah, katĕmu mne hanakanak.»

1) E^3: ontbreekt. 2) B. E^3: Çelāgṛha-rong. 3) B: sang hamūrwwa-n-mataruka. E^3: sang hamūrwwa bhrataruka. 4) E^3: ibhu Had ngaranya. 5) B. E^3: hinutuk. 6) B. E^3: ring kajñang kaṇḍĕ. 7) B. E^3: watu Gugutuk. 8) B. E^3: sirālakwa widū. 9) B. E: tpungākna gode lawehangku. 10) E^3: „Hing halumuh pinuk". 11) B: sapinku. E^3: samipinku. 12) E^3: tan kawruhak paranya.

«Ah, hapan lanang[1]) sapi pinun[2]).»

«Lah, paran dene mne katmu hanakanak.»

Rĕp tinĕpungakĕn[3]) lawehan lawan çirahnya, paripūrṇna sira muwah, mulih maring rāmanira. Ikang rāryyāngon katmu roro sapinya. Kunang ikang widu mangungsi maṇḍala hirikang Gṛha-rong[4]), amalaku sira winikon. Sinangāskāran hinaranan but Gĕnting, mataruka[5]) ta maṇḍala ring gunung Kawi; ngaraning taruka-nya: ring Braja-hning[6]), ring Arggha-maṇik, ring Jangkanang[7]), ring Bhamana, ring Gumantar[8]). Samangka[9]) kwehning taruka-nya maṇḍala; yekā sinangguh kasturi Gĕnting ngaranya.

Kunang sirāmpu Bharang, sah ta sira saking maṇḍala ring Bapa, mangulon ta larinira, mataruka maṇḍala ring Ḍupaka. Tinhĕr bherawapakṣa sira, sing pangan tanana liniwatan, mating-gal ta sirānak rabi, tyagāmbĕknira; matangnyan dewaguru pak-ṣa tyaga ngaranya. Sira tĕmbehan ing dewaguru pakṣa tyaga sang hyang maṇḍala-kāsturi Ḍupaka. Muwah mataruka maṇ-ḍala ring Wariguh ri lambung bhaṭāra Wilis lor, irika ta sira çuklapakṣa, loka sinangguh kāsturi Bā[ra]ng[10]) ngaranya; mangkana kacaritanya ngūni.

Kahucapa ta ki samgĕt[11])- bhagañjing, mabadḍa mapakṣa ṛṣi sira. Sah ta sira saking Ḍaha, mataruka ta sira maṇḍala pinggir ing awan, bhararak ḍami pinakahubhubnira[12]). Wineh ta sira tahi huyuh[13]) dening wwang liwat awan; matangnyan kaki Botahi panĕnggah[14]) ning wong ri sira. Rĕp tumĕdun tang wangunan[15]) saking ruhur hakaça, parĕng lawan tambak lalehan. Samangkana ta kang wong kapuhan[16]) tumon kasidḍyanira kaki Botahi. Ikang sapi bhulalak tansah ringwanira; yata matangnyan ingaranan maṇḍala ring Bhulalak ngaranya wkasan.

Amtang ikang sapi, ingwanira ta pinggir ing awan; mijil tānak-nya rare wadwan lituhayu[17]). Winawa tānaknira mulih, wine-haknira ta ring abtĕk[18]):

«[19]) Hana ta wwang hatadin[20]) den karekĕn hanaknya ring awan[21]).»

[1]) B. E^3: pan lanang. [2]) E^3: pinuk. [3]) B. E^3: ginpungakĕn. [4]). B. E: māṇḍala ring Çelāgṛha-rong. [5]) B. E^3: manaruka. [6]) B: ring Mrāja-hning. E^3: ring Prajā-hning. [7]) B. E^3: ring Jangkunang. [8]) B: ring Sumantar. E^3: ring Çūmāntar. [9]) B. E^3: Samangkana. [10]) E^3: ingevoegd: ngaranta. [11]) B: kita sangmgat E^3: kitāmgat. [12]) B. E^3: pinakāhubahubnira. [13]) B. E^3: wuyuh. [14]) B. E^3: kaki (E^3: kini) Botahi panĕngguh. [15]) B. E^3: wangunwangunan. [16]) B. E^3: Samang-kana wong kapohan. [17]) B: listuhayu. [18]) B: ring aṇṭĕk. E^3: ring nang abṭĕk. [19]) B. E^3: ingevoegd: „Mah ta rara, rikṣakani. [20]) B: hatawḍik. E^3: hataḍḍik. [21]) B. E^3: maring awan.

122

Mangkana lingira kaki Botahi. Atuha pwa kang rare, tanpahingan lituhayuning rūpanira. Sirāji Taki pwa nora binihajinira; inalapnirā tānaknira kaki Botahi, ikang ibu sapi; yata pinakaparameçwarīnira. Mangkana kacaritanya maṇḍala ring Bhulalak, yekā kasturi Botahi ngaranya.

Mamkas ta ring çiṣyanira [1]):

«Yan ana tĕmbe çaiwapakṣa mangaran sirāmpu Tapa-wangkĕng, kawi çakti biṣāngaji [2]), tan adoh saking Ḍahā, aywa ta kita tan prayatna; kami hika, waluya muwah maṇḍalangku ring Bhulalak.»

Mangkana pawkasira kaki Botahi.

Ana ta sira prabhū sama ta sira ring Ḍahā, sira haji Huṇḍal ngaranya. Mapalayanan ta sira lāwan aji Taki; kalah ta sira haji Huṇḍal. Tan satya sira ring raṇa, matakut ring pati, mambolot ta sirāsusupan. Ana ta hulunira pujut kalih çiki lawan walyan tunggal, yata tumūt tansah ring sira.

Mangungsi ta sira gunung Kawi, makuwukuwu ta sirāsusupan. Magawe ta sira sumur, matangnyan hana ring Uṇḍal ngaranya mangke, ikang sumur hana tkaning mangke. Manambut [t]a sira daluwang ring sāmpiran: «mandar [3]) lamun wikuha». Matangnyan hana ring Lamunwiku ngaranya mangke, ri himbang sang hyang Kawi mārĕp wetan. Ḍatang ta sira ri sang hyang Mahāmeru, harĕp ta sira hangera ring Taṇḍĕs. Tinakonakĕn ta nggonirāngaskāra, mawarah ta yan hanambut daluwang ri sampiran; tan wineh mangçu hapan [4]) sira durung wiku.

Tumurun ta sira saking Taṇḍĕs, makuwukuwu ta sira ring jurang ring Çiṇḍo. Motus ta sireng hulunira ḍatnga ring Kukub, sumambaheng bhaṭāra Mahāguru, hamintānūgraha pangaskāra [5]). Almĕh sira katatapa dwanirāhutus [6]). Lumampah tikang hulun apangaran si Kajar [r]wwa lawan walyan pangaran Bugoleng; ikang pujut pangaran si Tĕnggĕk yata kari matunggu ri sira, lawan asu lanang tunggal.

Kunang pangaran si Kajar lāwan Bhugoleng ḍatĕng ring Kukub, sumambah ri bhaṭāra Mahāguru, mawarah yen kotus de haji Huṇḍal. Irika ta bhaṭāra Ḍarmmarāja mangutus ta sira hulu-kĕmbang-pakalpan ḍatngeng aji Huṇḍal, kumirimi [7]) daluwang pangaskāra; nhĕr winawan payung kuṇḍala kalambi, dewaguruha [8]) ring Gĕrĕsik çrī maḥārāja.

[1]) B. E^3: Mangkana pamkas ta ring çiṣyanira. [2]) B. E^3: ngaji çakti ring sangaji (B: ajñi) [3]) B: „Māṇḍa. E^3: „Mādḍa. [4]) E^3: sirā mangguh hapan. [5]) B. E^3: ngaskara. [6]) B. E^3: dwanirāhutusan. [7]) B: humirimi. [8]) E^3: dewaguruhana.

123

Tan wihang lumampah sira hulu-kĕmbang-pakalpan, tan wineh malawasa; sinamayan rwang wngi. Çīghra ḍatang ri Çindo; mogha tan [1]) kapanggih sira haji Huṇḍal, kahaḍang sira lunghāmĕngamĕng. Inaṇṭi hasuwe taṇ ḍatang, mantuk sira hulu-kĕmbang-pakalpan; ikang ḍaluwang sangaskāra kinaryyāknireng watu, ikang watu pamasĕhan iṇḍing bhaṭārī Huma kacaritanya ngūni.

Lĕs lunghā hulu-kĕmbang-pakalpan; sapungkurira ḍatang çrī mahārāja; binadḍaknira [2]) kang daluwang pangaskāra, payung kuṇḍala kalambi hinanggonya. Ikang watu hinaranan ki Hulu-kĕmbang-pakalpan, [3]) [ana tkaning mangke, pamasĕhan iṇḍing bhaṭārī Huma kacaritanya; tinhör ring Ḍingḍing haraning maṇḍala tkaning mangke. Matangnyan maṇḍala ring Ḍingḍing tan marĕk ing Kukub tkaning mangke: ratu halmĕh katatap kacaritanya.] [4])

Ana ta çiṣya de bhaṭāreng Ḍingḍing, ki bhuyut Samaḍi [5]) ngaranya. Maçewa ta sira ḍarmma; sāmpun sirāmuṣpa ring ratri, wineh ta sirānugraha kawikun. Enak ta wisikwisiknira lawan bhuyut Samāḍi; kunang si Kajar si Tĕnggĕk Bhugoleng tan kari hasu hirĕng paḍa maturu ring longan, pada ta mangrĕngö wisikwisiknira. Enak pangrĕngĕnya ri sang hyang kawikun, paḍa tan wruh ri sang hyang ḍarmma.

Ki byut [6]) Samaḍi ri huwusnira wineh nugraha sang hyang kawikun, sinung ta sira payung kuṇḍala kalambi, kinwanira dewaguruha ring Manuñjang, taruka sang hyang Gaṇa ngūni; tinhĕr Ḍingḍing-Manuñjang ngaranya. Mangkana kacaritanya.

Kunang kahucapa ta si Kajar lawan si Tĕnggĕk, mangrĕngĕ sira wisikwisikira bhaṭāra ring ki [7]) buyut Samaḍi. Mangucap ta si Kajar, lingnya:

«Jhah, si Tĕnggĕk, mangrĕngö kita?»

«Mangrĕngö si [8]) pinun.»

«Enak ta pangrĕngöngku; wruh ngwang mangke kalingan ing wiku; wnang ngwang mangke wiku tanpaguruhā.»

Mangkana wuwusnya kalih. Ana ta daluwang lĕpihan ing çrī mahārāja, yata binadḍakĕnya kalih. Mwajar taya:

«Wiku ngaran ing ngwang kalih. Kajar, syapāranta wiku mangke?»

«Byut Jala [9]) ngaran ing ngwang mangke. Kita si Tĕnggĕk, syapa ngaranta wiku?»

---

1) B. E3: mogha ta. 2) B. E3: binaktaknira. 3) B. E3: ingevoegd: kacaritanya. 4) E3: ontbreekt. 5) E3: buyut Samaṇḍi. 6) B. E3: Si byut. 7) B. E3: bhatāriki. 8) B: sih. 9) E3: byut Jayalā.

124

«Byut Giri ngaran ing wang mangke. Matangnyan byut Jalagiri ngaran ing wang kalih. Byut Jala, panĕmbah kiteryyāku!»

«Ih, halmĕh si pinun, paḍa hi kita makas ture [1]). Byut Giri, panĕmbah kiteryyāku!»

«Ih, halmĕh si pinun, paḍa taya makas ture.»

Matangnyan wiku kasture ngaranya kalih. Lĕs lunghā taya kalih, ḍatang ring gunung Wlahulu [2]) hamangunakna tapa; matangnyan hana ring Arggha-kleṣa [3]) ngaranya mangke patapan ing byut Jalagiri. Maṇgkana kacaritan ing kasturi Jalagiri.

Ana ta rājaputra hinilangakĕn saking nagareng Galuh, sira tuhan Cañcurāja [4]) ngaranya. Masusupan ta sira, ḍatang maring byut Jalagiri, amalaku ta sira hinurip. Mojar ta byut Jalagiri:

»Lah, si kita sang rājaputra, yan arĕp ahuripa, pawiku ta kita hiri kami.»

Mwajar ta tuhan Cañcurāja:

«Almĕh si kami hawikuha ri rahadyan sanghulun, [apan rājaputra pinakanghulun] [5]).»

«Lah, hulih si [6]) kita mareng nagara, yan kita halmĕh winikwan.»

Mangkana lingnira byut Jalagiri. Wkasan manglalu ta sang rājaputra, sinangaskāran dening pujut, inaranan ta byut Çrī-manggala; winkaswkas ta de byut Jalagiri:

«Haywa ta kita wanwa lawan wiku waneh, agöng patakaning wiku. Balik tkani [7]) sakarĕpta; sing pangan tajana [8]) liniwatan; parabi; panganggo sahananing dṛwenta [9]). Wnang kita mangaskārani hanak rabi, wnang tanpabantĕn, wnang tanpamūjā-brata, wnang tan wruh ing çāstrāgama, wnang hanājāna [10]) kinawruhakĕn. Bhaṭāra juga panĕnggahakning hawakta.»

Mangkana pawkas byut Jalagiri ring byut Çrī-manggala. Jag lĕs lunghā byut Çrī-manggala, manaruka [11]) ta sira maṇḍala ri tpining sāgara kidul. Haraning tarukanya: ring Rājamaṇik, ring Panimbangan, [ring Gilingan] [12]), ring Wungkal-ibĕk; samangkana kwehning tarukanya maṇḍala, yekā kāsturi Çrī-manggala ngaranya. Mangkana kacaritanya ngūni.

Kahucapa ta walyan mangaran Bhugoleng, wruh yan lunghā si Kajar lawan si Tĕnggĕk. Enak ta pangrĕngönya ri sang

---

1) E^{3}: madasture. 2) B. E^{3}; Wlawulu. 3) B. E^{3}: ring arggha Kelaça. 4) B: tuwan Caṇḍurāja. E^{3}: tuwañ Caṇḍārajā. 5) *B*: ontbreekt. 6) E^{3}: sih. 7) B. E^{3}: Balikan tkĕning, 8) B. E^{3}: hajāna. 9) B. E^{3}: rājadṛwenta. 10) B. E^{3}: hajāna. 11) B. E^{3}: mataruka. 12) B: ontbreekt. E^{3}: ring Giringan.

hyang kawikun, lĕs lunghā Bhugoleng; amanggih ta ya wiku mati, yata pinupunya daluwangnya lawan jaṭanya, ginawenya badḍa rañjingrañjingan. Lunghā ta ya manangsinangsi, kahampir ta ya ring amahat; si Lulumpang-gurut [1]) ngaran ikang amahat. Maweh ta yānginuma twak, sinambinya [2]) maguywan-guywan; nhör mangucap wikuha si Lulumpang-burut. Mwajar Bhugoleng:

«Yen sih ḍak ṣangaskārani, yan sirārĕp [3]) wikuha.»

Rĕp sinangaskāran ta, nhĕr manginum twak maguywan-guywan, winarah ri sang hyang kawikun. Inaranan ta byut Lsung-burut [4]). Lĕs lunghā ta ya maring deçālas, mataruka maṇḍala ring Ārggha-tilas. Tumindak mangetan, mataruka maṇḍala ring Jawa [5]), mangalwar mataruka maṇḍala ring Rĕbhālas [6]), ri sukuning gunung Çundawiṇi. Aminta kalambi ring Tigāryyan, yekā kasturi Lsung-burut [4]) ngaranya. Mangkana kacariṭanya ngūni.

Kahucapa ta hikang asu hirĕng, enak ta pangrĕngönya ri sang hyang kawikun, wruh mangrĕngö ri sang hyang ḍarmma. Katwan lunghā si Kajar lawan si Tĕnggĕk Bhugoleng, lunghā ta ya muwah. Ana ta majagal [7]) mangaran si Dṛwyānak [8]), akweh ta celeng winawanya; kapanggih tang asu denya. Mwajar ta ya, lingnya:

«Ih, hasungku katmu mangko, alawas ta ya lunghā, ḍak pupuh ngūni, hoṣanya tanpasara [9]) manūtakĕn dadi lunghā. Atutuku hanmu.»

Mangkana lingnikanang ajagal; mojar tikang asu:

«Jhah, sugih amalaku [10]) dinol kamung, sumĕngguh asumu hiryyāku. Pira ta pirakpirakmu? Astu mātiha celengmu.»

Mangkana ling ikang asu; pjah ta celengnya. Mwajar kang ajagal:

«Uḍūh, masambhāwa kita hasu; wruh mwajar wwang, atyanta siddḍiçaktinyu. Māti kabeh celengku mangko; pangawak bhaṭāra kapwa sira.»

Rĕp manambah ta si Dṛwyanak [11]) ring asu, amintā warah nugrahā; mojar tta sang asu irĕng:

«Lah, si kamu ḍak wikwani; kunang pawkasangkwiri ko [12]):

---

[1]) B. E^3: Lulumpang-burut. [2]) B. E^3: sinambil. [3]) B. E^3: yan kitarĕp. [4]) B: Lpung-burut. E^3: Lphung-burut. [5]) B. E^3: ring Jiwa. [6]) B. E^3: ring Rĕgālas. [7]) B. E^3: mañjagal. [8]) B. E^3: si Wṛdḍyānak. [9]) B. E^3: doṣanya tanpaçaramā. C: doṣanya. [10]) B. E^3: sugih ta hapalaku. (E^3: hamalaku). [11]) B. E^3: si Wṛdḍyānak. [12]) B. E^3: pawkasangkwa riko.

pabhaṣma kita hawu; wnang ta kita tanpamūjā-brata; sing pangan tanana liniwatan[1]); panakrabi[2]) kita; wnang tan wruh ring çāstra; wnang tanpajapāmantra. Ajana kita nawruhakĕn[3]), bhaṭāra juga panĕnggahakning awakta, wnang kitāngaskārani hanak rabi. Aywa kita wanwāwiku waneh, apan agöng papapatakaning wiku. Mangkana pawkasangkwiri ko[4]).»

Tlas mangaskara si Dṛwyanak[5]), byut Arĕng ta ngaranya wiku. Jag lĕs lunghā ta[6]) sira mara ring Wlahulu. Kunang byut Arĕng mataruka maṇḍala, ngaraning tarukanya: ring Anaman, ring Andrala, ring Kpuh-rĕbah, ring Jun-maṇik; samangkana kwehning tarukanya maṇḍala. Sumambah ri bhaṭāra ri Tigaryyan, mamintānugrahā kalambi; matangnyan kasturi Harĕng[7]) ngaranya.

Ana ta kahucapa muwah rajāputri saking Ḍahā, sira tuhan Galuh çrī Wīratanu ngaranya, anak de mahārāja Taki. Kasingsal ta saking nāgaranira duk sira Tapa-palet hingilangakĕn saking Ḍahā, çrī parameçwarī sira tinuṇḍung. Karuwak ta[8]) rakryan rājaputrī; samana[9]) ta sang rājaputrī sah saking Ḍahā, umungsi ta maṇḍala ring Labdawara ring sira bhagawan Açoṣṭi. Tan ucapĕn lawasnirangkāna, [10]) tan daraṇa tāmbĕknira bhagawan Açoṣṭi tumon lituhayunira rākryan rājaputrī; yata linawananira rākryan Galuh çrī Wiratanu. Kāwaran ta heṣi[11]) wtangning rādyan Galuh; erang ta manaka ring Labdawara; lĕs lunghā ta sira ḍatang[12]) gunung Kāwi. Manak ta[13]) raray kĕmbar paḍa jalu, lituhayu paripūrṇna. Wruh ta sira yan raray mangirangirangana, yata tininggal tang raray ring alas. Lĕs lunghā ta sira mantuk maring nāgaranira.

Kari tang raray manangis makanangkanangan. Tuminghāl ta bhagawan Agaṣṭi, mawlas tumon āmbĕknira ring kasesinikang raray tininggalaknibhunya. Sināmbutnira tang raray, nhĕr dinus dinulangnira, iningunira ring yogha samāḍi. Atuhā tang raray wkasan, winawanira mangulwan maring Maçin, ḍatang ring arggha Kelaça, ring maṇḍala bhagawan Mārkandeya[14]), mantuka maring swargganira. Yata sinrahaknira tang payung kuṇḍala kalambi ri bhagawan Agaṣṭi, sira gumantyani dewaguru tumunggu ring ārggha Kelaça, gumanti[15]) bhagawan Mārkaṇḍeya. Sira

[1]) B. E^3: liniwatanyu. [2]) B. E^3: pānak parabi. [3]) B. E^3: kinawruhakĕn. [4]) B. E^3: pawkasangkwi ko. [5]) B. E^3: si Wṛdḍyānak. [6]) B. E^3: lunghāha. [7]) B. E^3: kasturi Tarĕng. [8]) B. E^3: Kataruwag ta. [9]) B. E^3: samangkana. [10]) B. E^3: lawasnirengkana. [11]) B. E^3: Kawḍaran ta haji. [12]) B. E^3: ḍatngeng. [13]) B. E^3: manaka. [14]) B. E^3: ingevoegd: Maharĕp ta bhagawan Mārkaṇḍeya. [15]) B. E^3: gumantyani.

bhagawan Agaṣṭi dewaguru ring Sukāyajñā. Kunang tikang raray kalih çiki kinahananira[1] sangaskāra, inaranan bhagawan Tṛṇawindu lawan bhagawan Anggira; inanugrahan ta sang hyang kawikun de bhagawan Anggaṣṭi.

Kahucapa ta bhagawan Mārkaṇḍeha, sah saking harggha Kelaça, midĕr ta sireng bhuwaṇa, amrabhajita[2] bhawanira. Kāmpir ta sira humah ing abhelawa, si Suka ngaran ikang ajagal. Tumon ta bhagawan Mārkaṇḍeya ring balung, igulan[3], kulit, wruh ta yan humah ning caṇḍala. Lĕs lungha ta sira; manututi ta si Sukā, mojar tta ya:

«Uḍuh, mangsula sang paṇḍita, pwangkulun, aḍahara sarwwaphala mulaphala sang yatiwara, pwangkulun. Hapa kalinganya tanpanolih[4])?

Tan sumahur bhagawan Mārkaṇḍeya, nhĕr lumaku. Mangetan ta larinira matūt jöng sang hyang Mahāmeru kidul; ikang ajagal tansah matūtburi ring sira. Rĕp marāryyan[5] ta sira ring alas, lĕsu gĕyuh[6] tāwaknira si Suka, apan kangelan tumūt i lampah sang paṇḍita; matangnyan ta haturu mangko[7]. Enak ta paturunika si Suka, lunghā ta bhagawan Mārkaṇḍeya mangetan larinira; tininggalakĕn ta sampĕtnira ri tunggakning nangka. Jag lĕs manganakĕn ta sirā bratā samāḍi ring sang hyang Mahāmeru, pitung we pitung wngi lawasnira, mangilanga caṇḍala[8] paknanya. Ri sāmpunira mangkana mantuk ta sira maring swargganira.

Kahucapa ta si Suka, sapatanginya norana[9] katon sang paṇḍita denya, satinghalnya ri tunggakning nangka ana kari daluwangnira. Sinambutnira tang daluwang, nhör binaddakĕnya; ikang tunggak sinambahnya, iniḍĕpnira sang paṇḍita. Ikang alas tinarukanya maṇḍala,[10] waṇa ngaraning alas,[11] aji[12] pinetnya, tinhör ngaraning maṇḍala ri Jiwaṇa ngaranya mangke. Sumambah ta ring bhaṭāra ring Sukāyajñā aminta[13] nugrahā ring bhāgawan Agāṣṭi; tlas pwaya sinung kṛttānugrahā[14] kalambi, mataruka ta māṇḍala ring jöng bhaṭāri Wilis. Ngaraning tarukan: ring Bhāṇa, ring Talutug, ring Aribhāṇa;[15] samangkāna kwehning tarukan[16] māṇḍala, yeka Sukāyajñā-pākṣa-Jiwana ngaranya. Mangkana kacaritanya ngūni.

[1] B. E^3: kinahanan ing. [2] B. E^3: amrabhāthita. [3] E^3: igalan. [4] B. E^3: tanpawali. [5] B: areryyan. E^3: araryyan. [6] B: bĕyu. E^3: biyu. [7] B. E^3: mangke. [8] B. E^3: pabilangā çaṇḍāla. [9] B. E^3: nora. [10] Einde gaping D. [11] B. E^3: bengarakaugalas. [12] B. E^3: haja. [13] Einde A en C, vervolg volgens B. [14] E^3: sinung nughraha. [15] D: ring Karibawana. [16] D: samangkana hulihnira taruka.

128

Kunang bhāgawan Agāṣṭi mantuk ta maring swārgganira; ikang payung kuṇḍala kalambi sinrahakĕn ta ring bhāgawan Tṛṇawinḍu, sira gumanti dewaguru ring Sukāyajñā, sira ta mungguh ring argghā Kelaçā. Kunang bhāgawan Ānggira wineh nugrahā payung kuṇḍala kalambi de bhāgawan Tṛṇawinḍu, kinon sira dewaguruha ring Sarwwasidḍa [1]) mapākṣa wukir. [2]) Manggālya ta bhāgawan Hanggirā, apan tan sukāwaçāngarakā sira; [3]) tinhĕr ta ngaranira Sukāyajñā-pāksa-Manggalya.

Mataruka ta sira māṇḍala, ikang lwah sinatnira bañunya, winetnira hiwaknya; tinhĕr ngaraning māṇḍala ring Panatmaku. [4]) Akweh ta çiṣyanira, manguñjangañjing [5]) ta sira maring gunung Bhurukah [6]), magawe ta sira wwat malaring lwah, [7]) artha pwa sira kayu mali. [8]) Sāmpun ta ya pinrangān mantuk ta sang hanguñjangañjing; [9]) ikang kayu halmĕh ta gawenĕn wat, ring wngi malayu hikang wawatang [10]) tumḍun ring lwah. Ring eñjing yata mara sang anguñjangañjing, [9]) ikang wawatang nora kapanggih; tunggaknya gunturnya [11]) matmahan watu, ana tkaning mangke. Tinūt [t]ampaknya malayu tumḍun ing lwah; tinhĕr ngaraning māṇḍala ring Layu-watang, [12]) mari haraning Panatan. [13])

Colophon.

Iti sang hyang Tantu panglaran, kagaḍuhana de sang matakitaki, kabuyutan ing sang Yawaḍipā, caturpakandan, caturpakṣa, kabuyutan ring Nanggaparwwatā. Mwah tanpasasangkalā, mulanikang manusā Jawa, ḍuk ḍurung sang hyang Mahameru tka ring Jawa, sawusira tibeng Jawa; mangkana nimitanya tanpasasangkalā, reh yan ing purwwa.

Tlaç [s]inurat sang hyang Tantu panglaran ring karang kabhujanggan Kutritusan, dina u(manis) bu(dha) maḍangsya, titi çaçi kaçā, rah 7, tĕnggĕk 5, ṛṣi panḍawa buta tunggal: 1557.

---

[1]) E[3]: ring Sarwwasidḍi. [2]) D: pakṣa hukir. [3]) D: apan tabĕharaka sira. [4]) D: ring Panatan. [5]) E[3]: panguñjangañjing. D: bujangga haji. [6]) D: Bareka. [7]) D: wat mangkaring lwah. [8]) E[3]: kayummalit. D: matwasi sira kayu mali. [9]) D: sang bujangga haji. [10]) D: iwa mangkana tang kayu malayu. [11]) E[3]: tungtungnya. D: tukunganya. [12]) D: ring Malayu-watang. E[3]: ingevoegd: taranya. Einde van E[3]. [13]) Einde van B. Colophon volgens D.

Bibliography

Boechari. 1985–86. *Prasasti koleksi Museum Nasional*, vol. 1. Jakarta: Proyek pengembangan Museum Nasional.

———. 2012a. An inscribed liṅga from Rambianak. Melacak sejarah kuno Indonesia lewat prasasti, pp. 331–40. Jakarta, Gramedia [Originally published in BEFEO 49 (2), 1959, pp. 405–8].

———. 2012b. A dated bronze temple bell from Pekalongan (North Central Java). *Melacak sejarah kuno Indonesia lewat prasasti*, pp. 341–48. Jakarta: Gramedia [Originally published in *Report ASAIHL seminar on fine arts of Southeast Asia, April 21–23 1963*, pp. 121–31. Denpasar: The Association of Southeast Asian Institutions of Higher Learning].

Bosch, F.D.K. 1915a. Inventaris der Hindoe-oudheden op den grondslag van Dr. R.D.M. Verbeek's Oudheden van Java (tweede deel). *Rapporten van den oudheidkundige dienst in Nederlandsch-Indië.*

———. 1915b. *Notulen van de algemeene en bestuursvergaderingen van het Bataviaasch genootschap van kunsten en wetenschappen* 53, pp. 105–6, 130–32.

———. 1920 Epigraphische en iconographische aanteekeningen. *Oudheidkundig Verslag,* pp. 98–106.

———. 1923.Oudheidkundig verslag over het derde en vierde kwaartal. *Oudheidkundig Verslag*, pp. 85–86.

———. 1926a. Oudheidkundig verslag over het eerste en tweede kwaartal. *Oudheidkundig Verslag*, pp. 3–36.

———. 1926b. Aanwinsten van de archaeologische collectie van het Koninklijk Bataviaasch Genootschap. *Oudheidkundig Verslag*, pp. 77–80.

Brandes, J.L.A. 1889. *Notulen van de algemeene en bestuursvergaderingen van het Bataviaasch genootschap van kunsten en wetenschappen* 27, pp. 73–74, No. VI,c.

———. 1904a. Naar aanleiding der mededeeling van Dr. J.L.A. Brandes. In Not. Dec. 1904, VIII (p. 129). *Notulen van de algemeene en bestuursvergaderingen van het Bataviaasch genootschap van kunsten en wetenschappen* 42, pp. cxvii–cxlviii.

———. 1904b. De verzameling gouden godenbeelden gevonden in het gehucht Gemoeroeh, bij Wanasaba.... *Tijdschrift voor Indische Taal-, Land- en Volkenkunde* 47, pp. 552–57.

———. 1904c. Enkele oude stukken, betrekking hebbende op Oud-Javaansche opschriften en bewaard in de Rijksuniversiteitsboekerij te Leiden. *Tijdschrift voor Indische Taal-, Land- en Volkenkunde* 47, pp. 448–60.

———. 1920. Pararaton (Ken Arok) of het boek der koningen van Tumapĕl en van Majapahit. *Verhandelingen van het Bataviaasch genootschap van kunsten en wetenschappen* 49.

Brumund, J.F.G. 1868. Bijdragen tot de kennis van het Hindoeïsme op Java. *Verhandelingen van het Bataviaasch genootschap van kunsten en wetenschappen* 33, pp. 1–309.

Budiman, A. 1978. *Semarang riwayatmu dulu*. Semarang, Tanjung Sari.

de Clercq, F.S.A. 1909. *Nieuw Plantkundig Woordenboek voor Nederlandsch Indië*. Amsterdam: J.H. De Bussy.

Clignett, C.W. 1844. Reis den naar Smeroe in 1836. *Tijdschrift voor Nederlandsch Indië* 3, pp. 159–65.

Cohen Stuart, A.B. 1875. *Kawi oorkonden in facsimile, met inleiding en transscriptie*. Leiden: E.J. Brill.

Cortesão, A. 1944. *The Suma Oriental of Tomé Pires*. London: Hakluyt Society.

Crucq, K.C. 1929. Epigraphische aanteekeningen. *Oudheidkundig Verslag*, pp. 258–82.

Damais, L.C. 1949. Epigrafische aantekeningen. *Tijdschrift voor Indische Taal-, Land- en Volkenkunde* 83, pp. 1–26.

———. 1955. Études d'epigraphie indonésienne IV. Discussion de la date des inscriptions. *Bulletin de l'Ecole française d'Extrême-Orient* 47, pp. 7–290.

Darusuprapta et al. 1991. *Centhini, Tambangraras-Amongraga*, vol. I. Jakarta: Balai Pustaka.

Eringa, F.S. 1984. *Soendaas-Nederlands Woordenboek*. Foris Publications Holland.

Friederich, R.H.Th. 1870. Over de omgeving van het Oengaran-gebergte. *Tijdschrift voor Indische Taal-, Land- en Volkenkunde* 19, pp. 501–20.

———. 1876. Rapport over reizen gedaan op Java. *Tijdschrift voor Indische Taal-, Land- en Volkenkunde* 23, pp. 43–52.

Gericke, J.F.C. and T. Roorda. 1901. *Javaansch-Nederlandsch Woordenboek*. Amsterdam: Johannes Müller; Leiden: E.J. Brill.

Gopinath Rao, T.A. 1971. *Elements of Hindu Iconography* (2 vols.). Varanasi: Shri Bhagwan Singh M.A. Indological Book House.

de Graaf, H.J. and Th. G. Th. Pigeaud. 1986. *Kerajaan-kerajaan Islam pertama di Jawa*. Jakarta: PT Pustaka Grafitipers.

Groeneveldt, W.P. 1887. *Catalogus der archeologische verzameling van het Bataviaasch genootschap van kunsten en wetenschappen*. Batavia: Albrecht.

Guillot, C. 2002. "The Tembayat hill: clergy and royal power in Central Java from the 15th to the 17th century". In *The potent dead: Ancestors, saints and heroes in contemporary Indonesia*, edited by H. Chambert-Loir and A. Reid, pp. 141–59. Honolulu: University of Hawai'i Press.

Guillot, C. and L. Kalus. 2003. L'énigmatique inscription musulmane du maqâm de Kediri (Xe s. H./XVIe s. E.C.). *Archipel* 65, pp. 25–42.

Guillot, C., L. Nurhakim and S. Wibisono. 1996. *Banten sebelum zaman Islam. Kajian Arkeologi di Banten Girang, 932? – 1526.* Jakarta: Pusat Penelitian Arkeologi Nasional, École Française d'Extrême-Orient [Original title: *Banten avant l'Islam. Étude archéologique de Banten Girang (Java – Indonésie) 932? – 1526*. Paris: EFEO, 1994].

den Hamer, C. 1893. Opgave van weinig bekende beelden, aanwezig in het scheidingsgebergte tusschen Pekalongan en Banjoemas. *Notulen van de algemeene en bestuursvergaderingen van het Bataviaasch genootschap van kunsten en wetenschappen* 31, pp. cxix–cxxii.

Hefner, R.W. 1985. *Hindu Javanese, Tengger tradition and Islam*. Princeton: Princeton University Press.

Hoepermans, N.W. 1913. Hindoe-oudheden van Java (1864–1867). *Rapporten van den oudheidkundige dienst in Nederlandsch-Indië*, pp. 73–372.

Indrajaya, A. and V. Degroot. 2012–13. Prospection archéologique de la côte nord de Java Centre: le district de Batang. *Bulletin de l'Ecole française d'Extrême-Orient* 99, pp. 351–83.

———. 2014. "Early traces of Hindu-Buddhist influence along the north coast of Central Java: Archaeological survey of the district of Batang". *Amerta* 32, no. 1, pp. 1–76.

Istari, R. 2015. Prasasti pendek dari Candi Sanggar dan kemungkinan penghormatan terhadap dewa Brahma. *Berkala Arkeologi*, pp. 59–72. Yogyakarta: Balai Arkeologi.

Jasper, J.E. 1927. Tengger en Tenggereezen. *Djawa* 7, pp. 23–37, 217–31, 291–304.

Junghuhn, F.W. 1849. Goenong Smeroe of Maha Meroe, de hoogste berg op Java. *Tijdschrift voor Nederlandsch Indië* 1, pp. 112–38.

———. 1854. *Java, zijne gedaante, zijn plantentooi en inwendige bouw, Deel IV*. Den Haag.

Juynboll, H.H. 1906. Ādiparwa. Oudjavaansch prozageschrift. 's-Gravenhage: Nijhoff.

———. 1909. *Catalogus van's Rijks Ethnographische Museum. Deel V, Javaansche oudheden*. Leiden: E.J. Brill.

Kern, R.A. 1927. De reis van koning Hajam Woeroek door Lamadjang in 1359 A.D. *Tijdschrift van het koninklijk Nederlandsch aardrijkskundig genootschap* 44, pp. 613–24. Leiden: E.J. Brill.

Kieven, L. 2013. Following the cap-figure in Majapahit temple reliefs. *Verhandelingen van het Koninklijk Instituut voor Taal-, Land- en Volkenkunde* 280. Leiden: Brill.

Knebel, J. 1902. Beschrijving der Hindoe-oudheden in de residentie Pasoeroean, afdeeling Malang. *Rapporten van de commissie in Nederlandsch-Indië voor oudheidkundig onderzoek op Java en Madoera*, pp. 253–383.

———. 1904. Beschrijving der Hindoe-oudheden in de afdeeling Prabalingga, Kraksaän en Loemadjang der residentie Pasoeroean. *Rapporten van de commissie in Nederlandsch-Indië voor oudheidkundig onderzoek op Java en Madoera,* pp. 93–134.

———. 1905–6. Beschrijving der Hindoe-oudheden in de afdeeling Madioen/Magetan der Residentie Madioen. *Rapporten van de commissie in Nederlandsch-Indië voor oudheidkundig onderzoek op Java en Madoera*, pp. 23–64.

Krom, N.J. 1913a. Oud-Javaansche oorkonden. Nagelaten transscripties van wijlen Dr. J.L.A. Brandes. *Verhandelingen van het Bataviaasch genootschap van kunsten en wetenschappen* 60.

———. 1913b. Het jaar van den val van Majapahit. *Tijdschrift voor Indische Taal-, Land- en Volkenkunde* 55, pp. 252–58.

———. 1913c. *Oudheidkundig Verslag*, pp. 93–94.

———. 1914. Inventaris der Hindoe-oudheden op den grondslag van Dr. R.D.M. Verbeek's Oudheden van Java (eerste deel). *Rapporten van den oudheidkundige dienst in Nederlandsch-Indië.*

———. 1916. Eenige gegevens over de Hindoe-oudheden van Oost-Java, volgens een handschrift van J. Hageman J. cz. (1861–1868). *Bijdragen tot de Taal-, Land-en Volkenkunde van Nederlandsch-Indië* 72, pp. 412–57.

———. 1919. Epigraphische Aanteekeningen III. *Tijdschrift voor Indische Taal-, Land- en Volkenkunde* 58, pp. 161–68.

Kusen. 1988. Prasasti Wanua Tengah III, 830 Śaka: Studi tentang latar belakang perubahan status sawah di Wanua Tengah sejak Rake Panangkaran sampai Rake Watukura Dyah Balitung. *Kegiatan Ilmiah Arkeologi IAAI Komisariat Yogyakarta.*

Lunsingh Scheurleer, P. 2008. "The well-known Javanese statue in the Tropenmuseum, Amsterdam, and its place in Javanese sculpture". *Artibus Asiae* 68, no. 2, pp. 287–332.

Maurenbrecher, E.W. 1923a. *Oudheidkundig Verslag*, pp. 89–90.

———. 1923b. Verbeteringen en aanvullingen op den inventaris der Hindoe-oudheden (Rapport 1923) voor de districten Malang, Penanggoengan en Ngantang van de afdeeling Malang, residentie Pasoeroean. *Oudheidkundig Verslag*, pp. 170–84.

van der Meulen, W.J. 1977. In search of 'Ho-ling'. *Indonesia* 23, pp. 87–111.

Monier Williams, M. 1899. *A Sanskrit-English Dictionary*. Oxford: Clarendon.

Muusses, M. 1923a. De Soekoeh-opschriften. *Tijdschrift voor Indische Taal-, Land- en Volkenkunde* 62, pp. 496–514.

———. 1923b. Inventaris der Hindoe-oudheden op den grondslag van Dr. R.D.M. Verbeek's Oudheden van Java (derde deel). *Rapporten van den oudheidkundige dienst in Nederlandsch-Indië.*

Nastiti, T.S. et al. 1994–95. Laporan survei di Kabupaten Lumajang, Propinsi Jawa Timur 1990. *Berita Penelitian Arkeologi* 44. Jakarta: Pusat Penelitian Arkeologi Nasional.

Nastiti, T.S. and M. Suhadi. 1996. *Laporan penelitian epigrafi di Kabupaten Madiun, Magetan dan Ponorogo, Provinsi Jawa Timur*. Jakarta: Pusat Penelitian Arkeologi Nasional.

Nawawi, A.C. 1990. Keadaan lingkungan arkeologis di daerah Lumajang sekitar masa pemerintahan kerajaan Majapahit dalam rangka penentuan hari jadi. *Seminar penentuan hari jadi Kabupaten Daerah Tingkat II Lumajang.*

Nitihaminoto, G. 1990. Pertumbuhan dan perkembangan kota-kota di Lumajang (tinjauan arkeologis dan geografis). *Seminar penentuan hari jadi Kabupaten Daerah Tingkat II Lumajang.*

Noorduyn, J. 1962a. Over het eerste gedeelte van de Oud-Soendase Carita Parahyangan. *Bijdragen tot de Taal-, Land- en Volkenkunde* 118, pp. 374–83.

———. 1962b. Het begingedeelte van de Carita Parahyangan. *Bijdragen tot de Taal-, Land- en Volkenkunde* 118, pp. 405–32.

———. 1968. Further topographical notes on the ferry charter of 1358. *Bijdragen tot de Taal-, Land- en Volkenkunde* 124, pp. 460–81.

———. 1978. Majapahit in the fifteenth century. *Bijdragen tot de Taal-, Land-en Volkenkunde* 134, pp. 207–74.

———. 1982. Bujangga Manik's journeys through Java; Topographical data from an Old-Sundanese source. *Bijdragen tot de Taal-, Land- en Volkenkunde* 138, pp. 413–42 [Republished in Noorduyn and Teeuw 2006, pp. 437–65].

Noorduyn, J. and A. Teeuw. 2006. Three Old Sundanese Poems. *Bibliotheca Indonesica* 29. Leiden: KITLV Press.

Orsoy de Flines, E.W. van. 1941–47. Onderzoek naar en van keramische scherven in de bodem in Noordelijk Midden-Java, 1940–1942. *Oudheidkundig Verslag*, pp. 66–84.

Pigeaud, Th. G. Th. 1924. *De Tantu Panggĕlaran. Een Oud-Javaansch prozageschrift, uitgegeven, vertaald en toegelicht*. 's-Gravenhage: Nederl. Boek en Steendrukkerij voorheen H.L. Smits.

———. 1938. *Javaans-Nederlands Woordenboek*. Groningen: Wolters-Noordhof (reprint 1989).

———. 1960–63. *Java in the 14th century, a study in cultural history* (5 vols.). The Hague: Martinus Nijhoff.

———. 1967. *Literature of Java*, vol. I. Leiden: Koninklijk Instituut voor Taal-, Land- en Volkenkunde.

Poerbatjaraka, R. Ng. 1926. De Calon-arang. *Bijdragen tot de Taal-, Land- en Volkenkunde* 82, pp. 110–45.

———. 1968. *Tjeritera Pandji dalam perbandingan.* Djakarta: Gunung Agung [Originally published in 1940 under the title *Pandji-verhalen onderling vergeleken.* Bandoeng: Nix & Co.].

———. 1992. *Agastya di Nusantara.* Jakarta: Yayasan Obor Indonesia [Originally published in 1926 under the title *Agastya in den Archipel.* Leiden: Brill].

Prijohoetomo, M. 1937. Manik Maya. *Javaansch Leesboek; vier verhalen uit de oudere Javaansche letterkunde*, pp. 1–47. Amsterdam: H.J. Paris.

Raffles, T.S. 1817. *The history of Java* (2 vols.). London: John Murray [Reprinted as one volume in 1988 by Oxford University Press].

Rangkuti, N. 2000. Pola permukiman desa Majapahit di Kabupaten Malang. *Laporan penelitian arkeologi.* Yogyakarta: Balai Arkeologi.

Rassers, W.H. 1982. *Pañji, the culture hero, a structural study of religion in Java.* The Hague: Martinus Nijhoff.

Reichle, N. 2007. *Violence and Serenity: Late Buddhist Sculpture from Indonesia.* Honolulu: University of Hawai'i Press.

Rinkes, D.A. 1996. *Nine Saints of Java.* Malaysian Sociological Research Institute.

Robson, S.O. 1979. Notes on the early kidung literature. *Bijdragen tot de Taal-, Land- en Volkenkunde* 135, pp. 300–322.

———. 1995. Deśawarṇana (Nāgarakṛtāgama) by Mpu Prapañca. *Verhandelingen van het Koninklijk Instituut voor Taal-, Land- en Volkenkunde* 169. Leiden: KITLV Press.

Santiko, H. 1995. Early research on Sivaitic Hinduism during the Majapahit era. *The Legacy of Majapahit*, pp. 55–72. Singapore: National Heritage Board.

Sarkar, H.B. 1971–72. *Corpus of the inscriptions of Java* (2 vols.). Calcutta: Firma K.L. Mukhopadhyay.

Satari, S. 1978. *New finds in northern central Java.* Jakarta: Proyek Pengembangan Media Kebudayaan, Departemen P & K.

Satari, S., R. Darmosoetopo, A. Sukardjo and R.M. Soesanto. 1977. Laporan hasil survai kepurbakalaan di daerah Jawa Tengah bagian utara, kabupaten Pekalongan, Batang dan Kendal. *Berita Penelitian Arkeologi* no. 9. Jakarta: Proyek Pengembangan Media Kebudayaan, Departemen P & K.

Scholte, J. 1920. De slametan Entas-entas der Tenggereezen en de Memukur-ceremonie op Bali. *Handelingen van het eerste congres voor de taal-, land- en volkenkunde van Java*, pp. 47–85. Weltevreden: Albrecht & Co.

Sedyawati, E. 1994. Gaṇeśa statuary of the Kaḍiri and Singhasāri periods. *Verhandelingen van het Koninklijk Instituut voor Taal-, Land- en Volkenkunde* 160. Leiden: KITLV Press.

Sell, E.A. 1912. Opgave der Hindoe-oudheden in de residentie Pekalongan. *Rapporten van de commissie in Nederlandsch-Indië voor oudheidkundig onderzoek op Java en Madoera*, pp. 153–200.

Setyawati, K., I. Kuntara Wiryamartana and W. van der Molen. 2002. *Katalog Naskah Merapi-Merbabu, Perpustakaan Nasional Republik Indonesia.* Yogyakarta: Universitas Sanata Dharma.

Sidomulyo, H. 2007. *Napak tilas perjalanan Mpu Prapañca*. Jakarta: Wedatama Widya Sastra.

———. 2010. From Kuṭa Rāja to Singhasāri: towards a revision of the dynastic history of 13th century Java. *Archipel* 80, pp. 77–138.

———. 2014. Kidung Pañji Margasmara. Kajian atas nilainya sebagai sumber sejarah. *Seminar Nasional Naskah Kuno Nusantara 2014. Cerita Panji sebagai Warisan Dunia*. Jakarta: Perpustakaan Nasional.

Sosrodanoekoesoemo, R. 1927. Literatuur en kunst in Madoera (Verslag van het congres van het Java Instituut). *Djawa* 7, pp. 163–71.

van Stein Callenfels, P.V. 1918. Oudheidkundig verslag over het eerste kwartaal. *Oudheidkundig Verslag*, pp. 9–12.

———. 1924. Stukken betrekking hebbend op Oud-Javaansche opschriften in de bibliothèque nationale te Parijs. *Oudheidkundig Verslag*, pp. 23–27.

Stutterheim, W.F. 1925. Een oorkonde op koper uit het Singasarische. *Tijdschrift voor Indische taal-, land- en volkenkunde* 65, pp. 208–81.

———. 1935. Enkele interessante reliefs van Oost-Java. *Djawa* 15, pp. 130–44.

———. 1936. *Oudheidkundig Verslag*, p. 14.

———. 1937a. *Oudheidkundig Verslag*, p. 18 and Figure 14.

———. 1937b. Het zinrijke waterwerk van Djalatoeṇḍa. *Tijdschrift voor Indische Taal-, Land- en Volkenkunde* 77, pp. 214–50.

———. 1940. *Oudheidkundig Verslag*, pp. 16, 35 and Figure 29.

Sugriwa, I.G.B. 1956. *Babad Pasek*. Denpasar: Balimas.

Suhadi, M. 2003. *Laporan penelitian prasasti di Museum Mpu Tantular dan di Museum Purbakala Trowulan*. Jakarta: Pusat Penelitian Arkeologi Nasional.

Sukarto Kartoatmodjo, M.M. 1990. Menelusuri sejarah hari jadi Lumajang berdasarkan data prasasti dan naskah kuno. *Seminar sejarah Hari Jadi Lumajang*. Kabupaten Daerah Tingkat II Lumajang.

Suyami et al. 1999. *Tinjauan historis dalam Babad Kadhiri*. Jakarta: Departemen Pendidikan dan Kebudayaan R.I.

Swellengrebel, J.L. 1936. *Korawāśrama, Een Oud-Javaansch proza-geschrift, uitgegeven, vertaald en toegelicht*. Santpoort: C.A. Mees.

Tjahjono, B.D., A. Indrajaya and V. Degroot. 2015. Prospection archéologique de la côte nord de Java Centre: le district de Kendal. *Bulletin de l'Ecole française d'Extrême-Orient* 101, pp. 327–56.

van der Tuuk, H.N. 1897–1912. *Kawi-Balineesch-Nederlandsch Woordenboek* (4 vols.). Batavia: Landsdrukkerij.

Verbeek, R.D.M. 1891. Oudheden van Java. *Verhandelingen van het Bataviaasch genootschap van kunsten en wetenschappen* 46.

Veth, P.J. 1869. *Aardrijkskundig en statistisch woordenboek van Nederlandsch Indië* (3 vols.). Amsterdam: P.N. van Kampen.

Wahyuni, I.A.M. and R.H. Galeswangi. 2011. *Kepurbakalaan di Kota Malang: koleksi arca dan prasasti.* Malang: Dinas Kebudayaan dan Pariwisata Pemerintah Kota Malang.

Weatherbee, D. 1985. Notes on the Mariñci inscription: a 14th century Majapahit copper-plate. *Bijdragen tot de Taal-, Land- en Volkenkunde* 141, pp. 349–52.

Wibowo, A.S. 1975. Penemuan candi di daerah Ampelgading. *Bulletin Yaperna* 5, pp. 48–61.

Wilkinson, R.J. 1959. *A Malay-English Dictionary (Romanised).* London: Macmillan.

Wirjo Asmoro. 1926. Iets over de "adat" der Madoereezen. *Djawa* 6, pp. 251–61.

Wisseman Christie, J. 2002. "Register of the inscriptions of Java (from 732–1060 AD), Part 2: May 855 – May 898 AD. Consultation Draft II" (unpublished).

Yamin, M. 1962. *Tatanegara Majapahit*, Vol. II. Jakarta: Prapanca.

Zimmer, H. 1946. *Myths and symbols in Indian art and civilization.* New York: The Bollingen Library.

———. 1952. *Philosophies of India.* London: Routledge and Kegan Paul Ltd.

Zoetmulder, P.J. 1982. *Old Javanese-English Dictionary* (2 vols.), with the collaboration of S.O. Robson. KITLV. 's-Gravenhage: Nijhoff.

———. 1983. *Kalangwan. Sastra Jawa kuno selayang pandang.* Jakarta: Djambatan [Original title: *Kalangwan. A survey of Old Javanese literature.* Den Haag: Martinus Nijhoff, 1974].

———. 1990. *Manunggaling kawula gusti: pantheïsme dan monisme dalam sastra suluk Jawa.* Jakarta: Gramedia [Original title: *Pantheïsme en monisme in de Javaansche soeloek-litteratuur.* Nijmegen: Berkhout, 1935].

LEXICOGRAPHICAL LIST

This list contains lexical items mentioned in the notes as either not included in the dictionary (Zoetmulder 1982), with meanings different from those listed, or of unknown meaning. References are to the page of the translation as published here, with the number of the footnote.

A

angsil: umangsil 39, 133
angśu: mangśu 61, 245
antara: mantara 29, 79

B

b(h)ararak 60, 240
bolot: mambolot 61, 242

C

cĕpĕl: acĕpĕl 31, 95
cup: kapacupi 23, 46

D

dom: adomdoman 55, 217

E

ĕṇḍĕk: ingĕṇḍĕk-ĕṇḍĕk 59, 235

G

gowantĕn 47, 167
gulawĕṇṭah 33, 109
guling: kaguling-gulingan 25, 57
guntur 67, 273

H

haṇḍawar 52, 204
hāraka: anghāraka 67, 266
hudipan 46, 161
hyangta 20, 30

J

jaya: angajaya 58, 232

K

kamawaśyahara 36, 123
kanang: makanang-kanangan 66, 259
kaluku 42, 144
kaṇṭora 47, 169
katu-katu 21, 39
kĕba-kĕba: pakĕba-kĕba 30, 89
kĕlah: makĕlah-kĕlah 15, 15
kĕlĕm: kumĕlĕm 22, 45
krĕci 51, 193
ktak 19, 21

L

labĕt: manglabĕt 26, 68
langon-langon 46, 159

lawu: lumawu-lawu 46, 163
lĕka-lĕka 34, 113
lĕnggita: malĕnggita 37, 128
lumbur 40, 140

M

masi 33, 107

N

nangsi: manangsi-nangsi 51, 190

P

pakan: makan 51, 194
papa: apa-apa 25, 56
parandene 60, 237
purungul-purungul 48, 172

R

rapus: dak rarapusane 26, 61
rātnadwada 56, 223
rūpajuti 45, 156
rurung, lurung 50, 186, 187

S

śarasantana 11, 11
sĕlang: panĕlangan 45, 155
su[ra]ngga 28, 74

T

tajang 31, 99
tĕtak: den tĕtakĕn 23, 47
tingkĕr: katingkĕran 45, 154
tuñci 18, 19
tuñjang 35, 118
turuk 20, 29

U

unte-unte: angunte-unte 51, 195

W

wakya: kawakyan 49, 178
wiḍak 27, 70
wiring 16, 17
wusungan 48, 175

GENERAL INDEX

A

Aḍidarwa (book), 54, 182
Adinusa, 106. *See also* Nuṣa
Āḍiparwa (text), 94
Agaṣṭi, Bhagawān, 37, 41, 66–67, 75, 108, 122, 125, 140, 182, 193. *See also* Anggaṣṭi
Agastya, 75
Agni, Hyang, 12, 182
Aji Saka, 84
Alas Persilan (forest), 172. *See also* Gunung Perceel
Amadanom, 144, 200
Amanguyu-guntung, 19, 182, 200
Amir Hamzah, 168
Amongbudi, Syekh, 115
Ampelgading, 119, 133, 136, 137
Analaga, Bhaṭāra Hyang, 44, 182, 189
Anaman, *maṇḍala*, 65, 182
Anantabhoga, Sang Hyang, 24, 182. *See also* Antaboga
Aṇḍawar, *maṇḍala*, 52, 145, 147, 162, 182
Andayaningrat (king), 159
Andrala, *maṇḍala*, 65, 182
Andungbiru, 163
Anggang-anggang, Mt., 45, 182
Anggaṣṭi, Bhagawān, 182
Anggaṣṭi, Hyang, 182, 200
Anggara, *wiku*, 28, 182
Anggira, Bhagawān, 66, 67, 108, 125, 182
Anggirah, hermitage, 50, 183, 188. *See also* Girah
Angrok, Ken (legendary hero), 78, 173–78
Antaboga (god of snakes), 98. *See also* Anantabhoga
Antrukan Pawon (waterfall), 119
Anungkāla, *rākṣasa*, 40, 41, 43, 140, 183
Anungkurāt, Bhaṭāra, 44, 183
Anyar (river), 166, 168
Ardiwijaya, 84. *See also* Kaṇḍyawan
Arĕng, Buyut, 65, 182, 183, 187, 191, 194. *See also* Kasturi
Arga-kleṣa, hermitage, 63, 183
Arga-maṇik, *maṇḍala*, 60, 183
Arga-tilas, *maṇḍala*, 64, 183
Argopura, Mt, 91, 168. *See also* Hyang
Aribhāṇa, *maṇḍala*, 67, 125, 183
Arjuna, Mt., 44, 93, 183
Aśoṣṭi, Bhagawān, 36, 65, 145, 183
Asta Jamar (grave site), 168
Asta Landaur (megalithic site), 170, 171
Astitijāti, 34, 184
Asuji (month), 51, 159
Atas Angin, Kyai, 127

B

Babad ing Sangkala, 79
Babad Kadhiri, 84
Babad Pasek, 153
Babad Tanah Jawi, 93
Bajul Semanggi (crocodile), 159
Bajwa-langit, Mt, 93
Bakal, Ki, 52, 184
Bakar, 51, 159, 184
Balai Arkeologi (Yogyakarta), 88
Balangbhangan, 93. *See also* Walambangan, Walangbangan
Balekambang, 98. *See also* Kentengsari
Bali (island), 68, 112, 164, 178, 195
Balitung, Dyah, 141
Bāmeśwara, Śrī, 151
Bañak-wiḍe, 144–45. *See also* Wiraraja
Bancak, Mt, 93, 154, 184. *See also* Bañcak
Bañcak, Mt, 50, 153, 154, 184. *See also* Bancak
baṇḍagiṇa menmen, 46
Bango-samparan, 175
Banjarnegara, 82, 99, 101, 105
Banten (west Java), 96
Banyubiru (bathing place), 133, 136
Banyukembar, 125
Bapa, *maṇḍala*, 57, 58, 59, 60, 176, 184. *See also* Tūryan
Barang, Mpu, 50, 53–57, 60, 75, 79, 154, 156, 162, 172, 175, 176, 182–84, 187–89, 191, 206–9, 211. *See also* Kasturi
Baron Sekeber, 126
Baruṇa (World Guardian), 17, 184
Basuki, *nāga*, 99
Batang, 98, 104, 105, 107, 109, 198, 203
Batur, 163, 164, 165, 168–71
Batur (inscription), 163, 170, 173
Bawang, 109
Bayeman, 161
Bāyu, Hyang, 12, 14, 184
Begawan, 141. *See also* Pangawān
Bĕsar, 52, 162, 173, 184
Besuksat (river), 120
Betapa (river), 121
Betoro Katong, 93
Bhagavata Puraṇa, 104
Bhairawa (sect), 53, 60, 75, 77, 150–52, 153, 156, 172, 184, 187, 200, 208
Bhamana, *maṇḍala*, 60, 156, 184
Bhāṇa, *maṇḍala*, 67, 125, 184. *See also* Bono
Bharāda, Mpu, 164
Bhatati, Mahārāja, 47–50, 53, 150, 184
Bhujangga, Mpu, 26, 184
Bhulalak, *maṇḍala*, 61, 175, 185
Blambangan (former kingdom in east Java), 101, 112
Blambangan (village in central Java), 101
Blandit, 142. *See also* Walaṇḍit
Bledug Kuwu (mud volcano), 88
Blitar, 175
Blora, 88
Bodḍa, *wiku*, 26, 185. *See also* Sogata
Boja, 86
Bojonegoro, 88, 90
Bonang, Sunan (Islamic saint, *wali*), 77
Bono, 125. *See also* Bhāṇa
Botahi, Kaki, 61, 185. *See also* Kasturi
Boyolali, 153, 154, 194, 198
Boyolangu, 125
Brahmā, Bhaṭāra, 10–12, 14, 16, 17, 18, 22–24, 34, 35, 37–40, 46, 53, 56, 76,

82, 84, 92, 100, 121, 129, 139, 140, 144, 175, 185, 190, 196, 201, 204, 205, 209, 210
Brahmā, Mt, 16, 56, 84, 93, 112, 113, 142, 147, 163, 177, 207, 208. *See also* Bromo
Brahmāloka, 47, 150, 185
Brajahning, *maṇḍala*, 156, 158, 185
Brantas (river), 175
Bret, Mt, 142, 185
Bṛnggiriṣṭi, *wil*, 45, 47, 142, 185
Brokoh, 104, 105
Bromo, Mt, 84, 93, 113, 116, 142, 162, 178, 185, 189, 207. *See also* Brahmā
Brumbung, 151
Brumund, J.F.G., 98
Bubukṣa, 34, 152, 185. *See also* Gagang-aking
Buddha, *wiku*, 28, 185
Buddha, Lord, 26
Bugoleng, *walyan*, 62, 64, 185, 190, 196
Bujangga Manik (Old Sundanese poem), 83, 85, 88, 98, 100, 101, 104, 108, 112–16, 121, 125, 129, 131, 140, 164, 166, 173
Bujuk Santi, 164
Bulak, 175
Bulon, *katyāgan*, 18, 104, 185
Bulu, 106
Buluh (riverbed), 172
Bululawang, 177
Burno, 121
Burukah, Mt, 67, 186
Butak, Mt, 156

C

Cakrawarti, Mahārāja, 56, 186
Calakuṇḍa, *cakra*, 38, 186
Calon Arang (text), 78, 164
Cañcurāja, Tuhan, 63, 186, 205
Candi Argokusuma (temple site), 86
Candi Argopura (temple site), 98. *See also* Gedong Alas
Candi Gayatri (temple site), 125
Candi Gedung Putri (temple site), 108, 119
Candi Jawar (terraced sanctuary), 137
Candi Kedaton (temple site), 163
Candi Panataran (temple site), 175
Candipetung, 106
Candipuro, 108, 119, 129
Candi Sukuh (temple site), 90, 91
*candrakap*āla (emblem), 151
Candra Kirana, 74. *See also* Sekartaji
Candrasari, Ken, 131, 134, 144
Cangcangan, 51, 117, 159, 161, 186. *See also* Penyancangan
Cangkaan, 170
Carita Parahyangan (text), 84, 85, 110, 111
*catur*āśrama, *katyāgan*, 75, 104, 108
caturbhasma, *maṇḍala*, 75, 78, 104, 122, 130, 131, 162, 164, 173
caturlokapāla (four world guardians), 17, 39, 184, 190, 194, 202, 211
caturyuga (four world ages), 111
Cemorokandang, 176
Cĕmpa, *ratu ring*, 59, 79, 186
Cĕmpa, *putri* (legendary princess), 79
Cepoko, 129, 187
Cintamaṇi, 25, 27, 28, 186, 188
Ciptagupta, Bhagawān, 12, 84, 186
Ciptangkara, Mpu, 12, 84, 186
Clignett, C.F., 133, 136
Crewek, 88
Cunggrang (inscription), 94

D

Daha, 53, 54, 56, 57, 58, 59, 60, 61, 65, 74, 77, 79, 116, 175, 176, 178, 182, 185–91, 195, 199, 206, 207–9, 210, 211. *See also* Galuh
Damais, L.C., 109
Dampit, 133, 144
Dayo, 79. *See also* Daha
Damalung, Mt, 18, 83, 101, 186, 198, 200. *See also* Mawulusan, Pamrihan
Dandang-gĕndis, 178. *See also* Kṛtajaya
Dander, 88
Danyangan (grave site), 145
Ḍarma (the holy), 39, 62, 64
Ḍarma (god), 38
Ḍarmarāja, Bhaṭāra, 37–42, 62, 186, 194, 205, 207, 209
Ḍarma-ūtpṭi, Sang Ṛṣi, 42, 186. *See also* Ḍarmarāja
Demak, 73, 77, 100
Deśawarṇana, *kakawin*, 75, 93, 104, 122, 130, 140, 144, 162, 172
Dewaputra, 44, 186
Dewata-kaki, 186
Dieng Plateau, 75, 82, 85–86, 96, 105, 106, 187, 193, 206
Ḍihyang, 76, 82, 83, 92, 96, 101, 122, 128, 187. *See also* Dieng Plateau
Ḍingḍing, *maṇḍala*, 20, 62, 112, 113, 115, 116, 118, 119, 129, 145, 146, 183, 187, 202, 203, 209
Ḍingḍing-Manuñjang, *maṇḍala*, 63, 145, 187, 197, 203. *See also* Manuñjang
Doro, 110
Drawa Puruṣa Prameya (religious text), 153
Dṛĕwyānak, 64, 65, 187
Duk, Mt, 129, 159, 161, 184, 187
Dupak, 176, 177
Ḍupaka, *maṇḍala*, 60, 176, 187. *See also* Dupak
Durgā, Bhaṭārī, 45, 46, 142
Durgādewī, Bhaṭārī, 45, 142, 187, 191
Durgā-Mahiṣāsura-mārdinī, 140

E

Ĕndok, Ken, 175
Er Hangat (inscription), 96, 105. *See also* Ratanira

F

Friederich, R.H. Th., 86, 98

G

Gabus, 88
Gaḍa (weapon), 27, 187
Gaḍa-wĕsi, Mt, 45, 182, 187
Gading, 164, 166, 172, 173
Gaḍing, 166
Gagang-aking, 34, 152, 187. *See also* Bubukṣa
Gajendra (elephant), 104
Galuh, 47–50, 63, 74, 150, 184, 186, 187, 191, 206–9. *See also* Daha
Galuh (kingdom in west Java), 111
Galuh, Raden, 74. *See also* Candra Kirana, Sekartaji
Galuh Śrī Wīratanu, Tuhan, 65, 74, 208
Gambyok, 175
Gaṇa, Sang Hyang, 20–23, 26, 35, 41, 63, 85–86, 109, 111–12, 140, 145, 187, 194, 197, 202, 210. *See also* Gaṇeśa
Ganḍamaḍana, Mt, 41, 45, 187
Gandamayi (old woman of), 142. *See also* Gondomayi
Gandariya, 101

Gandulan, 106, 108
Gaṇeśa (elephant-headed god), 85–86, 106–7, 119, 133, 135. *See also* Gaṇa
Gantĕn, 41, 140, 144, 188
Gapura, 109
Garga, *dewata*, 23, 85, 188
Gĕḍe, *maṇḍala*, 172
Gedong Alas, 98. *See also* Candi Argopura
Gĕgĕr-katyāgan (hermitage), 20, 21, 112, 116, 188
Gĕlang-gĕlang (variant Gĕgĕlang), 93
Gemuruh, 125. *See also* Gumuruh, Guruh
Gĕnĕng (inscription), 151
Genijaya, Hyang, 153
gĕnta (ritual bell), 178–80
Gĕnting, Buyut, 60, 156, 158, 183–85, 188–89, 190. *See also* Kasturi
Genting (Merjosari), 156
Gerbo, 137
Gĕrĕsik, *maṇḍala*, 30, 62, 129, 159, 188. *See also* Gresik
Ghono, Syekh, 109
Ghorī, Bhaṭārī, 41, 140, 188
Gianyar (Bali), 195
Gilingan, *maṇḍala*, 64, 188
Girah, 50, 183, 188. *See also* Anggirah
Giri, Buyut, 63, 207. *See also* Jala, Jala-Giri
Girindrawardhana dyah Raṇawijaya, Śrī (Majapahit king), 80
Gondomayi, Mt, 142. *See also* Gandamayi
Gono (toponym), 86
Gonoharjo, 86
Gonoriti, 86
Gora, Sang Hyang (weapon), 188
Goromanik, Mt, 125–27
Gorontol, *rabut*, 176. *See also* Grontol
Gresik, 129–30. *See also* Gĕrĕsik
Grobogan, 88–90, 198
Grontol, 176. *See also* Gorontol
Gubugklakah (inscription), 145, 164
Gucialit, 116–19, 129, 145, 179–80
Guḍuhā, Sang Hyang (weapon), 26, 188
Gulingaṇḍara, Mt, 25, 188
Gulung-gulung (inscription), 141
Gumantar, *maṇḍala*, 60, 156, 189
Gumuruh, 122, 124, 189. *See also* Gemuruh, Guruh
Gundil (mountain ridge), 168
Gunung Perceel, 172. *See also* Alas Persilan
Guru, Bhaṭāra, 19–21, 24, 27, 28, 36–37, 39, 42, 45–47, 54, 74, 76, 82, 91, 93, 104, 106, 108, 109–12, 119–22, 128, 130, 140, 142, 144, 152, 159, 182–84, 185–202, 204–11
Guru, Mbah, *punden*, 164
Gurudeśa, 11, 12, 83, 189
Guruh, *maṇḍala*, 30, 122, 125, 189. *See also* Gemuruh, Gumuruh
Gutuk, *watu*, 60, 189
Guwar-gawir (religious text), 153

H

Hageman, J., 164, 168
Hahāh, *maṇḍala*, 30, 128, 129, 189
Hamer, C. den, 98
Hantang (inscription), 150
Hanuman, 133, 136
Hari, Bhaṭāra, 36, 38, 189
Haricaṇḍana, Bhaṭāra, 55, 56, 189
Harjo Ta'i, *dukun*, 180
Hayam Wuruk, 163. *See also* Rājasanagara

Hiang, Mt, 108, 112. *See also* Hyang
Himad, 141, 142, 177
Himalaya (mountain range), 73, 92, 197
Hindu (tradition), 76, 111, 150, 185
Hoepermans, N.W., 83, 108, 126
Horsfield, T., 88
hudipan, 46
Huluwanwa, *katyāgan*, 18, 104, 106, 108, 185. *See also* Lowanasari, Lowano
Hyang, Mt, 53–55, 75, 91, 92, 150, 156, 162, 164, 166, 172, 173, 184, 189–92, 193, 200, 206, 210. *See also* Hiang

I

Ibu-tĕngahan, 57, 59, 189
Ijo, Mt, 22, 112, 116, 189
ijo-ijo, 46
Ileru, 19, 109, 189
India, 92, 152, 186, 190, 207. *See also* Jambuḍipa
Indra (World Guardian), 17, 190
Indrokilo (inscription), 106, 128
Islam, 73, 77, 128, 178
Iśwara, Bhaṭāra, 11, 12, 16, 30–35, 37–40, 45, 46, 57, 76, 83, 86, 100, 122, 128, 129, 140,
144, 156, 185, 189, 190, 198, 200, 203–4, 207, 208
Itip-ing-lĕmbu, Mt, 25, 190
I-tsing, 109

J

Jabon, 120
Jabung (Malang), 141
Jagatnātha, Bhaṭāra, 11, 37, 39, 190
Jagatpramāṇa, Bhaṭāra, 10, 18, 82, 190
Jagatwiśeṣa, Bhaṭāra, 37, 190
Jala, Buyut, 63, 190. *See also* Giri, Jala-Giri
Jala-Giri, Buyut, 63, 64, 183, 190, 205, 210. *See also* Kasturi
jalagrahā, 59
Jala-parwata, *maṇḍala*, 144, 190
Jambuḍipa, 10, 14, 31, 32, 54–56, 76, 79, 91, 92, 183, 186, 190. *See also* India
Janaḍipa, Mpu, 50, 150, 190
Jangkanang, *maṇḍala*, 60, 156, 190
Jangkang, 163
Jasper, J.E., 113
Jaṭa, Mt, 35, 145, 190
Jatipitutur, Ki, 88
Java (*mangajawa*), 35. *See also* Yawaḍipa
Jawa, *maṇḍala*, 64, 190
Jayabhaya, Mapañji, 150
Jayakatyĕng, Śrī, 93
Jayengresmi (prince of Giri), 88
Jayangsari, Raden, 115
Jenggolo-manik (hill), 119. *See also* Maṇik
Jĕru-jĕru (inscription), 141
Jetis, 106
Jipan, Pangeran, 127
Jiput, 175. *See also* Jiwut
Jiwaṇa, *maṇḍala*, 67, 125, 190
Jiwut, 175. *See also* Jiput
Joho, iv
Joko Linglung (mythical serpent), 88
Jolotundo (bathing-place), 94, 95
Jumat, *dukun*, iv
Jun-maṇik, *maṇḍala*, 65, 191
Junrejo, 176
Junwatu, *maṇḍala*, 176
Junghuhn, Franz (botanist), 113, 133
Jurang Limas (ravine), iv
Juru, Raden, 159

K

Kabalon, 176. *See also* Kebalon
Kabhayan-panglayar, Ki, 51, 52, 54, 145, 147, 156, 159–63, 168, 170, 172, 173, 191
Kabyang (hermitage), 19, 112, 121, 191
Kacuṇḍa, Ḍang Hyang, 35, 145, 191
Kadiran, 112, 113, 116
Kaḍiri, 74, 121, 150, 151, 173, 178, 186, 187
Kagĕnĕngan, *dharma*, 176
Kailāśa, *pitāmaha i*, 96. *See also* Kelāśa
Kajar, Si, *pujut*, 62–64, 190, 191
Kajen, 122
Kaki-dewata, 21, 191
Kāla, *rākṣasa*, 38–41, 43, 46, 140, 191. *See also* Anungkāla
Kālakūṭa (poison), 15, 93, 191
Kālāmukha (sect), 152. *See also* Kāpālika, Pāśupata
Kālarūdra, Sang Hyang, 46, 191, 195
Kālawijaya, 152
Kalijaga, Sunan (Islamic saint, *wali*), 77
Kalipadang, 133, 140, 144, 200. *See also* Padang, Paḍang
Kalotan, Mpu, *pangambehan*, 47–50, 150, 152, 191
Kalpataru, 191
Kalyasĕm, Mt (cemetery), 47, 48, 53, 54, 162, 163, 172, 173, 182, 191
Kāmadewa, Sang Hyang, 19–20, 86, 108–10, 192
Kamalkuning, 166. *See also* Kaman-kuning
Kamaṇḍalu, Sang Hyang, 15–17, 95, 126, 129, 139, 161, 192
Kaman-kuning, 166. *See also* Kamalkuning
Kāmeśwara, Mpu, 147
Kambangan, *nūṣa*, 49, 50, 152, 192
Kambang-rawi, 166. *See also* Sĕkar-rawi
Kambe, Mt, 93
Kampil, Mt, 35, 145, 192. *See also* Pilan
Kampud, Mt, 15, 24, 44, 93, 187, 192, 196, 203, 204. *See also* Kelud
Kandangan, 113, 115, 116, 117, 121, 180
Kaṇḍawa, *maṇḍala*, 163, 164. *See also* Khaṇḍawa
Kaṇḍawan, Hyang, 110, 111. *See also* Kandiawan, Kaṇḍyawan
Kandiawan, Sang, 110. *See also* Kaṇḍawan, Kaṇḍyawan
Kaṇḍayun, Hyangta, 20, 110, 192. *See also* Wṛtti-kaṇḍayun
Kaṇḍyawan, Rahyang, 12, 13, 84, 85, 110, 111, 192. *See also* Kaṇḍawan, Kandiawan
Kanyawan, Sang, 12, 84, 85, 192
Kāpālika (sect), 77, 150, 152. *See also* Kālāmukha, Pāśupata
Kapila, *dewarṣi*, 17, 192
Kapuhunan (inscription), 96
Kapulungan, *mpungkwing*, 151
Karanganyar (Pekalongan), 109
Karanganyar (regency), 90
Karangkobar, 82
Karangnongko, 144
Karivarada (legendary tale), 104. *See also* Varadaraja
Karmaṇḍeya, Bhagawān, 34, 192. *See also* Mārkaṇḍeya
Karuman, 175
Karung-kalah, Sang, 12, 13, 84, 192
Karurungan, Mt, 50, 154, 192
Kasingi, Dewi, 33, 86, 193
Kasongo, 88

Kasturi (ascetic order), 57, 75, 76, 130, 137, 156, 157, 173, 184, 185, 188, 193, 196, 204, 205, 208, 209
Kasturi, *maṇḍala*, 58, 59, 60, 75, 122, 130, 131, 156, 175, 193
Kasturi Arĕng, 65, 157. *See also* Arĕng
Kasturi Barang, 60, 157. *See also* Barang
Kasturi Botahi, 61, 157. *See also* Botahi
Kasturi Gĕnting, 60, 157. *See also* Gĕnting
Kasturi Jala-Giri, 63, 157. *See also* Jala-Giri
Kasturi Lĕsung-burut, 65, 157. *See also* Lĕsung-burut
Kasturi Palet, 59, 157, 200. *See also* Tapa-palet
Kasturi Śrī-manggala, 64, 157. *See also* Śrī-manggala
Katiha, 20, 110, 111, 193
Katingalan, Mt, 93
Katong, Mt, 15, 93, 193
Katu, *rabut*, 176
Katu-katu, 21, 193
Katung-malaras, Sang, 12, 13, 84, 193
Kawedenan, 154, 176, 177
Kawi, Mt, 37, 44, 60, 61, 65, 108, 125, 156, 158, 175, 182–85, 188, 189, 190, 193, 195, 209
Kayutaji (hermitage), 19, 111, 113, 119, 121, 193
Kḍu, 106. *See also* Kedu
Kĕba-kĕba, Bhaṭārī, 30, 193
Kebalon, 176. *See also* Kabalon
Kediri, 74, 79, 151, 175. *See also* Kaḍiri
Kedman, 36, 193
Kedu, 84, 106
Kedungkandang, 176
Kedunglo, 108
Kedungsumur,168
Kĕdyangga, Mt, 25, 190
Kekep, Mt, 156
Kelāśa, Mt, 15, 19, 20, 34, 40, 66–67, 86, 95, 96, 98, 100, 105, 108, 109, 110, 122, 125, 183, 198. *See also* Kailāśa
Kelaśabhumisampūrṇawan, 40, 194
Kelud, Mt, 93. *See also* Kampud
Kemulan, Mt, 128
Kendal, 86, 87, 98
Kendalbulur, 125
Kenep, 112
Kĕṇḍĕng, Mt, 50, 153, 154, 194
Kenongo, iv
Kentengsari, 98
Kepanjen, 175
Kĕpuh-rĕbah, *maṇḍala*, 65, 194
Kepung, 151
Kertowono, 118, 119
Keśawa, Bhaṭāra, 22, 36, 194
Kĕtĕk-Mĕlĕng, 16, 17, 194. *See also* Kamaṇḍalu
Ketu, *dewarṣi*,17, 194
Khaṇḍawa (forest), 164. *See also* Kaṇḍawa
Kidal, 133. *See also* Kiḍal
Kiḍal, 131
Klakah, 161
Klego, 153
Kombala, *ranu*, 43, 194
Kotaanyar, 166
Kowera (World Guardian), 17, 194
Kraksaan, 166
Krejengan, 166
Kṛtajaya, 178. *See also* Dandang-gĕndis
Kubukubu (inscription), 141
Kuḍampilan, 51, 159, 194
Kudus, Sunan (Islamic saint, *wali*), 79

Kukub, *maṇḍala*, 35, 36, 39, 42, 50–52, 55, 62, 75–77, 113, 116, 119, 122, 129–34, 137, 140, 144, 145, 147, 159, 161, 178, 194. *See also* Śūnyasagiri
Kulikuli, Sang, 20, 110, 111, 194
Kumāra, Sang, 20–22, 45–47, 112, 116, 142, 194
Kumāra-gimbal, Mpu, 26, 194
Kumāra-gohphala, Sang, 24, 25, 194
Kumāra-raray, Mpu, 26, 185, 188, 195, 205. *See also* Budḍa, Sogata
Kumāra-sidḍi, Mpu, 26, 195
Kumukus, Mt, 14, 44, 93, 195
Kuna, Mpu, 26, 195
Kupang, 18, 104, 105, 106, 109, 126, 195
Kurambitan (inscription), 127
Kuruṣya, *dewata*, 23, 85, 195
Kuśika, *dewata*, 23, 85, 195
Kuṭi (inscription), 101
Kutri-tusan, *kabhujanggan*, 68, 195

L

Labdawara, *maṇḍala*, 36, 65, 145, 193, 195
Lamajang (ravine), 131, 133. *See also* Majang Tengah
Lamajang Kidul, 112
Lamdaur (grave site), 145
Lamunwiku, 61, 195
Lawajati, 142. *See also* Lowokjati
Lawu, Mt, 46, 83, 90, 91, 93, 96, 154, 193, 195
Lawu, Sunan, 93
Layu-watang, *maṇḍala*, 67, 196
Lĕbĕng, Mt, 44, 196
Ledokombo, 69, 92, 113, 116, 181
Leiden University, 93, 130
Lĕmah Abang, Seh (Islamic saint), 77. *See also* Siti Jenar
Lĕmah-bang, Ki, *rākṣasa*, 54, 196
Lemahduwur, *kramat*, 133, 140
Lĕmah-tulis, 164
Lemongan, Mt, 91, 92, 161, 162, 172, 196. *See also* Limohan
Lesan, 164, 166
Lĕsung-burut, Buyut, 64, 183, 190, 196, 203, 206. *See also* Kasturi, Lulumpang-burut
Limbangan, 86
Limohan, Mt, 13, 91, 196
Lingga, 122. *See also* Linggoasri
lingga (gold), 126
lingga (origin of), 82
Linggasuntan (inscription), 141–42
Linggoasri, 122. *See also* Lingga
Lodra, Kāla, 196
Lombok (island), 168
Lowanasari, 106, 108. *See also* Huluwanwa, Lowano
Lowano, 106
Lowokjati, 142. *See also* Lawajati
Lowokwaru, 175
Lulumbang, 176, 177. *See also* Lumbang-lumbang, Lumbangsari
Lulumpang-burut, Si, 64, 196. *See also* Lĕsung-burut
Lumajang, iv, 108, 113, 115, 117, 118, 120, 129, 145, 161, 179, 180, 196, 202
Lumanglang, Yakṣa, 41, 196
Lumangling, Yakṣa, 41, 196
Lumangut, Yakṣa, 41, 196
Lumbang-lumbang, 177
Lumbangsari, 177

M
Madakaripura, 144
Madiun, 93
Madumali, Dewi, 33, 196
Maduretna, Ratu, 154
Magetan, 154, 176, 177, 184
Mahābhārata (epic), 94
Mahādewa, Hyang, 12, 83, 197
Mahāguru, Bhaṭāra, 50–52, 62, 197. *See also* Guru
Mahākāla (deity), 140
Mahākāraṇa, Bhaṭāra, 10, 11, 13, 14, 17, 35, 197. *See also* Guru
Mahāmeru, Sang Hyang, 14–17, 19, 24, 28, 30, 31, 34, 35, 39–43, 45, 52, 61, 66, 68, 75–76,
91, 92–96, 99, 100, 104, 110, 111, 116, 119, 121, 125, 128, 129, 131, 140, 144, 145, 147, 159, 161, 162, 178, 182, 183, 188, 191–93, 195, 197, 199–202, 204, 206, 207, 210. *See also* Semeru
Mahapunggung, Sri, 84, 85
Majang Tengah, 133. *See also* Lamajang
Majapahit, 73, 79, 80, 99, 119, 140, 142, 151, 159, 161, 178
Makuṭa, 21, 197
Malang, 75, 108, 125, 131, 133, 137, 141, 144, 156, 173, 175, 176, 177, 178, 185, 200, 209
Mamanggis-lili, 142. *See also* Manggis
Manah i Manuk (inscription), 131
Mandala (river), 166
Maṇḍalagiri, Sang Hyang, 10, 197
Maṇḍalikā, Mt, 93
Mandara, Mt, 95
Mandaragiri, Sang Hyang, 14–17, 30, 35, 42, 45, 197
Mandara Giri Semeru Agung, *pura*, 115
Mandaraparwata, Sang Hyang, 10, 197
Manden, 106. *See also* Mandisari
Mandiki (club), 38, 197
Mandisari, 106. *See also* Manden
Mangdulur, Yakṣa, 41, 197
Manggis, 142. *See also* Mamanggis-lili
Manginte, Yakṣa, 41, 197
Makukuhan, Ki, 84. *See also* Mahapunggung, Mangukuhan
Mangukuhan, Sang, 12, 13, 84, 197
Mangulihi (inscription), 96
Mangulihi, *samgat*, 96
Manguyu (ascetic order), 18, 74, 109, 197
Maṇik, Mt (hermitage), 21, 35, 112, 119, 145, 197. *See also* Jenggolo-manik
Manik Maya (text), 84, 93, 96
Manjing (river), 140
Manuñjang, Mt, 35, 63, 145, 197. *See also* Ḍingḍing-Manuñjang
Maraṇak, Ki, *rākṣasa*, 54, 198
Marapi, Mt, 25, 198. *See also* Marapwi, Merapi
Marapwi, Mt, 101, 198. *See also* Marapi, Merapi
Mariñci (inscription), 75
Mārkaṇḍeya, Bhagawān, 66, 75, 108, 122, 125, 182, 190, 192, 198, 205. *See also* Karmaṇḍeya.
Maśin, 18, 19, 66, 106, 108–10, 122, 128, 198. *See also* Masin
Masin, 30, 106, 109, 110, 198. *See also* Maśin
Matsya Puraṇa, 94
Maulana Mahribi, Syekh, 128
Maurenbrecher, E.W., 156
Mawulusan, Mt, 18. *See also* Damalung, Pamrihan

Māyana *maṇḍala*, 29, 34, 122, 198
Medang (river), 88
Mĕḍang, 36, 85, 90, 128, 152, 198
Mĕḍang-agung, 85
Mĕḍang-gaṇa, 12, 20, 33, 84–86, 110, 111, 152, 198. *See also* Mĕdang-kana
Mĕḍang-gowong, 85
Mĕdang-jati, 111
Medang Kamulan (settlement in central Java), 88
Mĕḍang-kamulan, 12, 84, 85, 86, 88–91, 152, 198
Mĕdang-kana, 111. *See also* Mĕḍang-gaṇa
Mĕḍang-kumuwung, 85
Mĕḍang-tamtu, 85
Mĕḍang-tañjung, 50, 152, 154, 198
Mendala, 122
Mendikil, 88
Menjangan (river), 113
Mepeles-awi, 110. *See also* Pileku-sewu, Pinaleśawi
Merapi, Mt, 98, 101, 198. *See also* Marapi, Marapwi
Merapi-Merbabu (corpus), 83, 101
Merbabu, Mt, 83, 98, 101
Merjosari, 156, 158
Merjosari (inscription), 156, 158
Metri, *dewata*, 23, 85, 198
Meulen, W.J. van der, 85, 86, 95–96, 126
Miroloyo, *kraton*, 126
Misari, *dukun*, 179, 180
Mo-ho-sin, 109
Mojokerto, 80, 94
Momorong, 166. *See also* Morong
Morong, 166. *See also* Momorong
Moyanang (hill), 122. *See also* Māyana
Mpu Tantular Museum (Sidoarjo), 120–21
Mṛṣa, Sang Hyang (weapon), 26, 199
Mūla-malurung (inscription), 93, 151
Mulyosari, 137
Munggir, 120
Muñcang (inscription), 177
Muria, Mt, 100, 210
Muusses, M., 90, 133

N

Naga Pertala, 98, 99, 100, 128
Nāmaśiwaya, Bhaṭāra, 52, 199
Nandaka (dagger), 38, 199
Nandiguru, Bhaṭāra, 199
Nandiśwara (deity), 140
Nangga-parwatā, *kabuyutan*, 68, 199
Nangka-parwata, *maṇḍala*, 35, 40, 199. *See also* Panasagiri
Nārada, *dewaṛṣi*, 17, 199
Narajñāna, Mpu, 50, 150, 199
National Library (Jakarta), 83
National Museum (Jakarta), 86, 108, 109, 120, 124, 125, 126, 133, 136, 145, 156, 158, 163
Ngadirejo (Temanggung), 106
Ngadirejo (Magetan), 176
Ngadisari, 116
Ngadoman, 101
Nganjuk, iv
Ngantang, 158
Ngargo, 86, 98
Nglegok, 175
Nglimut, 86
Nglorok, 124
Nīlakaṇṭa, Bhaṭāra, 95, 199
Nini, Aji, (queen), 59, 199. *See also* Ra Nini
Niṣada, Mt, 16, 199
Nongko (toponym), 144
Nongkojajar, 144

Nongkopait, 144
Nongkorejo, 144
Nongkosewu, 144
Nongkosongo,144
Noorduyn, J., 80, 84, 90, 98, 100, 112, 131, 154
Nuṣa, 105. *See also* Adinusa

O

Orsoy de Flines, E.W. van, 88

P

Pace, iv
Pacelengan, 51, 159, 161, 199. *See also* Pawijungan
Pacira, *katyāgan*, 18, 104, 108, 113, 199. *See also* Pasirian
Padang (river), 133, 144. *See also* Kalipadang
Paḍang, 41, 133, 144, 200. *See also* Kalipadang
Paguhan, 47, 200
Paiton, 166
Pajarakan, 162, 164, 166, 172
Pajaran (river), 118
Pājaran, *batur*, 164
Pakel, 118, 179, 180
Pakisaji, 175
Pakuan (royal court in west Java), 112
Pakuluran, 126
Palĕmaran (inscription), 101
Palot, Mpu, 176
Palyat, Bhaṭāra Mahāmpu, *bhujangga*, 47–50, 150–51, 156, 172, 200
Pamanguyon-agung, 19, 20, 21, 74, 112, 116, 200. *See also* Amanguyu-guntung
Pamotan (river), 133
Pamrihan, Mt, 18, 83, 100, 101, 200. *See also* Damalung, Mawulusan
Panasagiri, *maṇḍala*, 35, 36, 145, 199, 200. *See also* Nangka-parwata
Panatan, *maṇḍala*, 67, 200
Panatmaku, *maṇḍala*, 67, 200
pañātūr-mukā(four "openings" on the Mahāmeru), 41, 119, 140, 200
Pañcajanya (conch), 38, 200
pañca kuśika ("five deities"), 85
Pandan, Mt, 93
Pandansari Lor, 141
Pangawān, *kahyangan*, 40, 41, 140, 141, 144, 177, 200. *See also* Begawan
Pangeran, Bhaṭāra, 44, 200
Pangkeśwara (hermitage), 30, 200
Pangkur, 175
Panimbangan, *maṇḍala*, 64, 201
Pañji, 74, 85, 93, 126, 168, 175
Pañji Margasmara, *kidung*, 131, 134, 140, 142, 144
Parakan, 106
Parameśwara, Bhaṭāra, 13, 15, 16, 18, 19, 20, 23, 27, 28, 30, 34, 40, 42, 46, 54, 150, 201
Parameśwara-śiwa, 32, 201
Parameśwarī, Bhaṭārī, 10, 19, 25, 26, 30, 201
Pararaton (text), 78, 79, 144, 173–78
Parijñana, *walija*, 50, 152, 201
Paruk (river), 161
Parwatī, 120, 125, 175. *See also* Umā
Pasanggaman, Mt, 25, 201
Pasirian, 108, 199. *See also* Pacira
Pasrujambe, 120, 121, 137
Pāśupata (sect), 152. *See also* Kālāmukha, Kāpālika
Pasuruan, 133, 136, 141, 144, 176

Patean, 86
Patĕmon, 101
Pati-pati, Sang Apañji, 151
Pāwaka, Bhaṭāra, 22, 201
Pawijungan, 161. *See also* Pacelengan
Pawinian, Mt, 82, 201. *See also* Pawinihan
Pawinihan, Mt, 11, 82, 201. *See also* Pawinian
Pawitra, Mt, 16, 43, 93, 94, 201. *See also* Penanggungan
Payaman, 51, 52, 159, 161, 201
pederat, 46
Pekalongan, 97, 98, 104, 109, 122, 124, 126, 127
Penanggal, 108, 120, 121
Penanggungan, Mt, 94, 201. *See also* Pawitra
Penawungan (hill), 117, 207. *See also* Tawungan
Pengging, 159
Penyancangan (hill), 117, 159, 161. *See also* Cangcangan
Perawan-sunti (spout figure), 126
Petapan, Mt, 168
Petirejo, 106. *See also* Ptir
Petirgunung, 106. *See also* Ptir
Petungkriyono, 83, 98
Petungombo, 133, 136, 140
Phala (hill), 43, 201
Pigeaud, Th., 104, 110, 111, 112, 121, 144, 153, 163
Pilan, Mt, 22, 112, 145, 201. *See also* Kampil
Pileku-sewu, 110. *See also* Mepeles-awi, Pinaleśawi
Pinaleśawi, 20, 110, 111. *See also* Mepeles-awi, Pileku-sewu
Pintang Mas (inscription), 96. *See also* Kapuhunan
Pinton, Mt, 19, 111, 121, 201
Pires, Tomé, 78–79
Plaosan, 164
Poerbatjaraka, R. Ng., 95, 122, 175
Poncokusumo, 144–45
Ponorogo, 93
Pulosari, Mt, 96
Prahu, Mt, 82, 96, 98, 109
Prapañca, Mpu, 75, 78, 93, 104, 122, 130, 131, 140, 141, 144, 162, 163, 172, 173
prasen ("zodiac beaker"), 145, 178, 180
Aratañjala, *dewata*, 23, 85, 201
Pratasti Bhūwanā (manuscript), 110, 111
Prendengan, 109
Probolinggo, 117, 129, 159, 161, 162, 164, 166, 168, 169, 171, 172, 181, 187, 207
Pronojiwo, 119, 129, 144, 202. *See also* Pūrṇajiwa
Pṛthiwī, Bhaṭārī, 24, 56, 202
Ptir, 106. *See also* Petirejo, Petirgunung
Pulutan, 90
Puṇḍutan-śawa, 39, 202
Pūrṇajiwa, 41, 140, 144, 202. *See also* Pronojiwo
Purwodadi, 88, 90
Puṣpa, Mt, 93

R

Rabunan, 168, 170–72
Raditya, *wiku*, 28, 202
Raditya, Sang Hyang, 17, 202. *See also* Śiwa-(r)aditya
Raffles, T.S., 86

Raga-runting, Mpu, 153. *See also* Rogo-runting
Rāga-runting, *raṇḍa*, 50, 152–53, 202
Ragḍang, 51, 159, 161, 202
Rahadyan, 44
Rāhu, *rākṣasa*, 18, 95, 126, 202
Rahung, Mt, 98
Rājamaṇik, *maṇḍala*, 64, 202
Rājapati, Sang Hyang, 23, 202
Rājasa (dynasty), 78, 178
Rājasanagara (Majapahit king), 142, 144, 161, 162, 163, 172, 173. *See also* Hayam Wuruk
Rajĕgwĕsi, former district in East Java, 90
Rambutgono, settlement in Central Java, 86
Rancangkapti, 115
Ra Nini, 142
Ranobawa, 112, 113, 115, 119, 131. See Ranubhawa
Ranubhawa, *patapan*, 19, 112, 113, 116, 118, 121, 202
Ranugedang, 161
Ranu Kumbolo (inscription), 147, 194
Ranupane, 147
Ranupuhan, Sang Hyang (holy stream), 20, 112, 116, 119, 202
Ranuyoso, 117, 161
Ratanira (inscription), 105. *See also* Er Hangat
Ratih, Bhaṭārī, 20, 110, 202
Rātmaja, *rākṣasa*, 16–18, 126, 129, 161, 203
Rātmaji, *rākṣasa*, 16–18, 126, 129, 161, 203
Ratmojo, Mbah (grave site), 161. *See also* Repatmojo
Rawunglangit, 110. *See also* Wawu-langit
Rĕban, *mpungkwing*, 128
Rĕban, *pakṣa*, 31, 128, 203
Reban, 106, 128, 203
Rĕbhālas, *maṇḍala*, 64, 203
Rĕbhawinuk, *cakra*, 38, 203
Rĕnĕb, 44, 203
Rengganis, Dewi (legendary female ascetic), 86, 98, 161, 168, 170
Repatmojo, 161. *See also* Ratmojo
Rĕrĕban, Mt, 28, 122, 128, 203, 204, 206
Rogojembangan, Mt, 98–100
Rogo-runting, Eyang, 153. *See also* Raga-runting
Rogoselo, 104, 110, 125–28
Rokom, 126
Rondokuning, 166
Rorawa (hell), 41
Ṛṣi, *pakṣa*, 59, 60, 203
Ṛṣi-angarĕmban, 26, 75
Ṛṣi-mabadḍa ("sage-with-headband"), 57, 156
Rudra, 38, 203

S

Sāgara, *maṇḍala*, 55, 75, 122, 130, 162, 163, 172, 173, 203
Sāgara, *wan*āśrama, 131, 162, 172–73
Sagara Dalĕm, 131, 173. *See also* Sāgara
Sagĕnggĕng, 175, 176. *See also* Segenggeng
Śaiwa (sect), 48, 50, 61, 73, 76, 83, 140, 150, 152, 184, 203
Salatiga, 101
Salingsingan (inscription), 127, 128. *See also* Slingsingan
Salud Mangli, 105. *See also* Simangli
Samaḍi, Ki Buyut, 62, 63, 145, 157, 170, 203

Samagawe, 101
Samaya, Kāla, 210
Sambadagni, Mt, 24, 204
Sambu, Kāla, 38, 204
Samĕgĕt-bagañjing, Ki, 8, 58–60, 204
sampĕt (ritual sash), 59, 66, 178, 180
Samudramanthana (legend), 76, 94, 98, 100, 137, 139
Samuḍung, 141
Saṇḍang-garbha, Sang, 12, 13, 84, 204
Sandijñāna, *sang hyang kuñci*, 52, 53, 55, 204
SaneśCara, *wiku*, 28, 204
Sangara, Jaka, 159
Sanggara, *maṇḍala*, 54, 204. *See also* Sāgara
Sañjaya, Mt, 18, 100–1, 204
Sapaka, *dewarṣi*, 17, 204
Sarayu (river), 52, 161, 204
Sarjawa-Jambuḍipa (hermitage), 37, 204
Sarwasidḍa, *maṇḍala*, 28, 34, 67, 122, 125–26, 204. *See also* Sorosido
Sarweśwara II (Kaḍiri king), 121. *See also* Śṛnggalañcana
Satari, S., 83, 99, 104
Sawela Cala, 84. *See also* Kaṇḍyawan
Segaran (lake), 162, 172
Segenggeng, 175, 177. *See also* Sagĕnggĕng
Segono, 86
Sĕkar-rawi, 166. *See also* Kambang-rawi
Sekarsari (hermitage), 168, 169, 170
Sekartaji, Dewi, 74. *See also* Candra Kirana
Śelagraha-rong, *maṇḍala*, 59, 60, 200, 204
Sell, E.A., 98
Selobrojo (inscription), 158
Semarang, 98, 100
Semeru, Mt, 69, 76, 94, 108, 113, 114, 116, 119–21, 125, 129, 131, 133, 137, 144, 178, 197, 199. *See also* Mahāmeru
Sendang Ramesan (volcanic pool), 88
Senduro, 113, 115–16, 120
Senjoyo (river), 101
Sentono Kates (grave site), 118
Sĕrat Centhini, 88, 89, 109, 115, 116
Sĕrat Kanda, 84, 93, 159
Serayu (mountain range), 101
Serayu (river), 101
Śewa, *wiku*, 26. *See also* Śaiwa
Śewaśāsana (sacred text), 128
Sidḍawangsitadewa, Sang Ṛṣi, 37–39, 205
Sidḍayoga, Mpu, 32–34, 74, 86, 205
Sidḍayogi, *wiku*, 33, 205
Silurah, 106, 107
Simangli, 105, 106, 107. *See also* Salud Mangli
Simojayan, 133, 140
Sindoro, Mt, 98, 101
Śiṇḍo (ravine), 62, 116, 129, 205
Siṇḍok, Pu, 141, 142, 177
Singhasāri, 131, 133, 134, 142, 145, 151, 178
Singosari, 141, 142, 176, 185, 209
Sinutug, 126
Siti Jenar, Seh (Islamic saint), 77. *See also* Lĕmah Abang
Śiwa, Lord (Bhaṭāra), 18, 154, 189, 197, 201, 203, 205
Siwalan, 109, 122, 124
siwalan palm (Borassus flabellifer), 124
Śiwāmba ("water of life"), 15–17, 37, 76, 93, 100, 205
Śiwa-(r)aditya, Sang Hyang, 45, 58, 202

Śiwarāśi, Sang, 141
Slingsingan, Pangeran, 127, 128. *See also* Salingsingan
Smarī, Bhaṭārī, 19–20, 57
Sogata, 26, 205. *See also* Boḍḍa, Kumāra-raray
Sogata, *pakṣa*, 50, 53, 54, 154, 156, 185, 205, 209
Sokarini, Mt, 93
Soma, *wiku*, 28, 205
Sorosido, 126. *See also* Sarwasiḍḍa
Sragi/Sranggi, 109
Srangin (grave site), 161
Śrī, Bhaṭārī, 12, 13, 50, 59, 84, 85, 152, 192, 198, 199, 202, 205
Śrī-manggala, Buyut, 63, 64, 205. *See also* Kasturi
Śrī Manggala II (inscription), 127
Śrī Sĕdana (legendary tale), 85
Sri-wedari (legendary female figure), 86
Śṛnggalañcana (Kaḍiri king), 121. *See also* Sarweśwara II
Stein Callenfels, P.V. van, 106, 163
Stutterheim, W.F., 85, 175
Sudamala, *kidung*, 142
Suḍarṣana (discus), 38, 205
Suji, Mt, 93
Sujiwana, Mpu, 11, 84, 205
Suka, Si (butcher), 66, 125, 205
Sukamṛta (inscription), 151
Sukawela, *maṇḍala*, 28, 122, 206
Sukayajña, *maṇḍala*, 28–31, 34, 66, 67, 75, 86, 108, 110, 121, 122, 123, 125, 128, 130, 131, 206
Sukayajña-pakṣa-Jiwaṇa, 67, 125. *See also* Jiwaṇa
Sukayajña-pakṣa-manggalya, 67, 123
Sukorejo, 98
Śukra, *wiku*, 28, 206
Sumber, 129, 161, 181, 187
Sumberurip, 125
Sumbing, Mt, 98, 101
Sumergo, 164
Sunda (land), 96
Suṇḍawiṇi, Mt, 56, 64, 206
Śūnya(sa)giri, *maṇḍala*, 30, 34, 129, 130, 144, 206. *See also* Kukub
Supiturang (plantation), 137
Suroloyo, 126
Surugajah, 86, 98
Susuṇḍara, Mt, 101. *See also* Sindoro
Swarga, 43, 206
św ari, 46

T

Tagwas, Dyah, 105
Taji Gunung (inscription), 106
Tajuk, 101
Taki, Mahārāja, 53, 56, 57, 59, 61, 65, 74, 186, 199, 206, 207, 209, 210, 211
Talun, *maṇḍala*, 52, 53, 162, 163, 170, 172, 173, 206
Talun, *batur i*, 164
Talutug, *maṇḍala*, 67, 125, 206
Tamansari (Kendal), 98
Tamansatriyan, 137, 138
Tambangan, 51, 159, 206
Taṇḍĕs, *patapan*, 21, 35, 61, 62, 112, 113, 115–16, 145, 206
Tanjung, 153–54
tanjung tree (Mimusops elengi), 152, 154
Tantu Panggĕlaran, Sang Hyang, 10, 68, 73, 178, 206
Tapa-palet, Mpu, 53, 54, 56–59, 65, 175, 176, 207. *See also* Kasturi

Tapa-wangkĕng, Mpu, 53, 54, 56, 57, 58, 175, 176, 207
Tapi, *gĕgĕr*, 57, 207
Tarĕnggabāhu (discus), 38, 207
Tarokan, 175
Taruṇa-tapa-yowana, Sang Ṛṣi, 42, 43, 50, 159, 207
Tasik-lĕbu ("sea of dust"), 43, 207
Tatar, Mt, 93
Tawungan, Mt, 22, 112, 117, 207. *See also* Penawungan
Tĕkĕn-wuwung, Sang Hyang, 31, 32, 205, 207
tĕkĕs, 46
Telogo Indro, 164
Telomoyo, Mt, 101
Temanggung, 87, 106
Tempeh, 108
Tempuran, 99, 100
Tempursari, 119
Tĕnggĕk, Si, *pujut*, 62–64, 207
Tengger, 69, 76, 84, 92, 93, 113, 115, 116, 117, 121, 122, 129, 141–42, 144, 147, 161, 170, 177, 178, 181, 194, 212
Tesirejo, 121
Tigalana (religious text), 56, 207
Tigapatra, *maṇḍala*, 40, 144, 207. *See also* Tigāryan-parwata
Tigarahaṣya (religious text), 56, 207
Tigāryan-parwata, *maṇḍala*, 35, 57, 64, 65, 76, 144, 156, 208. *See also* Tigapatra
Tigatĕpĕt (religious text), 56, 208
Tingkir, 101
Ṭiris, 161, 162, 172
Tirtoyudo, 125, 133, 137, 138
Tlogomas, 175
Tlogopakis, 98, 99. *See also* Naga Pertala
Tlogosari, 140, 176
Trawas, 94, 95
Tribhuwana Wijayottunggadewī, 142, 163
Trikurungan, Sang Hyang (weapon), 26, 208
Trinity of Lords (*trisamaya*), 16, 34, 35, 38, 40, 51, 76, 129, 144, 185, 190, 210
Triśṛngga, Mt, 41, 208
Triwungan, 166
Tṛṇawindu, Bhagawān, 66, 67, 75, 108, 125, 208
Trowulan, 80
Trowulan Museum, 138
Tru i Tĕpussan (inscription), 106
Tugu Hotel (Malang), 137, 139
Tuhan, Bhaṭāra, 44, 208
Tulungagung, 125
Tulungrejo, 120
Tumapĕl, 176
Tumburu, *dewarṣi*, 17, 208
Tunggĕng, Mt, 39, 208
Tunggul Amĕtung, 176
Tunjung, 145
Turen, 75, 131, 133, 156, 177. *See also* Tūryan
Turen (river), 86
Turuk-manis, Sang, 20, 110, 208
Tūryan, *maṇḍala*, 58, 60, 75, 76, 131, 156, 175, 176, 178, 208. *See also* Bapa
Tutur, 144, 176
Tyāga, *pakṣa*, 60, 75, 187, 208

U

Ubhusan, *watu*, 53, 162, 170, 208
Udara, Patih, 159
Udyogaparwa (text), 150

Ulu-kĕmbang-pakalpan, Ki, (rock), 62, 209
Umā, Bhaṭārī, 18–22, 24, 25, 27, 43–45, 47, 62, 74, 76, 82, 109–12, 116, 119–21, 128, 142, 209. *See also* Parwatī
Umalung, 101. *See also* Damalung
Unan-unan (Tengger festival), 115, 181
Uṇḍal, Aji, 61, 62, 77, 116, 129, 209
Uṇḍal (well on Mt Kawi), 61, 209
Ungaran, Mt, 86, 98, 154, 192
Untehan, 51, 159, 209
Utan Sungi Petung, 133, 135, 136

V

Varadaraja (legendary tale), 104. *See also* Karivarada
Verbeek, R.D.M., iv, 83, 154
Viṣṇu Puraṇa, 94
Volkenkunde Museum (Leiden), 101, 133, 135, 137

W

Wadas, 106
Wadung Prabhu (menhir), 115, 117, 170
Wagir, 176
Waju-kuning, Mpu, *pangambehan*, 47–50, 150, 152, 209
Walambangan, 101. Mt, *See also* Balangbhangan, Walangbangan
Walaṇḍit, 141–42, 177. *See also* Blandit
Walaṇḍit (inscription), 142
Walaṇḍita, Mt, 45, 142, 209
Walangbangan Mt, 18, 100, 101, 209. *See also* Balangbhangan, Walambangan
Waluh-bang, Mpu, 50, 53, 57, 154, 156, 209
Wanalaba, 101
Wanayasa, 99
Wanasari, 109. *See also* Wanisari, Wonosari
Wangkal (Gading), 164, 166
Wangkḍi, Mt, 141
Wanisari, 19, 109, 209. *See also* Wanasari, Wonosari
Wanua Tĕngah III (inscription), 98, 106, 108
Warag, 53, 57, 156, 209
Warak, Rakai, 98
Warida, Jaran, 131
Wariguh, *maṇḍala*, 60, 209
Warungasem, 109
Warunggama, 43, 210
Waśaṇa, *maṇḍala*, 53, 54, 162, 163, 170, 172, 173, 191, 196, 198, 203, 208, 210
Watu Gajah (statue), 104, 105
Wawu-langit, Sang, 20, 110, 111, 210. *See also* Rawunglangit
Wawu-langit, Mahārāja, 33, 193, 196
wayang (Javanese "shadow play"), 46, 78
Weatherbee, D., 75
Wĕdi, Mt, 141
Wela (river), 110
Wĕlahulu, Mt, 18, 63, 65, 100, 210
Welirang, Mt, 44, 93, 195. *See also* Kumukus
Wĕngan, Sang, 20, 110, 111, 210
Widodaren (inscription), 139
Wihanggamaya, Mt, 40, 140, 210
Wija, Mt, 22, 112, 210
Wilis, Mt, iv, 15, 30, 43, 60, 67, 83, 93, 125, 128, 210
Winduprakāśa, 11, 210
Winihatya, Mt, 24, 210
Winongan, 133, 136

Wiraraja, 144. *See also* Bañak-wiḍe
Wirosari, 88
Wisnu (river), 122
Wiṣṇu, Bhaṭāra, 10–14, 16–18, 23, 24, 28–31, 34–40, 46, 53, 56, 76, 79, 82–85, 92, 100, 104, 121, 122, 128, 129, 139, 140, 144, 145, 176, 210
Wiṣṇu (golden image), 56, 79, 176, 211
Wiṣṇuwardhana (king), 151
Wiśwakarma, *dewarṣi*, 17
Wiśwakarma, Sang Hyang, 11, 12, 83, 85, 211
Wonokerso (Malang), 175
Wonokerso (Tengger), 113, 116, 117
Wonokerto, 118
Wonosari, 109, 110. *See also* Wanasari, Wanisari
Wonosegoro, 154
Wonosobo, 125
Wṛhaspati, *wiku*, 28, 211
Wṛtti-kaṇḍayun, Sang, 12, 13, 84, 110, 111, 192, 193, 211
Wulan, Sang Hyang, 17
Wungkal-ibĕk, *maṇḍala*, 64, 211
Wunut, 106
Wurawan, *bhūmi*, 93. *See also* Gĕlang-gĕlang
Wurung, *ranu*, 43, 211

Y

Yama (World Guardian), 17, 211
Yawaḍipa, 11, 12, 13, 28, 47, 82, 211
Yawaḍipāntara, 11

Z

Zoetmulder, P.J., 74, 77, 118

Stuart Robson is a leading specialist in the fields of Old Javanese Language and Literature. He has occupied the position of Senior Lecturer in Javanese at the University of Leiden in the Netherlands (1979–91), Associate Professor of Indonesian at Monash University, Melbourne, Australia (1991–2001), as well as Visiting Professor at the Tokyo University of Foreign Studies (2014–15). His significant contributions to the advancement of scholarship over the years include a study of the Middle Javanese Pañji *kidung* Wangbang Wideya (earning him the degree of Doctor of Letters in 1971), collaboration with P.J. Zoetmulder in the preparation of the Old Javanese – English Dictionary (1982), and an English translation of Prapañca's *kakawin* Deśawarṇana (1995). In 2019 he won the A.L. Becker "Southeast Asian Literature in Translation" Prize for his publication entitled *The Old Javanese Rāmāyaṇa: a New English Translation.* Robson is currently Adjunct Professor of Indonesian Studies in the School of Languages, Literatures, Cultures and Linguistics at Monash University.

Hadi Sidomulyo is an independent writer and historian, focusing on Javanese history of the pre-colonial period. His time spent as consultant to the Indonesian Department of Culture and Tourism, first in Yogyakarta (1986–89), and later in Surabaya (1989–94), stimulated a special interest in the study of historical topography. Between 1998 and 2001 he conducted a ground survey of the route followed by the fourteenth century king Rājasanagara of Majapahit through eastern Java, as recorded in Prapañca's Deśawarṇana. The results were later published under the title *Napak Tilas Perjalanan Mpu Prapañca* (2007). Since then he has written a series of articles dealing with problematic aspects of Javanese history, among them "From Kuṭa Rāja to Singhasāri: towards a revision of the dynastic history of 13th century Java" (2010), "Kṛtanagara and the resurrection of Mpu Bharāda" (2011), "Gravestones and candi stones: Reflections on the grave complex of Troloyo" (2014), and "Notes on the topography of ancient Java" (2018). He is presently engaged in an intensive exploration of the archaeological remains on Mt Penanggungan, East Java.

www.ingramcontent.com/pod-product-compliance
Lightning Source LLC
Chambersburg PA
CBHW061225150426
42811CB00057BB/1303
* 9 7 8 9 8 1 4 8 8 1 9 9 9 *